MARCO⊕POLO

VIETNAM

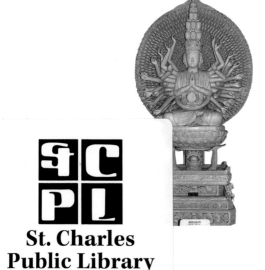

www.marco-polo.com

Do You Feel Like ...

... new discoveries in Vietnam? Make it a cultural programme or a bit of nature? Here are some suggestions for different tastes.

BOAT TRIPS

HO CHI MINH

SIGHTS FROM A TO Z

PRACTICAL INFORMATION

CHAM HIGH CULTURE

- **Da Nang**
  The Cham Museum houses the most important exhibits on the Cham culture. **page 201**
- **My Son**
  The UNESCO site of ruins near Hoi An seems to take visitors on a trip back in time. **page 328**
- **Po Nagar and Po Klong Garai** ▶
  The last imposing Cham holy sites in Vietnam
  pages 345, 348

BEASTLY

- **Riding an elephant**
  … in the highlands near Buon Ma Thuot or in Da Lat **pages 162, 197**
- **Bird watching tours**
  … in Vietnamese mangroves and swamps, like those in Cat Tien National Park or in the Mekong Delta. **pages 174, 198**
- **Cuc Phuong National Park**
  Visit a primate project. **page 223**

MOVIE SETTINGS

- **Sa Dec**
  Marguerite Duras' autobiographical novel *The Lover* is about forbidden love in this harbour town on the Mekong Delta, where the author met her first lover.
  page 175
- **Hotel Continental**
  Graham Greene's novel *The Silent American* is set mainly in and around the colonial hotel in Saigon. **page 396**
- **Dry Ha Long Bay**　　　　▶
  Indochine with Cathérine Deneuve in the leading role was filmed here.
  page 218

BACKGROUND

ENJOY VIETNAM

PICE CATEGORIES
Restaurants
(main course)
££££ = from £15
£££ = £8–£15
££ = £4–£8
£ = up to £4

Hotels (double room)
££££ = from £130
£££ = £90–£130
££ = £30–£90
£ = up to £ 30

TOURS

BACKGROUND

Much appears exotic and strange in Vietnam. On the following pages, useful and interesting background on the country's natural environment, its people, religion and history will help to understand this fascinating land more fully.

Good Morning, Vietnam!

First came the Chinese, a thousand years the French, followed by the Japanese, who were in turn soon replaced by the Americans. Today, they all come at the same time, but on a peaceful mission – as tourists. Throughout its 4000-year history, Vietnam has suffered war and foreign rule like no other country in the world.

But this small country is now rising from the ashes like the proverbial phoenix, a David that has battled and defeated multiple Goliaths. It appears be leaving the world's poorest countries behind – at first glance at least. In the streets, everywhere you go, there is hammering and drilling, planing and filing, cooking and frying. Here, an improvised bicycle repair stand is made from a wooden stool, an air pump and a water bucket; there, a mobile cart offers a modest range of refreshments – perhaps ten cans of drink. Like other innovations inspired by difficult times, the Vietnamese people have turned their numerous war zones into lucrative tourist attractions, the most famous being the tunnels of Cu Chi and the legendary Ho Chi Minh Trail. Vietnam appears to have succeeded in overcoming the division of North and South and the whole nation of »sons of gods and dragons« are unified in the pride in their historical ancestry. The monuments, palaces and temples, copiously covered in moss and patina, bear witness to a thousand-year-old culture. Vietnam enchants its visitors with its natural heritage, such as the prehistoric landscape of Ha Long Bay – seemingly inhabited by mythical creatures – and the many parts of the country that even napalm and explosives could not rob of their beauty, such as the widely ramified Mekong Delta in the south or the mountainous regions in the north.

Paddy fields: a green mosaic covers the land

THE »GALÁPAGOS OF SOUTHEAST ASIA«

Although Vietnam is one of the most densely populated countries in the world, with a population of approximately 90 million, the World

Wildlife Fund considers it to be one of the most biologically diverse countries in Asia. In remote areas and particularly in mountainous regions a variety of zoological oddities are to be found here. Animal researchers even refer to Vietnam as the »Galápagos of Southeast Asia«. Since the 1980s researchers have discovered species long thought to be extinct, such as Delacour's langur, the grey-shanked douc langur and, most recently in 2011, a colony of white-cheeked gibbons. A new deer species, the giant muntjac was also found, along with a new breed of antelope, the saola. These are two out of only six newly discovered mammalian species found worldwide in the 20th century!

Dragons are symbol of wisdom and power

TRADITION MEETS THE MODERN AGE

The Vietnamese people have an unyielding desire for their country to emerge into the 21st century at the forefront. Moving further away from the tourist centres, however, there is less and less evidence of this attitude. While rural areas are still characterized by peasants wading through paddy fields, mobile-carrying businesspeople are a common sight in the cities, where remnants of the colonial backdrop are eclipsed by tower blocks, or are even being torn down to be replaced by even more skyscrapers. But in spite of the move to modernity, countless mythological figures have survived the millennia. The Vietnamese pantheon of gods is huge: temples and pagodas are overcrowded with gods and demons, Buddhas, guardian angels, princes of darkness, dragons, unicorns and other creatures, and all demand to be pacified with offerings. Ancestors play the most important role. To prevent the soul from mutating into a poltergeist, the bereaved families offer tea, rice and vegetables, and burn small presents made of cardboard on holidays and commemorative anniversaries for the deceased. Still today, the temples exude an atmosphere of timelessness – a world where drum beats ring out through the dim light and thick incense. Traditions inspired by Confucianism and practised for centuries have survived so many wars, they will no doubt stand up to the test of modern invaders.

Facts

Nature and Environment

Which indigenous animals are under threat? How can a Communist country and a capitalist economy coexist? Where can hand-crafted souvenirs be found? The facts and figures presented on the following pages will help you gain a better understanding of Vietnam.

Vietnam form is determined by **natural borders**. The South China Sea to the east and vast highlands to the northwest and west offer protection from the neighbouring countries. Vietnam's two lowland regions, the Red River delta in the north and the Mekong Delta in the south, are limited to a smaller area and make up the two »rice bowls« of Vietnam. Due to the positioning of these fertile lowlands and the shape of the country, Vietnam is sometimes referred to as the »bamboo pole with two bowls of rice«. The name is derived from the way in which loads are carried with the help of a bar and one basket on each side in Vietnam (and China).

»Bamboo pole with two bowls of rice«

The north is framed by the deeply fissured landscape of the Tonkin plateau which continues into the Chinese province of Yunnan and into Laos and covers nearly three quarters of North Vietnam. Rising up close to the border, **Fansipan** is the highest mountain in Indochina at 3143m/10,312ft. The mountain area (1000m/3300ft–1500m/5000ft) encloses the Red River Delta and its tributaries that open into the Red River northeast of the capital Hanoi. Due to the difference in altitude, the Red River picks up a lot of debris and silt on its 1200km/746mi journey, which results in the creation of the country's most fertile soil. In the past, redirecting waterways and breaching the natural river dams regularly resulted in disastrous flooding, which could only be kept under control by means of artificial dykes. Bac Bo forms the heart of Vietnam with a population of approximately 40% of the 90 million inhabitants, who are scattered quite unevenly across the different regions.

The North (Bac Bo)

While the mountain areas are close to deserted, the **Red River Delta** is occupied by nearly 2000 inhabitants per sq km (approx. 5000 per sq mi), making it one of the world's most densely populated regions. This area is home to approximately 15% of Vietnam's people. The Red River Delta was granted UNESCO status as a biosphere reserve in 2004.

With a great deal of industriousness, the Vietnamese have worked their way from a bombed out country to the status of the world's third largest rice exporter

Central Vietnam (Trung Bo)

Central Vietnam, historically the region of Annam, constitutes the 900km/559mi-long »bamboo pole« of the country. In the north of the region, the mountains form a narrow cordillera that runs parallel to the South China Sea and in places stretches to the coast. The lowlands are therefore limited to small bays with big cities, for example Hue and Da Nang. The mountains in the southern part of Central Vietnam expand into highlands. The altitude drops continuously from north to south. Central Vietnam is quite sparsely populated as it has few mineral resources and agricultural cultivation is limited to the narrow coastal strip – 40% of the landmass is home to only 25% of the population. The more densely populated regions are the small lowland areas along the coast around Hue, Da Nang and Nha Trang, while the population of hill tribes is considerably smaller.

The South (Nam Bo)

South Vietnam, also known as Cochinchina, constitutes approximately 35% of Vietnam and consists of broad, low hills in the north that gradually merge into the **Mekong Delta** in the south. The Mekong River flows through Vietnam for the last 200km/124mi of its

Sunset over Nha Trang

length and creates a delta on the coast that, at 45,000 sq km/27,900 sq mi, is three times bigger than the Red River delta in the north. It is the country's second biggest rice bowl. In contrast to the Red River, the Mekong has a storage basin in the form of the giant Tonlé Sap (Cambodia), which helps to regulate the course of the river and makes the Mekong Delta less prone to flooding than in the north.

Several archipelagos in the South China Sea and Gulf of Siam belong to Vietnam. One of the most scenic attractions in the north, close to the Chinese border, features thousands of bizarre-looking limestone islands jutting out from the sea in Ha Long Bay. Much further south, off the coast of Cambodia, Phu Quoc, is the largest Vietnamese island. Also in the far south, the islands of Con Dao can be found in the South China Sea. The oil and gas reserves which lie here have become the country's greatest source of foreign currency.

Islands and archipelagos

FLORA

Year-round humidity combined with high temperatures creates very fast-growing, lush vegetation in the tropical rain forest. There is no distinct time of blossoming, ripening or defoliation – everything appears to happen in parallel. Due to the tropical climate, organic material decomposes rapidly and it is possible for a tree to regenerate itself with its own foliage.

Rain forests

In the flood-hazard zones of the river deltas and sea coasts there are lots of bog and mangrove forests. The movement of the tides means they are flooded twice a day, when only the upper trunks and tree tops remain above water. The trees have high stilt roots as well as respiratory roots that loom out of the water at low tide.

Mangrove forests

The tropical lowland forests feature the highest diversity of species, with 40 to 100 different types of trees. The dense canopy formed by the tree tops, over five to six levels, **filters out the sun** and in the forest interior a permanent half-light predominates. Ground vegetation is scarce, but epiphytes, creeping plants and many types of orchid strive to reach the sun. In addition, an abundance of parasitic plants use trees not only as a means to access more sunlight, but also as a source of nutrients, which will eventually lead to the death of the host plant. Above 700m/2300ft–900m/2950ft lowland forest gives way to **tropical mountain forest**. The lower temperatures make it species-poor and growth rates slower. Tree ferns and low palm trees are characteristic of the moist and moderately warm climate of these elevations, and there are also deciduous trees such as oaks, as well as conifers.

Dry forests in the highlands and lowlands

Deforestation Deforestation started in the lowland regions of the Red River and the Mekong Deltas, which are ideal for rice cultivation. These rice valleys are so closely connected to our image of Vietnam that they are hardly considered man-made. It was not until the overpopulation problems of the 20th century that deforestation had an impact on the mountain forests. The method of slash-and-burn shifting cultivation is used to clear forested land units for agriculture. These lands are then cultivated until they are incapable of further yields and, while the soil is left to regenerate, the farmers move on to clear land in a different location. At the end of this period, and once the soil has recovered, they return to the point of origin to start a new rotation cycle. When the population grows, however, either the rotation cycle speed has to be increased – leading to the soil not being able to recover completely – or bigger land units need to be cleared, which results in increased deforestation. Consequently, forest stands were reduced from 80% to 50% between the beginning and the middle of the 20th century. Today, tropical forest coverage is no more than 12%.

Consequences of war A further cause for the enormous reduction of forest stands was the Vietnam War. The United States waged both a military and an **ecological war**. They bombed dams and dykes, caused artificial landslides and destroyed vegetation by spraying defoliant. These measures were used primarily in the forests of the Mekong Delta to uncover the natural hiding places of the Vietcong, who were operating from within the thick forests.

> **?** MARCO ◉ POLO INSIGHT
>
> *Insecticide*
>
> During the Vietnam War, 80 million tons of Agent Orange, Agent Blue and Agent White were dropped on Vietnam, particularly over the southern part of the country. This led to the poisoning of approximately 5.4 million acres of woodland and one fifth of all farmland.

In the past, forests were cleared to develop new cropland. Recently however, the forest itself has become the focus of attention, as a supplier of tropical **precious woods**, such as teak or sandalwood. These are chiefly used as exports. The great variety of plants in the tropical rain forests make the cutting and transporting of every single tree an extremely complex operation, as large areas need to be cleared. Since the early 1990s, major efforts have been made to undertake reforestation, even though this does not entirely compensate for the annual deforestation. In addition, reforestation with fast-growing softwood trees, such as **eucalyptus**, does not offer the same ecological protection as a tropical rain forest rich in plant species.

Crops Approximately 7000 different plant species have been counted in Vietnam. The exact number is estimated to be closer to 12,000 species, of which approximately 40% are native species. About 2300 herbal plants are used in everyday life as foodstuffs, pharmaceuticals and animal feed. The most important crops are rice (▶MARCO POLO Insight p.324), tea, coffee, caoutchouc (natural rubber) and tobacco. Others include sweet corn, sweet potato, manioc, peanuts, cotton, sugarcane, and soy beans. The Mekong Delta is rich in fruit and vegetable plantations in which mainly delicious fruits such as rose apples, pineapples, rambutan, jackfruit, pomelos, mangos, pawpaws and bananas are grown. There are also approximately 1500 wood species, including palm, bamboo, teak, oak and spruce, as well as mangrove trees along the coast. Also to be seen are colourful and exotic flowers such as frangipani, hibiscus and hundreds of wild orchid species.

FAUNA

Vietnam is a veritable paradise for zoologists. In no other country have as many animal species been (re)discovered in recent times: the grey-shanked douc langur in 1997, for example, and a colony of white-cheeked gibbons in 2011). Approximately 280 **species of mammal** can be found in Vietnam, a lot of them endangered, such as the Asian elephant. 180 reptile species, 80 different amphibian species and 2600 fish species have also been recorded. Researchers have also listed between 773 and 850 types of bird, 11 of which are indigenous, and approximately 6000 different insect species further enrich the Vietnamese fauna.

The significance of the water buffalo as a working animal is not to be underestimated

Elephants Some 100 wild elephants can be found in various provinces such as Lai Chau, Da Lat, Kon Tum, Dak Lak and Tay Ninh. Cat Tien National Park is one of Vietnam's most important habitats for elephants. With the Javan rhinoceros already hunted to extinction in Vietnam by 2010, elephants are in similarly serious danger on account of their tusks. According to the WWF, the price paid for ivory in Vietnam is higher than anywhere else in the world: US$750 per pound. Almost all of the ivory is sold illegally to China, Were it not for the millions of Chinese and their absurd superstitions concerning the healing powers of animal ingredients, the threat to so many valuable wild animals around the world would be vastly diminished. In 2011, in Binh Duong province, such greed even led to the slaughter of a domesticated elephant for its tusks. The ivory trade has been outlawed in Vietnam since 1992, but with one loophole. Ivory which predates the ban can still be sold – and the WWF states that it is virtually impossible to ascertain the age and origin of the merchandise. Elephants have been domesticated in Vietnam for centuries, particularly by hill tribes, who use them for heavy labour. They are bred in the Central Highlands close to Buon Ma Thuot in the village of Ban Don. The village hosts a folk festival in spring that lasts several days and features costumes, dances and elephant races. These seemingly slow animals accelerate to almost 40kmh/25mph without any difficulty.

The first photo of a Vu Quang ox (Saola) shows a female calf in Hanoi's Botanical Gardens

Tigers

The tiger population in the wild in Vietnam has declined by 95% since the 19th century. Today, the maximum number of tigers is said to range from 50 to 100 in Vietnam's national parks and in areas bordering Laos and Cambodia. Due to the increasing loss of their natural habitat, their chances of survival are diminishing. Until a few centuries ago, these felines were **hunted on a large scale**. Tigers are hunted for their fur, bones and other body parts. Tiger bones are found in Vietnam in a well-known rheumatic balm, while Laos uses the skin of tigers in the treatment of dog bites and tiger teeth to reduce fever. In 1993 and 1994, the trade in tiger parts and derivatives was banned in the main countries of consumption, namely China, Taiwan and South Korea – all in vain, with two pounds of tiger bone fetching more than US$6500.

Monkeys

There are a large number of monkey species in Vietnam's forests, the most widespread being the macaque monkey. Among the gibbon species, the crested gibbon is native to Vietnam. During the early 1990s Delacour's langurs was rediscovered in Cuc Phuong National Park. One of the critically endangered species is the Tonkin snub-nosed monkey; approximately 300 of these animals are said to exist in the northern limestone regions, and sightings of the monkeys are extremely rare since they often hide in the treetops.

Antelope

In 1992, the amazing discovery of this antelope in Vu Quang Nature Reserve in the northwest of Vietnam made world headlines. This elusive and nocturnal bovid (Pseudoryx nghetinhensis or the Vu Quang ox), with its long, sharp, furrowed horns, was identified during a joint survey by the WWF and the Ministry of Forestry of Vietnam, and is one of only **six newly discovered large mammalian species** in the world during the 20th century! Experts estimate a population of 300 to 400 specimens.

Turtles

The Ho Guom turtle is the biggest freshwater turtle in the world and can weigh up to 130kg/285lbs. In Vietnam it enjoys renown mainly for its role in the Le Loi legend (▶Hanoi). Only a few specimens are said to live in the lakes of Hoan Kiem and Hoa Binh – a female was caught in a net in 2011 and treated medically.

Domestic and working animals

One of the most important traditional domestic animals in Vietnam is the water buffalo, which was introduced from China about 2000 years ago. The water buffalo is the quintessential pack and draught animal of Vietnam, without which the country's agricultural landscape is unimaginable. Cattle, geese, chickens, goats, cats, dogs and pigs also find a place in the rural homestead. The pot-bellied pig is a typical Vietnam variety – for the most part, they run wild in villages and on farms. Inhabitants of rice-growing regions will keep domestic animals merely for their labour needs, but hill tribes and inhabitants of drier areas also rear livestock (cattle, sheep). The Hmong are well-known for **breeding horses and cattle**, and dairy farming is becoming increasingly important. In the Central Highlands near Buon Ma Thuot, elephants are trained as working animals and ridden by tourists.

Bird life
Roughly 800 different bird species live in Vietnam, eleven of which, such as the Collared Laughingthrush, are native. Some bird species are critically endangered since their habitat, mainly marshland, is becoming more and more confined. Most ornithologists head for **Vietnam's national parks**, whose lagoons and marshes attract rare birds such as cranes, cormorants, pheasants, peacocks, hornbills and short-toed eagles. Among the most important areas are Cat Tien National Park, the forests of the Tam Dao Plateau near Hanoi, Cuc Phuong National Park, the My Hoa Bird Reserve near Ben Tre, the Truong Son Mountains and the areas surrounding Da Lat.

NATURE CONSERVATION AND PROTECTION OF ANIMALS

Measures
Vietnam today is home to more than 30 national parks and over 130 nature reserves. It was not until 1992–93 that the Vietnamese government passed a law for the protection of its flora and fauna. A ban on timber exports has been in force since 1992. Two years later, Vietnam signed up to the (Washington) Convention on International Trade in Endangered Species of Wild Fauna and Flora (**CITES**), which officially prohibits trade in endangered species. However, the enforcement and control of this treaty leaves a lot to be desired. International animal rights groups have been supporting the Vietnamese government since the mid-1980s in their attempt to protect their extensively rich fauna. All rare and endangered species have been listed on the »red list« since 1990. At present, the list consists of approximately 78 animal species, 83 birds and 54 reptiles and amphibians, making hunting for these animals strictly prohibited. Throughout Asia, however, superstition is still widespread and there is a strong belief in the healing power of animal-sourced substances and extracts. **Breeding programmes** have been put in place to protect wildlife from being hunted to extinction. These programmes also create a source of income for local people. Since the 1970s, many farmers and hunters have been entrusted with the breeding of endangered species, such as snakes, crocodiles and elephants. The idea behind this initiative is that, thanks to their extensive knowledge of the animal's natural habits, former poachers and members of hill tribes will become valuable animal-rights campaigners. Other government

projects include support and development of caoutchouc and cinnamon plantations, set up to bring alternative sources of income to certain areas and diversify the sources of income of the inhabitants, for example former tree fellers.

Population · Politics · Economy

Vietnam's .population of 90 million, over 25 million more than that of the UK, makes it one of the most populous countries in Southeast Asia. Between 1960 and 1993 the population doubled in size, though it is unequally distributed. The contrast between the densely populated lowland regions and the all but deserted highlands is striking. From 1963, North Vietnam has attempted to curtail population growth through **family planning** education. The directive aims to limit the average family size to two children, to increase the marital age of women and to determine that the first child should not be born before a woman reaches the age of 22. In addition, the recommended age difference between the two children should be at least five years.

Population growth

Befitting the high birth rate, Vietnam's population is overwhelmingly young. Two thirds of Vietnamese are younger than 35, hence they were born after the war. This is also a reason for the rapid change in society which can be observed in Vietnam today, and the pragmatic stance towards the United States, once Vietnam's arch enemy. It is the young who are primarily responsible for heavy migration to

Very young population

More than half of all Vietnamese are under 20 years of age

▶ Vietnamese spelling:

Việt Nam

Location:
Far southeast of the
Indian subcontinent

Area:
332,800 sq km/128,500 sq mi

Population:
approx. 91 mil.

Population density
280 people per sq km/730 per sq mi
(60% in rural villages)
Average age: 28 years
Population growth: approx. 1 % per year

CHINA
Hanoi
LAOS
THAILAND
995 km/618mi
Vietnam
Bangkok
CAMBODIA

©BAEDEKER

▶ Religion

Exact numbers are difficult to obtain as religion was and is still seen as a rival to stately influence.

Religions in Vietnam

Local / others   Christs

Buddhists   not religious

30   45
9
16

according to Pew
Research Center
Washington D.C.

1
7
10

82

according to
governmental census

▶ Flag

Introduced in North Vietnam in 1955. Red signifies success, the star symbolizes the leadership of the Communist Party. The five points represent workers, farmers, soldiers, intellectuals and the youth.

▶ Government

Socialist republic with one-party system (Communist Party of Vietnam, CPV)

Head of state: president Truong Tan Sang (since July 2011; vice president: Nguyen Thi Doan)

Prime Minister: Nguyen Tan Dung (since June 2006)

Parliament: National Assembly (500 seats)

Administrative structure: 58 provinces, 5 municipalities

Economy

GDP per capita: 4000 US$ (2013)
Unemployment rate: 1.3 % (2013)
Export: 128 bil. US$ (2013)
Chief export commodities: textiles and clothing, crude oil, seafood, electronic goods

Employment structure:

Industry and craft **21**

Services

% 48

31

Agriculture and fishery

Real growth: 5.3% (2013)
Tourists: approx. 4 mil. (2012)

▶ Climaste in Hanoi

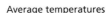

Average temperatures

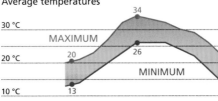

MAXIMUM

MINIMUM

34

30 °C

20 20 °C 26

13 10 °C

0 °C

J F M A M J J A S O N D

Precipitation

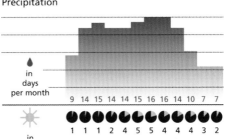

in days per month

9 14 15 14 14 15 16 16 14 10 7 7

1 1 1 2 4 5 5 4 4 4 3 2

in hours per day

J F M A M J J A S O N D

▶ Land of 1000 unknown species

Over one thousand species have been discovered in Vietnam over the past decade – including animals long believed to be extinct.

Saola (Vu Quang bovine)
Discovered in 1993 and in danger of extinction. Their number is estimated at just a few hundred.

Swinhoe's soft-shell turtle
Thought to be extinct in the wilds, discovered in North Vietnam in 2008.

Irrawaddy dolphin
An endangered species, according to WWF figures the population is down to a mere 85 animals.

Southern white-cheeked gibbon
Listed as critically endangered, a colony of this almost extinct species was discovered in 2011.

urban centres (Saigon, Hanoi, Nha Trang, Vung Tau, Hai Phong, Da Nang). A million people, most of them young, leave the countryside for the cities every year, many illegally. They dream of a higher standard of living – moped, mobile phone and Facebook included. Average income per annum is estimated at around US$1300/=£860 – poverty has been reduced by more than half in the past two decades but the urban-rural divide is still sharply pronounced.

Education system

Vietnam enjoys a relatively well developed education system. Attendance up to 6th grade is free. Thus, since 1979, the **illiteracy rate** has decreased from 16% to less than 6%, although the standard of literacy is still relatively low. According to a World Bank study, various issues still need to be addressed, including oversized classes, an insufficient number of lessons, unskilled and underpaid teachers, and a high number of school drop-outs after 5th grade, as parents find it difficult to cover the cost of school uniform, books and school fees. More than a few teachers will award higher grades for a little »extra« or sell students test results on cheat sheets. Recent years have seen an increasing number of (expensive) private schools opening, raising concerns that education standards for the majority are declining as tuition becomes the exclusive privilege of the wealthy classes.

Sa Pa is primarily home to Red Dao and Black Hmong

Approximately 88% of the country's population is Vietnamese. Thus, Vietnam – like Cambodia and Thailand – is one of the Southeast Asian countries with a relatively **uniform population structure**. The Vietnamese people originated from an ethnic mixture of Austro-Indonesian peoples who travelled overseas to the north and Mongolian tribes who travelled overland, crossing large rivers and interjacent mountain ranges. Their economy has always been based on the cultivation of wet rice, which is limited to lowland regions. Only very few Vietnamese people live above 100m/328ft. While **settling** these lands and adapting to heavy seasonal fluctuations in water level and the frequently changing courses of rivers, they tamed the bodies of water by building dykes. With the exception of Hanoi (and later Saigon), no real cities emerged in Vietnam until the French colonial occupation. Even today, 80% of Vietnam's population live in villages, which are strictly hierarchically structured so that every individual serves the community.

The Vietnamese people

Ethnic minorities in Vietnam only account for 12% of the population, but this still amounts to around nine million people. In Vietnam, there is a marked contrast between the small, densely populated lowland regions inhabited predominantly by Vietnamese and the vast but scarcely populated highlands inhabited mainly by ethnic minorities. Minority groups are a colourful mix made up of very different population groups with a variety of origins. There are a total of **54 different ethnic groups**, their numbers ranging from a few thousand to several million. The lowland minority groups often have features in common, and foreigners cannot distinguish between them since they are, in their appearance, very similar to the Vietnamese. The main differences lie in tradition, religion, lifestyle and habits. Ethnic minorities living in mountainous regions, however, can easily be identified as independent groups on the basis of their physical appearance and clothing (▶MARCO POLO Insight p.26.

Ethnic minorities

POLITICS

The Socialist Republic of Vietnam emerged in 1976 as a result of the unification of the Democratic Republic of Vietnam – formerly North Vietnam – and the Republic of South Vietnam. The preamble of the constitution, based on a phrase attributed to the former US President Abraham Lincoln, reads: »The Socialist Republic of Vietnam is a state of the people, by the people, for the people«.

State

According to the constitution, the Communist Party of Vietnam (CPV) – with more than 3 million members – is the country's only political power. Not only does it determine the political guidelines,

Communist Party

Vietnam Ethnicities

Some 10 million of Vietnam's people belong to one of the 54 recognized ethnic minorities in the country. Most of them live in the central region or the northern highlands. The Red Dao and Black Hmong will be seen at the market in Sa Pa, whilst the Flower Hmong will be close by in Bac Ha. Those who wish to learn more about the individual groups should pay a visit to the Museum of Ethnology in Hanoi.

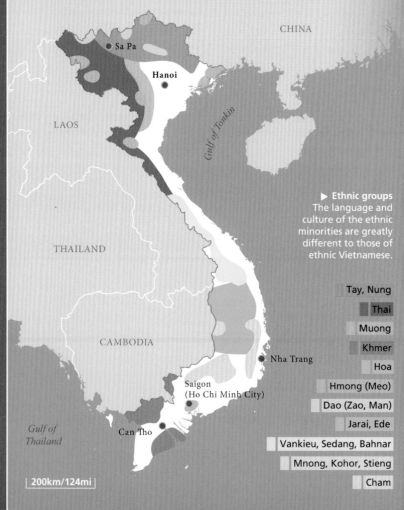

CHINA

Sa Pa

Hanoi

LAOS

Gulf of Tonkin

THAILAND

► **Ethnic groups**
The language and culture of the ethnic minorities are greatly different to those of ethnic Vietnamese.

CAMBODIA

Nha Trang

Saigon
(Ho Chi Minh City)

Can Tho

Gulf of
Thailand

Tay, Nung

Thai

Muong

Khmer

Hoa

Hmong (Meo)

Dao (Zao, Man)

Jarai, Ede

Vankieu, Sedang, Bahnar

Mnong, Kohor, Stieng

Cham

200km/124mi

Vietnam Museum of Ethnology
The Museum of Ethnology in Hanoi offers an excellent insight into the world of the hill tribes. Inside, everyday artefacts and clothing illustrate the traditions of the individual groups, whilst the open-air section presents stilt houses, tombs and tribal art.

www.vme.org.vn

Vietnamese population
There are 54 officially recognized ethnic groups in Vietnam; inofficially there are probably more than 100. The largest groups are listed here.

Ethnic Vietnamese **90.1 %**

Tay, Nung **2.6 %**

Thai **1.5 %**

Muong **1.3 %**

Khmer **1.2 %**

Hoa **1.0 %**

Hmong (Meo) **0.9 %**

Dao (Zao, Man) **0.7 %**

Jarai, Ede **0.3 %**

Bahnar **0.2 %**

Vankieu, Sedang **0.1 %**

Stieng **0.1 %**

Mnong, Kohor **0.1 %**

Cham **0.1 %**

A Colourful Mix

About ten million inhabitants of Vietnam belong to one of the numerous ethnic minorities. While the lowland peoples often differ from one another only in terms of their traditions, religion or way of life, the hill tribes can be identified as separate groups by appearance alone.

The **Chinese** (Hoa Hoa) are the largest minority group. Most of them live in the south of Vietnam and engage mainly in commerce and trading. When South Vietnam was taken over by the north, the Chinese gained 100% control of wholesale trading, as well as almost all import and export business and 80% of heavy industry, as well as textile production and food processing. However, their situation deteriorated rapidly when businesses were nationalized in 1978. This took place at the same time as tension increased between China and Vietnam, which resulted from the Vietnamese policy on Cambodia and even led to war between the two countries in 1979. The consequence was mass flight, reducing the Chinese population by over one million to half of its previous level. As boat people (▶ MARCO POLO Insight p.62) the refugees fled to their Chinese motherland or overseas. However, government economic reforms that began in the late 1980s allowed the Chinese to take up their traditional fields of activity once again.

Woman of the Nung people

The Cham

The Cham, who also live in the lowlands, are descendants of the people of **Champa**, a once-mighty kingdom that lay in today's Cambodia before it was conquered in conflicts with Vietnam and the Khmer kingdom. In the centuries after the occupation of their state, the Cham population was increasingly absorbed by the Vietnamese, so that today only about 100,000 people identify themselves with this ethnic group. Once Hindu, the Cham are now Muslims, and thus not only an ethnic but also a religious minority.

The Khmer

The Khmer populate the Mekong Delta, which was occupied by Vietnam in the 18th century. Their numbers, now about 900,000, were swelled by refugees from Cambodia during the rule of the Khmer Rouge (1975-1979). Like their kin across the border, they are adherents of Theravada Buddhism, and consequently differ considerably from the Vietnamese in their attitude to life. As they are entirely devoted to gaining a better reincarnation, they do not strive for material wealth. Their belief that each person must search for his or her own way to enlightenment means that they lack the marked communal feeling of the Vietnamese. This is evident even in their settlements, as Khmer villages consist of scattered wooden houses built on stilts.

Hill Tribes

In their appearance and habits the hill tribes are so different from the Vietnamese that they are instantly recognizable as being separate ethnic groups. The French called them **Montagnards**, a term that has survived and is used by the hill tribes themselves. The Vietnames, however, often refer to them as »moi«, i.e. wild people, which expresses their reservations towards a lifestyle that in some respects differs greatly from their own. In contrast to the Vietnamese, they do not live from cultivating rice in paddy fields, but keep livestock and practise shifting cultivation, **clearing land by burning** and moving on. They live not in compact villages but in loosely scattered settlements in houses built on stilts or, in some places in the south, in longhouses. The cultivation of coffee, tea and tobacco, which flour-

ish only in tropical highlands, is being extended. The introduction of these new crops is intended not only to reduce the widespread growing of opium, but also to encourage the hill tribes to settle in one place. In order to tie the mountain regions more closely to the heartlands of Vietnam, more and more Vietnamese are being settled there, which is increasingly making the hill tribes a minority in their own regions. The entire mineral resources of the country are situated in the mountain regions of the north.

Hill Tribes of the South

The largest group among the minorities in the mountains of the

Lao woman with handcrafted silver jewellery

south are the **Jarai**, of whom there are 250,000. They keep cattle and livestock, and originally planted dry rice, vegetables and sweet potatoes in shifting cultivation, but today increasingly grow tea, coffee and tobacco. Their origin in Southeast Asia is still evident from the fact that they dwell in longhouses of the type that are built on the island of Borneo.

Hill Tribes of the North

The northern hill tribes wear their own costumes much more often than those of the south. This distinguishes them not only from the Vietnamese but also from each other. For tourists, it is a real experience to walk around a market and admire their colourful costumes. Many of the women wear silver jewellery, which is quite un-

Woman of the Flower Hmong people

typical for the Vietnamese. The largest group are the **Tay**, of whom 1.2 million live in the area bordering China. They are regarded as having been strongly »Vietnamized« and are well represented in politics and government. Other minority groups include the **Nung**, who come from southern China and engage in shifting cultivation and livestock keeping, as do another group, the **Thai**, who are subdivided into the Red, White or Black Thai according to their clothing and are also tob e found in Laos, China and Thailand. The **Muong** are thought to be descended from the original inhabitants of Vietnam, i.e. have been settled in the country for a very long time, while the **Hmong** (Meo) did not come to Vietnam from southern China until the 19th century.

Meo girl with typically magnificent hair

but its members also occupy all political and administrative high offices. The party is omnipresent in all levels of society. Every citizen is urged to join either the party or one of its sub-organizations. The **Sixth National Party Congress**, held in 1986, made history with its reform programme, when the new economic policies of Doi Moi were introduced. At the Seventh National Party Congress in 1991 these policies were officially enacted, the acquisition of property certified and private property guaranteed. Since the National Party Congress only meets approximately every five years, its duties are assigned to the Central Committee in the interim. It consists of over 170 members and has bi-annual meetings known as plenum.

The National Assembly – a unicameral parliament with approximately 500 ministers – is the highest legislative political body in Vietnam. It is elected, or rather validated, by the people every five years. Nevertheless, **compulsory voting** prevails in Vietnam. The National Assembly meets bi-annually for a fortnight to discuss bills that have often been previously mandated by the Politburo or the party itself. These meetings end, sometimes after controversial debates, in the eventual unanimous passing of these bills. The National Assembly decides on issues of war and peace and presides over the Supreme Court. Even the appointment and release from duty of high state officials, such as ministers, judges etc., is part of their responsibility. The 17 members of the **State Council** the highest institution of the National Assembly and the highest representative of the state, are elected from the ranks of the National Assembly. With the amendment of the constitution in 1992, collective governance was replaced by a state president. Since July 2011 this role has been fulfilled by Truong Tan Sang and vice president Nguyen Thi Doan.

National Assembly and State Council

The Council of Ministers appoints the government and consists of a prime minister and departmental ministers, whose responsibility it is to implement and enforce the bills passed by the National Assembly.

Council of Ministers

ECONOMY

Since time immemorial, Vietnam's economy has been based on **wet rice cultivation** in the lowlands, the Red River delta in the north and the Mekong Delta in the south (►MARCO POLO Insight p.324). Commercial fishing also plays an important role: in part due to the country's long coastline, but also because of the fish farming that is practised in the numerous and extensive irrigation reservoirs in rice-growing areas. Even today, around half of all Vietnamese (48%) still work in agriculture, although the industrial sector (22%) and service

Structure of the economy

sector (30%) have caught up in recent years. This movement out of classic underdevelopment is likely to continue in tandem with rapid social change. Average yearly income is roughly US$1300/=£860 (US$200 in 1993), poverty levels have dropped in the past two decades from 60% to 10%, at least in urban centres. Vietnam thus qualifies as a »middle income« state. One of the main sources of foreign currency is tourism, with some four million tourists and a total of six million visitors (in 2012, with business travellers and relatives visiting families included) indicative of great potential for growth. The conditions for **agriculture** in Vietnam are not at all bad. Fertile lowlands allow for extensive rice cultivation, which not only covers national requirements but also makes Vietnam one of the **world leaders in rice exports**. The further range of traditionally cultivated products (coffee, tea, caoutchouc pepper, cashew nuts) are among the chief export goods, along with fishing and aquaculture (especially Pangasius and shrimp farming in the Mekong Delta).

Women planting small rice plants

Industry Conditions are also good for the creation of a stronger industrial sector in Vietnam: the country is rich in mineral resources, such as hard coal and metals, e.g. iron ore, bauxite, manganese, chrome, zinc and silver, and possesses energy reserves in the form of charcoal and crude oil.

? *Leading the way with pepper ...*

MARCO ⦿ POLO

... and coffee. Vietnam is the world's leading producer of black pepper and neck and neck with Brazil in coffee production – it is also one of the top exporters of rice (behind India) and cashew nuts, caoutchouc and tea?

By the year 2020, Vietnam aims to gain the status of an industrial nation. Prime export products are crude oil, electronic goods, furniture or wooden artefacts, textiles and shoes. The most important imports come from China (machinery and engine parts, steel, cloth and electronic goods). The tertiary sector (service industry) has advanced just as swiftly in recent years – in 2012 it contributed an estimated 38% of gross national product. In particular, small family-run businesses supplying any number of goods or services shape daily life in every Vietnamese city.

Tourism is one of the main catalysts for growth, as Vietnam's popularity as a destination increases. Some 4 million international guests arrived in 2012, with many **new hotels** built to meet demand, not only for business travellers and tourist groups but also for individual excursionists. As so often, the south is the real driving force in this respect. Proximity to Thailand has undoubtedly been an integral factor as a commercial sector has developed which caters to individual tourists with small private hotels, a wide variety of culinary delights and private minibus transportation.

The Vietnamese invasion of Cambodia in 1979 and the ensuing war with China ruled out any further trade relations with its northern neighbour. In addition, the United States imposed a **trade embargo** on Vietnam, which was also joined by the ASEAN states. As a consequence of this, Vietnam turned to the states of the Warsaw Pact and became a member of the Council for Mutual Economic Assistance. Against this backdrop, Vietnam fell into a severe economic crisis at the end of the 1970s when even rice – Vietnam's main food resource – had to be imported.

Foreign trade

Much like in the Soviet Union, the year 1986 was a turning point for Vietnam. With the death of the head of state, Le Duan, younger, less dogmatic politicians came into power.
At the **Sixth National Party Congress** in December they decided on a new, progressive economic policy that came to be known as doi moi: the economic structure was to be changed from a closed to a free market economy, which meant that the state and party should

New economic policy Doi Moi reforms

withdraw from the economy and only uphold political offices. Families in the agricultural sector were assigned long-term tenancy agreements of the once collectivized soil. Production and sales was now their own responsibility, while ordering fertilizers and machinery or agricultural implements continued to be incumbent on the cooperatives. In the industry sector, too, planning requirements were not imposed as of 1987; the procurement of raw materials as well as production and financing were now managed by the businesses themselves. The United States lifted the economic embargo in 1994 and officially entered a diplomatic relationship with Vietnam in 1995. In 2000, the two countries signed an economic agreement. In 1995 Vietnam had joined the Association of Southeast Asian Nations (ASEAN states) – once founded as an association of anti-Communist countries.

Problems Despite the positive progress of the recent years, the transition towards a free market economy entails plenty of challenges for Vietnam, the biggest obviously being the number of **unemployed people**. With the closing down of a number of unprofitable state-owned companies many employees have been laid off, although, according to official figures, these account for just 4%. Another issue is the increasing gap between poor and rich. Through economic reforms, a small number of people became well-off very quickly, yet the vast majority of the population lives barely above the poverty line. Prices have risen dramatically as inflation hit 20% (in 2008 and again in 2010/11), widening the divide even more severely. According to the CIA World Fact Book, some 15% of Vietnamese still live below the poverty line with a daily income of less than US$1 (an improvement, at least, on the 37% in 1998).

Religion

Spiritual diversity As a country situated both politically and culturally in an area of conflict between southern and eastern Asia, virtually all world religions have left their mark on Vietnam. Unlike its neighbouring countries Laos and Cambodia, where Buddhism is omnipresent, a far greater spiritual diversity prevails in Vietnam. The country itself brought about the worshipping of ancestors and animism. Several influences came from the outside, such as Buddhism, both from China in the form of Mahayana (Greater Vehicle) and from India in the form of Hinayana (Inferior Vehicle). Hinduism was the religion of the Cham in Central Vietnam, whose descendants are still followers of Islam. European missionaries eventually brought Catholicism to the country. There are also several mostly regionally operating sects, which in the recent past had greater significance, also in the political arena. Unlike in Europe, philosophy is an important part of daily life, first and foremost Confucianism and Taoism.

The different spiritual streams do not compete but rather comple- **Religious** ment each other. While it is nearly impossible for Europeans to be **tolerance** both Christian and Buddhist, or for an Indian to be both Hindu and Christian, for a Vietnamese it is no problem to embrace both religions. Hence, **double entries** when stating religious denomination are quite common.

Ancestor worship can be considered prototypical for Vietnam as it **Ancestor** was not introduced to the country from abroad. It never faced rejec- **worship** tion from other religions, but was always practised alongside other sets of belief. Based on the notion that humankind consists of more dead than living beings, a worthy way of worshipping the deceased is given great importance. It is not death that is at the focus of attention here, but rather the deceased themselves who, according to Vietnamese belief, live on as spirits and require continuous care from the living. The spirit not only provides a connection between the living and

The ancestors are commemorated at small altars in apartments and pagodas

the dead, but also a bond with future generations. The burning of incense and offerings (e.g. food) at the ancestor altar on major holidays or birthdays and death anniversaries is a sign of respect toward the deceased. The ancestral spirits are summoned for important decisions, and informed about all new developments. Ancestor worship is the foundation of all religiousness of the Vietnamese, particularly of their belief in ghosts and demons.

Belief in ghosts and demons Being primarily a rural people and therefore strongly dependent on favourable or unfavourable natural conditions, the Vietnamese developed a very distinct form of animism. It is founded on the idea that the universe is divided into **three realms**: heaven, earth and humankind. Ong troi, the honourable heaven, watches over their balance together with the gods of the earth, water and mountains. Within this hierarchy there are four sacred animals, which make an appearance on numerous monuments in Vietnam. The dragon symbolizes the king (as well as power and intelligence), and the phoenix represents the queen, beauty and peace. Long life is assigned to the tortoise, which also secures the protection of the empire. Finally, the mythical Kylin, a kind of unicorn, is associated to wisdom. The belief is that nature is animated by ghosts and demons that can either be good or evil towards humans. Offerings are a way to appease them. These spirits can live everywhere, for example in stones, plants or animals. Every house and village has their own guardian spirits, which are worshipped at temples and community houses. Sometimes the spirit may be a legendary character such as the Bach Ma mountain, a Taoist deity or a historic figure.

? MARCO POLO INSIGHT

Significant offerings

Did you know that in temples the plates with fruit offerings are deeply significant? A coconut, for example, symbolizes frugality, while a papaya means pleasure. The custard apple grants a wish, prunes promise old age, the pink dragon fruit provides power and strength, and »dragon eyes« (longans) are said to have relaxing properties.

CONFUCIANISM

Approximately 2500 years ago, the Chinese philosopher Confucius designed a strictly hierarchical social model which allocates each individual to his proper place within the community, with closely defined rights and duties. The stricter an individual adheres to the model, the better the society functions and the stronger is the empire. According to Confucius the state is much like a **big family** – both are structured following the same set of rules. Within his society model he distinguishes five different forms of shared existence: ruler – subject, master – servant, husband – wife, elder brother – younger brother and friend – friend. While the first four pairs describe a relation of dominance and subordination, the last is a relation of equals. A sense of duty is the basic requirement for all members of society. Subordinates also need to be loyal and obedient towards their master or ruler and to accept their place, while the latter function as role models and need to care for their subordinates.

Confucius searches for nobleness in human beings; a noble person embodies all **virtues** such as education, tolerance, a sense of duty, public spiritedness, and justness. The more a person matches this ideal, the more he or she is entitled to become a leader in a state. However, these virtues are not innate, but need to be acquired through education and study. Therefore, irrespective of social class, education is of the utmost importance for Confucius. He therefore disapproves of a hereditary monarchy, instead making a case for the strict selection of rulers on the basis of tests.

Confucian idea of man

The major impact of Confucianism in later years is mainly due to the fact that Confucius's teachings were also understood by the general

Impact

Respect for elders is a pillar of Confuzianism

public. To him, a philosophy that could not be practiced had no right to exist. By providing only a few clear rules, he allowed the people to practice them as well. However, his teachings were not spread until centuries after his death. They were to serve as a **state philosophy** for over 2000 years. In 1908, during the final stages of the Chinese Empire, Confucius was even canonized. Confucianism came to Vietnam in the 2nd century and became the predominant philosophy here. Up until 1915, aspiring civil servants had to pass exams in Confucian teachings in **Mandarin** before they could take up a position (▶MARCO POLO Insight p.264).

Change | Though Confucianism remained the predominant philosophy for a long time, it slowly degenerated. For example, in Vietnam rulers were not elected; instead the system of dynasties was maintained, which often led to incompetent people governing the country. While the rulers were willing to claim Confucian rights, they did not live up to the corresponding duties. Alongside this there emerged a scholarly guild that considered it their duty to preserve the untainted teachings, but not to develop them any further. As a consequence, Confucianism froze in a backward-oriented movement that glorified the past and was less and less able to face new developments. Not least because of this trend, Europe's colonial powers easily gained ground in Vietnam in the 19th century.

Confucianism today | To this day, Confucianism plays an important role in daily life in Vietnam. Any changes that have occurred over the past 100 years have been unable to dissipate the hierarchical structures of state and family. This becomes especially noticeable in any conversation, where the first question is always about **age**. The rule of thumb is the older, the better. This helps establish a ranking between the two people, which allows assessment of one another. Furthermore, Vietnam has separate concepts for the elder and younger brother and for the elder and younger sister. This is also helps determine the hierarchical position of each family member. The effectiveness of Confucian ideas was confirmed through the victory of the north over the south: while the former were resolute in their organization both socially and politically, the latter were split into numerous groups and cliques who only had their own interests in mind.

TAOISM

Natural philosophy according to Lao Tse | Unlike Confucianism, Taoism is a natural philosophy which can be traced back to the Chinese philosopher Lao Tse, who lived in Northern China in the 6th century BC. The central idea of his philosophy is the Tao (Dao), which can be literally translated as **»the path«**. Lao

The ruler of the north is said to have power over the winds

Tse's underlying idea is that all things have an innate force that cannot be perceived by our senses. It acts not through its strength, but through its apparent softness and subtlety. Water, for example, though the weakest medium, can still erode the strongest stone. Lao Tse does not weigh good against evil, as both are inherent in the Tao, and water can only work in interaction with the stone. This belief is emblematized through **Yin and Yang**, the ancient representation of male and female which creates harmony by mutual permeation and interaction.

The ideal of Taoism is the sovereign human (the sage). He has authority without being authoritarian. He guides humans solely through his presence and provides certainty that everything is in order. He acts much like a conductor who, with only few movements of his baton, makes an entire orchestra play together. Lao Tse rejects laws, orders and prohibitions as they demonstrate a lack of **sovereignty**. Although his teachings were written down in the ancient book of Tao Te Ching (Dao De Jing), Lao Tse is against written proclamations, as these would already be selective and therefore a restriction. Advice is not given as it would involve an assessment of good

The figure of the Jade Emperor in the main sanctuary at the Temple of the Jade Mountain on Hoan Kiem Lake in Hanoi

and evil. Instead, Lao Tse propagated his views in sometimes paradoxical aphorisms. For example, about the perfect leader he writes: »When the effective leader is finished with his work, the people say it happened naturally.«

Taoism and spirituality is one of the central themes: the religion expresses its spiritual nature in the worshipping of gods, spirits and demons of nature. They are integrated into a hierarchical system led by the **Emperor of Jade** Ngoc Hoang. He is supported by Bac Dau (Star of the North) who watches over the dead, and Nam Tao (Star of the South) who keeps an account of the living. Their subjects are the four mothers representing the cardinal points of the compass, but also the four elements heaven, earth, water and wood. There are only a few purely Taoist temples in Vietnam. Taoist and Buddhist deities are often found side by side or worshipped in community centres or at family altars.

BUDDHISM

Founder of Buddhism — Buddhist teachings go back to **Siddhartha Gautama**, a prince who lived in northern India at the foot of the Himalaya during the 5th century BC. Raised in wealth and luxury, while out on a ride he came across an old man, a diseased person and a corpse, as well as a monk. To him, these encounters were crucial experiences: he decided to abjure courtly life to find the **meaning of life**. He followed various philosophical teachings without ever finding a satisfactory response to his questions. At about 30 years of age, however, he gained knowledge through his own meditation and became Buddha, which translates as »the enlightened one«. In the centuries to follow he travelled through India to propagate his teachings before, at about 80 years of age, he died, or rather entered nirvana.

Cycle of life — Like all eastern religions, Buddhism also considers life as a cycle – an eternal succession of birth, death and rebirth. According to Buddha's teachings, life means suffering and the purpose of humanity is to break this cycle. In this context suffering means not physical pain but **futility and illusiveness**, because everything worldly perishes. The reason for human imprisonment within this eternal cycle of life is that they are attached to earthly concerns, above all to material objects. Only when they succeed in detaching themselves from perishable things in life will they achieve enlightenment and break this endless cycle. The enlightened will not be reborn but instead enter nirvana **nirvana**. Nirvana does not mean paradise in a Christian sense, but rather signifies leaving all earthly existence behind in a state of highest meditation.

According to Buddha, the ability to reach enlightenment is inherent in all humans and only needs to be called forth. In order to reach enlightenment, Buddha came up with a set of rules called the Eightfold Path, which consist of: 1. the right view, 2. the right intention, 3. the right speech, 4. the right action, 5. the right livelihood, 6. the right effort, 7. the right mindfulness, 8. the right concentration. Buddha did not in the least assume that humans reach enlightenment during the course of one life, but that they need to work their way up from reincarnation to reincarnation until one day in a far existence they enter nirvana.

The Eightfold Path

Composure and confidence are Buddhist character traits. Believers know they do not miss out on anything, since whatever they are refused in this life can be made up for in the next. They are not ascetics, but do not strive for wealth as they believe anything earthly (material) is perishable. At the same time they are confident that they can, one day, leave their earthly existence behind. They are **lenient** toward all fellow beings as they, just like the Buddhists themselves, are also travelling the tedious path to enlightenment.

Buddhist concept of man

Buddhism came to Vietnam in the 2nd century from two directions – from the north via China in the form of Mahayana (the Greater Vehicle), and from the south via India in the form of Hinayana (the Inferior Vehicle). Mahayana, which is widespread in East Asia, represents the **main school of Buddhism** in Vietnam. According to its interpretation there are not only Buddhas, but also Bodhisattvas. These people have already reached the state of enlightenment, but voluntarily do not enter nirvana in order to help others on their way. They help not only monks but also perfectly ordinary mortals to reach enlightenment.

Mahayana Buddhism

Hinayana, which is common mainly in Burma, Thailand, Laos and Cambodia, teaches that every individual needs to find the path to enlightenment on their own. Furthermore, a person can only reach enlightenment as a **monk**. Therefore, the path to nirvana is only open to a few people, hence the name »the Inferior Vehicle«.

Hinayana Buddhism

Altar with various Buddha statues and an abundance of offerings

Impact of Buddhism

Buddhism was most strongly promoted from the 10th to 12th century when it became a state religion in Vietnam. Many temples and monasteries were built during this time. However, from the 13th century onwards it was repressed by Confucianism which accused it of not being state-friendly and lacking commitment to social engagement. Buddhism became a religion of the individual, but it found fewer followers within the educated social classes than among the common people.

Buddhism and spirituality

Since most people were not familiar with the theoretical framework of Buddhism, they found help and refuge in Bodhisattvas. At the very top of the hierarchy of Buddhist deities are Buddhas of three generations (the past, the present and the future). The Buddha of the past A Di Da (Amitabha) supports people during catharsis. The Buddha of the present Thich Ca Mau Ni, on the other hand, relates to the historical Buddha Siddharta Gautama and is considered a teacher, while Di Lac (Maitreya), the Buddha of the future, is always portrayed laughing and round-bellied. One of the most popular figures among the Bodhisattvas is the goddess of charity (Quan Am or Guan Yin). The Buddhist healers, however, were combined with other deities from various religions to form an entire pantheon of gods. Therefore a lot of Buddhist temples often also feature Taoist deities or elements of ancestor worship (▶MARCO POLO Insight p.402).

CHRISTIANITY

European discoverers were generally followed directly by missionaries – both in Asia and America. Unlike in America, however, Christianity had to compete with religions that were already in existence. The first records of missionary activities date from the early 16th century: as early as 1533 the »teachings of Jesus« were forbidden. This was followed by proselytizations through Dominicans from Spain, Portugal and France and from the 17th century also by Jesuit priests, who had previously been expelled from Japan. Alexandre de Rhodes(▶Famous People) is especially worthy of mention at this point. He was first active in Annam (Central Vietnam) and later also in Tonkin (North Vietnam). Alongside his activities as a missionary he developed the first Vietnamese to Spanish/Portuguese dictionary bringing Latin writing to Vietnam, which is still in use today. At the end of his stay, the estimated Christian community in Vietnam numbered approximately 300,000 people.

Proselytization of Vietnam

Although persecution of Christians took place throughout the 18th century, the number of believers rose to 400,000 by the beginning of the Nguyen dynasty in the early 19th century. Due to a tendency to follow the teachings of Confucius, further persecution was recorded between 1825 and 1883, when approximately 100,000 Christians were killed.

Persecution of Christians

When the Communists assumed power in 1975, Christians were forced to accept the same restrictions as other religious communities, such as limited mobility, working on Sundays, closing of seminaries, etc. However, despite the changing course of history, today about 6 million Vietnamese people are Christians, mainly Catholics. Thus, Vietnam has the second highest number of Christians in Asia – second only to the Philippines.

Christianity after the unification

ISLAM

The number of Muslims in the Vietnamese population today amounts to approximately 1%. The Cham are the main followers of this religion. From the fourth to the 14th century the Cham formed a re-

Islam »light«

Welcome to Everyday Life

Experience Vietnam off the beaten track and meet »regular everyday folk« -and pick up some tips from a designated local expert.

HOMESTAYS

The homestay concept in Vietnam covers community homestays with direct links to families through to homestays with pool and staff. Staying with the hill tribes of Sa Pa, in the Mekong Delta or in a dormitory or private room on one of the small islands less frequented by tourists. The further away from the tourist trail, the more authentically original the family-based accommodation becomes and the likelihood increases of being served Vietnamese coffee rather than Nescafé.

Bookings are usually made via (local) travel agencies as part of a trekking tour or Mekong boat voyage (Sa Pa Tourism or Cuu Long Tourist). Guest families can also be found on:
www.homestaybooking.com
www.couchsurfing.org

SHADOWBOXING WITH VIETNAMESE

Keeping Yan and Yang in balance through shadowboxing in Vietnam requires an early start to the day. Between 5.30am and 7am each morning, the grounds of Hoan Kiem Lake are busy with students of tai chi and other keen athletes – it is possible to join in any number of activities, such as aerobic gymnastics to a cha cha beat, guaranteed to work up a sweat, or badminton as the royal statue of Ly Thai To looks on.

Hanoi: Hoan Kiem Lake
Saigon: Tao Dam Cultural Park (approx. 8am–9am) or Le Van Tam Park (Hai Ba Trung, corner of Dien Bien Phu)

SUPPORT SOCIAL PROJECTS

Guests who stay at the tiny »Baguette & Chocolat« will not only enjoy fine food in front of the fireplace, they will also be supporting a social project for street children of the Hoa Sua School.

Dine in »socially correct« fashion at KOTO with former street kids and purchase souvenirs at Craft Link or next door at the Hoa Sen Gallery (all three can be found in Van Mieu Street) – the takings go to ethnic minority groups.

www.hoasuaschool.com, ▶*p. 249*
www.craftlink.com.vn, ▶*p. 249*
KOTO, ▶*p. 252,*

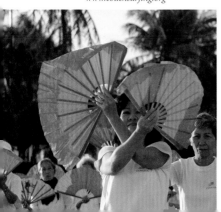

HO HO HO CHI MINH

Every year, many thousands of Vietnamese pay their respects to their highly revered father of the nation. Vast parties and large family groups from all over the country flock to Hanoi. Tourists also join the long queues outside the Ho Chi Minh mausoleum and reverentially file past the glass sarcophagus of the leader of the revolution – not in shorts, spaghetti tops or mini-skirts, of course. At 9pm precisely, the flag is lowered with full military pomp.

Hi Chi Minh Mausoleum, Ba Dinh Square, Hanoi

MAKE LANTERNS OR LEARN TO COOK IN HOI AN

There are still some three dozen lantern makers and lantern manufacturers in Hoi An. Long Vy not only exports to Hollywood, he also offers workshops for tourists, as does the non-profit organization Life Start Foundation, as well as drawing classes with local artists. If the delicate handicraft required for the fine silk material is too taxing, then Hoi An also boasts esteemed cookery courses.

Long Vy lanterns
6 Phan Chau Trinh, Hoi An
Tel. 0510/360 66 11 and mobile no. 090/8646 47 31
www.hoianlantern.com.vn (only bookable in Vietnamese: courses from 60,000 VNDBooking via hotel will be more expensive)
or
Life Start Foundation
77 Phan Chau Trinh, Hoi An
www.lifestartfoundation.org.au
Mobile no. 0167/35 59 44
(half day US$25)

gional power in Central Vietnam with Hindu beliefs. After their sub-ordination by the Vietnamese they converted to Islam. This new belief was also brought to Southeast Asia between the 7th and 10th century by Arab traders and seafarers, though it did not find many followers. Today, the Cham represent an **isolated island of faith**, unconnected to the central ideas of Islam. The religious command-ments are therefore fostered less than in Arab countries. Vietnamese Muslims do not go on a pilgrimage to Mecca, and the prayers that are normally performed five times a day are performed only on Fridays; the month of Ramadan is shortened to three days. Furthermore, other common forms of religious faith are fostered in Vietnam along-side Islam, such as, for example, animism or the worship of ancestors.

SECTS

Caodaism
As previously mentioned, several different religions are practiced side by side in spiritually diverse Vietnam. The denomination of the Cao Dai goes one step further. With approximately two million be-lievers today, it is limited to **South Vietnam** and aims to unite all of Vietnam's religions into one. The Cao Dai sect was founded in the 1920s by the spiritualist Ngo Van Chieu. Cao Dai sees itself as the third and last revelation of religions that have already manifested themselves twice – first through Moses and the mythical creatures of Eastern religions, later through the historical figures Confucius, Lao Tse, Buddha, Jesus, and Muhammad. The third revelation comes in the shape of the Cao Dai, the Supreme Being, which will guide people to salvation. Their symbol shows an eye framed by rays of light watching over the earth. Its teachings take elements from all other religious doctrines, but to an outsider seem somewhat randomly se-lected. During spiritualistic sessions its members try to make contact with the Supreme Being. Historical figures can act as a medium, such as the French author Victor Hugo or the founder of the Chinese Re-public, Sun Yat-Sen. The Cao Dai are tightly structured and are ori-ented towards the Catholic Church, with one difference being that women can also become priests. Their headquarters, the so-called high tower, is located in the Tay Ninh province northwest of Saigon, close to the Cambodian border.

Hoa Hao sect
The Hoa Hao sect was founded in 1939 by the monk Huynh Phu So and named after his native village in the Mekong Delta. He preached a **reformative Buddhism** that renounces pomp and prestige and propagates a simple life. Due to his bond with spiritualists, Huynh Phu So was pronounced insane by the French and sent to a mental home where he managed, however, to persuade the director of the institution of his religion. During the Second World War, with the

help of the Japanese, he built a strong army, which controlled parts of the Mekong Delta. After a falling-out with the Vietminh, Huynh Phu So was assassinated in 1947. Nine years later the sect's military branch was destroyed by the Diem government. The number of followers of the Hoa Hao sect is estimated at approximately 1.5 million believers. It is difficult to determine the exact number, since it does not maintain any temples and its followers do not attract attention through any particular style of clothing.

The all-seeing eye

History

Small and Tough

The Chinese, the French, the Japanese and later even the mightiest power on earth, the USA – all staked claims of various kinds on the small nation in Southeast Asia. And all their exertions ultimately ended in defeat and enforced retreat.

EARLY EMPIRES AND CIVILIZATIONS

7th to 3rd century BC	Bronze Age (Dong Son culture) and the Van Lang Empire of the legendary Hung Kings
3rd century BC	Union of several princedoms to form the Au Lac kingdom
111 BC	Start of 1000 years of Chinese domination
931–938	Victory over China, independence instituted

There are different theories about the ethnological origin of the Vietnamese. Today it is generally suggested that the Viet were a highly fragmented ethnic group of Melanesian-Indonesian origin that settled in the south of China. In the 4th century BC their families gradually moved to the southern **Red River delta**. Much of the first millennia of the approximately 4000-year history of the Vietnamese is lost in legends in which dragon kings and mountain fairies as well as the Han and Viet peoples play a major role. In the third millennium BC, 100 Viet principalities allegedly emerged from the Bach Viet kingdom of the dragon lord Lac Long Quan and the immortal fairy Au Co. Yet all Viet tribes were almost completely Sinicized (i.e. they underwent the process of becoming Chinese) in the 3rd and 2nd century BC under the influence of the Han Chinese. The Van Lang kingdom is thought to have been one of the last legendary dynasties, though this theory has not yet been scientifically proven.

Early-history legends

The Dong Son culture was named after a village in North Vietnam (Thanh Hoa province), where in 1924 archaeologists found hatchets, daggers and belt buckles. Some of the most fascinating relics of the Dong Son era are **bronze drums** (▶p.227), of which more than 150 were discovered in Vietnam.

Dong Son culture

In the 3rd century BC Vietnam left the realm of myths and legends with the newly founded kingdom of Au Lac. Some princedoms in the Red River Delta had presumably merged under An Duong Vuong (also Thuc Phan) around 257 BC in order to fend off Chinese invasions.

Kingdom of Au Lac

King Tu Duc's life is described on his tomb stele in Hue

Independent kingdom of Nam Viet

The Chinese commanding General Trieu Da defeated Au Lac after several unsuccessful attacks. He founded the Nam Viet kingdom around 200 BC and laid the foundation for the Trieu dynasty. The capital of his kingdom, which was largely independent of China, was situated close to what is now Guangzhou (Canton).

CHINESE COLONY AND INDEPENDENCE

Chinese protectorate of Giao Chi

In 111 BC Emperor Wu of Han captured Nanyue and turned it into the Chinese protectorate of Giao Chi. This marked the beginning of roughly 1000 years of Chinese domination of the »barbarians« in Vietnam. Their submission resulted in the exploitation of resources in Vietnam, regular tribute payments and the continuous immigration of the Chinese. Under the Chinese, everyday life changed so dramatically that the Viet nobility finally revolted and fought for its national identity. In AD 40 the **Trung sisters** and their followers made a

These stakes are said to have pierced Chinese ships at the battle on Bach Dang River (Museum of History, Hanoi)

stand against the Chinese. They appointed themselves queens and ruled for three years until they were defeated by the Chinese army; many Viet noblemen either emigrated or were banished. Although the Chinese called the Vietnamese region of Annam the »pacified south« from the 7th century onwards, there were still more uprisings and upheaval against the Chinese occupiers. During the 2nd century, Indian pilgrims started bringing the **teachings of Buddha** to Vietnam. Later, most Vietnamese adopted the Dhyana doctrine of the Indian monk Bodhidharma (6th century), the founder of Zen Buddhism.

As the downfall of the Tang dynasty weakened the Chinese empire, the Vietnamese general Ngo Quyen, after years of battle, brought independence to Vietnam in 939 and founded the Ngo dynasty – the **first purely Vietnamese dynasty**. Co Loa, the old seat of the Au Lac kingdom, was to be its capital. After Ngo Quyen's death in 944, generals and princes competed for power until one of them, Dinh Tien Hoang, prevailed in 968 and established the Dai Co Viet kingdom.

Dai Co Viet kingdom

THE GREAT DYNASTIES

1009–1225	Ly dynasty introduces the civil service system.
10th century	Confucianism becomes the state religion.
1288	Tran Hung Dao defeats the Mongols.
16th century	Trinh and Nguyen split the country in two.
1771–1802	Tay Son uprising
1802	Hue is made capital under Emperor Gia Long (Nguyen).

The Ly dynasty was the first major dynasty in Vietnam. In 1010, on the order of the first king, Ly Thai To, the capital was moved to Thang Long (now Hanoi). Many important and **far-reaching reforms** were implemented during his reign: he created a civil service system, financed through tributes and taxes and consisting not only of members of the royal family. In addition, general conscription was introduced, science and culture thrived, and the Chinese-Vietnamese script Chu Nom developed. Early dyke constructions successfully held off the yearly floodings of the Red River delta. The rulers of the Ly dynasty were greatly devoted to Buddhism; when it came to the education of scholars, however, they promoted Confucian philosophy, which became a **state religion** in the 10th century. The common people mixed Buddhist, Confucian and Taoist beliefs with animist elements – this »People's Buddhism« is still largely practised today. The third king of the Ly dynasty, Ly Thanh Tong, defeated the Cham in the 11th century, occupied their provinces in the north and renamed the entire country Dai Viet.

Ly dynasty

Tran dynasty The Tran clan, related to the Ly dynasty, established a new dynasty in Dai Viet. One Tran family member in particular became widely known through his glorious victories over the Mongols: in 1288, Tran Hung Dao drove out the outmanned army of the **Mongol ruler Kublai Khan** at the Bach Dang River. But the Tran dynasty also expanded its empire peacefully, for example by the marriage of one of the king's sisters to the Cham king in the south in the early 14th century. The kingdom of Champa became a tribute-paying vassal state, until Cham troops invaded the capital, Thang Long, in 1371 and 1377, destroyed the imperial palace and annexed the southern provinces.

Diarchy of the Trinh and the Nguyen In 1527 the ambitious provincial governor Mac Dang Dung had temporarily seized power over the gradually collapsing Le dynasty – though his dominance was only short-lived. The Le dynasty, reinstated in 1533, thereafter practically ruled in name only, for it was members of the feudal families Trinh and Nguyen that actually pulled the strings. Vietnam saw a time of thriving arts, and its **ceramics** in particular were greatly sought-after and mimicked throughout Asia. The initially more powerful Trinh took control over the marionette king from the Le dynasty by marrying into the imperial family and by taking over strategically important military posts in the north of the country. From the late 16th century the Nguyen also extended their influence as they built their palaces in Central Vietnam. For decades, the two families fought a civil war, until around 1673 they divided Vietnam in two. The Nguyen managed to continually expand their territory southward to the Gulf of Siam, receiving military support from the Portuguese, who meanwhile had arrived with their ships. At the end of the 17th century they had an enormous fleet of 133 vessels. In 1678, the Nguyen clan chose Phu Xuan (now Hue) as their seat of government. From here the clan invaded Cambodia in 1767 and evicted the Khmer from the Mekong Delta, where they had earlier founded the city of Gia Dinh (Saigon) around 1694.

Dynastic Urns of Hue: symbols for the emperors of the Nguyen dynasty

Tay Son uprising The uprising against the Trinh and Nguyen dynasties began in 1771, headed by three brothers from Tay Son, who with the help of dissatisfied soldiers and peasants rebelled against the high taxes, disastrous corruption and **poor economic conditions** in the country. Eventually, in 1776–77, they were actually successful as the Tay Son rebels were able to conquer the territories of the Nguyen dynasty. In turn, the Chinese of the Qing dynasty used these years of upheaval to stage another attack on the separated nation, worn down by peasant uprisings and internal power struggles. This attempt was in vain, however, and in 1789 the Chinese were expelled again by one of the Tay Son brothers (who now called himself Emperor Quang Trung).

The only surviving Nguyen prince, Nguyen Anh, defeated the Tay Son brothers after two decades of battle and thus ended his exile in Siam – albeit with French assistance. He reclaimed first Saigon, then Hue, and proceeded to march on Hanoi. In 1802, under the name Gia Long, he pronounced himself the first emperor of the last Vietnamese dynasty, the Nguyen dynasty. During military campaigns the neighbouring countries of Laos and Cambodia were turned into vassal states. Hue was made capital of the reunited empire of Viet Nam (from 1804). During this period, Vietnam faced claims to power from two foreign rivals: China and France. Under the rule of the Emperor's son, Minh Mang and his successor, Thieu Tri, Franco-Vietnamese relations deteriorated noticeably.

Nguyen dynasty

UNDER FOREIGN RULE

1862–63	French colonization begins.
1940–45	Japan occupies Vietnam.
1946–54	First Indochina War
1954	Geneva Conference: division of Vietnam

FRENCH COLONIAL RULE

French battleships landed in Da Nang (formerly Tourane) in 1858. By only one year later, the French had conquered Gia Dinh (Saigon); later, towards the end of the 19th century, they took the north, including Hanoi. The colonial army gradually occupied all of Indochina (Cambodia, Laos and Vietnam). In 1862–63, the country's governance was contractually taken from the Nguyen and given to France. Vietnam was split into the colony of Cochinchina in the south, the Annam protectorate in the centre and Tonkin in the north. In particular, it was the **rich mineral resources** (especially coal and tin) as well as agricultural products (such as caoutchouc, rice, tobacco, tea and coffee) that made the operation in the Far East worthwhile.

French colonial master in a rickshaw with coolie

However, the country's infrastructure – the road network, railroads, docks, mines, and factories – was also developed with French assistance. These projects were financed by taxes and the state's monopoly on the opium trade.

First resistance movements

During the 20th century, signs of an anti-colonial movement became increasingly noticeable. It stemmed particularly from the educated upper class, some of whose sons and daughters even went to French schools and universities. In 1930 the Communist Party of Vietnam (later CP of Indochina) was founded in Hong Kong. In Central Vietnam the resistance against the French reached its most violent later that yearwith an uprising of the farmers and workers in **Nghe An**. The French colonial rulers put the nationalist movements and revolts down with utmost brutality and banished all opposing factions to the prison island of Con Dao, including nearly all leaders of the Vietnamese CP. Eleven years later the Communist League for the Independence of Vietnam, or Vietminh (Viet Minh) was founded, with Ho Chi Minh (▶Famous People) as its leader. In the following years the United States provided weapons for the Vietminh to support their fight against Japanese occupation.

During the Second World War, Vietnam experienced yet another period of co-sovereignty: although the Japanese occupied the country from 1940, they still tolerated the French administration. Japan granted independence to Vietnam only in 1945, having disarmed and interned the French colonial army at the end of the war after all. The Nguyen Emperor Bao Dai (▶Famous People) was now allowed temporarily to rule the country under Japanese supervision, a situation that persisted until the Japanese capitulated in August of the same year.

Second World War

With the capitulation of Japan, Ho Chi Minh took the opportunity to call for an **armed revolt**. In Hanoi, on 2 September 1945, he proclaimed the nation's independence – the Democratic Republic of Vietnam (DRV) was born. Bao Dai had to abdicate, and, for the first time in Vietnam, elections were held in January 1946, with a victory for the Vietminh.

Declaration of Independence

FIRST INDOCHINA WAR

Even though the former French colonial rulers, in signing the French-Vietnamese Agreement of Hanoi, had recognized the independence of the DRV, they occupied Saigon and Hanoi again only shortly afterwards. The bombardment of the Hai Phong harbour in November 1946 was the official beginning of the First Indochina War between France and Vietnam, a guerrilla war that was to last several years. Ho Chi Minh's government was forced to go underground and hide in the north in the inaccessible mountains near Cao Bang. In 1948 the former emperor, Bao Dai, was reinstated by the French as regent of the formally independent state of Vietnam. In this way this once purely colonial conflict evolved into an international proxy war and split the entire world at the time of the Cold War: while China and the Soviet Union supported the north with weapons and considered its government to be legitimate, the western states took sides with France and its marionette leader Bao Dai.

The Vietnamese Struggle for Independence

The French army failed for years to make any real headway against the liberation movement. In 1954, the decisive battle took place in the far north, near Dien Bien Phu. Soldiers of the Vietnamese People's Army (VPA) besieged, bombarded, starved and eventually defeated the French troops in their own stronghold. During this 55-day siege, which ended on 7 May 1954, about 3000 French soldiers died. The legendary Vietnamese commander-in-chief, General Vo Nguyen Giap, later also repeatedly challenged the US troops.

Battle of Dien Bien Phu

DIVISION OF VIETNAM

Geneva Conference

In April 1954 the immediate opponents of the war, the neighbouring countries Laos and Cambodia as well as the four world powers (the USA, the Soviet Union, China and Great Britain) met at the **Geneva Conference** in Paris to determine the future of the Southeast Asian nation. The provisional **demarcation line** at the 17th parallel at Dong Ha was only meant to divide the country up until the all-Vietnamese elections in July 1956. But Dong Ha became a permanent border for the next 21 years. The Geneva Conference was signed by neither South Vietnam nor the United States.

The North – Democratic Republic of Vietnam

Under Ho Chi Minh the Communists ruled in the north of the newly separated country from the capital Hanoi. The socialistic Democratic Republic of Vietnam became a one-party state (the CP) where all urban and rural family businesses were put under state control. Those in power began systematically to cleanse the country north of the 17th parallel, which caused about one million North Vietnamese to **flee** to the south. Every day alleged traitors were denunciated or executed. A rigorously enforced land reform in 1955/56 increased the feeling of insecurity among the population and led to more uprisings in the north.

The Republic of South Vietnam

The Republic of South Vietnam was proclaimed in the capital of the pro-West south, Saigon, in October of 1955. The anti-Communist and Catholic Ngo Dinh Diem became head of state. Fearing a likely victory for the Communists, he simply cancelled the all-Vietnamese elections of 1956 that had been agreed upon at the Geneva Convention. Instead Ngo Dinh Diem had himself appointed president after a manipulated referendum in the south. The French army only left South Vietnam in 1956. Starting in the mid-1950s, however, the United States sent military help and advisors to solve the conflict with the north. Meanwhile, the South Vietnamese head of government gradually transformed into a **dictator** who took action against Buddhists and political dissidents with relentless violence. In 1963, Buddhist monks publicly **self-immolated**, while South Vietnamese students demonstrated in the streets (Famous People, Thich Quang Duc).

VIETNAM WAR (►MARCO POLO INSIGHT p.58)

1963	Overthrow of South Vietnam's dictator Ngo Dinh Diem
1964–75	Second Indochina War
1975	North Vietnamese invade (FNL) Saigon and seize power.

The Vietcong (Vietnamese Communists) was a guerrilla organization from South Vietnam and had been part of the resistance from 1956 onwards. The regular troops of South Vietnam were already considerably weakened due to widespread corruption and numerous cases of defection. Driven underground by political persecution, in 1960 the South Vietnamese opposition founded the NLF, the **National Liberation Front**, with Communist support from Hanoi. With the beginning of the 1960s, the US continuously sent more military advisors to South Vietnam: their number increased from 2000 (at the end of 1960) to 16,300 (at the end of 1963). The reason for this action was the so called domino theory: Western politicians (the Americans in particular) feared a Communist victory in Vietnam would cause a domino effect in the neighbouring countries. After several attempted coups that all failed, the military removed Ngo Dinh Diem from office and executed him in 1963. All of this was supported by the CIA and silently approved by President John F. Kennedy.

Preparations for war

The so-called **Gulf of Tonkin Incident** is considered to be the official cause for the Vietnam War (Second Indochina War). In August 1964 the US destroyer »Maddox« engaged in a gun battle with two torpedo boats off the North Vietnamese coast. Later American investigations revealed that the »Maddox« had been involved in a secret manoeuvre with the South Vietnamese navy. US President Lyndon B. Johnson

Gulf of Tonkin Incident

One of the most forceful photographic images ever: Nick Ut pressed the shutter as a crying girl from Trang Bang ran towards him

Green Hell

The war in Vietnam may have brought an end to partition, but it took many years for the North and South Vietnamese to come together effectively. For the USA, defeat at the hands of the »jungle warriors« was a traumatic experience, both in political and social terms.

▶ **Parties in conflict and losses**

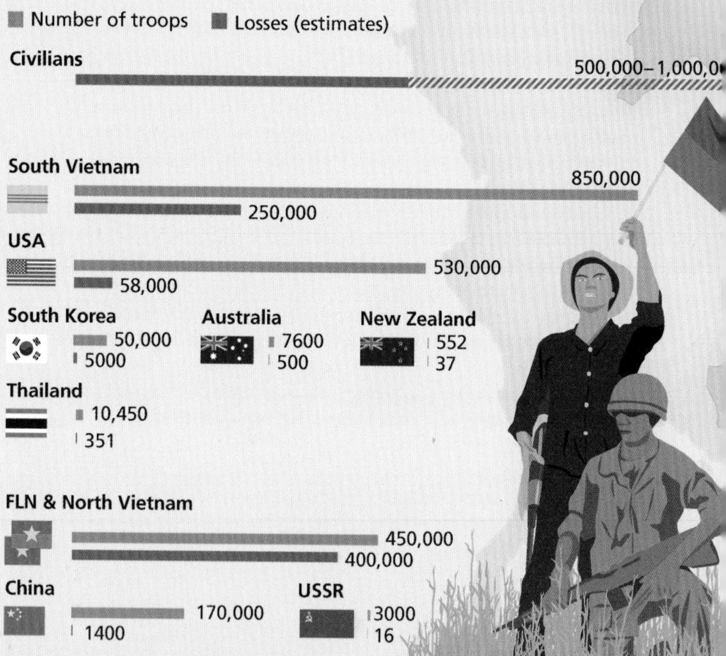

■ Number of troops   ■ Losses (estimates)

Civilians
500,000–1,000,0▮

South Vietnam
850,000
250,000

USA
530,000
58,000

South Korea
50,000
5000

Australia
7600
500

New Zealand
552
37

Thailand
10,450
351

FLN & North Vietnam
450,000
400,000

China
170,000
1400

USSR
3000
16

▶ **Chronology of the Vietnam War**

7 May 1954
The French Army surrenders at Dien Bien Phu in North Vietnam: end of French colonial rule in Indochina, partition of Vietnam.

1955
The USA dispatches 350 official military advisors to South Vietnam.

1956
South Vietnam's regime blocks open elections, fearing a victory for the Communist Viet Minh.

1962
U.S. Air Force unleashes »Agent Orange« defoliation programme.

August 1964
A provoked torpedo attack by North Vietnamese boats on a US warship in the Gulf of Tonkin is used by the USA as a pretext to commence with the bombardment of North Vietnam.

8 March 1965
Regular US ground forces land in Vietnam.

▶ **Key military operations**

Siege at Khe Sanh   21.1. – 8.4.1968

| USA / South Vietnam | ■ 45,000 / 2016 |
| North Vietnam | 34,100 / ~12,000 |

North Vietnamese troops were unable to take the US base close to the border with Laos. After the siege, the US Army actually gave up Khe Sanh.

Tet Offensive   ✕   30.1. – 23.9.1968

| USA / South Vietnam | ~1 mil. / >9078 |
| Viet Cong / North Vietnam | ~500,000 / 45,276 |

Although the Tet Offensive ended in a heavy defeat for the Communists, the public mood shifted in the US, as the Viet Cong had taken the war into the cities of the south, catching the US Army totally by surprise.

▶ **Material battle**
More bombs descended on Vietnam, Laos and Cambodia than in all the theatres of World War II combined.

Vietnam:
🔹🔹🔹🔹🔹🔹🔹🔹🔹🔹 5 mil. t

Cambodia:
🔹🔹🔹🔹🔹 2.7 mil. t

Laos:
🔹🔹🔹🔹 2 mil. t   🔹 = 500,000 kg

NORTH VIETNAM

○ **Hanoi**

Demilitarised Zone

17th Parallel

○ Hue

Da Nang ○

My Lay

LAOS

Ho Chi Minh Trail

▶ **Ho Chi Minh Trail**
The Viet Cong's most important supply route was heavily bombed by the USA.

SOUTH VIETNAM

CAMBODIA

○ Saigon

©BAEDEKER

31 January 1968
Tet Offensive

March 1968
When news of the My Lai Massacre emerges, the USA seek peace talks, which begin in May in Paris.

31 October 1968
Bombardment of North Vietnam ceases

1969
Gradual withdrawal of US combat forces as »Vietnamization« of the war begins.

March 1972
Following the withdrawal of the US Army, North Vietnamese troops march into the South.

Mai 1972
Resumption of the bombardment of North Vietnam

27 January 1973
Paris Peace Accords to establish peace, but proves ineffective.

30 April 1975
South Vietnam capitulates.

used this incident as a pretext for sending reinforcement troops to South Vietnam and for ordering the bombing of North Vietnam, both with the consent of the US Congress. Oddly, the so called Tonkin Resolution had already been sitting in the President's drawer months before the alleged attacks – as theNew York Times reported with extracts from the top secret »Pentagon Papers«. The Americans never officially declared war on North Vietnam. The task force **»Operation Rolling Thunder«** was the starting point for the US entry into North Vietnam. In March 1965, 25,000 soldiers went ashore in the area of Da Nang. Within the following four years their number rose to a half a million.

»Tiger traps« against US tanks

With state-of-the-art weaponry, the US military was to drive the Communist soldiers out of South Vietnam and defeat the north. The Vietcong, however, employed **guerrilla tactics** against US troops and fought on familiar territory, partly supported by the rural population. Due to their repressive governance in the years before, the rulers in Saigon had long lost the sympathy of many farmers in the hard-fought areas. A multitude of casualties within the civilian population did the rest – a lot of South Vietnamese refugees joined the Communists. In order to cut down the supplies to the Vietcong, a great part of the rural population was eventually relocated to the cities or to so called fortified villages. »Charlie«, as the US troops soon came to call the South Vietnamese underground fighters, inflicted huge losses on the Americans by means of land mines, tiger traps, surprise attacks and acts of sabotage. The **tunnels of Cu Chi** enabled the Vietcong to become virtually invisible. Using this underground complex the Communist fighters even managed to close in on Saigon. Today these tunnels are open to the public. During the day, US troops seemed to prevail, but at night the Vietcong fought back and was able to strike serious blows against the world power. An overall victory by the Communist guerrillas, however, was impossible due to the superiority of American, South Vietnamese and soldiers from allied nations (among them Australia and South Korea). More than 600,000 allied troops fought against 200,000 Communist soldiers from the north and south. To bring this **military stand-off** to an end, US Army Chief of Staff, General Westmoreland even called for the use of nuclear weapons.

In order to win this jungle war, US Army Chief of Staff, General Westmoreland ordered the release of **»Agent Orange«**, a chemical pesticide containing dioxins. Vast areas were declared »free-fire zones«. The favourite target of these defoliation operations was the so-called **Ho Chi Minh Trail** (▶DMZ). The US forces dropped napalm and conventional bombs on this 16,000km/10,000mi-long, heavily branching network of trails, part of which crossed over to

Laos and Cambodia. North Vietnamese fighters ceaselessly travelled these trails bringing (military) supplies from the north to the south and immediately returning for new assignments.

The turning point of the war took place on 31 January 1968, the Vietnamese New Year's Day or »Tet«. Despite the ceasefire agreed for this holiday, the fighters of Ho Chi Minh and the Vietcong attacked positions of the American and the regular South Vietnamese forces. Though the attacks were not a military success and the Communists suffered huge losses (approximately 30,000–50,000 casualties), the consequences for the American government were severe. The news footage showed several Vietcong soldiers on the US embassy grounds, thus proving the American war propaganda about a near end of the war to be all but lies. These pictures came as a shock to the American public. In 1968, United States public opinion finally shifted. More and more war veterans and injured GIs joined the **anti-war movement**, and millions of people in America and Western Europe gathered in the streets to protest against the Vietnam War. The same year, President Johnson announced official peace negotiations that finally began in May in Paris, even though the ceasefire, one of the conditions for negotiation, lasted only a short while – operations soon continued and were officially extended to the neighbouring countries of Laos and Cambodia. Vietnamization of the conflict was conducted under President Richard Nixon as of July 1969: the gradual withdrawal of the US Army was to be counterbalanced by the rearmament of the regular South Vietnamese troops.

Tet Offensive

MARCO ⊕ POLO INSIGHT ?

The war in numbers

A total of 9.7 million tons of bombs were dropped in aerial warfare (the same amount detonated in ground offensives) in Indochina – more than three times as many as in the whole of the Second World War. The Americans spent approximately US$150 billion on the war. The total number of military and civilian fatalities is estimated at up to 3.5 million.

In no other war did the uncensored media coverage have such a resounding impact – an entirely different impact, however, from what had been planned by American military strategists. Reports about the **My Lai Massacre** (16 March 1968) changed public opinion for good. During a 90-minute »search and destroy« operation US soldiers killed 504 villagers: elderly people, women, children and babies. The pictures of Trang Bang (1972) had an even more powerful and symbolic impact on the world's public, and continues to do so to this day. Amongst other things, they showed a naked girl, crying as she ran from the destruction of her village by napalm bombs and towards photographer Nick Ut (▶photo p.57).

Media coverage

Flight by Sea

After the end of the Vietnam War in 1975 about two million so-called boat people fled the country, which was now a Communist state. Those who left the Socialist Republic of Vietnam were mainly ethnic Chinese, well-to-do business people who were persecuted by the new regime.

Many had worked for the Americans or for multinational companies during the war. Now thousands of them were dispossessed and sent to »re-education camps«. Some lost their work permits for decades: former traders and business people were now expected to earn their living in the »New Economic Zones«, as fishermen, on factory production lines or making deliveries by bicycle. Many more fled to avoid prison, as they or members of their family had fought »on the wrong side«.

Dangerous passage

Take the example of Huynh Hanh, who was just 17 years old when he precipitately fled Vietnam in 1977. After the Communist takeover in the south his brothers, who had served in the South Vietnamese army, were regarded as traitors. His father's pharmacy in Saigon was immediately confiscated. Hanh was forced to flee alone. The fishing boat in which he escaped to Thailand was tossed to and fro by waves that were metres high. There was only one day's supply of **drinking water** on board for 24 refugees. Pirates, attracted by thei scant possessions, attacked by boat. Via camps in Thailand and Italy Hanh eventually reached Germany, where his refugee status was recognized. He served an apprenticeship there, and before

long his father joined him. Today the rest of the family is scattered around the world. Hanh returned to Vietnam when his grandmother was on her deathbed. Confucian ethics require children and grandchildren to honour and look after relatives until they die. In conversation Hanh, now a car mechanic in a German company in Saigon, appears more European than Vietnamese. He complains about **arbitrary behaviour of the authorities** and the widespread poverty in his old and new homeland.

It came as a shock to return there after 18 years living in a consumer society run with German efficiency and discipline. His first impression was that the ideology of Karl Marx had given way to **ubiquitous corruption**: at the airport he had to pay 100 dollars extra for a visa in clandestine transaction in order to be allowed to re-enter his home country without difficulties.

Quota refugees

Around 33,000 boat people from Vietnam were stranded in the Federal Republic of Germany and taken in as so-called quota refugees. Following dramatic television images of shipwrecks and people drowning in the South China Sea, there was an overwhelming response to help the refugees in the late 1970s. In 1978, for example, Lower Saxony put an end to the tortuous odyssey of 1000 boat people who had been on the »Hai Hong« off the Malaysian coast with no prospect of entering Malaysia, the country which had been hit the hardest by the influx of refugees.

West German donations succeeded in launching the rescue ship the »**Cap Anamur**« and the Vietnamese were granted financial aid and offered language courses and training in the Federal Republic. But soon this receptivity had to be restricted to family members – the limit of 38,000 quota refugees was not to be exceeded.

Reluctant return

After a repatriation agreement of 1990, and with financial support from the EU, it was mainly so-called economic refugees who returned home, few of them willingly. Each of them received US$410 for **reintegration**, at the time more than the average annual income in Vietnam.

The presence of the United Nations High Commission for Refugees in Hanoi and Saigon was intended to prevent discrimination against those who returned. However, it was not possible for a handful of United Nations observers to monitor the situation of 100,000 repatriated Vietnamese scattered over the whole country. They were by no means welcomed with open arms. The return of the boat people at the same time as the repatriation of workers contracted abroad to other Communist countries led to a **huge rise in the numbers of unemployed**. Most of them had difficulties in finding work, in addition to their problems with a lethargic bureaucracy and corruption. This was why many of them did everything they could to avoid repatriation, even resorting to self-mutilation and threats of suicide, as happened when the last boat people were forcibly deported from Hong Kong.

A refugee boat capsizes as it docks with the »Cap Anamur«, but all on board were saved. The German aid ship saved the lives of around 9000 Vietnamese refugees in the 1970s.

Prolonged
end to the
Vietnam War

In spite of peace talks which began in 1968 and secret negotiations, the war continued for several more years, with heavy bombings of the city of Hanoi. It was not until 27 January 1973 that the opponents signed the **Paris Peace Accords** that were to end the war and guarantee the withdrawal of the US forces. A national reconciliation, however, was yet to come. After the withdrawal of the US troops in 1973 the North Vietnamese government pushed for a victory over South Vietnam and launched a large-scale attack at the beginning of 1975. Thousands of South Vietnamese soldiers defected and fled when the North Vietnamese troops could not be stopped from closing in on **Saigon**. President Nguyen Van Thieu stepped down and fled as well – to Great Britain. On 30 April 1975 the North Vietnamese and Communist troops marched into Saigon and conquered the presidential palace with no resistance of note offered by the South Vietnamese army. The Republic of South Vietnam surrendered unconditionally. The outcome, however, can only be described as horrible: millions of casualties, and hundreds of thousands injured, crippled or missing.

In addition, approximately 10 million homeless refugees and former soldiers roamed the devastated country. Roughly 1600 US soldiers remain unaccounted for to this day; they are the so called MIAs (»missing in action«). Even today the 80 million litres of **defoliant** which were sprayed claims its victims who can be found both among the children of US veterans and in the babies with numerous deformities born in Vietnamese hospitals. Dioxins have a long-term effect on the food chain and, years after the end of the war, are cited as a cause of cancer.

The whole country was bombed to the ground. Endless factories, schools and hospitals, traffic infrastructure, villages and almost half of all cities lay in ruins. Much of the country's wildlife and the better part of the Vietnamese forest were destroyed as well.

UNITY AND THE SOCIALIST PERIOD

1976	Socialist Republic of Vietnam is founded.
1978	Ban on private trade
1979–89	Occupation of Cambodia, overthrow of terror regime
1979	China attacks Vietnam, severe economic crisis
1986	Reforms decided at Sixth National Party Congress
1994	End of the US trade embargo
2001	The moderate Nong Duc Manh becomes the new head of the Communist Party.
2003	Tourism crippled by SARS and bird flu
2007	Vietnam becomes a member of the World Trade Organization (WTO).

As expected, the first ever Vietnamese elections in April 1976 were won by the Communists. On 2 July 1976 the Socialist Republic of Vietnam (SRV) was founded and the north and south were reunited. Ho Chi Minh did not live to see this triumph: the North Vietnamese president had died back in 1969. The reintegration of the capitalistic south after 20 years of separation was now rigidly executed by the Communist Party. In addition to the nationalization of the South Vietnamese economy, the new republic also set up so called re-education camps. The effects of this radical change in the south were catastrophic. Religious freedom was seriously restricted and political persecution did not spare artists, journalists and intellectuals. The nationalization of agricultural holdings and the expropriation of private merchants led to the largest flood of refugees – in particular, the population of Chinese origin fled overland and across the South China Sea. About 2 million people left Vietnam between 1975 and 1990, mostly as boat people (▶MARCO POLO Insight p.62). In terms of foreign policy, Hanoi moved closer to the Soviet Union, much to the displeasure of the Chinese.

Consequences of reunification

Vietnam's old ambitions for expansion towards Laos and Cambodia were gradually beginning to show again. In January 1979 the Vietnamese army marched into the Cambodian capital Phnom Penh, overthrew Pol Pot's regime of terror and ended the genocide. A ten year period of occupation began, with the Cambodian government controlled by the Vietnamese until September 1989. The Chinese, who had supported the terrible regime of the Khmer Rouge, countered the Vietnamese advance into Cambodia with an invasion on Vietnam. This conflict, the Sino-Vietnamese War, took place on the North Vietnamese border in the spring of 1979.

Occupation of Cambodia

PRESENT-DAY VIETNAM

The collapse of the Vietnamese economy had already been looming since 1979, and for obvious reasons: the country's infrastructure and industry had been destroyed; there had been natural catastrophes; military expenses were huge and economic aid from China had stopped in 1978; all exacerbated by an international embargo and crippling inflation (around 1000%), the exodus of educated elements of the population and an increase in corruption. Even the rulers in Hanoi realized that profound **reforms** had become inevitable. During the 1980s a new political generation came into power which led to the »renovation of thinking« (Doi Moi). At the Sixth National Party Congress in 1986 the delegates agreed on a programme of economic reforms that should for example promote decentralization and the market economy. At the latest by the collapse of the Soviet Union

Reforms – Doi Moi

and the Eastern Bloc in 1989, Vietnam had no choice but to put these reforms into action. At the beginning of 1988 there was yet another **famine** in the north. As a consequence the government abolished the agricultural cooperatives for good: now farmers were allowed to lease some land and sell their goods on their own. The new constitution from 1992 guaranteed the right to private property.

Phase of opening and normalization

Since the 1990s, foreign observers have regarded Vietnam, with its double-figures growth rate, as another Asian »tiger« or »dragon« – just like Hong Kong, Taiwan, South Korea, Singapore and Thailand. The export industry in particular flourished when the country turned away from the strongly supported heavy industries and embraced once again the typical Vietnamese agricultural industries. Vietnam is now one of the **biggest exporters of rice** worldwide, despite the fact that the exporting of rice was only re-established in 1989! The horrendous rate of inflation had dropped down to a normal level. Vietnam attracted foreign capital with its enormous oil deposits, liberal laws, a highly motivated workforce and low wages.

Towards the 21st century

In 1990 President Bush was the first US president to pick up talks with government representatives from Vietnam. Four years later, the United States lifted their trade embargo from 1975 for good. The **opening of the American embassy** in Hanoi in 1996 saw relations between the former enemies largely return to normal. In November 2000 Bill Clinton was the first US President to visit Vietnam after 25 years. During his speech, which was broadcasted live on television, he emphasized America's intention to further improve the relations between the two countries. An unparalleled and prolonged economic miracle (since 1991) and a solid period of »turbo-capitalism« lasted for a number of years until the global financial crisis finally caught up with Vietnam in 2008/2009. Inflation rose at times to 20%, whilst property and share prices plummeted. The Dong was devalued on three occasions, many companies went bankrupt. Thanks to money transfers from Vietnamese overseas (approx. US$9 billion in 2011), foreign investment (US$11 billion) and development aid (almost US$4 billion), Vietnam was able to pull out of the crisis fairly quickly. Growth, however, had slowed in the meantime (approx. 6% in 2011). A darker side to the boom economy also manifested itself in the form of high unemployment and migration. The potential for conflict was heightened by the ongoing population growth (around a million per year) and the widening gulf between rich and poor.

Prospects

Whilst Vietnamese living in urban areas have benefitted a marked improvement in income levels and Vietnam is no longer one of the poorest countries in the world, energy prices (electricity), rent and transport (petrol) costs have risen sharply since 2011. With society in such a state of upheaval, the traditional family unit is gradually dissolving. The political system is still ruled by the **one-party government** in Hanoi – neither an opposition party nor true democratic change towards a multi-party system in Vietnam is anywhere to be seen, and political opponents are, as ever, threatened with many years of imprisonment. In spite of all the economic liberalization, the comrades of the Vietnamese Communist Party, the sole political power in Vietnam, still have a firm grip on the country. The removal from office of Vice-President Ngo Xuan Loc at the end of 1999 was a huge success for the anti-corruption campaign. In 2013 an official anti-corruption department takes up the challenge.

Vietnam is shifting from an agricultural nation into a service economy. **Tourism** plays an increasingly significant role, particularly through visitors from neighbouring countries (China tops the list with around one million of its people visiting Vietnam each year) and through tourists en route from Thailand via Laos and Cambodia on Indochina voyages. 2011 saw visitor numbers exceed the six million mark for the first time. Including business travellers, that number rose to 6.8 million in 2012. Between 2012 and 2015, a host of five star hotel chains with pool villas and condominiums will have opened for business along the 20 miles of coastline (China Beach) at Da Nang, Hoi An and Hue, including InterContinental and Hyatt Regency. Regrettably, the no holds barred approach to construction has little time for sustainability or environmental concerns, as on Phu Ouoc. Since the international airport opened there in 2012, numerous buildings have shot up on the island – which for many years had enjoyed a reputation as one of Vietnam's last undiscovered treasures.

Arts and Culture

Art History

Which was the golden age of Vietnamese art and architecture? What are sapeke clappers? How are the pictures that can be seen everywhere during the Tet New Year's Festival produced? Find all the answers here.

ARCHITECTURE AND SCULPTURE

When travelling through Vietnam, a great variety of architecture can be observed: simple thatched houses made of bamboo, elegant colonial mansions, clinical socialist buildings made from prefabricated slabs and postmodern high-rise buildings with reflective glass fronts. The most impressive buildings are palaces and emperor's tombs, temples, pagodas and community houses. They were built from more »durable« wood, stone or bricks and often adorned with carvings and sculptures. Of the numerous fortresses built during the 18th and 19th centuries only ruins or watchtowers have remained – with the exception of **Hue**. The citadel of Hue, in particular, clearly exhibits the foreign influences of the time, taking Beijing's Forbidden City and French fortresses as models. Here, and for nearby burial sites, it is not only aesthetics but also geomancy that play an important role. The aim was to achieve absolute harmony of art and nature in order to positively influence destiny. During their period of colonial rule, the French built administrative and prestigious buildings as well as city mansions adorned with stucco and colonnades in both **Hanoi** and **Saigon**. As befitting the tropical climate, shutters and patios were added. The residential buildings outside the centre and at resorts, such as Da Lat and Sa Pa, were given a more rustic look with tiled roofs and timber constructions. To this day, a third of Hanoi's colonial buildings, such as the opera and the residence of the British ambassador, still show traces of Art Deco, combined with some Asian elements. During the 1930s Vietnamese architects developed

Vietnam's architecture in overview

MARCO POLO INSIGHT

?

Geomancy

According to Chinese teaching more than a thousand years old, every place has both good and bad characteristics. When constructing burial sites, palaces or temples, as well as normal dwellings, the aim is to balance the elemental forces »yin« and »yang«. The characteristics of each location can be »measured« with the aid of a compass-like instrument featuring a magnetic needle.

Calligrapher in Thien Hau Pagoda in Cholon

the puristic design used for the building of Bao Dai's mansions in Da Lat, Vung Tau and So Son.

Sculpture   Vietnam's sculpture focused almost exclusively on **religious themes** and complemented the elaborately built pagodas and burial sites. Sacred buildings – often adorned with carved columns and gracefully curved roofs – often unites symbols of different persuasions. Besides Buddhas and Bodhisattvas, Taoist deities, spirits of ancestors and national guardians can be found (►MARCO POLO Insight p.402). Their design is a display of formidable craftsmanship, be it artistically shaped lattice work, imaginative paintwork, remarkable wooden sculptures or overwhelming roof ornaments. The rock stelae in some pagodas are equally impressive. They tell of the laying of the foundation or another important historical event. The most interesting characters and reliefs emerged, without a doubt, during the culture of the Cham people.

Cham Shrines

Hanoi

100 mi
150 km
©BAEDEKER

Than Hoa

Vinh

Ron
Dong Hoi

Quang Tri

Hue
Da Nang
LAOS   ← **Amaravati**

← **Vijaya**
Qui Nhon

CAMBODIA

← **Khautara**
Nha Trang

Tay Ninh   Phan Rang
Panduranga
Saigon   Phan Ri
Phan Thiet

The old and fascinating towers found between Phan Thiet and Da Nang are relics of the Cham dynasty, which ruled over parts of Central and South Vietnam for more than 1400 years. According to Chinese records, a man named Khu Lien collaborated with local princes near Quang Triin in 192 BC to fend off the Han Chinese in the north and to establish an independent state. Soon **Champa** united the coastline from Phan Thiet to Dong Hoi, and at the end of the 4th century it extended across four provinces: Amaravati (surroundings of Hue and Da Nang), Vijaya (around Quy Nhon), Kauthara (around Nha Trang), and Panduranga (today ranging from Phan Thiet to Phan Rang). Simhapura (lion citadel) was named capital of the first united empire. Around the same time the building of the My Son temple site began. Due to its location between the Khmer in the south and Viet groups in the north (which were still under Chinese rule at the time),

Champa had to incessantly ward off its neighbours. Between the 3rd and the 5th century there were repeated conflicts with the Chinese. The battles against the Khmer were most severe during the 12th and 13th centuries and culminated in the partial destruction of Angkor, in what is now Cambodia. Under Binasuor the kingdom expanded even further, though following his death in 1390 the Viet had already seized control over the region around Indrapura. The Viets finally took over Vijaya in 1471. The Cham were forced to move their capitals south and their power decreased immensely. Over the following centuries they ruled nominally in the area between Phan Rang and Phan Thiet. When the last independent Cham king died in 1697, this once power-ful empire was hardly more than a Viet vassal state. The emperor Minh Mang also put an end to this around 1820. Approximately 100,000 descendants of the Cham still live in Vietnam today.

If there ever was a golden age of Vietnamese art and architecture, it would be that of the Cham empire. Sadly, due to weathering in the hot tropical climate, pillage, and bombings, only around 20 of the once 250 sites have been preserved. The most interesting Cham sites are Po Klong Garai, Po Re Me (both ▶Phan Rang), Po Nagar (▶Nha Trang), Thap Doi (▶Quy Nhon) and My Son. The excellent collection in the Cham Museum in Da Nang gives a good overview. The earliest pieces belonged to the **My Son temple** and date back to the 8th cen-tury. Although they resemble Indian arts of the time, they have a distinctive character, especially in its naturalistic portrayal of hu-mans. The religion of the Cham was Hinduism, riddled with Bud-dhist elements and popular beliefs. Islamic influences were added in the late 14th century. Monuments and sculptures were mainly used for religious purposes. Dead rulers were worshipped as god-kings and affiliated to Hindu deities, especially Shiva. Ganesha, Vishnu and Lakshmi were also borrowed from Hinduism. The universal mother, Uroja, seems to be based on local beliefs. Often she is portrayed as a bust or nipple (▶photo p.332). She can, however, also show traits of Shiva's spouse, Bhagavati – in the Po Nagar Towers near Nha Trang she is revered as a woman. Kala and Makara sculptures and the boat-like roof construction in some buildings also exhibit Javanese influ-ences. To honour their gods appropriately, Cham kings had impres-sive brick buildings built. At the centre of a typical complex stood the **kalan (tower)**, whose interior housed the sanctum with an image of a deity, mostly a lingam, the phallic symbol for Shiva. During cleans-ing rituals it was doused in holy water, which drained off through a gorge at the base, symbolizing the female counterpart (the yoni).

Culture of the Cham

While originally the Vietnamese term »chua« only described a Bud-dhist pagoda, the concept is now also used for temples of other reli-gious beliefs. Most Buddhist sanctuaries also display guardian spirits

The Vietna-mese pagoda

The Vietnamese Pagoda

It was during the Ly and the Tran dynasties (11th 14th centuries) that pagoda architecture reached its high point, but only a few buildings have been preserved from this time. Wood was the main construction material, and because it quickly weathered in Vietnam's ho, damp climate, the shrines had to be renewed at regular intervals. This often meant not only rebuilding but also restructuring.

❶ The best time to visit is the 1st or the 15th day of the lunar month (half oon or full moon), as most believers come at these times.

❶ Gate (Tam quan)
A three-element gate leads into the temple site. Some gates are magnificent constructions with a tiled roof and rows of columns; others consist of simple posts with crossbeams.

❷ Temple building (chua)
The temple is divided into three parts – the increasing religious importance moving from the entrance to the main altar is underlined by means of ascending levels.

❸ Main entrance
Open on festive days. The best impression of the site is gained from here.

❹ Front hall (tien duong)
Items for temple festivals, along with statues of ancestral spirits or local deities and tutelary spirits, are kept in the front hall.

❺ Central hall (thien huong)
In the centre of the incense offering room stands an altar, at which prayers are said and offerings laid. The Buddha child is enthroned on the altar, often accompanied by other statues.

❻ Main altar hall (thuong dien)
The statues here throng around a steeply towering altar rising up to the entablature: the three generations of Buddhas, the Jade Emperor and his disciples, the Kings of Hell. There may also be statues of the donors.

❼ Living quarters
The monks live in the galleries or in a building behind the pagoda, and pilgrims also find accommodation here.

❽ Bell tower
In the courtyard – as a simple wooden framework or elaborate pavilion

❾ Stupas
Monuments for the ashes of the monks and abbots. The height of the stupa depends on their age and rank.

Vietnamese Pagoda

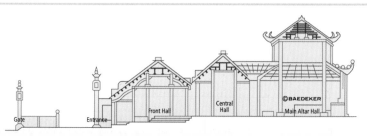

Gate Entrance Front Hall Central Hall Main Altar Hall ©BAEDEKER

The st
pagod
Chine
plan i
reclini
head.
aroun
usuall

he entranc
f three ele
eft gateway
eing is reco
e right the
arthly thing
rough the
ternal char

or Taoist and Confucian deities (►MARCO POLO Insight p.404). Most buildings that can be visited today are from the 18th and 19th centuries. During restorations they were often not only reconstructed, but also remodelled. A three-part gate (tam quan) in the south leads to the temple buildings, which are situated in the middle of a park, sometimes even around a lake or with a bell tower. The chua is always tripartite and subdivided into a bigger hall and three altar chambers. From the outside it becomes obvious that despite their size and the abundance of ornamentation, the curved roofs appear relatively light – this effect is created by means of elevated roof endings and adorned ridges. In the atrium, often simple in design, wardens and regional deities are found. The central hall, which is slightly elevated, is followed by the main sanctuary. An altar and tables with incense and food oblations are stored in the second chamber. Once again a variety of statues are found here, such as childlike portrayals of Buddha or the laughing Buddha of the Future. Their arrangement differs from one temple to another and can amount to up to 100 statues. Generally an uneven number must be placed on the individual steps, while the most significant figure stands in the middle. The Buddhas of the three generations reside at the very top. At the rear of the complex are the living and sleeping rooms of the monks or nuns. Sometimes inconspicuous altars in the halls commemorate the deceased members of the order; other pagoda gardens feature small stupas with burial sites of the former residents of the monastery.

Music, Theatre and Film

Art forms like music and theatre often portray strange or surprising images - films on Vietnam, however, seem comparatively familiar to us

MUSIC

Court music At the time of the Vietnam Empire, music was one of the six liberal arts (along with ceremonies, shooting, horseback riding, law and arithmetic). Along with chess, poetry and painting, it was considered one of the four **»joys in life«**.

According to Confucian belief that music has an ennobling effect on people, Vietnamese rulers always appreciated and promoted the art of music. When the last Vietnamese emperor abdicated in 1945, the royal court of musicians, mime artists, singers and dancers disappeared as well. Feudal and aristocratic culture was to have been finally overcome. In the meantime, however, numerous groups have committed themselves to the court art form. Such performances can be seen in Hue.

Buddhist priests proclaim their sutras and prayers in a mixed form of loud reading and singing, while the mostly evenly-spaced rhythm of the prayers is underlined by bells or a small gong. Very often, priests will also use tambourine-shaped wooden drums, ornately decorated with carvings. At some ceremonies they are also accompanied by fiddles, lutes, wooden rattles or a small one-skinned drum. At funeral services in southern Vietnam, five musicians provide ceremonial or funeral music to enhance the ambience for the various ritual acts. They usually play ceremonial drums, a buffalo horn beaten with a wooden stick, an oboe, gongs and cymbals, as well as the one-skinned goblet drum. Singing during these ceremonies is, however, strictly restricted to the pallbearers: whilst carrying the coffin they chant songs to »accompany« the soul of the deceased.

Religious ceremonial and cult music

At the beginning of the 18th century **»music from Hue«** was at the height of its popularity. It is performed either by a solo musician or by small ensembles consisting of three to six different instruments. Most commonly string instruments are used, but there are also flutes, drums and sapeke clappers (see below). Today this virtuoso music is being performed publicly again, at the former Imperial Palace in Hue for example. The **»music of lovers«** from southern Vietnam stems from the same tradition as the music from Hue. Singing is an essential part of both types of music; while the music from Hue is mainly sung by women, male vocalists are also to be found in the south. Larger audiences will hear such music in »cai luong« theatre performances – so-called renewed or reformed theatre. One of the most popular and tear-jerking songs in southern Vietnamese music is calledLonging for the Past (vong co).

Classical music

The most essential element in folk music consists of tunes (hat) about the life of the ordinary people and the »Vietnamese soul«, which expresses itself through melodies, songs, poetry and lyricism and is often filled with sentimentality, profound melancholy and fierce patriotism. Many folk songs are about unhappy love, the transience of

Folk songs

life – and work too. In Vietnam, all professions and crafts have their own tunes. Traditionally, those of farmers and peasant workers are represented the most.

Music of ethnic minorities More than 6% of the population of Vietnam belong to ethnic minorities. Most of them live in isolation in the Central Highlands or in the mountainous regions of the north. All of them maintain their own traditions of music and dance, which are related to Indonesian, Thai or Burmese forms.

Sapeke clapper An example of an authentic Vietnamese percussion instrument is the sapeke clapper (Sinh Tien). Made of wood, it combines the characteristics of clappers, rattles and ratchets. It is played by rubbing a wooden stick along its notches or beating it rhythmically. Sapeke clappers can be heard in both classical and folk music. If, in water-puppet theatre or in »hat cheo« theatre, musicians wish to create an evening atmosphere in the countryside, they will use a wooden instrument resembling sugar tongs. When the flexible tongs are pressed together and the small tines hit against each other and start to vibrate, it sounds like croaking frogs.

Monochord One rather unique instrument is the monochord (dan bau), a narrow, stretched zither with only one string, which is attached to a peg at one end and to a wooden hemisphere at the other. This hemisphere is connected to a flexible, slightly bent bamboo rod. The player can change the pitch by bending the rod sideways with his left hand. With his right hand he plucks the string with a bamboo plectrum, while constantly changing the tension of the string. This instrument is most common in North Vietnam.

THEATRE

Folk theatre (hat cheo) Hat cheo is a popular boulevard theatre found in central and North Vietnam. Plays were mostly performed in the courtyard of the town hall. Both costumes and make-up are extremely simple – all props easily fit into one box. Actors usually embody common stereotypes, such as the poor and the rich man, the old woman, the clown, the monk or the hero. Lines are often filled with sarcasm directed at the wielders of power, which has led to conflicts and occupational bans more than once in the past. The performances protest against vices and praise (Buddhist) virtues by depicting fates of the common people and the lives of heroes, often spiced with the most current social criticism. They play scenes and sketches or dance and sing folk songs. Even ancient songs of the various professions are still preserved. To this day, improvisational art – in which audiences often enthusiastically participate – is an integral part of the performance. A musical ensemble is also an important element for the performance of this kind of musical play.

Classical theatre, or hat tuong, dates back to the 12th and 13th centuries and is influenced by Chinese opera. It later became an integral part of court entertainment. Even Emperor Tu Duc himself wrote texts for the »hat tuong«. Generally, tuong plays are meant to strengthen **patriotism** and loyalty to the rulers. Topics are mainly derived from the country's history, for example the story of the Trung sisters or the liberator Le Loi. In South Vietnam this type of theatre is called hat boi, which denotes songs that are performed in costumes and using gestures. The costumes of the courtly hat tuong are far more sumptuous than those of the cheo plays, and there are more ceremonial elements involved. The gestures of the actors are highly stylized, their message being that of **Confucianism**. As soon as the actors enter the stage the audience immediately recognizes the identities of the characters by their costumes and make-up: a red-painted face is associated with courage, honesty and loyalty, a white-painted face implies brutality and deceitfulness.

Classical theatre (hat tuong)

Concert at the Royal Theatre in Hue

Marionettes in the Water

Many countries have a tradition of puppets and puppet theatre, but water puppe theatre is exclusive to Vietnam. Little is known about its origins, but performan in noble courts and temples are mentioned in voyagers' reports as long ago as th 11th century. There is a magic to the few remaining shows performed today – if there is a chance to see the puppets in action in Saigon or in Hanoi at Hoan Kiem Lake, be sure to take it!

▶ **The puppets**
are carved from the soft, light wood of the
fig tree, then waterproofed with varnish and
resin. Their limbs are moved by wires.

1–5kg/
2lb – 11lb

30cm–1m
12in–39in

▶ **The orchestra**
provides musical accompaniment
and vocals for the puppets.

Thang Long
Water Puppet
Theatre, Hanoi
Vietnam 2012

©BAEDEKER

▶ **Water puppet theatre construction**
Since the 1980s, the stage has consisted of a pool and an elaborate backdrop.
The »floating« puppets tell their story, controlled by puppeteers holding poles
3 to 4 metres (10 to 13 feet) in length. The poles remain beneath the surface of
the water, barely visible to the audience for the duration of the performance.

backdrop	
aOrchestr	Stage: Pool approx. 4sq m/7 sq ft
	Audience

▶ **Performance**
Up to eight puppeteers are
at work behind the thin curtain
of woven bamboo.

Water pup-
petry (mua
roi nuoc)

Water puppetry from North Vietnam is an art form that is unique in the world. Though it incorporates influences from cheo plays and even classical theatre, its main themes stem from old legends and the everyday lives of Vietnamese peasants. The wooden puppets float, dance, plough and plant above and in the water and enact small, yet exquisitely satirical tales. This fascinating form of theatre is accompanied by musicians playing an array of percussion instruments made of metal and wood, string instruments and various types of bamboo flutes. They also sing and lend their voices to the puppets (▶MARCO POLO Insight p.78, p.368). The origins of water puppetry lie within the religious ceremonies and water rituals of the rural population. This unique technique most likely developed when the puppeteers of the **Red River Delta** tried to perform their plays in spite of heavy rain and immense flooding during the monsoon season. The earliest records of water puppetry performances date back to the 11th century, but it is commonly believed that this folk art existed much earlier in the rural areas. In the 16th century the first permanent theatre venues were then built, including Thay Pagoda (Quoc Oai, Son Tay Province ▶Hanoi, surroundings) and the Dong Temple (Dong Anh, Hanoi). The latter still features the small temples for the water god from which the puppeteers controlled their puppets.

VIETNAM IN FILMS

Hollywood
and Vietnam

Utterly exhausted, completely filthy and carrying heavy backpacks, a group of young US soldiers is fighting its way through the jungle. Heat, mosquitoes, fear and despair are omnipresent. The Vietcong is everywhere and nowhere. The tension becomes unbearable. Then suddenly, mortar bombs pierce the humid air and the sweat-drenched bodies of the soldiers. Screaming, blood; wounded and dead. Hollywood goes Vietnam. We have all seen films like this. Countless directors from the 1970s and 1980s used America's war against Vietnam as a backdrop for brutal battle scenes set against an exotic landscape – although most of these films were shot in studios and images of landscapes from Thailand and the Philippines simply edited in later. Because, up until recently, the Socialist Republic of Vietnam was closed to filmmakers. Still, the **clichés** of most Vietnam films, which have little or nothing to do with the actual country, are often mistaken for reality. The image of the »slit-eyed«, unpredictable Vietcong has been more deeply engrained in the minds of audiences around the world than many will care to admit.

Films about
the Vietnam
War

Prototypical for this genre are *The Green Berets* starring John Wayne (USA 1967) and *Missing In Action* (USA 1984). The latter revolves around freeing American soldiers, given up as lost by their military

Scene from *Apocalypse Now*

superiors, from a Vietnamese prison camp, a plot more or less repeated in *Rambo: First Blood Part II* with Sylvester Stallone.
Not so easy to analyze, the **most famous film about the war** in
Vietnam is undoubtedly *Apocalypse Now* by Francis Ford Coppola.
Shot in 1979 for a record sum of US$ 30.5 million on the Philip-
pines, the film was awarded the Palme d'Or of Cannes as well as an
Academy Award for best cinematography. The story: an American
captain is ordered to assassinate an insane colonel who is acting up
as ruler deep in the jungle. The journey upriver – inspired by Joseph
Conrad's *Heart of Darkness* – develops into a surreal odyssey which
depicts war as a drug-fuelled spectacle with a popular music soundtrack where any sense of good and evil, right and wrong, is thrown
into question. *Full Metal Jacket* (directed by Stanley Kubrick, USA
1987) also accompanies battles and Vietnam war scenes with familiar pop songs, bringing the experience closer to home. The protago-
nist Private Joker has to surrender his ideas of morality.
In *Platoon* (written and directed by Oliver Stone, USA 1986), the
tough guys are also the top dogs: there are lengthy waits in the torrid
sun, dangerous patrols, sudden battles. The film was highly praised,

especially in the USA, as the first of its kind to avoid patriotic pathos as a smokescreen for soldiers' fears and the extreme situations in which they found themselves. Historical accuracy, however, is not the movie's strongpoint. The glorification of the My Lai Massacre, which took place on 16 March 1968, is visualized through laughing GIs as they cross lush green rice fields with little children in their arms or on their shoulders, leaving behind them a village they themselves set ablaze. Only a soldier buttoning up his trousers hints at the rape of countless Vietnamese women. If there is little to be learned of historical facts, all the more attention is given to the suppression of wartime events in USA society, along with some insight into the psyche of the soldiers.

Veteran films A second group of films illustrates the trauma of war even more explicitly: the veteran film. These productions zoom in on physical and psychological injuries, tied to the question of why American GIs ended up in the Vietnamese jungle in the first place. The films show crippled war veterans returning home from a Vietnam which destroyed not only their health, but also their personality.
Coming Home (USA, 1978), recounts the love triangle of a Vietnam warrior's wife (Jane Fonda) who, during her husband's absence, has an affair with a Vietnam War invalid.
Heroes (USA, 1977) or *Welcome Home* (USA, 1989 with Kris Kristofferson) also number among the genre of the broken returnee.
Most widely known, however, is *Born on the 4th of July* (USA, 1989) by Oliver Stone, the story of a now paraplegic GI and his transformation to become a committed opponent of war. *Ashes and Embers* (USA, 1982), on the other hand, describes the major difficulties in readjusting experienced by black American soldiers, underdogs in both the army and society at large.

Recommended exceptions One exception to the stereotypical filmic representation is *Dear America – Letters from Vietnam* (USA, 1987), based on letters written by American soldiers to their girlfriends, mothers and wives.
The film contains original battle footage and American news coverage from that time – thus preventing any false romanticization about adventures in the trenches. Another very worthwhile film is *Good Morning, Vietnam* (USA, 1987). It demonstrates that it is even possible to make a comedy about this topic, and what's more one with depth and substance. The new DJ Adrian Cronauer (Robin Williams) at an army radio station quickly becomes a favourite with his listeners for his saucy comments, but his smart mouth gets him into trouble with his superiors. When Cronauer's Vietnamese friend is debunked as a member of the Vietcong, the DJ is relocated. This tragicomedy shows empathy for the victims on both sides of the war,

and manages to be thought provoking in spite of the breathtaking speed of the film.

What Asian romantic films lack in authenticity, they make up in thrilling exoticism and popular cliché. *The Lover* (France/England, 1991), based on the autobiographical novel by the French writer Marguerite Duras, depicts the famous Chinese movie star Tony Leung as a rich man who initiates a young French woman into the secrets of love. Another romantic film set in 1930s Indochina is the French melodrama *Indochine* from 1991, starring Cathérine Deneuve. It was the first European film that was actually shot at the original sites of Ha Long Bay, Dry Ha Long Bay and the caoutchouc plantations near Saigon. Set in the time shortly before colonialism ended, the colonial plantation owner recounts the story of a love triangle between her adoptive Vietnamese daughter and their joint lover.

Romantic films

After making several conventional Vietnam War films (*Platoon* and *Born on the 4th of July*) director Oliver Stone also made one from a Vietnamese point of view. The extensively modified adaptation of the novel *Born in Vietnam* by Le Ly Hayslip bore the film title *Between Heaven and Hell* (USA 1993). The novel is the autobiographical story of Hayslip's youth in a village which is increasingly penetrated by the war. She grows up amidst bombings and Vietcong training, and is suspected of collaborating with the South Vietnamese. As a maid she flees to the city where she is made pregnant by her employer and fired by his wife. She works on the black market to earn a living for herself and her son, until finally a great opportunity presents itself: a soldier, played by Tommy Lee Jones, falls in love with her and takes her back to the United States.

Vietnamese perspectives on the war

Neither the novel nor the film end here, for the story goes on to examine her social difficulties in a foreign culture and the longing to return home, even while being aware that her relatives are exposed to starvation and great danger. In 1986, directly after the opening of Vietnam's doors to the outside world, Le Ly visits her family and is painfully struck again by the sharp contrast between Vietnam and the United States. In the end, this film does not skimp on American emotionalism either.

FILMS BY VIETNAMESE DIRECTORS

Regrettably, there are hardly any films made from the perspective of Vietnam's own people. A notable exception is *Where War Has Passed* directed by Vu Le My. This film, which won an award in 1997 at the Ecomedia Festival, depicts the consequences of the destructive war machine. In this documentary, victims speak about their suffering,

Vu Le My

and reveal that malformed children are still being born. They describe the pains and diseases they still have to cope with today. Children, their bodies and souls scarred, vegetate without any limbs or eyes, or with massive heads, even though they were born long after the end of the war. There is no financial and medical support from external sources.

Tran Anh Hung Arthouse cineastes may be more familiar with the films by the Vietnamese director Tran Anh Hung. His first film, *The Scent of Green Papaya* (France, 1993), aesthetically depicts the life of a female servant in Vietnam at the start of the 20th century. Although this film, like so many others, was shot not in Vietnam but at French studios, it conveys an impressive and near-authentic feel. Tran Anh Hung's second film *Cyclo* (1995) deals with present-day Vietnam. Buzzing streets, slums and the bars of Saigon provide the settings for this fast-paced, sinister and brutal film. Youth gangs fight their battles and the city shakes as if running a fever. Cyclo and his sister find themselves witnesses to a murder. The fast pace and the atmosphere draws the spectator into the bewildering speed of the city. It shows how Vietnamese society is changing dramatically, with families losing their once strong ties. This affectionate and poetic film, along with the documentary *Where War Has Passed* by Vu Le My, portrays the most realistic picture of modern Vietnam.

Arts and Crafts

Vietnam is rightly considered a paradise for lovers of arts and crafts. It is worth remembering to leave enough space in bags or suitcases for the fantastic souvenirs and artefacts which can be found here!

Varied in nature and common throughout the country, the finest selections are sold in the cities of Saigon, Hue and Hanoi. This is because almost all inhabitants of the nearby villages make a living from those individual skills in which they have specialized. Gift shops tend to offer lacquerware, pottery, embroidery, wood carvings and intarsia crafts, whereas the local markets are the point of sale for beautiful bamboo and wickerwork items. The hill tribes have specialized in weaving, dyeing and embroidered textiles.

Lacquerware Originally from China, lacquerware has been in use in Vietnam for at least 1500 years and is sold throughout the country. The black or brown lacquer is produced from the sap of the sumac tree.

However, the differences in quality and manufacturing standards are immense. Well-made items were once characterized by up to 200 coats that were air-dried and polished for hours – a process which may have taken months or even years. Today, pieces should be coated at least a dozen times. Only then will the motif be applied or carved into the inlays (seashells or eggshells). In Song Be province, southwest of Saigon, craftsmen have been manufacturing these goods for centuries.

During the Vietnamese Tet Festival, the most important holiday of the year (►MARCO POLO Insight p.114), coloured woodcarvings (tranh tet), printed on silk or paper, are displayed above entrances to houses and apartments. They are supposed to ward off evil and bring happiness and fortune. Originally a rural tradition, the pictures have become absolutely commonplace throughout Vietnam since the 15th century. The most treasured works come from the **village of Dong Ho**, approximately 50km/31mi from Hanoi. Every year, more than 500,000 of these prints are manufactured in Dong Ho by small family-run businesses and one cooperative. The manufacturing of the woodcarvings can be observed and admired in Hanoi on Hang Trong Street, in the craftsmen's quarter of the old town. First, the artists create a draft. They then copy it onto a block of wood and carve a printing plate. After printing, the outlines of the motifs appear in black and the surfaces are coloured with a paintbrush. Traditional materials for manufacturing the colours are blossoms, fruits, bark, leaves, ashes and ground minerals – such formulations, developed especial-

New Year's pictures

Classically designed lacquerware and furniture

MARCO POLO TIP

Looking over the artist's shoulder

Those interested in the specific production process of lacquer-ware should pay a visit to the state and family-run businesses in Hanoi and Saigon where such goods are produced. The Hanoi Art Museum has dedicated a small exhibition to this special technique.

Insider Tip

ly by the artists in Dong Ho, are well-kept secrets. Nowadays, more and more synthetic (and cheaper) paints are replacing the natural ones. Finally, the pictures are coated with a glossy surface, which was originally supposed to be made of finely ground pearl oysters. These prints depict events in the nation's history, folk tales, scenes of ordinary life (for instance a peasant woman with a water buffalo), heroes, guard-ian sprits and blessed animals: the rooster protects the house from evil, the goose stands for gentleness, the frog for courage, the pig for wealth and fertility, the peacock announces beauty and peace, while flowers bring happiness. For the entire year all these lucky charms decorate the houses until they are replaced by new ones at the next Tet celebration, when once again there will be »fireworks in the yard and the picture of the rooster on the wall…«.

Ceramics and porcelain The production of ceramics has a long tradition in Vietnam. Origi-nally, plated shapes were coated with clay and burnt; however, over the years, the procedures and shapes have progressed and gradually been refined. What is striking is that each dynasty apparently pre-ferred different techniques, colours and motifs: items are coloured jade or blue, are more or less transparent, and the type of glazing is variable. The art of glazing stems from China. During the Tran dy-nasty (1225–1400), bricks, tiles and ceramics were mainly coloured green, ochre and shades of brown, whereas in the 15th century the fashion was for blue and white ceramics, which are still manufac-tured today. In Hue during the reign of the Nguyen princes, bright blue porcelain was developed which showed Chinese influence in shape and decoration. To this day, Hue and the artisanal villages of Bat Trang and Tho Ha outside Hanoi (▶p.280) have remained the pottery centres of Vietnam.

Water puppetry figurines Water puppetry figurines (▶MARCO POLO Insight p.78, p.368) are carved out of the soft and light wood of the common fig tree. The figurines are between 30cm/12in and 1m/3ft tall, and take the shape of boats, balls, buffalos, ducks, dragons, peasants, children, kings and fairies. In order to protect them from the water, the puppets are coat-ed with a waterproof resin and lacquer. Additionally, this layer is sup-posed to protect against woodworm. On top of this lacquer, paint as well as gold and silver are applied. The bodies of the puppets are made of one piece of wood, and the head and arms are fitted with joints to make them flexible. When performing the show in ponds or

Bat Trang: decide directly on the street what takes your fancy ...

pools, the majority of the heavy puppet (1kg/2lbs–5kg/11lbs) lies submerged in the water. The puppets are moved with 3m/10ft–4m/13ft-long wooden or bamboo rods. Quite often they are also attached to little rudders and strings. The rods allow the puppeteer to move the puppet forwards and backwards or from side to side. The head, arms and other extremities are controlled by using the strings. The exterior of the puppets may look stylized, but their movements and expressions are often very realistic.

Vietnam's forests contain many precious woods such as mahogany, teak, ironwood and rosewood. The work of Vietnamese woodcarvers can be seen in the adornments of old community houses and the ornamentation of Chinese pagodas. In the old town of Hanoi and in the workshops of Hoi An, visitors can observe how little masterpieces (roof ornaments, figurines and furniture) come to life, some even crafted with mother-of-pearl intarsia. Smaller figurines (mostly water buffalos and elephants) made of buffalo horn, ivory or tortoiseshell are also sold, but beware: according to the Washington Convention on International Trade in Endangered Species of Wild Fauna and Flora (CITES), such items may not be imported to Europe or the United States.

Other wood-carvings

Silk painting and silk embroidery

Typically Asian motifs such as landscapes, flowers and village life are predominant in silk paintings and embroidery. Silk painting most likely developed in the 13th century and was originally a type of calligraphy, which was gradually complemented by small nature scenes. Tablecloths, blouses and kimonos are often decorated with dragons, birds and Chinese characters. The silk shops in Ho Chi Minh City and in the old town of Hanoi (Hang Trong), as well as the tailor's shops in Hoi An, are famous for these kinds of silk paintings. More elaborate silk embroidery may be marvelled at or purchased at the gallery in the Bao Dai Villa (Da Lat).

Weaving of conical hats

In all parts of Vietnam, men and women work in the streets and fields. To protect themselves from the sun they wear conical hats: regardless of the time of day, they efficiently keep the head in the shade. They are made of young palm leafs, attached and weaved into a frame (photo ▶p.126). The more simple hats are sold throughout the country, though the nicest hats are those from Hue. Here, romantic silhouettes and verses are laid between the palm leafs and shine through when holding the hat against the sunlight. There are also hats featur-

Beautiful and colourful: the Flower Hmong and their fine art weaving

ing colourful embroidery. The bands with which the hat is held in place are available in cotton, velvet and silk.

The ethnic minorities in Vietnam possess a wide range of handicraft skills, for example in manufacturing textiles, jewellery and baskets, to name but a few. The **Muong** are definitely worthy of mention for their **fine art weaving**, as are the unique indigo-dyed and embroidered **dresses of the Bahnar**. Those with a special interest in this subject should pay a visit to the Vietnam Museum of Ethnology in Hanoi, where many of the techniques are explained. The Craft Link shop and Hoa Sen Gallery on Van Mieu Street (next to the Temple of Literature) are well worth a visit for anyone interested in taking a look or perhaps purchasing something from the multitude of local artisanal products (textiles, wooden figurines, woven or lacquered goods etc.). The profits from these shops are used to finance projects in the hill communities and support children living on the street.

Arts and crafts of the ethnic minorities

Famous People

BAO DAI (1913–97)

Bao Dai (born Nguyen Vinh Thuy) was the last emperor of the Nguy-   Last emperor
en dynasty, which ruled in Vietnam from 1802 to 1945. However,   of Vietnam
when Annam, the heartland of the empire, became a French protectorate in 1883, the monarchs became rulers in
name only. Following the death of his father,
Khai Dinh, in 1925, Bao Dai officially became
king. At that time, however, the 13-year old was
being educated in Europe. It was seven years
before he returned to his home country in order to fulfil his ceremonial duties. During the
Second World War, Vietnam came under Japanese rule and around the same time the **Viet
Minh** or National Liberation Movement was
formed. This was a movement of opposition
against the imperialist powers of Japan and
France. In line with the Japanese surrender,
Bao Dai was forced to abdicate on 24 August
1945. Initially however, he was to remain as an
»advisor« to the Viet Minh government, which
proclaimed the independence of the country
on 2 September 1945. In March 1946, Bao Dai
decided to travel to Hong Kong and then to
Geneva, where two years later he was persuaded by the French to return to Annam to help
them expand their influence. On 14 June 1949
they even made him »head of state« within
their sphere of influence (central and southern
Vietnam). Bao Dai then assigned the Catholic
Ngo Dinh Diem to be his close advisor. During
the following years, his position was very vague
as he spent most of his time on the Côte d'Azur.
France left Indochina for good after their defeat

at the Battle of Dien Bien Phu in 1954, leaving
the destiny of the country to be discussed at the Geneva Conference,
while Bao Dai preferred to remain at his villa in Cannes. The negotiations resulted in a shaky ceasefire and the separation of the country at the 17th parallel. Diem became president of South Vietnam
with support from the United States. When Diem abolished the emperor's guards, Bao Dai lost his last remaining foothold in Vietnam.
The result of a referendum held on 23 October 1955 led to the former
emperor being dispossessed in 1957. It seems that by then he had
already accumulated sufficient funds abroad, as he then lived in exile

Ho Chi Minh and President Ton Duc Thang (Ho Chi Minh Museum)

on the French Riviera, his preferred domicile. Bao Dai died on 31 July 1997 in Paris at the ripe old age of 83.

HO CHI MINH

▶MARCO POLO Insight p.265

MARIE-CHARLES DAVID DE MAYRÉNA (1842–90)

Adventurer The story of the Frenchman Marie-Charles David de Mayréna is one of the most curious episodes in Vietnam's colonial history, and it shares some similarities withHeart of Darkness by Joseph Conrad. The novel is about a European who appoints himself ruler of a remote part of the Belgian Congo, a storyline that was later also used by Francis Ford Coppola in his filmApocalypse Now. The life of the rather dubious de Mayréna was rather diverse. His exploits included a spell in the French Army a career as a banker and ultimately the life of a planter in South Vietnam. In 1888, the governor sent de Mayréna on an expedition into the mountains accompanied by hundreds of carriers and soldiers. What exactly happened next is unknown, but in the end the only person with him (in Kon Tum) was Alphonse Mercurol. With the help of French missionaries, he met with the tribal chiefs of the Sedang, who were soon fascinated by him, possibly because of his blue eyes and imperious presence. De Mayréna took advantage of the situation and appointed himself Marie I, King of Sedang, while Mercurol became the Marquis of Hanoi. His residence was a straw hut; he designed his own flag, created laws, formed an army and declared war on the neighbouring Jarai tribe. But in spite of it all, he became bored of his majestic lifestyle after only a few months. He packed up and set off to make money out of his title. Surrounded by courtiers, he lived in expensive hotels in Saigon. In Europe, too, he tried to convert his very presence into hard cash by selling fake titles and concessions. Over time, he could not prevent cracks appearing in his stories, and he became less and less credible. Eventually he returned to Asia in 1890 where he henceforth lived a moderate life on the Malaysian island of Pulau Tioman up until his death. De Mayréna is said to have died of a snake bite.

PHAN THI KIM PHUC (BORN 1963)

UNESCO One of the most memorable press photographs of the last century ambassador shows a young unclothed girl fleeing her burning village together with other children. She screams whilst appearing to run towards the observer. The picture came to symbolize the Vietnam War and the horrors of war in general (►photo p.57). The Vietnamese **photographer Nick Ut** arrived in Trang Bang on 8 June 1972, shortly after a Napalm bomb attack. Surrounded by gruesome scenes such as these, he pressed the shutter release button. Nine-year-old Phan Thi Kim had suffered third-degree burns during the attack, which still affect her today. After

MARCO POLO INSIGHT

? »The Girl In The Picture«

It would not be greatly exaggerated that the shocking effect of this photograph may have at least accelerated the withdrawal of the United States, if not made it unavoidable. More about the life of Phan Thi Kim Phuc can be read in her biography by Denise Chong (Penguin, 2001).

lengthy hospital stays and studies in Cuba, the mother of two now lives in Canada. In 1997 Phan Thi Kim Phuc was appointed a UNESCO ambassador. The previous year she had forgiven the American responsible for the attack on her village during a personal encounter.

ALEXANDRE DE RHODES (1591–1660)

Missionary

Vietnam is the only Asian country to have a writing system based on Latin letters. This came about when Alexandre de Rhodes, a French Jesuit missionary, came to Vietnam in 1627 as part of the proselytization of Southeast Asia. Apart from various European languages, he could also speak Chinese and was able to preach in Vietnamese after only six months of being there. In order to make the Gospel available to a greater audience he developed the »quoc ngu« script, a phonetic alphabet based on Latin letters which is still in use in Vietnam today. He then published a catechism and transliterated Vietnamese into Latin characters, hereby creating a complete Latin-Portuguese-Vietnamese dictionary, written in Latin and Chinese characters. Not only did the missionaries aid alphabetization and teach Christian beliefs, they also taught the Vietnamese basic skills such as shipbuilding and the manufacturing of clocks and firearms. Constantly travelling between Hanoi, Macao, Paris and Rome in order to raise money and support for his work, Rhodes also became famous in Europe. His activities were the reason that the Vatican sent more French priests to Indochina to carry out missionary work – a fact that would later clearly help the French when trying to gain ground and expand their power as colonial rulers. Rhodes had been a welcome guest at the court of Hanoi since 1627, though this was slowly starting to change. The monk's uncompromising views on Vietnamese traditions such as Buddhism, ancestor worship and polygamy, as well as increasing audiences during his sermons, were particularly disturbing for Confucian scholars. In 1630, Rhodes went to Macao after eventually being forced to leave the country. During the following years, he illegally returned to South Vietnam on various occasions until he was finally expelled in 1645. Alexandre de Rhodes died in Isfahan (Persia) in 1660 at the age of 69.

THICH QUANG DUC (1897–1963)

Monk

During the early hours of 11 June 1963, several Buddhist monks from Xa Loi Pagoda in Saigon headed to the corner of Cach Mang Thank Tam/Nguyen Dinh Chieu Street. Having arrived from Hue, 66-year old Thich Quang Duc sat down on the street in a position of meditation. As a protest against the **discrimination of Buddhists** by the government of the Catholic President Diem, his companions doused

Thien Mun Pagoda, Hue: the Austin in which Thich Quang Duc drove to Saigon is kept in a small garage

him in petrol and set him on fire. As the flames started to slowly consume the body of Thich Quang Duc and passers-by threw themselves on their knees, Western journalists and photographers also joined the crowd. The day after this gruesome event, the story featured on the front pages of newspapers throughout the world. However, the violation of monasteries, the demolitions and the slaying of many hundreds of nuns and monks continued, and Diem imposed martial law. Xa Loi Pagoda became the centre of protest and mass demonstrations. More than 30 monks and nuns followed in the footsteps of Thich Quang Duc as a protest against Diem's politics and the interference of the United States in South Vietnam. Two young US citizens also burned themselves publicly in November 1968, one of them in front of the Pentagon and the other near the Headquarters of the United Nations. The entire world was shocked about these **suicides**, and even more appalled by the cynical reaction of the president's sister-in-law, the legendary Madam Nu who commented: »Let them burn, we will applaud them.« Nevertheless, Thich Quang Duc's **self-immolation** initiated the beginning of the fall of President Diem. The world public turned away from him, and shortly afterwards he and his brother were killed during a military coup.

THE TRUNG SISTERS (DIED 43 AD)

The Trung sisters are the most famous and most admired heroines in Vietnamese history. Their rebellion against the Chinese in Vietnam, whose rule lasted for almost 1200 years, is still the most renowned and the most celebrated. Vietnam was seized by the Chinese in 111 BC and was declared a protectorate of Giao Chi. Trung Tac was married to Lord Thi Sach, who was executed by the Chinese in AD 40. Together with her sister Trung Nhi she colluded with other sovereigns and successfully assembled and commanded an army that caused the Chinese governor to flee. The Trung sisters soon declared themselves **queens** of the now independent Vietnamese territory.

Freedom fighters

Their leadership, however, was short-lived: three years later the Chinese troops returned, this time putting a bloody end to the rebellion. Trung Tac and Trung Nhi were allegedly captured and beheaded, though another version of the story suggests that the sisters drowned themselves in the Hat Giang River to escape captivity.

Vietnam still honours the sisters as symbols of this war of independence. Almost every city has a street named after them, many temples are dedicated to them and various monuments have been built in their memory. During the annual commemoration service on the second day of the fifth lunar month, the statues of both queens are carried into the river for a ritual ablution.

ALEXANDRE YERSIN (1863–1943)

Alexandre Jean Emile Yersin was born to French parents on 22 September 1863 in Rougemont in the Swiss Canton of Voud. After finishing his degree in medicine, he went to France where he met and for some time worked with Louis Pasteur. As a surgeon, he travelled to the Far East where he ended up in Nha Trang in 1891. Two years later, during one of his expeditions, he discovered the mountain village of Da Lat. Due to the beauty and moderate climate there, he recommended Da Lat as an eligible holiday location, advancing its status as a popular destination for the French. The following year, in 1894, he went to Hong Kong to help fight the cholera epidemic. Soon after returning to Nha Trang he built a laboratory, which in 1902 became the first Pasteur Institute outside France. At the institute, independently of the co-discoverer S. Kitasato, he managed to isolate the **pathogen that causes the plague** and developed an antiserum that was named after him. In addition, he set up a cattle farm to produce serums and vaccines. During the 50 years that he lived in Nha Trang until his death, Yersin made important reforms to the Vietnamese health system, often against the will of his employers. Apart from his medical successes, he also excelled in other areas: he has been credited with the importation of the coffee and rubber plants to Vietnam and was a driving force in promoting the industrial manufacture of rubber. Once he had retired from his active working life, he primarily concerned himself with astrology, photography and the characteristic water conditions of the Nha Trang Bay. On 1 March 1943, Alexandre Yersin died at the age of 79. He was buried in Suoi Dua, a village south of Nha Trang.

Tropical doctor (▶MARCO POLO Insight p. 338)

Yersin is better known in Vietnam than in Europe

ENJOY VIETNAM

What will turn up on your plate if you order »Thit Heo« in a restaurant? Which places will kids love? What are the best souvenirs to bring back from Vietnam – and where can they be found? Practical tips for a successful holiday.

Accommodation

A Place to Suit Every Taste

Accommodation ranges from simple guesthouses and mini hotels, former colonial houses and mid-range hotels to first-class hotels and ultra-modern luxury residences, which have now opened in tourist regions far away from the towns, as in Dry Ha Long Bay or on remote islands such as Con Dao.

In the cities of Saigon and Hanoi and the beach towns of Da Nang, Nha Trang and Phant Thiet/Mui Ne and on Phu Quoc, there is a place to suit every pocket. Especially stylish and ideal for a jaunt back in time are the renovated colonial residences where Graham Greene and William Somerset Maugham checked in and found inspiration for their novels. Homestays with minority groups are growing increasingly popular, up in the mountains around Sa Pa or on the Mekong Delta.

Guesthouses and mini hotels offer simple, small and mostly clean rooms without air conditioning, often with sheets and towels, but without daily room service. They are particularly suitable for **backpackers**, but there are also true bargains to be found including en-suite shower or bath and hot water! While some rooms do not even have windows, others come with a balcony.

Guesthouses/ mini hotels

Lower-range mid-range hotels do not always meet European demands in terms of service, cleanliness and fixtures. Sometimes the tap drips incessantly,and the air-conditioning sounds like a motorway next to the hotel. In this price range, rooms are equipped with shower, balcony and cupboard as well as TV, telephone, fridge and radio. Sometimes the room only has one window looking onto a courtyard or the hallway. Most hotels have their own restaurant, an elevator and sometimes even a pool. Often hotel staff do not speak English well.Those searching for accommodation meeting certain international standards should choose the higher end of the mid-range category or luxury standard. These will reflect all tourist comforts.

Mid-range hotels

In this price range, rooms are equipped with a shower and/or bath, air conditioning, satellite TV and hotel videos, telephone, minibar, and room safe. The hotels also offer swimming pools, karaoke bars, discos, 24-hour coffee shops, fitness facilities and business centres, i.e. every form of entertainment and service imaginable. Reservations

Luxury/ First class

Coco Beach Resort in Mui Ne boasts 34 of these log cabins

are often handled as **flat-rate bookings** by foreign travel agents, which usually means better prices, as walk-up rates are subject to tax and service charges amounting to 15%. A lot of foreign business people stay for longer periods and can therefore expect better rates.

Luxury hotels Top-class accommodation meets the best international standards (5 stars) with all amenities and excellently trained staff. The rooms are luxuriously decorated and hotels come complete with a swimming pool and several speciality restaurants.

Special hotel recommendations

PRICE CATEGORIES
Double room

££££	from 4,2 mil. VND (£130)
£££	2,84 – 4,2 mil. VND (£90 – 130)
££	1 – 2,8 mil. VND (£30 – 90)
£	500,000 – 1 mil. VND (£15 – 30)

»Six Senses Ninh Van Bay« has an idyllic bayside location at Nha Trang

PURE LUXURY
Six Senses
Ninh Van Bay ££££
Ninh Van Bay, Ninh Hoa (approx. 50km/30mi north of Nha Trang on the Hon Heo peninsula) Khanh Hoa
tel. 058/372 82 22
www.sixsenses.com/SixSenses NinhVanBay
Robinsonade on a remote peninsula: 35 rustic villas on the beach or on the hillside. Exclusivity (private pools) and incomparable service (butler) meet nature at its purest (no nails). It almost comes as a surprise to find that the telephone and music system are not made of bamboo. And of course every Robinson here has Wi-Fi.

SPA HOTEL
Fusion Maia ££££
Truong Sa
Khue My district (China Beach)
Da Nang
tel. 0511/396 79 99
www.fusionmaiadanang.com
Holiday in a seventh heaven spa: »Asia's first all-inclusive spa hotel« on the infinite China Beach has a team of 60 professionals who have been pampering their guests since

2012 – scrubs, wraps, foot reflex zones, beauty treatments, Swedish or Thai massage, you name it. 84 pool villas in tropical gardens with minimalist-cool design. Nirvana can wait!

NATURAL OASIS *Insider Tip*
Jungle Beach Resort £

Hon Heo peninsula, Ninh Phuoc village, Ninh Hoa
(approx. 60km/37mi north of Nha Trang)
tel. 058/362 23 84, mobile tel. 091/342 91 44
www.junglebeachvietnam.com
Communal hammock Homestay: Canadian host Sylvio and his Vietnamese wife welcome nature lovers, hippies and anyone from around the world seeking heavenly solitude. Spartan, all-inclusive bamboo huts (3 vegetarian meals) with walls that can be rolled up, sea views and communal latrines. The »1000 Stars Room« (a bed beneath the stars), the huts and two suites (air-con) are all on the wide expanses of the beach.

KIDS & CO.
Coco Beach Resort
£££–££££

km 12.5, 58 Nguyen Dinh Chieu, Ham Tien, Mui Ne,
Phan Thiet
tel. 062/384 71 11
www.cocobeach.net
Family-run hotel which feels just like home. Jutta and her husband were pioneers when they opened this idyllic hotel, the first in Mui Ne, in 1995. Just 34 wooden huts stand on the broad, clean beach (three 2-room »villas« for families) – no television, but air conditioning and Wi-Fi. Babysitters, children's playground and for the older kids windsurfing, kiting and bodysurfing lessons on the beach. If the wind gets up, retire to the garden pool, also with kids' pool.

In Saigon's backpacker district

Colonial Atmosphere

No other place conjures up the colonial era of Vietnam or Indochina quite like the Sofitel Legend Metropole in Hanoi. As the name suggests, this noble hotel is rich in legend, a classic which has impressed its guests for over a century: William Somerset Maugham and Noel Coward in the 1930s, Charlie Chaplin and Graham Greene, Ho Chi Minh and, in the Vietnam War, Jane Fonda and later Mick Jagger and Fidel Castro.

Illustrious names and tragicomic anecdotes bring the history of the honourable residence to life through the decades. A French officer once shot a waiter in the Beaulieu Restaurant during a power cut – mistaking him for an assassin in the dark...

There have been other darker moments as well as glorious ones, the hotel was used for a time as a prison. During the war, guests retreated to a bunker beneath the swimming pool as the US bombardment continued overhead. Joan Baez sang against the thrum of the B52s and the bombings, whilst »Hanoi Jane« Fonda stayed for two months at the »Thong Nhat«, as the hotel was known in 1972, on her protest trip through North Vietnam.

Princes, presidents and pop stars pass through the lobby until this very day. The suites are named after some of the most famous guests, such as Charlie Chaplin, who honeymooned here with Paulette Goddard in 1936 after their wedding in Canton. High-tech gear and iPods come as standard in the suites, of course.

Nostalgic Charm

Neoclassical charm and historic decor still abound in the hotel; a well-travelled, oversize **Louis Vuitton trunk**, for example (not a fake, for once!) with all its compartments and faded stickers from Paris to Shanghai. Vintage telephones are still in service in the stairwell and suites. Guests who imagine they are only for show are taken aback to learn that they are directly connected to the main switchboard. Not to mention the old shoeshine chair in the lobby, the cabinets, ceiling fans, black and white postcards from the turn of the last century and the chandeliers above the bath. A journey into Vietnam's colonial history is thus not restricted to the historic »Metropole Wing« of the hotel alone. The parquet floors creak in the original historic wing, opened in 1901, and old charcoal drawings bear witness to the expeditions of pith helmeted colonial rulers in days gone by, aboard sampans or pulled along on rickshaws. How easy it is to think back to the »good old days«. The German manager of the Metropole, Kai Spieth, finds himself doing just that, time and again. »Sitting in the Graham Greene Suite, one can readily imagine him writing the 500 words he set himself as a daily target, just like clockwork.« Such inspiration is well worth the US$2000 (a night, just to be clear) for many a CEO or corporate boss). Graham Greene sipped daiquiris listening to chansons in the club restaurant in the garden, followed years later by Roger Moore, dry Martini in hand. Perhaps this is where William Somerset Maugham scribbled his notes, now the scene for guests swiping and typing on their iPhones – with such exotic cocktails as coriander mojitos never far away. The **afternoon chocolate** buffet in Le Club is an irresistible must.

Those Were the Days...

Without doubt, the Sofitel Legend Metropole is one of Asia's finest residences, its staff of 600 both attentive and friendly, without being overbearing or subservient. The »good old days« are well and truly over, which is a shame in one sense at least: in the 1920s, a room cost between US$7 to US$12. At todays prices, one could have lived here for two months back then – with full board! Those were the days...

Sofitel Legend Metropole ££££
15 Ngo Quyen,
near Hoan Kiem Lake
tel. 04/38 26 69 19
www.sofitel.com

The pool has its own style, too

Children in Vietnam

Fun and Games

The miles of beaches of Phan Thiet/Mui Ne, Nha Trang and Da Nang are, of course, ideal destinations for holidays with children. But Saigon and Hanoi can also be thrilling for kids, once visitors have adjusted to the incredible volume of traffic. The often dim, smoky pagodas may be a little unsettling for small children, as tall, grim guardians peer down at them. Then again, with a guide who speaks their language, the legends associated with the site can be of interest to them. .

Sadly, the exotic world of Vietnam is also associated with a certain lack in hygiene. Though most children don't mind this, parents should take steps, even before the trip, and have their children vaccinated (e.g. against typhus and tetanus, besides vaccinations for all common children's diseases). Those travelling in malaria regions (outside cities) should gather information in advance at tropical institutes on medication and preventive measures (mosquito nets, repellent, light clothes covering the entire body) at least 6 weeks prior to departure. See **www.fco.gov.uk/en/travelling-and-living-overseas** for the latest information.

Travel preparations

Parents of babies should definitely bring a few specific items: passport, vaccination record and, though there is a growuing number of retail markets, baby food, disposable nappies and sun lotion. A child carrier which can be strapped on is a useful accessory on treks

Those taking their children to Vietnam must first survive the lengthy flight time (from Europe, 11 to 13 hours or longer), which often involves changing several times. Once in Vietnam, cross-country travel can be extremely strenuous: long rides in crammed (mini) buses; loud, hectic and dangerous traffic; and accommodation that is not always well equipped and clean.

En route

Better not to give the little ones ice cream (or only in top hotels). Older children should be fine in restaurants: pizza, pasta or chips and cola are served in all tourist areas. For hygienic reasons, steer clear of: meat grilled on street stalls, seafood, fish sauce, fresh coconut juice, unpeeled fruit, raw salad and raw, unpeeled vegetables. Drink plenty due to high temperatures but do not drink tap water! Better to use (sealed) bottled water for cleaning teeth as well.

In Vietnam babies and children up to two years of age (or under 80cm/32in) usually fly free of charge. Children up to the age of ten may be eligible for 50% discount on bus travel, tours and amusement

Discounts

A friendly hello on a boat trip

parks. A little known fact: most hotel swimming pools can be used during the day by families who are not hotel residents (for a fee of around £3 per person).

Fun for kids

Water Puppet Theatre

Thang Long Theatre
57B Dinh Thien Doang (Hoan Kiem Lake), Hanoi
Tel 04/39 36 43 35
http://thanglongwaterpuppet.org/en/
Shows: daily 3pm, 4.10pm, 5.20pm, 6.30 and 8pm
Tickets: approx. £3.50–7 (purchase early!)

Rong Vang Golden Dragon Water Puppet Theatre
55B Nguyen Thi Minh Khai, Saigon
tel. 08/39 30 21 96
Shows daily 5pm, 6.30pm and 7.45pm, tickets approx. £4.50
An art form dating back 1000 years, loud, cheerful and rich in colour: water puppet theatre relates the ancient tales and legends of Vietnam. The best performances are in Hanoi and Saigon (there are also shows in Hue and daytime ones in Saigon at the tiny theatre in the History Museum and the main post office in the afternoons (▶MARCO POLO Insight p.78, 368).

Dam Sen Water Park

3 Hoa Binh, District 11, Saigon
Tue-Sat 9am-6pm, Sun 8.30am-6pm
Admission: adults approx £2.70 (depending on time of visit), children: approx. £1.90

www.damsenwaterpark.com.vn
Amusement park for all ages with rowing boats, giant waterslide, Space Spiral and miniature railway, even dinosaurs. Restaurant and fast food outlets (generally quiet on weekdays but not all rides may be open, totally crowded at weekends, expect to queue with Vietnamese families).

Elephant Rides

at Lak Lake, in the villages of Ban Jun and Ban Don, Buon Ma Thuot (can be booked as an expensive tour, e.g. via Dak Lak Tourist in Buon Ma Thuot, tel. 0500/385 22 46, www.daklaktourist.com.vn).
Price: £7.50-15 per hour (prices for rides are negotiable depending on the season and haggling skills, official tours: £15-22.50 per hour).
High up on an elephant, visit the »elephant villages« of the M'Nong, reputed as traditional elephant breeders for centuries, and swing through the Vietnamese highlands. Two to three persons can ride in the basket atop one beast as he wades through the lake, unhurried. Feed them with bananas after the ride (also possible in Yok Don National Park, ▶p.165).

Chocolate Buffet

15 Ngo Quyen, Hanoi
tel. 04/38 26 69 19
www.sofitel.com

Families with a sweet tooth and discerning palate will enjoy an afternoon in the noble Sofitel Legend Metropole: an endless chocolate buffet with more than 20 different creations from the »Maître Chocolatier« in the legendary »Le Club« (daily 3pm-5pm, approx. £12; ▶MARCO POLO Insight p.104).

Lake of Sighs and Da Lat
3 between 6km/3.5mi from Da Lat
daily 8am-6pm
Admission: approx. £0.80
The »Lake of Sighs« (Ho Than Tho) and Ho Da Thien (lake) both lie in the »Valley of Love« amongst a beautiful, hilly landscape. Both amusement parks feature typical Vietnamese activities such as pony rides, canoe trips, pedalos and a Wild West Park with cowboys and Indians at the Cam Ly waterfall. Kids will have fun exploring the Da Lat Crazy House too (▶pp.194/195).

Zoo and Circus
Saigon Zoo
Le Duan, District 1, Saigon
daily 7am-8pm
admission: approx. £0.40

Saigon Circus: Rap Xiec
1 Hoang Minh Giam, in Gia Dinh Park, Go Vap district, Saigon
tel. 08/35 88 17 40
Sat and Sun 7.30pm (2 hours)
admission: approx £4, kids approx. £3
Zoos, animal parks and circuses are amongst the most love attractions in many a Vietnamese town. In Saigon, crowds gather to catch

Sliding through the sand in Mui Ne

a glimpse of the white tigers and Komodo dragons. Clowns, magicians, artists, tightrope walkers and jugglers perform in the Saigon Circus, where elephants, horses, monkeys and dogs also show off their routines.

Saigon Pony Club
Lane 42 Le Van Thinh, District 2 Saigon
Mobile tel. 091/373 33 60
16 ponies await large and small guests. Stroke them, learn to ride them or just watch (riding lessons from 6 years upwards, approx. £7.50). Not far way, the X-Rock Climbing Center poses a challenge to kids from the age of four and up (75 Nguyen Dinh Chieu).

A Wealth of Myths and Symbols

Few nations in the world like to celebrate as much as the Vietnamese: from honouring great grandmother or other ancestors to the village patron saint or celestial spirits. Earth, Water and Forest are revered, Buddha, the Moon Goddess and Ho Chi Minh are remembered. The Party is celebrated, there is no shortage of reasons.

Myths and legends also play an important role. Full moon days are the most commonly chosen, as for thousands of years the dates for traditional festivals have been calculated according to the position of the moon. The lunar year has twelve months and starts in the middle of January. Each year is marked by another animal of the Zodiac (goat 2015, monkey 2016, cock 2017). Using this 4600-year-old calendar, astrologers still calculate the lucky days – and the unlucky ones. And so crucial decisions and actions are taken on the advice of astronomers and the lunar calendar, anything from a voyage or moving house to opening a new business, building a house or signing a contract.

All of Vietnam is caught up in the country's new year festivities in January/February (see calendar below and ▶MARCO POLO Insight p.114). Travellers take note: transportation (flights especially) will be booked up long in advance for this period, the same goes for many hotels, who may now charge double, whilst many restaurants, shops, museums and galleries might be closed. Tourist offers will also be fully booked or »on ice«. For at least a week, all of Vietnam will be visiting relatives and many Vietnamese return home from abroad.

Festival calendar

PUBLIC HOLIDAYS
1 January: New Year's Day
3 February: Foundation Day of the Communist Party (1930)
30 April: Liberation Day for the Southern Republic / Fall of Saigon and Reunification Day (1975)
1 May: International Labour Day
19 May: Birthday of Ho Chi Minh (1890)
2 September: Independence Day (1945)

3 September: Anniversary of Ho Chi Minh's death (1969)
24/25 December: Christmas with midnight Mass (for Christians, mainly in the south)

JANUARY–FEBRUARY
Tet Festival
The most important festival in Vietnam is the Vietnamese New Year (tet nguyen dan), which is celebrated for at least three days

Oblations are presented at festivals

between mid-January and mid-February (sometimes early March): with offerings and gifts, family visits, festively decorated streets and houses and the consumption of tasty sticky rice cakes ▶MARCO POLO Insight p.114).

MARCH/APRIL
Elephant race festival

Insider Tip

Held on the Serebok River in Buon Don (Dak Lak province), where the M'Nong demonstrates their skills with locally bred elephants around the 3rd month of the lunar calendar. During the races the portly looking animals can reach speeds of up to 40kmh/25mph along a 1km-2km/half a mile to 1 and a quarter mile track.

APRIL/MAY
Phat Dan –
Buddha's birthday

Buddhists in Vietnam celebrate Buddha's birthday on the 8th day of the 4th lunar month – temples are filled with incense smoke, offerings and people praying

Insider Tip

MAY
Po Nagar Festival

A festival of the Cham people with boat races and traditional »boi« chanting (Thap Ba)

APRIL–JUNE
Ba Chua Xu –
Pilgrimage to the Nui Sam

The pilgrimage to Nui Sam Mountain (Chau Doc) takes place from the 22nd to the 26th day of the 4th lunar month.

The Dragon Dance is a New Year's tradition, bringing positive energy and happiness

Ancestors are honoured with prayer and burning incense sticks at festivals

JULY/AUGUST
**Trang Nguyen (Vu Lan) –
Festival of Forgiveness**
A holiday commemorating ancestors and their wandering souls: on the day of the »Festival of Forgiveness« (15th day of the 7th lunar month) the Jade Emperor and the Princes of Hell deliberate over the sins of their earthly children, while the souls of the wandering dead return home for the day

AUGUST
Hon Chen Temple Festival
This temple festival takes place twice every year, during the 3rd and 7th lunar month: 10km/16mi west of Hue, at the Perfume River, the faithful gather to attend plays and processions and to worship the Holy Mother Thien Y A Na – the river is lit up by small lightships and illuminated boats.

SEPTEMBER
Festival of buffalo fighting
This famous festival on the 9th day of the 8th lunar month is for worshipping the tutelary deity of the Hai Phong fishermen, Dieu Tuoc Ton Than. Various rituals are followed by a (normally bloodless) buffalo fight. Sadly the winner does not benefit from its victory – both buffalos are slaughtered and eaten in honour of the tutelary god.

OCTOBER/NOVEMBER
**Ghe-Ngo Festival
(Ok Om Bok)**
On the 14th/15th day of the 10th lunar month the Khmer in the Mekong Delta celebrate the full moon festival, Ok Om Bok, by making offerings to the Moon Goddess, who bestows luck and wealth on the people. Lanterns and flying lampions light the sky while offerings are presented to the Mekong River or one of its many tributaries in the delta on small banana leaf floats. The Ghe Ngo boat race takes place on the Soc Trang River at the same time.

Happy New Year!

The celebrations begin a full week before the first day of the New Year: on the 23rd day of the twelfth lunar month, in a ceremony held in the home, offerings such as fruit, flowers, food and paper gifts are laid on the domestic altar.

This puts the Hearth God Tao Quan in a good humour when he leaves the house and ascends to heaven, where he makes his annual report to the celestial ruler, the Jade Emperor, about the state of affairs on earth. He does not return until the evening of the New Year, which means that for one week the Vietnamese themselves have to protect their house against evil spirits. To this end they hang lights around the house and red banners on the streets, and adorn their living rooms with red and gold decorations, flowers and orange trees. In the villages bamboo poles draped with old clothing are often placed in the garden in order to drive away evil spirits. **Tet, the New Year's festival**, is the highlight of

the year. As the lunar calendar is used in Vietnam, Tet is celebrated from the first to the seventh day of the first month, i.e. in late January or early February. Officially three days around New Year are public holidays, but most Vietnamese take a whole week.

Time for the Family

Tet means not just the changing of the years, but an occasion for big family gatherings and feasting. It is the time to pay debts, make up disagreements, buy new clothes and send **greetings cards**. The Chinese characters painted on red silk paper that are hung up inside the house or on the front door are also wishes for good luck. All year round the inhabitants of the village of Dong Ho near Hanoi make traditional **New Year's pictures** (▶p.85) showing scenes from legends and myths or symbols of fortune such as round, ripe fruit, fish or well-nourished children. Until 1995 fireworks and rip-raps were an indispensable part of the Tet celebrations, but since then the government has banned this centuries-old tradition, as serious accidents involving a number of fatalities had taken place.

A New Year's celebration without a **great banquet** is unthinkable. Banh chung and banh day are an inseparable part of the feasting: these round cakes of sticky rice, filled with pork and soy beans and wrapped in banana leaves, symbolize earth and heaven. Even if the family cannot really afford it, everything that the food market has to offer will find its way onto the table, because the first day of the year is meant to set the pattern for the whole twelve months to come.

Honour Your Ancestors

The **temples** buzz with activity, especially at midnight when the new lunar year begins. Many people gather at this hour to honour their ancestors and welcome the good spirits back to earth with choice dishes and a host of joss sticks. **Presents** are then exchanged in the family circle.

Symbols

This is a time for superstition, too. Everything that happens around Tet is symbolic. Not only the first visit, but also the first sound that is heard in the New Year (apart from fireworks!) is thought to foretell what will happen in the coming year: a cock's crow, for example, means a lot of work and a bad harvest, while the barking of dogs signifies trust and optimism. A very bad year is in store for anyone who hears the cry of an owl, which is a harbinger of epidemics and ill fortune for the whole community. It is also unlucky at this time of the year to break glass, wash clothes, curse or engage in dirty talk – these are things that attract the evil spirits!

The sale of calendars for the new year

Food and Drink

Delicious, Fresh and Inventive

Food represents an entire life philosophy in Vietnam – and rice in particular, cultivated here for centuries. The Vietnamese have three wholesome meals a day at precisely the same hour. An ethnologist even concluded when observing food rituals: »The Vietnamese are concerned about a filled rice bowl not only in their present life, but also for their next one.« This also explains the many food donations during ancestral worship at home.

The meaning of food is deeply rooted in Vietnamese history, which for millennia was marked by wars, droughts, floods, plagues and other catastrophes. Necessity is the mother of invention, and this is the reason that all kinds of animals still end up in the cooking pot.

Just as the country is split into three main regions – the north, the central region, and the south – there are also three culinary traditions. The northern style is strongly influenced by **Chinese cuisine**. Stir-fries, stews, rice pudding and soups are especially popular in this region, where the climate is cooler and drier. The lack of herbs and spices here also make meals less aromatic. In the the central region around Hue, the former Imperial capital, cooking was a refined art and came to play a significant part in a refined way of life. Special attention was paid to decoration and **presentation of food**, said to please the royal palate. The cooks

Regional preferences

MARCO ⊕ POLO INSIGHT ❓

Price Categories

££££	over 600,000 VND/ £15
£££	300,000 – 600,000 VND/ £8 – 15
££	150,000 – 300,000VND/ £4 – 8
£	up to 150,000 VND/£4
(for a main dish)	

from Hue are known for their pork sausage, their sweet-and-sour rice cake and their soup ingredients with a mix of fried tomato puree, chilli and prawn sauce. Around Hue, many European types of vegetables are used as well: artichokes, cauliflower, asparagus and potatoes. Southern cuisine is less complex but spicier than up north. Exotic fruit and top-quality vegetables grow well on this fertile land, and are served uncooked with meals. In this region quick stir-fries and sautés are preferred to fried or slowly stewed dishes; spicy curries are very common. The **French influence** of the colonial rulers is most evident in the use of asparagus, tomatoes and potatoes, which are prepared

»Banh bao« are steamed rolls with various fillings: in China they are known as Dim Sum

Vietnamese-style. Grilled dishes are equally popular here. In the south, it is customary to wrap fried or grilled meals with raw vegetables and herbs into a salad leaf. This little package is then dipped into a hot sauce.

Three big meals Most Vietnamese start their day with a noodle soup. Even in the morning they are spiced with freshly cut chilli peppers. A wholesome breakfast is usually served bright and early. Boiled rice is served at lunch and dinner along with a mixture of spicy and mild dishes of meat, fish and vegetables. A characteristic of Vietnamese cooking is the use of additional ingredients of different consistencies to create flavours for the individual palate and taste. Colour contrast and the mixing of different aromas also play a major role.

Restaurants The furniture in restaurants is often fairly simple and tourists should not be put off by wooden benches, plastic chairs and cutlery, or dirty table cloths. Foreigners are often given spoons and forks instead of chopsticks. In larger towns there are English and/or French menus, but waiters in Vietnamese restaurants rarely speak English. Sometimes menus do not list any **prices**, so make sure to ask the waiter when ordering. Often prices are stated for different portion sizes – the smallest portion is usually enough for one person. Green teacomes free of charge everywhere, while snacks such as salted almonds or dried fish in chilli sauce are normally extra, as is the damp towel.

Restaurants fill up relatively early with local customers (lunchtime is around noon, dinner time between 6pm and 8pm). Vietnamese like to eat in big groups with business partners or the entire family. The more people there are, the more opulent the meal: all ordered dishes are served at the same time, and every guest can try each dish by putting some into a rice bowl using chopsticks (never take too much!).

Eating out with the Vietnamese can be quite **lively** at times and is often accompanied by loud (live) music. Particularly at traditional, but also at finer restaurants, be prepared to hear the typical atmospheric noise of slurping, spitting and burping. People often smoke or talk loudly on their mobile phones.

In simple street restaurants and cookshops without menus, diners simply point to their chosen vegetables and dishes displayed behind glass. No need to worry: restaurants in all the tourist areas offer international and often upmarket cuisine, whilst vegetarian and tofu dishes are everywhere to be found. It is acceptable to leave a tip, but in the better hotels and restaurants, a service charge is already included. Tips are not expected in cookshops. Do not leave chopsticks sticking in the rice, it is considered a bad omen.

Most restaurants serve poultry, marinated pork, beef, grilled pork ribs, thinly sliced beef and minced meat as well as fish in all shapes and sizes. Bun cha are noodle dishes with grilled meat, usually served with raw vegetables on the side. The key ingredient is the **sauce**: it is said to be best in Hanoi and includes peppermint leaves. Anything from the sea, e.g. crab, shrimp, crayfish, lobster, mussels, snails, prawns, squid, mackerel, carp, tuna and shark, is a high-protein food that is affordable to many Vietnamese; in Vietnam, fish and shellfish are fairly inexpensive, delicious and always served fresh in coastal towns. Fruit is recommended for **dessert**: pineapple, water melon, banana, lychees, longan, mango, papaya and pomelo are just some of the delicious fruits grown in Vietnam. Better restaurants also offer

Restaurant food

Dishes are usually decorated with a fine eye for detail

Typically Vietnamese Dishes

Vietnamese cuisine is greatly varied – and rich in spices and nuanced flavours. Most Vietnamese recipes are based on rice and noodles. Traditionally, three or four dishes are served: rice or noodles, a fish or meat dis, vegetables and a soup.

Pho: »Pho«, one of the most popular dishes in Vietnam, consists of rice or wheat noodles, thinly sliced beef, chicken or prawn and a few soybean sprouts as topping. Boiled meat broth is poured on top – a steamy and very spicy affair. On request, a raw egg is cracked on top. The soup is spiced with pepper, mint, coriander, ground chili and lemon juice, but those who wish to can add a bit of fish or soy sauce, as well as herbs. The soup is eaten with a spoon and chopsticks, the local way is to eat it, however, is to slurp it on the side of the street.

Hot Pot: This Vietnamese-style fondue is prepared in a large tin samovar or clay pot. Waitresses put the ingredients (fish, seafood, vegetables and glass noodles) into the bubbling soup stock and cook them at the table.

Mooncakes: During every full moon festival shops and food stands stock up on golden-brown banh nuong and banh deo – small, round mooncakes. This typical Vietnamese treat is made of fried sticky rice, rice flour and sugared water.

Spring rolls: Small and zesty spring rolls (cha gio), either fried or fresh, can be stuffed with vegetables, minced meat, prawns, shrimp, glass noodles, chopped onion or soybean sprouts and are usually wrapped at the table in salad leafs or thin rice paper (that was first dipped in water). This small package is then dipped in a sauce made from fish sauce, chili, pepper and lemon juice (nuoc cham). A bowl with salad and herbs, such as coriander, lemon balm, mint, lemon grass and basil, is also provided on the table.

Nuoc Mam: This typically Vietnamese fish sauce is used for seasoning. It is prepared in a small bowl at the table with a mix of fresh chili and garlic, sugar, pepper and lime juice. It can be used for various dishes such as spring rolls and tastes far better than the ketchup or chili sauces in plastic bottles that are often offered to foreign guests.

Bun Cha: For this Hanoi specialty meat filets, pork belly or meat balls are prepared on a charcoal grill and served with long thin rice noodles (bun) in a spicy broth of fish sauce. It's best to try this dish from one of the street vendors, just follow the wads of smoke and the mouth-watering barbecue flavor!

fried bananas, pineapple flambéed with rice wine or traditional co-conut desserts. Another common dessert is the rainbow drink, a cold sweet beverage made of ground mung beans, agar agar and coconut milk. Naturally, Western desserts such as crème caramel, ice cream or fruit sorbets can be ordered as well. In cities, many restaurants also offer good, though sometimes very sugary, cakes made of dough or sticky rice.

INDIVIDUAL DISHES

»Moi ong xoi com« (»Enjoy your rice«) is an old saying further illus-trating its importance. Today people are more likely to say »Chuc an ngon!« or »Xin moi!« for »Enjoy your meal«. Unfortunately, most tourists in all Asian countries order fried rice, which is offered eve-

Some cooks without a regular stall carry their fare on their shoulders, serving their delicacies on the street

rywhere – blissfully unaware of what they›re missing.These rice and vegetable fry ups, however, are considered to occupy the lower rungs of the Vietnamese culinary ladder. The Vietnamese mostly eat boiled rice and the ingredients are either mixed on the plate or served on the side (►MARCO POLO Insight p.324).

The Vietnamese simply love Fish sauce (nuoc mam), and it is far more than a substitute for salt. Nuoc mam is produced in factories in the Mekong delta and on the island of Phu Quoc (►p.121, 358-359). The recipe is very simple: salted sardines are stored and fermented in barrels for one year. At home, the bottled brew is refined with lemon juice, vinegar, fresh chilli, sugar, pepper, garlic and coriander.

Fish sauce (nuoc mam

In Vietnam there is a soup kitchen on every corner, and the streets are lined with travelling cooks who carry their kitchen over their shoulder or in a little cart. Soup kitchens serve traditional and very cheap soups for breakfast at low benches and stools. Soup is also an integral part of lunch and dinner. The northern spicy soup called **pho** (►p.120) has become a national dish: There are also sweet-

Between Asia and Europe

Vietnamese cuisine is a culinary highlight within Asia, as the fusion of Asian and European styles results in light, delicious food. Compared to the spiciness of Indian or Thai food, Vietnamese dishes are fairly mild. The dominating flavour is determined by the addition of many fresh herbs, especially coriander.

and-sour (Chinese) soups, as well as purely sour soups with shrimp or fish, tomatoes and onions (**canh chua**). Noodle soups are eaten with spoons and chopsticks; tables are usually set with chopsticks. Mien is a Chinese glass noodle soup with meatballs, chao is a thick rice soup, and the sweetish che soup is prepared with coconut milk.

Spring rolls (►p.121) are the most popular starters. Western travellers who are in Asia only for a short time should be wary of raw vegetables, salads and herbs.
Vietnamese omelette is served with vegetables and meats in plentiful variety. Samosas stuffed with shrimp or meat are another speciality along the coast. At the side of the street, a kind of pancake with meat (banh bao) is sold. Crispy flatcakes made of sesame and rice flour are baked over charcoal,while spicy sa giang chips made of shrimp paste and flour (banh phong tom) are offered as a small starter in some restaurants and exported all over the world. Street stalls offer **baguette sandwiches** (com tay cam or banh mi pate), with often extremely spicy toppings with cheese, chicken, fish or pork, vegetables and onions. Meat grilled over charcoal is another popular roadside snack, as are scalloped bananas from the street vendors› baskets.

Starters,side dishes and snacks

Food is not just a question of nutrition in Vietnam, it also serves the balance of body and soul

Noodles   The Vietnamese eat different types of noodles – either yellow (mi, made of wheat flour and eggs) or white (banh, made of rice). The thin, transparent glass noodles are mainly used for soups.

DRINKS

Tea   Tea is usually brewed early in the morning to last the entire day, and is kept warm under a quilted tea cosy. It is offered to guests along with nuts, dried fruit and cake.

Water etc.   It is also usual to find mineral water, **soft drinks** such as Coke and Sprite, sweet soybean milk (sua dau nanh), which is probably not enjoyed by many Westerners, **freshly squeezed fruit juices** and coconut milk. Many street stands (and restaurants) have a choice of coconuts that will be cracked open with a machete. Freshly squeezed sugar cane is commonly sold by street vendors. Under no circumstances drink tap water (▶p.444)!

Coffee   Some time is required for traditional, tasty coffee, one of the country's biggest exports, it has to be said – and a sweet tooth is advantageous: the coffee slowly seeps through a metal filter into the glass, in which a thick layer of condensed milk has already been poured (»ca phe sua nong«). Those desiring iced coffee should order »ca phe sua da«. Black coffee is called »ca phe den nong«, in single cup filters: »ca phe phin«.

The Vietnamese word for **wine**, ruou, is used for various alcoholic beverages. One well-known national drink is called ruou de or choum. It is a strong, clear, alcoholic spirit made from sticky rice and is quite similar to Japanese sake. People drink it warm and normally only on special occasions when raising a toast.

Signs on every street corner advertise Tiger beer from Singapore: the company brews its relatively strong **beer** in Vietnam. Another joint venture ist the French beer, BGI, is also brewed in Vietnam. However, Vietnamese bottled beers are tasty too: Ba-Ba-Ba (333) was the follow-up to Saigon Export and is mostly available in cans. Naturally, (expensive) beers imported from Europe are also available.

Vietnamese coffee is served thus

►Language, p.449

Menu

Shopping

Beautiful Handicrafts

The number of irresistible gifts worth taking back home is endless: from classics like chopsticks and conical hats to pretty silk blouses and silk lanterns, or basketry and lacquerware, ceramics and fabrics.

In recent years, the range has grown even broader, with imaginative and trendy additions as well as »sustainable« souvenirs. How about a pair of flip-flops with bamboo soles and cinnamon straps from Hoi An (just the right Ayurvedic recipe to combat sweaty feet)! Or a life-size Buddha in Da Nang marble for the terrace at home? In Hanoi, where else, cool propaganda posters with »Uncle Ho« can be snapped up. Everything a tourist's heart desires, but training is required in one tactic – in spite of »special price for you «: haggling is the order of the day in Vietnam! Keep calm and smile whilst negotiating.

A special feature of Vietnamese handicrafts: disabled craftspeople work in many of the workshops, or the goods on sale come from the hill tribes, with proceeds going to projects supporting the disabled and minority groups. A transaction thus serves a good cause. Vietnam is, however, infamous for replicas and copies: expensive fashion brands, for example – a Louis Vuitton bag for €10, or where else might one purchase a Picasso for a mere £25?! »Brand names« spotted at Saigon's Ben Thanh Market are invariably fakes (70% discounts can be negotiated, the cheaper it gets, the more »fake« it seems..).

> **MARCO ⊕ POLO TIP**
>
> **Insider Tip**
>
> *Stop! Not permitted!*
>
> When buying souvenirs, be sure to avoid any kind of animal product, such as snake skin, crocodile skin, reptilian claws, brandied snakes, tortoise shell, tiger fur, corals, mother-of-pearl or live tropical fish.

In Vietnam the art of decorative woodcarving has been practised for more than 1000 years. The colourful or black-and-white woodcarvings are even popular among the Vietnamese, especially for the Vietnamese New Year celebrations, and mostly depict motifs with lucky charms, such as pigs or cockerels. These craftwork products are excluded from the wood export ban. The traditional **wood-carving village of Dong Ho** is near Hanoi (▶Sights, p.280), whilst Hoi An is home to many workshops.

Woodcarving

How are the conical hats made from palm leaves?

Ceramics CeramicsPottery has also been around in Vietnam for nearly 1000 years. The roofs of many houses and temples were covered with colourful ceramic tiles. Each dynasty had its own distinct style of pottery, such as the blue ceramics of the 17th-century Nguyen dynasty from Hue. The history museums in Hanoi and Saigon provide a good overview. In **Binh Hoa**, north of Saigon, there is a handicrafts centre with factories and family businesses manufacturing ceramic goods. Among the most popular souvenirs are the handmade elephants. Beware of so-called »antique« goods from centuries-old dynasties. If they really are genuine antiques, customs officials will certainly not turn a blind eye to them – without the correct paperwork, such items will be confiscated. Many shops can arrange documentation and ship goods via plane or sea.

Silk Sericulture and silk weaving have also been practiced in Vietnam for a millennium. Silk fabrics and **tailored clothing** are particularly inexpensive in Saigon. Within one or two days tailors can sew an item of clothing based on a model. Compare prices and ask for discounts for more than one item of clothing. Those travelling via **Hoi An** should definitely visit the tailor's shops on Le Loi Street. They make suits, kimonos and dresses cheaply overnight – still, better not to leave it until the last minute before departure, as some minor alterations may be required after fitting.

Vases and bowls are not the only ceramics to be found. This laughing Buddha is made from the same material

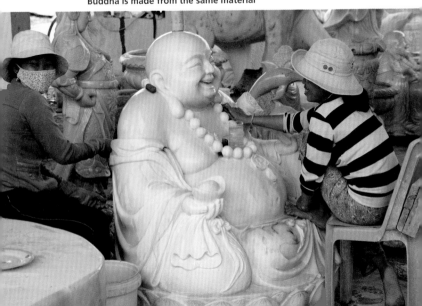

This handicraft, which originated in China, is now offered everywhere in Vietnam and has been practised for at least 1500 years. The black or brown lacquer is acquired from the resin of the sumac tree. Mother-of-pearl goods are particularly common and some are even quite cheap: jewellery boxes, writing utensils, betel nut bowls, ashtrays, china, chopsticks, musical instruments, altars, murals, cupboards and entire sitting room suites. Besides the traditional motifs and colours there are also more minimalist designs on offer, which seem more modern and less unconventional: pots, bowls and trays.

Clothes can be tailored cheaply in Ho An

A lot of souvenir items and everyday utensils are made of rattan and bamboo, e.g. classical instruments. Hand-woven rugs and blankets also make good souvenirs. At markets there is a whole range of different green teas and spices on offer. Gold, silver and gemstones (ruby and jade) should only be bought by those who really know what they are buying, and in licensed shops only. Souvenir opium pipes may cause problems when leaving the country as selling them is technically not allowed.

Rattan and bamboo

Products crafted by the various different peoples of Vietnam make ideal souvenirs, particularly embroidered and woven fabrics or silver jewellery.

Handicrafts of the hill tribes

Sport and Outdoors

Not Just Water Sports

A majestic coastline 3200km/2000mi long – what could be better than enjoying aquatic activities, on or in the water, riding the waves or breezing along on the wind. Surfing, kiting, paddling or diving, the range of activity choices has increased apace in recent years on the islands and mainland. Caving, canyoning, abseiling, rock climbing and deep water soloing are the latest trends to promise adrenalin rushes. Be sure to look out for proper equipment and be mindful of providers' safety standards. Not only sporty types and adventurers will love Vietnam: other activities are also in vogue, from shadow boxing (t'ai chi) and cookery courses to lantern making in Hoi An.

Golf is now hugely popular in Vietnam. The establishment of several golfing facilities in the country in recent years was encouraged in particular by Asian and US tourists. In the highlands, however, golf was already played in imperial times – Bao Dai himself was known to swing a driver at the golf course in Da Lat.

Golf

Most first-class beach resorts in coastal towns offer a whole range of fun in the water: paddle and sail boats, catamarans, surfboards and parasailing, sometimes even water skiing.

Beach resorts

Western-run diving schools (with PADI certificate) have opened up on the coasts of Vietnam and on the islands of Phu Quoc, Con Dao (Six Senses) and Whale Island. The best time to dive is from May to June, but diving along Vietnam's coasts is possible even in winter (in Central Vietnam typhoons may occur from August to December; rainfall increases between October and November/December when the water visibility in Nha Trang is not as good). The best and deepest water visibility can be found around **Phu Quoc** (up to 50m/165ft), where there is at least one dive centre. Day tours including two dives cost around £30.

Diving

The best spots for kitesurfing and windsurfing are at Phan Thiet/Mui Ne, Da Nang and Vung Tau. Mui Ne has developed into the biggest surf scene with clubs and schools and the annual Fun Cup in February, when hundreds of competitors from all over the globe gather here. Little rain, good winds (in terms of strength and direction) and a fine array of hotels with many bars and pubs amount to ideal surfer

Kitesurfing and windsurfing

Phan Thiet is an Eldorado for windsurfers

conditions. The best months for surfing are September/October to December, kitesurfing from November to March/April.

Kayaking The best kayaking region is to be found in the paradisiacal setting of Ha Long PBay and around the island of Cat Ba with its thousands of small islands jutting out of the emerald-green water like stone dinosaurs. A canoe ride leads through mangroves and caves directly to the beaches.

Two-day tours can be booked everywhere in Ha Long city and Hanoi from £22 per person, whereby the experience and safety standards tend to be superior when booking through trusted and renowned agents such as John Gray's Seacanoe from Thailand (www.johngrtayseacanoe.com although this costs a princely £190 for two people). Professionalism can really be a matter of life and death due to the tides and dangerous currents in the lagoons: life-threatening situations have arisen in the past through budget operators using poorly trained (Vietnamese) personnel. Never attempt paddling into laguna caves without assistance. People usually sleep on the boat or in tents on the beach. Kayaking tours are also on offer in Da Lat and the Cat Tien and Yok Don national parks, whilst the demanding disciplines of »white water rafting« and »expedition rafting«, canyoning and (advanced) abseiling are avsailable at the waterfalls around Da Lat (through Phat Tire Ventures, for example).

Rock climbing An eldorado for rock climbers: Ha Long Bay and Lan Ha Bay at Cat Ba, more recently tours have been added in the Dry Ha Long Bay, the Nha Trang region and Da Lat. The views over the water are spectacular, most climbs are challenging in nature. Those who prefer to map out their own climb will need to bring their own equipment and chalk for their hands. Experienced captains and guides who know the tides are essential in Ha Long Bay, as some of the caves and island lagoons in the limestone cliffs can only be accessed at certain times (and there may be treacherous currents). Deep water soloing involves jumping from the cliff face back into the water. Information and tours (with qualified climbers and equipment) can be found at Asia Outdoors in Cat Ba.

Trekking and hiking tours Trekking and hiking tours are not allowed everywhere without official permission and a Vietnamese trekking guide. It is not a good idea to roam Vietnam's forests alone, if only because of the (as yet) unexploded bombs dating back to the war. There are often police checkpoints in hiking areas or national parks, and frequently summits may turn out to be in a military area. Actual trekking tours last up to a week with eight-hour hikes every day. The group sleeps in very simple wooden huts provided by members of hill tribes, e.g. the Hmong, Muong or Thai. Canoe trips, dinghy excursions or elephant rides are

Beach volleyball with a breathtaking backdrop of Ha Long Bay

sometimes included in the programme. Those booking a one-day hiking tour with bus transportation are sure to end up in an ethnic minority village marketed specifically at tourists. During the **rainy season**, the high number of leeches and muddy paths make trekking tours a rather unpleasant experience. Precautions against malaria and extensive mosquito protection are an absolute must in rural areas, particularly in the rainy season. The Sa Pa region has developed into the most popular trekking terrain, boasting the best infrastructure (from easy walks to challenging climbs up Vietnam's tallest mountain, Fansipan, 3143m/10,312ft, in October/November and between March-May. Treks are also possible across the plateau of Tam Dao, in Hoa Binh/Mai Chau, Cao Bang, on Cat Ba Island, in the national parks of Ba Be, Cuc Phuong and Cat Tien and in the highlands of Da Lat and Dak Lak (elephant rides also on offer).

Caving is a new adventure sport. At 19km/12mi the most famous and longest cave is the Phong Nha Cave (▶Sights, p.216), which has been protected by UNESCO since 2003. Now cavers can discover the legendary grotto on the heels of the old explorers. In addition, the karst

Caving

region around Bac Bo is considered one of the best places for caving tours, particularly in the province of Lai Chau near Tam Duong, the area around Son La, Ha Giang and Cao Bang.

Other activities Those interested in table tennis, badminton or volleyball can join Vietnamese sports enthusiasts in some early-morning exercise in the parks and squares of Saigon and Hanoi. Fans of Tai Chi can study the movements of (mostly older) Vietnamese (from 5.30am to 7am at Hoan KIem Lake in Hanoi, for example, or Saigon's Le Van Tam Park (Hai Ba Trung, on the corner of Dien Bien Phu), or Tam Dam Cultural in Saigon: there are only a few courses specially for tourists so far, combined with Ha Long Bay cruises or in spa hotels). Badminton and peteca are also played here using one's feet. Those interested in horse races should consider mingling with the crowds at the race course in Phu Tho on the weekend – no extravagant hats, but pure fun with plenty of betting-crazed Vietnamese. Saigon and Hanoi offer bowling centres, cinemas and many other types of entertainment.

Hikers in the highlands accompanied by Red Dao

Useful addresses

GOLF
Vietnam Golf Club
Long Thanh My Ward, District 9,
Saigon
tel. 08/62 80 01 01
www.vietnamgolfcc.com

Further information:
www.vietnamgolfresorts.com
www.vietnamgolftours.com

DIVING
Rainbow Divers
90A Hung Vuong, Nha Trang
Hotline tel. 0908/78 17 56
www.divevietnam.com

WINDSURFING/ KITESURFING
Jibe's Beach Club and Water-Sports Center (Fullmoon Resort)
Ham Tien, Mui Ne Beach
Phan Thiet
tel. 062/384 70 08
www.windsurf-vietnam.com

KAYAKING, RAFTING, CANYONING
Buffalo Tours in Hanoi
94 Ma May, Hoan Kiem Lake,
Hanoi
tel. 04/38 28 07 02
www.buffalotours.com

Buffalo Tours in Saigon
81 Mac Thi Buoi, District 1,
Saigon
tel. 08/8 279170
www.buffalotours.com

Phat Tire Ventures
109 Nguyen Van Troi, Da Lat
tel. 063/382 94 22

Mobile tel. 098/661 88 61
www.phattireventures.com

ROCK CLIMBING
Asia Outdoors (formerly Slo Pony Adventures)
222, 1/4 Street (promenade
c/o Noble House Guesthouse)
Cat Ba Island
tel. 031/368 84 50
Mobile tel. 090/347 34 01
www.asiaoutdoors.com.vn

TREKKING
Footprint Vietnam Travel
10A 1 Ly Nam De (4th floor)
Hanoi
tel. 04/39 33 28 44
https://footprint.vn/travel-tips

Saigon Tourist
▶Information, p.447

CAVING
Phong Nha Farmstay
Phong Nha Farmstay
Cu Nam (35km/22mi outside
Dong Hoi)
tel. 052/367 51 35
Mobile tel. 094/475 98 64
www.phong-nha-cave.com
Australian Ben's caving tours to
the Phong Nha caves are also
open to tourists.

Footprint Vietnam Travel
▶Trekking

VETERAN TOURS
Vietnam Tourism
▶Information, p.447

Inserimex Travel
125 Bui Thi Xuan, Hanoi

tel. 04/39 36 46 04
www.inserimextravel.com.vn
Inserimex Travel in Da Nang:
Block 21-23 Area B4, Tran Hung
Dao, tel. 0511/395 19 06

MOTORCYCLE/MOPED
Saigon Tourist,
Vietnam Tourism
Both ▶Information

Xo Tours
tel. in Saigon: 093/308 37 27
https://xotours.vn/
Pillion ride with moped taxi driver
in a white Ao Dai dress

Dalat Easy Rider
(c/o Easy Rider Café)
70 Phan Dinh Phung
www.dalat-easyrider.com

Further information
www.minskclubvietnam.com

www.freewheelin-tours.com

CYCLING TOURS
Sinhbalo Adventure Travel
283/20 Pham Ngu Lao, District 1,
Saigon
tel. 08/38 37 67 66
www.cyclingvietnam.net

Footpring Vietnam Travel
▶Trekking
Some tour organizers offering cycling tours will have the busy
highways (e.g. N 1 and steep
mountain roads) covered by bus,
while cycling is reserved to quieter minor streets and the bikes
taken out of the bus

LANGUAGE HOLIDAYS
Hanoi Language Tours
https://www.myhanoitours.com/
category/theme/language/

Golf at Phan Thiet

SPECIAL ACTIVITIES

Vietnam markets its war history to tourists like no other country in the world. An example of this comes in the form of veteran tours. Veteran soldiers from (Western) allied countries visit the old battle-grounds and army bases, museums, markets of war items, the De-militarized Zone and the rest of the Ho Chi Minh Trail. Old ruins and fortresses such as Khe Sanh in the north and tunnels such as those at Cu Chi are also part of the programme. Participants even get to meet the enemy of the past, members of the Vietcong. *Veteran tours*

To some, it is a dream come true: riding on a motorcycle through Vietnam, from top to bottom or vice versa on National Highway 1. Often travellers will encounter an entire fleets of motorcycles, unfor-tunately an impossible amount of traffic altogether. As these tours may not yet officially be done alone – either on motorcycles or by car – many travel agents specialize in tours on two-wheels. Organizers take care of all the **necessary paperwork**, as a British or even an in-ternational drivers licence is often not accepted. Participants of these two to three-week-long motorcycle tours can choose between a Har-ley Davidson, BMW, Honda or Kawasaki, or various vintage bikes (Minsk). Road conditions require decent driving skills and quick reactions. *Motorcycle tours*

The most attractive routes lead through the mountains in the north and along the new Ho Chi Minh motorway through the hilly, often sparsely populated hinterlands close to the Lao border (from Buon Ma Thuot and Kontum via Aluoi and the DMZ to Huong Khe at Vinh, for instance) – the brand new motorway features a number of steep passes cutting through beautiful landscapes.

One trend to emerge began with the »Easy Rider« bikers from Da Lat (p.190) who organized tours on little Honda mopeds (riding pillion) – indeed there are now countless copycat agencies throughout the country offering pillion rides, on Vespas for example (www.vietnam-vespaadventures.com), even in chaotic cities like Hue and Saigon (definitely wear a helmet and check out insurance, some profession-al operators, such as Xo Tours, see above, provide insurance pack-ages for foreign passengers). Those wishing to ride themselves will find that suitable insurance is so far only available in connection with a Vietnamese driving license! Mopeds for tourists can be seen as a fundamentally risky proposition (the fatalities toll in Vietnam's rap-idly increasing traffic is one of the world's highest).

Those undertaking the north-south route by bicycle can manage the approximately 1700km/2754mi-long stretch between Saigon and Ha-noi within three to four weeks, depending on the number of stops. Either bring a bike by plane or simply buy a new one in Saigon. Trav- *Bicycle tours* ellers wishing to join a group tour should enquire at travel agents. The most popular tours follow the Mekong Delta or Dry Ha Long Bay. Watch out for heavy, even dangerous, traffic on the N 1. Newly laid coastal roads (north of Phan Rang, for instance) or the new Ho Chi Minh motorway are a welcome alternative, although the latter also runs through hilly, barely populated hinterland with no tourist infrastructure (see above, motorbike tours).

Helicopter tours
Those with little time but plenty of money to spare can experience a great way to see Vietnam – by air in a chartered helicopter. Destinations include Saigon, Cu Chi, Tay Ninh (landing on the Black Lady Mountain), Da Lat, Vung Tau (flying over the oil platforms in the South China Sea), Con Dau, and Hanoi, but also less accessible mountain regions such as Dien Bien Phu and Ha Long Bay in the north. Flying from Hanoi past the **limestone giants in the Ha Long Bay** is a spectacular experience. Prices for a one-day trip begin at US$1000. Tours can be booked via Vietnam Tourism (►Information).

Cookery courses
Nowadays, the secrets of Vietnamese herbs and cooking skills can be learned almost everywhere in the country. With cooking spoon and wok in hand, join the trend which began some years ago in Hoi An, home to innumerable cooking schools. Many restaurants in Hanoi, Saigon and Nha Trang offer courses of varying lengths, some including visits to the market.

BEACH HOLIDAYS

Beach towns in Vietnam
A coastline 3200km/2000mi long, with white sandy beaches fringed with palms and casuarina trees, is attracting an increasing number of beach holiday tourists to Vietnam. The infrastructure at many beach resorts, however, is not yet up to scratch. Many still lack nearby airports and many Western guests find comfortable access to the paradisiacal beaches lacking – there is no bungalow under palm trees directly on the beach like in Thailand or on the Philippines. Vung Tau, Da Nang, Nha Trang and Phan Thiet (Mui Ne) are the most well-known beach resorts with the best infrastructure Several **islands** are currently being transformed into beach resorts, such as Lang Co, Con Dao, Tuan Chau (Ha Long Bay), Qui Nhon, Van Dou (Bai Tu Long Bay) and Phu Quoc. Unfortunately, when it comes to the expansion of tourist infrastructure, Asia often favours high-rise hotels complete with golf course, karaoke disco and Disneyland-type leisure facilities. Broad coastal strips in the south and almost the entire length of the Mekong delta are covered by mangroves and are unsuitable for swimming due to the muddy waters. Searching for an empty beach paradise in Vietnam is a rather futile endeavour, for it

is a **densely populated country**, a fact that becomes very apparent all along the coast. If the odd small wonderland is found, it is likely that it is not even connected to the electricity grid, as is the case on the idyllic Lao Cham islands off the coast of Da Nang. Tourists in Vietnam can expect to hear roaring fishing boats at dawn, when entire town communities come together to pull the nets out to shore and trade the freshly-caught fish and sea food, often directly next to people's deck chairs (e.g. in Phan Thiet/ Mui Ne). At popular beaches countless travelling hawkers offer a variety of goods and services (from coconuts and pineapples to T-shirts and massages). Deck chairs and sunshades outside the hotels always cost extra.

Drinks and fruits are served on the most remote of beaches

The mountainous island of Con Dao ▶Sights, p.435) is a designated protected area and owes its popularity to a prison facility built by the French in the 19th century. Today the former prison is open to the public as a museum and memorial site. Here thewooded island mountains dramatically drop into the ocean and there are wide and deserted sandy beaches. Daily flights per week connect the island with Saigon, Hanoi and Can Tho (the best time to go: between March and July). Six Senses only recently opened up a dream oasis here.   Con Dao

The beautiful long sandy beach of Cua Dai (approx. 5km/3mi west of Hoi An) along with the nearby islands of Cham and Cam Kim offer some fabulously comfortable beach resorts between the Song Do River and the dunes, including the luxurious Victoria Resort and one of Asia's finest luxury residences in the form of The Nam Hai. Snacks and drinks are sold at food stands under casuarina trees. (Book as early as possible for the high seasons from August to October and December to February.)   Cua Dai

Da Nang is about to become an international beach town with numerous bars and karaoke clubs. The softly curved and seemingly endless beach south of Da Nang, China Beach (▶Sights, p.206), has become world famous. It is where the first US ground troops landed with their tanks in March of 1965, and where, ten years later, refugee boats set sail to unknown destinations. Now top-class hotels are   Da Nang/ China Beach opening their doors to foreign visitors. There may soon be as many hotels and guesthouses here as there are palm trees. Between August and October **typhoons** may rage in the area. Dangerous currents occur during wintertime in particular. Best time for bathing: from April/May to July. Despite predictions to the contrary, the world's most renowned hotel chains have not rushed in since the year 2000, with only a handful of new ventures appearing, even in Central Vietnam's Da Nang with the International Airport and the 30km/18mi of »China Beach«. The Hyatt's long-term project only reached fruition in 2012/13 when they opened for business with villas and condominiums, then the InterContinental and JW Marriott in 2014. Lang Co peninsula saw the Banyan Tree Lang Co open up in 2012 (p.208).

Around Ha Long Bay

The **Tuan Chau** peninsula was literally built from scratch in 2002 (approx. 10km/6mi south of Ha Long City). The beach resort island gives an artificial impression. There is a connecting dam to the mainland and views to the cliffs of Ha Long Bay and the skyline of Ha Long City. There are some modern first-class hotels on the small strip of beach, with more inexpensive accommodation to be found on the second row up the slope. Travel agents here mainly seem to target Asian families. Events such as dolphin shows take place at the apparent smaller imitation of the Sydney Opera House located on the beach. An 18-hole golf course is in planning.

On the biggest, largely rocky, national park island of **Cat Ba**, which has been a **biosphere reserve** under UNESCO protection since 2005, there are several idyllic, tiny beaches (Lan Ha, Cat Co and Cat Vang) though they become crowded during summer weekends. Most hotels are situated along the promenade of Cat Ba City. The only truly stunning luxury hotel so far is located on the small beach Cat Co 3, though more are currently being built on the bay nearby. On the islands dotted around Ha Long Bay there are some attractive beaches, with luck, equipped with sunshades. The silted beaches of Bai Chay in Ha Long City are unsuitable for swimming, as is the crowded beach of Do Son near Hai Phong (which has a casino).

More deserted beaches can be found in the nearby (to the east) and less crowded **Bai Tu Long Bay**, e.g. on the still rural peninsula of Van Don (simple to mid-range accommodation and a lower mid-range eco hotel with a small private beach set before imposing cliffs) and the two sandy beaches on the island of **Quan Lan**, so far only equipped with stilted huts and simple stone bungalows. Construction work continues apace, however. Best time for swimming in the entire Ha Long/Bai Tu Long Bay: May to September/October (rainy season in July and August, the odd typhoon between August and October). Winter (December/January to March/April) is too cold and rainy for bathing.

The best view of the small peninsula (50km/31mi south of Hue, ▶Sights, p.208) with its long sandy beach, can be enjoyed when crossing the Hai Van Pass (Cloud Pass) – provided the cloud cover allows a look down on this phenomenal coastal stretch, where the blue ocean rolls into the golden shore, fishing boats rest under palm trees and a deep-blue lagoon extends into the hinterland. The small fishing town lies next to an upper mid-range beach resort. Take care when swimming: there are sometimes **dangerous currents** here.

Lang Co

A magnificent crescent-shaped beach stretches along the coast near the famous Cham ruins at Phan Rang (approx. 100km/60mi south of the beach town of Nha Trang): Ninh Chu. A few comfortable hotel with bungalows and a food stand are located on the mostly empty beach. Ca Na, a little further south (approx. 25km/16mi.), is equally attractive with its beautiful and deserted beach – though it is directly behind the highly frequented N 1 motorway. There are some simple small houses and a diving resort at Ca Na. The shiny new 702 coastal road runs from Ca Na past Mui Dinh Beach, the lengthy Ninh Chu Beach and the idyllic Vinh By Bay to Bing Tien at Cam Ranh, where there is now an international airport (so far the only direct flights are from Moscow). So it comes as no surprise that the empty, yet wonderful stretch of coastline in Ninh Thuan province is currently being developed as leading luxury brands such as Aman Resorts and Inter-Continental set up shop here: fishing bays between striking rock formations, sand dunes and sparkling white beaches.

Phan Rang, Ninh Chu and Ca Na

Vietnam's most famous beach resort was developed in the harbour town of Nha Trang (▶Sights, p.336) during the French colonial occupation. A 5km/3mi-long sandy beach stretches along the quayside, dotted with shady palm and flamboyant trees. At night it gets very busy in the many beach restaurants, cafés, food stands and bars. Water skiing, windsurfing, scooting, diving, snorkelling, sailing and parasailing are just some of the aquatic sports on offer. There are one-day boat trips to the off-shore islands and their beautiful beaches, e.g. the universally popular **Bamboo Island** (Hon Tre) and the **coral reefs** of Hon Mun.
Beyond Nha Trang there are a few more isolated sandy beaches, e.g. **Doc Let** on the Hon Khoi peninsula some 50km/31mi north, which has two fairly simple beach resorts. The Hon Gom peninsula (approx. 60km/37mi north of Nha Trang) has recently been made accessible by the opening of a new road. On its eastern side are sandy beaches with dunes and casuarinas. Only a five-minute speedboat ride away from the island village of Dam Mon is Whale Island (**Hon Ong**), with small, wonderful coves set amidst striking rocks (like those in the Seychelles) and hidden bays with crystal-clear water. So far, there is only one lovely bungalow resort here (with electricity). The resort is

Nha Trang

A dream: the beach at Nha Trang

under French-Vietnamese management, and meals at the (seafood) restaurant are included. Visitors can follow in the flippered footsteps of Jacques-Yves Cousteau, who used to dive here back in the 1930s. With luck, **whales or whale sharks** can be spotted between April and July. Guests can also go snorkelling, windsurfing, sailing, or simply relax (best time to swim: June to October, diving from February to mid-October).

The vast **Hon Heo** peninsula (marked on some maps as Hon Khoi, approx. 50km/31mi north of Nha Trang) now boasts an exceptionally beautiful luxury hideaway, the Six Senses Ninh Van Bay in the bay of the same name. By contrast, many backpackers and old hippies congregate across the jungle-like peninsula on the open sea to the other side. On the mainland a little further north is another broad, deserted beach with casuarina trees, situated within a cove near the fishing village of **Dai Lanh** (approx. 70km/43mi north of Nha Trang). Behind the dunes stand a few hotels and camp sites, so far mainly frequented by Vietnamese tourists.

Phan Thiet/ Mui Ne   The beach with the most hotels and bungalow resorts in all price ranges is located some 10km/6mi from Phan Thiet (▶Sights, p.352). People come here for aquatics and action on the miles of sandy beaches (especially windsurfing, given the right conditions). There is also a golf course and the famous Mui Ne sand dunes are worth investigating, as are the remains of a Cham sanctuary.

Phu Quoc   This remote island close to the Cambodian coast – at 625 sq km/241 sq mi, the biggest island in Vietnam – was long considered an insider's tip. With several building projects in the pipeline, however, this is no longer a secret destination. A new airport was opened in 2012, unleashing a new wave of tourism. Phu Quoc is situated in the Gulf of Thailand. During the holiday season, planes land several times a day from Saigon (flight time 1 hour) and flights from Can Tho andRach Gia (30 minutes). Also from Rach Gia (in approx. 2 hours) as well as Hat Tien, both coastal towns in the Mekong delta, (night) ferries and modern speedboats ply to the island on a daily basis. Phu Quoc itself is covered by dense **protected rainforest** on hilly or mountainous terrain, and features countless uninhabited beach coves primarily in the south and west – with 40km/24mi of sandy beaches fringed with shady palm trees. In recent years, several cosy resorts with pools have opened directly on the beach, as well as simpler bungalow accommodation. Day-trip destinations include waterfalls,caves, pepper plantations and more than 100 off-shore islands – fishing boats take tourists here to snorkel above coral reefs. The area is one of the best diving grounds in all of Vietnam, with visibility of up to 50m/164ft.

In the south of the harbour town of Quy Nhon there are numerous attractive sandy beaches and coves hidden between dunes and rocks, and a newly developed international beach resort with great potential for tourism. The presence of the former Quy Nhon US Army base, including an airport and a lengthy runway, raises hopes that international tourism will thrive. So far, there is one luxury hotel in a small beach cove, as well as hotels in town and smaller places offering accommodation for backpackers.

Quy Nhon

The beach town of Vung Tau is still mainly frequented by Saigon locals, as it only takes two hours by car or one hour by speedboat to get there. At weekends and on holidays the many hotels and beaches are crowded with Vietnamese families, couples and people on company outings. The four beaches, however, do not quite meet Western requirements concerning swimming, hygiene or beauty. Only surfers find the beaches, such as Bai Sau, ideal. Attractions include numerous souvenir stands, a few temples and a large statue of Christ rising into the sky from the hill above the sea. Somewhat less touristy and more peaceful is the small town of Long Hai in the north, which offers equally long, but fairly quiet beaches.

Vung Tau

TOURS

Vietnam can look back on 4000 years of history, offering a wealth of historical and cultural sites as well as unspoilt nature in the highlands and nearly 2000 miles of coastline. The tours suggested here lead to the most appealing destinations.

Tours Through Vietnam

Fancy a drive to explore the whole country? Or perhaps a hike in the mountains? Visit the Mekong Delta, Ha Long Bay, or both? The following four suggested tours should make it easier to decide.

Tour 1   **Through the Whole Country from South to North**
Start off in Saigon in the south and, heading northwards, visit famous colonial and imperial cities, historic ruins, palm-fringed beaches and the most beautiful landscapes in the far north of the country.
▶page 150

Tour 2   **From Saigon into the Highlands**
This short but varied tour leads into the mountains with a stop at one of Vietnam's most fauna-rich national parks (Cat Tien). The trip ends at Nha Trang, or with a relaxing visit to the beach at Phan Thiet.
▶page 153

Tour 3   **In the Mekong Delta**
Water as far as the eye can see: the Mekong Delta boasts floating markets and fruit orchards, fish farmers and rice-paper producers, temples and pagodas.
▶page 155

Tour 4   **Mountains and Sea**
From the capital of Hanoi, tour 4 heads first for the mountains, either for some hiking or just to buy souvenirs from the hill tribes, who still today dress in traditional costume. From there, the UNESCO-listed Ha Long Bay beckons. One of the most magnificent settings in the country, it boasts dripstone caves and craggy limestone mountains in the middle of the sea – a place that could almost be home to mystical dragons.
▶page 157

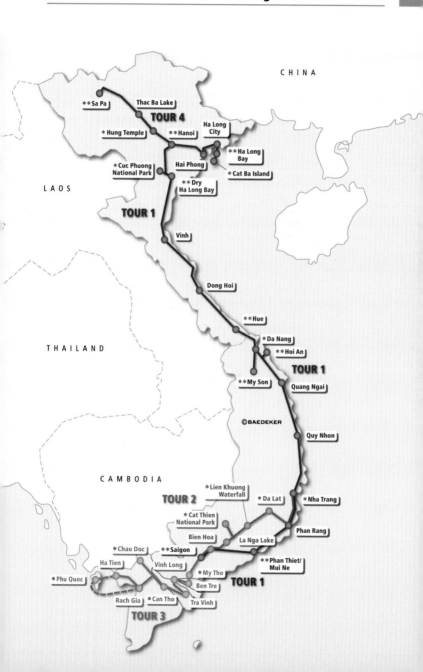

Travelling in Vietnam

Variety | With its incomparable array of experiences and attractions, Vietnam presents four fascinating »faces« as a travel destination. From the port city of Da Nang in central Vietnam, for example, it is possible to visit three different **UNESCO World Cultural Heritage Sites**: the temple city of My Son, the imperial city of Hue and the ancient city of Hoi An. Hot on the trail of the colonial rulers, fans of famous authors such as Graham Greene or Marguerite Duras make pilgrimages through colonial buildings and weather beaten villas, where the floorboards creak and the bathtubs are perched upon lions' feet.At the same time, **signs of the war**, which obviously did not spare the historical sites, are ever present. During the 1990s, Vietnam turned many remnants of the war into lucrative tourist attractions: US dollars are required to gain admission and crawl through the Vietcong tunnels in Cu Chi, veterans' reunions at the former line of demarcation, motor rallies along the Ho Chi Minh Trail, and boat tours through the mangroves of the Mekong Delta, once completely torched by napalm. Today, much of the havoc wreaked by the war is no longer visible. Yet, as harmless as the rice-paddy scenery appears, a third of all the bombs dropped during the war remain unexploded. The »third face« of Vietnam is made up of the many **beaches and coastal areas**. The more than 3000km/1860mi-long coast holds unbelievable potential. The beaches of Vietnam have only been a destination for foreign tourists for the last couple of decades – the rapid increase in the number of luxurious and inventive beach resorts in recent years is quite amazing. A fourth kind of vacation can be enjoyed in Vietnam, too: **a hiking holiday in the mountains**. »Ecotourism«, however, can sometimes come in strange forms. Don't be surprised if, during a several-day backpacking trek through the mountain villages around Sa Pa, neon lights compete with the starry night sky and your Homestay hosts serve Nescafé instead of Vietnamese coffee. The mountainous region around Sa Pa with Vietnam's highest peak (Fan Si Pan, 3143m/10,312ft), the high plateau of Tam Dao as well as the area around Mai Chau and Cao Bang in the north are the most popular hiking areas in Vietnam. Others include the highlands near Da Lat and Dak Lak, and the national parks of Yok Don, Cuc Phuong, Cat Ba Island and Bach Ma.

By car or by bus | A hired car with a chauffeur is the best way to get to know the country on your own, and of course also the most expensive option. However, almost the entire country can be travelled relatively comfortably on **organized minibus tours**, departing from tourist hubs: all the bathing areas, cultural highlights, cities and national parks can be reached in this way (the special, very inexpensive Open Tour Tickets allow passengers to break the journey at various points). Contact with the local residents is more likely when using public bus services (or when travelling with private minibus firms not aimed at tourists); this requires rather more time, however.

Travelling through a country by bike can often be a rewarding and **By bike** intensive way of experiencing the land and its people. However, Vietnam does not offer any designated cycle paths like those in Europe, which means cyclists are always on the same roads as cars, herds of oxen and so on. This can sometimes be a rather hair-raising experience, bearing in mind the often adventurous **Asian driving style**. On quieter side roads, in the Mekong Delta for instance, cycling in Vietnam can be recommended. Those who dare to brave the big cities like Hanoi and Saigon on a bike should have especially strong nerves, be experienced and fit. A good alternative to cycling alone is to join the guided tour groups. Cyclists ride without a pack, supported by a bus. Numerous UK and American firms offer such tours, which run mostly through the Mekong Delta or the Dry Ha Long Bay.

The N1 winds its way around serpentine bends across the Hai Van Pass – an alternative route uses the Hai Van Tunnel

Tour 1 Through the Whole Country from South to North

Distance: approx. 1750km/1090mi
Duration: approx. 14–21 days

No other tour promises so many highlights: from the lively metropolis of Saigon in the humid south to Hanoi, the capital and administrative centre in the cooler north, natural attractions and historically significant sites lie along this route. Stops are possible at a number of bathing areas, as is a trip into the mountains.

The first part of the tour leads from ❶**Saigon** on a four or five-hour drive past rice paddies, sugarcane fields, fruit stands and herds of cattle to Vietnam's expansive coast – an opportunity to go for a swim. About 20km/12mi away from the fishing harbour town of ❷**Phan Thiet** are a number of very good hotel and bungalow complexes built along the beaches of the Mui Ne peninsula, where the sand dunes are famously photogenic.

The Cham Temple complex at Nha Trang is dedicated to Po Nagar, the Mother Goddess

On the way north, it is worth stopping near **❸ Phan Rang** to visit the remarkable Cham towers (Po Ro Me, Po Klong Garai). Further along, the route runs past the harbour of Cam Ranh, which was used as a base by the US Marines during the Vietnam War. Close to the resort of **❹ **Nha Trang** there are more Cham buildings (Po Nagar) to visit. For those staying for a number of days, the Oceanic Institute, which has an aquarium, a fish farming facility and offers diving expeditions to the outlying islands, should be an obligatory part of the itinerary. Along the coast runs the spectacular beach and pass route: around 80km/50mi north of Nha Trang the bumpy surface of the Dai Lanh Pass runs above the coast, offering a marvellous view of the mountainous peninsula of Hon Gom. For the next 100km/60mi the mountains run closer to the coastline – a beautiful section of the route. The journey continues to **❺ Quy Nhon**, a coastal town with a number of the Cham towers influenced by the Khmer building style(Thap Doi; around 3km/2mi from the town centre) and one of the best spa resorts in the country. Fishing harbours and palm-fringed beaches border National Highway 1 for 170km/106mi until **❻ Quang Ngai** is reached. From here, after taking the bridge across the river, turn into a country road leading toward the sea and travel the 14km/9mi to Son My in order to see the memorial to the victims of the massacre at **My Lai**. On National Highway 1 near Thanh Phuoc An a road branches to the right towards **❼ **Hoi An**. The small town on the Thu Bon River

? Don't miss!

- Mui Ne: stop for a swim at the golden beach
- Nha Trang: boat tours, diving and snorkeling are on offer at this bustling resort.
- Da Nang: climb the Marble Mountains and visit the Cham Museum
- Hoi An: the little city impresses with Chinese temples and trading houses.
- Hue: soak up the imperial atmosphere in palaces and tombs
- Ninh Binh: jagged limestone mountains rise up from the paddy fields in Dry Ha Long Bay.

has played an important role as an Asian trading port for around 1000 years. It is worth a visit to see the pretty trading houses, the Chinese temples and the Japanese Covered Bridge. 30km/19mi further on is ❽*Da Nang, today Vietnam's fourth largest city, which looks back upon a millennium of history. China Beach, several miles in length, and the Marble Mountains are worth a visit. Rough roads lead from Da Nang to the ruined temple city of the Cham, ❾**My Son. Do not under any circumstances leave the marked paths – My Son was heavily bombed during the Vietnam War. A section full of magnificent panoramic views comes next: the coastal road runs between Da Nang and the old imperial city of ❿**Hue over the Hai Van Pass at an altitude of 496m/1627ft – in good weather, the Cloud Pass offers a breathtaking view of the peninsula and Lang Co lagoon. Since 2005 roughly one hour has been cut from the journey between Da Nang and Hue thanks to the 6.3km/3.0mi Hai Van Tunnel

The former Demilitarized Zone (DMZ) lies further north, at the 17th parallel in the area of the Ben Hai River. At Ho Xa the road branches off to Vinh Moc and the authentically preserved Vietcong tunnels there. Further along the N 1 is a chance to stop at ⓫Dong Hoi and visit the famous Phong Nha Caves. From there it is another 197km/122mi to ⓬Vinh. 15km/9mi west in Kim Lien stands the restored house in which Ho Chi Minh grew up. Continuing toward ⓯**Hanoi, the National Highway reaches the Red River delta, a fertile and densely populated plain that has been visited by floods for thousands of years. Before that however, the road crosses the ⓭**Dry Ha Long Bay, a fantastic landscape with steeply rising, wildly overgrown giant limestone formations lying between the rice fields in the area around the city of Ninh Binh (93km/58mi south of Hanoi). Nearby it is possible to take a rowing boat through the canals, e.g. to the caves of Tam Coc.

Around 50km/31mi past Ninh Binh, the bumpy country road 12 A leads to ⓮*Cuc Phuong National Park the oldest and most visited national park in Vietnam. It is also possible to spend the night in the nature reserve, which is primarily known for its giant trees and its caves.

From Saigon into the Highlands   Tour 2

Distance: approx. 600km/370mi
Duration: approx. 7 days

This route is among the most varied in Vietnam. It runs from the southern Vietnamese metropolis to one of the most diversely inhabited national parks in the Central Highlands at Da Lat, and continues over a breathtaking mountain pass back toward the coast to Nha Trang or Phan Thiet. This »green« route will delight anyone keen on nature, flora and fauna. But be prepared for damp weather.

Along National Highway 1, around 30km/19mi northeast of ❶**★★ Saigon**, a first stop can be made at ❷**Bien Hoa**, a centre for handicrafts. Some miles further on, take National Highway 20 into the mountains. It runs past caoutchouc plantations and expansive fields with fruit trees. ❸**La Nga Lake** (also the Tri An reservoir) is home to houseboats and floating villages, where fishermen live. Those wishing to visit ❹**★Cat Tien National Park** (approx. 150km/93mi north of Saigon) should take the dirt road leading off to the left in Ma Da Gui.

From the national park, the dirt road leads back toward National Highway 20. This winds slowly upward to an elevation of 1500m/5000ft in the province of Lam Dong, where the pass runs

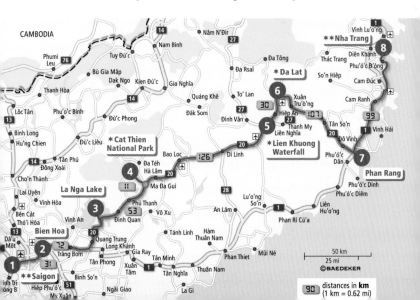

through thick jungle. Along the side of the road are a number of picturesque temple shrines and waterfalls. The high plateau is reached at the town of Bao Loc, where nearby tea factories and silk-worm farms can be visited. The ❺＊**Lien Khuong Waterfall** is a nice place to take a short break. Billboards as high as buildings eventually signify the beginning of the quiet mountain town of ❻＊**Da Lat** – its surroundings are ideal for hiking and very popular with Vietnamese honeymooners. A side trip lasting several days can be made from here, for example westward from Da Lat along the inconsistently surfaced N 27 to the provincial capital of Buon Ma Thuot. The best coffee in Vietnam is said to come from this region. Visitors can find simple accommodation here, or stay with the Stieng, Ede or Mnong hill tribes. It is also possible to visit the village of Ban Don (Buon Don, approx. 45km/28mi northwest), where elephants are bred. The same road leads back to Da Lat. Leave Da Lat initially heading southeast on the N 20 before joining the N 27 at the fork after approx. 25km/15mi towards the coast and ❼**Phan Rang**. The journey leads past the Don Duong reservoir (also Da Nhim) and the huge hydroelectric power station. The Ngoan Muc Pass offers fantastic scenery – in good weather the coast 60km/37mi away is even visible. The pass road gradually winds from an elevation of around 1000m/3300ft down to the coast, where palms and cacti once again define the landscape.

Looking towards the Lien Khuong Waterfall

About 6km/4mi outside the coastal town of Phan Rang are the Cham sanctuaries of Po Klong Garai and Po Ro Me from the 13th and 14th centuries. Now follow National Highway 1 north to the fishing and resort town of ❽＊＊**Nha Trang**. On the way are two more Cham towers (Hoa Lai) and, further north, the harbour Cam Ranh, which was used by the Americans as a Marine base between 1964 and 1973. Along this stretch, take a break at one of the restaurants built on stilts at the sea front. Alternatively, it is possible to head back from Phan Rang on the N 1 along the coast south toward Saigon, stopping off for a swim after 150km/95mi close to Phan Thiet. Dunes, salt mines and fishing villages define the coastal scenery here.

Market traders at the poultry market in Long An, Mekong Delta

In the Mekong Delta

Tour 3

Distance: approx. 200km/125mi
Duration: approx. 2 days

It is just a quick hop from the vibrant city of Saigon to the amphibian world of the Mekong Delta – the »rice bowl of the nation«. Pay a visit to the towns of Ben Tre and Can Tho – or take a couple of days to float along the nine arms and canals of the Mekong. The tour offers a vivid insight into how commerce and change are writ large in this emergent economic region.

National Highway 1 runs south to the Mekong Delta. The branching arms of the river and canals criss-cross the landscape, which is characterized by rice fields, bamboo thickets, fruit plantations, orchid gardens and farms for fish and shrimp. The first stop en route from Saigon is the provincial capital of ❷ *My Tho*, where it is possible to visit Vinh Trang Pagoda and a snake farm. Take the ferry further to

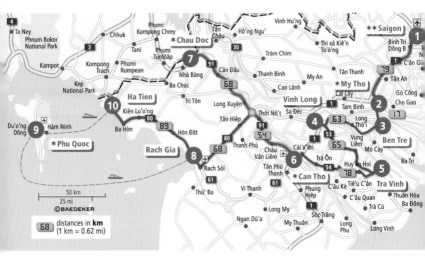

❸Ben Tre, where the famous fish sauce is produced and coconuts are processed. Day trippers can head back after a boat trip through the canals, which are lined with mangroves. If time allows, spend the night in **❹Vinh Long** in the heart of the Mekong Delta – the little town lies between the two arms of the Mekong, the Tien and Hau rivers. East of Vinh Long is **❺Tra Vinh**, where a number of Khmer pagodas can be marvelled at: Ba Om is said to be over 1000 years old. Cai Be is home to a floating market – a colourful attraction that can also be reached by boat. Hub of the Mekong Delta is the university city of **❻*Can Tho** with the famous, yet touristy, floating market of Can Rang. If it is too crowded, there is another floating market at Phung Hiep, which can be reached by boat or by bus, some 30km/18mi further on.

Another possibility is to travel further west (by boat or along Highway 91) to **❼*Chau Doc**, near the Cambodian border, where the Sam mountain, a popular destination for pilgrims, towers upward. The route back takes the same road to Long Xuyen. From **❽Rach Gia** a modern speedboat brings visitors to Vietnam's largest island, **❾*Phu Quoc**, in 2½ hours (aircraft faster still) – the island constitutes the westernmost region of southern Vietnam and lies in the Gulf of Thailand. Those who wish to can take the relatively bad N 80 road a further 90km/56mi to the far southwest and the harbour of **❿Ha Tien**. The area is known for its tortoise farms and the bizarre rock formations in the sea. Modern boats also leave from here to Phu Quoc (beware the budget ramshackle ferries, especially in the monsoon season!) – or one could continue towards Cambodia (border crossing Xa Xia/Prek Chak).

Mountains and Sea

Tour 4

Distance: approx. 1100km/680mi
Duration: 6–10 days

Mountains and sea – both can be combined on this magnificent tour. It starts by taking the train to the area around the picturesque little mountain town of Sa Pa, where it is possible to walk along the rice terraces and haggle over the price of souvenirs with the hill tribesmen. Over three or four days, the route then runs back along the coast via Hanoi – always in the direction of the sea – to Ha Long City, where the excursion boats and junks await to take visitors on a (sailing) voyage into the world of dragons.

Take the (night) train (7–10 hours) to reach a little mountain village, Lao Cai, near the Chinese border, and then board a bus or hire a taxi for the additional 38km/24mi to Sa Pa. Alternatively, make the somewhat tedious trip by bus from ❶**Hanoi** (a total of 380km/236mi, approx. 8–10 hours including breakdowns), which offers even more views of the marvellous landscape. It is possible to take a side

Hang Quat in the Old Town of Hanoi has everything imaginable for altars and shrines

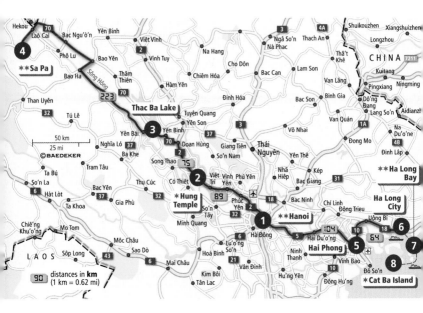

trip along the way to ❷*__Hung Temple__ northwest of Hanoi (along the N 2 towards the industrial city of Viet Tri, where after a further 12km/7mi a sign points to the sanctuary of the legendary kings). The journey continues back on the N 2 to Doan Hung, then turns left onto road no. 70 and passes ❸__Thac Ba Lake__. It slowly becomes apparent how the landscape is changing: suddenly there are terraced fields, palms with almost circular fronds and imposing houses on stilts. The last leg before Lao Cai (38km/24mi north of Sa Pa) runs along the Red River, with China lying on the opposite bank.

Heading southwest, the route leads to the highest mountain in Vietnam, Fan Si Pan (3143m/10,312ft), the immediate neighbour of ❹**__Sa Pa__. Here it is possible to take mountain hikes or walks, or simply to visit the market, where the Hmong and Red Dao offer their goods. Head back to Hanoi along the same route or by train, then take a car or a bus along the N 5 a further 100km/60mi east to ❺__Hai Phong__. From here it is another 60km/37mi on the new highway to ❻__Ha Long City__ (the double city of Bai Chay and Hong Gai); Hai Phong is potentially worth a stopover, or take the ferry from here to Ha Long City. Boats and junks set sail here and steer past the approximately 2000 bizarrely fissured rocky islands of ❼**__Ha Long Bay__ in the Gulf of Tonkin with their caves and floating villages. ❽*__Cat Ba Island__, the largest island in Ha Long Bay, and its national park are worth exploring. Those with more time who are interested in less

Colourful hill tribes market at Sa Pa

touristy places in the north of Vietnam can plan to make a trip by ferry to the island of Quan Lan and the Van Don peninsula in the neighbouring Bai Tu Long Bay.

SIGHTS FROM A TO Z

Many treasures await in Vietnam: patina-covered palaces, pagodas and temples, the primordial landscapes of Ha Long Bay and the Mekong Delta. And after the hustle and bustle of Hanoi or Saigon, visitors can unwind by enjoying water sports at fantastic beaches.

Buon Ma Thuot

E 6   E 6

Province: Dak Lak (capital)
Region: Central Highlands
Population: 200,000

Waterfalls, magnificent rolling hills and elephants – these are the main attractions of the remote Dak Lak highlands around the provincial capital of Buon Ma Thuot. The nearby Yok Don National Park also lures the adventurous with its wilderness and wildlife, hiking trails and elephant safaris.

Delightful highland region
Coffee, tea and rubber plantations characterize the largest province in the country, but there are also rice and maize fields as well as herds of cattle. Despite the migration of many Vietnamese to this region, the hill tribes still play an important role, especially the Ede and the Mnong. The area is also known for its elephants. As late as the 1930s, the area around Buon Ma Thuots was considered a **hunting paradise**; to this day there is still a large game population in the forests. The lakes, above all Dak Lak in the south, are known for their high fish count. However, in certain parts of the forest, the effects of the deployment of Agent Orange and deforestation can hardly be overlooked.

WHAT TO SEE IN BUON MA THUOT

Victory Monument
Buon Ma Thuot's central square is dominated by an enormous monument commemorating the events of 10 March 1975, when Vietcong and North Vietnamese troops »liberated« the city, leading inevitably to the defeat of South Vietnam.

Dak Lak Museum

The Dak Lak Museum (folklore and ethnology, at 12 Le Duan Street), where much can be learned about the province, its flora, fauna and culture, is worth visiting. The exhibition about the region's ethnic minorities – there are said to be 31 groups – is outstanding. Primarily on display are items of clothing and musical instruments, but equipment used for taming elephants as well as a model of an Ede stilt house are also on show. The unique gong collection amongst the musical instruments is one of the main crowd-pullers. Gong music was granted (intangible) UNESCO World Heritage status in 2005. On the second floor, the museum of the revolution displays photographs, paintings, propaganda and weapons from both Vietnam Wars.

❶ 12, Le Duan, daily 7.30am-4pm, admission: approx. 20,000 VND

The Republic of Vietnam is one of the largest producers and second largest worldwide exporter of coffee, mostly arabica and robusta. Hence the Vietnamese coffee house chain Truong Nguyen Coffee, here in the Vietnamese highlands, has collated more than 10,000 exhibits from Germany with the aid of the Hamburg collector and traditional coffee roaster Jens Burg – a little highlight in global coffee history, wonderfully presented in a beautiful wooden pile dwelling in longhouse style. In 2010, the Hamburg coffee museum was relocated in its entirety, so to speak, to Vietnam in 40 shipping containers, now displaying the coffee cultures of Europe, Africa and South America. Amongst the exhibits brought in from Hamburg are magnificent, gleamingly polished coffee machines from the 19th century, antique coffee grinders, old cash registers, the unavoidable Sarotti Moor and old-fashioned coffee pots.

*Trung Nguyen Coffee Museum & Coffee Bar

❶ Le Thang Tong, daily 7am–5pm; admission 12,000 VND

AROUND BUON MA THUOT

Around 20km/12mi southwest of Buon Ma Thuot (N 14), on the Serepok River, lies the »virgin waterfall«. Here, the adventurous can practice rock climbing and abseiling (bookings at the tourist office), survey the idyllic scenery either on foot or on the back of a horse or an elephant, explore caves, take a boat trip, or go fishing. Simple **accommodation** is offered in bungalows or a traditional long house; a local bar provides sustenance and refreshment.

Trinh Nu Waterfall

The beautifully situated, mist-spraying Dray Sap Falls can be reached by travelling southwest from Buon Ma Thuot via Doc Lap. A worthwhile stop can be made after 14km/9mi, turning left to the village of Buon Tur, the inhabitants of which are from the Ede ethnic minority, and subsist from cattle breeding and growing vegetables. Although the village has been heavily influenced by Vietnamese culture, traces of the **Ede cultural identity** can still be found. The matriarchal system is still intact, and women occupy the prominent position as the head of the household and centre of family life. Living together with their extended families in 30m/98ft-long pile dwellings, each couple and their children have their own small living area. Cows, pigs and fowl scurry about below.

Buon Tur

A few miles away , in the midst of the rain forest, lie the arch-shaped Dray Sap Falls. With a height of almost 15m/49ft and a width of over 100m/328ft, the view of the falls is somewhat obstructed by the clouds of spray, which explains the name – Dray Sap means **»waterfall of mist«**. The spray is especially refreshing at the left side of the pool, which can be reached by walking through bamboo thickets and

Dray Sap Falls

Buon Ma Thuot

INFORMATION
Dak Lak Tourist
53 Ly Thuong Kiet
tel. 0500/385 22 46
www.daklaktourist.com.vn
Also at Hotel Dam San
(see below, daily 7am–5pm)

TRANSPORT
Buon Ma Thuot Airport
(10km/6mi outside the city)
tel. 0500/395 50 55
(Flights from Saigon and Hanoi)

EVENTS
Elephant Festival

Every year in March, these heavy crea-tures compete in a race along the Sere-pok River. There is also a canoe race and a wealth of folklore displays with music and culinary delights. Further elephant spectacles are held in Ban Don, where the thick-skinned giants even play foot-ball. Elephant rides: approx. 700,000 VND per hour

MARKET
Those who enjoy observing everyday market should not miss the vast daily food market on Quang Trung Street.

Those who prefer not to go without Eu-ropean products should visit the **Metro** (4-5km/2-3mi along Gia Phong Street) – the retail chain is now present in almost all major Vietnamese towns and even in the Vietnamese highlands.

WHERE TO EAT
Quan Ngon £–££
72-74 Ba Trieu
tel. 0500/85 19 09
Large restaurant serving Vietnamese food in a stilt house and garden. Along-side the usual dishes, regional speciali-ties such as smoked game and poultry are served.

Pho Nuong £
150 Hung Vuong, Tu An Ward
tel. 0500/396 99 99
Typical al fresco establishment close to the Dam San Hotel with a large (English language) menu, quick and friendly ser-vice.

Hanoi Bakery £
Two branches: 123-125 D Le Hong Phong and 24 Ha Huy Tap (on the corner of Le Thanh Tong)
tel. 0500/385 36 09
Two branches of the renowned bakery: ice cream, colourful tarts and cakes, croissants, chocolate, yoghurt and sweets, as well as hearty sandwiches and snacks.

WHERE TO STAY
Dakruco Hotel £—££££
30 Ngyuen Chi Thanh
tel. 0500/397 08 88
www.dakrucohotels.com

Tall tower block visible from afar, northeast of the centre, with 114 spacious, well-equipped rooms in all categories (Wi-Fi), some with balcony, rooms facing the road are louder, often booked by wedding parties. Small pool, spa and tennis court.

Dam San Hotel £—££
212-214 Nguyen Cong Tru
tel. 0500/385 12 34
https://www.damsanhotel.com
Best hotel in town, slightly east of the centre: attractive rooms with parquet floors, satellite TV and bathtub; pool, tennis courts, good restaurant.

climbing over rocks. A dam has reduced the volume of water flowing through the river, so the best time to visit the falls is at the end of, or after, the rainy season.

● Daily 7am-5pm, admission approx. 20,000 VND

With a total area of 115,000ha/444 sq mi, Yok Don National Park is the largest in Vietnam. It lies near the border with Cambodia, just 37km/23mi west of Buon Ma Thuot. Many types of pharmaceutically useable plants grow in the mixed forests, as do orchids and a number of varieties of bamboo. Elephants particularly enjoy the leaves of the bamboo trees – 80 to 100 of the thick-skinned creatures are said to live in the grassy forests of the national park . Game wardens claim to have counted a number of tigers and even **leopards** in an area which is closed to visitors. More commonly found are gibbons, Sambar deer, wolves, wild buffalo and crocodiles, as well as hornbills, peafowl and pheasants. Nearly 500 plant species, around 50 mammal species – about half of which are endangered – and 245 registered bird species can be encountered in the area. It is especially popular to undertake an expedition on an elephant, which

*Yok Don National Park

MARCO POLO TIP

Insider Tip
Sample rice wine

A speciality of the highlands is the honey yellow ruou can, a mild (20% proof) wine made from rice, glutinous rice or grain, traditionally drunk communally through long, pliable »straws« (can) from an earthenware jug (che). Smoked venison, roast veal, roast chicken or tasty com lam (glutinous rice cooked in bamboo) are perfect complementary dishes.

can be booked for a few hours or even for an entire day. Alongside the pretty landscape and the particularly diverse wildlife of the area, remnants of the Ho Chi Minh Trail and a number of battlefields can be seen. It is best to plan a trip to Yok Don National Park as far as possible from the rainy season (April to October). Overnight accommodation can be found in the nearby villages and in a camp with huts.

❶ Admission: approx. US$2.00, guide US$20–30. A number of simple rooms and tents may be found at the headquarters (tel. 0500/378 30 49, www.yokdonnationalpark.vn) with English language guides, canteen, two restaurants and a basic guest house in the village of Ban Don.

*Elephant Village Ban Don

The elephant village of Ban Don, just 2km/1.2mi from Yok Don National Park and approximately 45km/28mi northwest of Buon Ma Thuot, is known throughout the land. Settled in the vicinity are Khmer, Thai, Lao and Jarai. Ban Don itself is primarily inhabited by the Mnong and Ede minority groups, both of which are organized according to a matriarchal system. Wild elephants are hunted by the Mnong and domesticated with the help of tamed animals. Later they are mostly used for the **transportation of precious woods**. Around 50 of the animals live permanently in Ban Don.

On the edge of the village, which is often overrun with tourists, lies the grave of the legendary Khonsonuk (1850–1924), who in his day was the most famous elephant hunter far and wide. Among the 244 elephants he tamed, there was said to be a white one which was a present to the King of Siam. Elephant tamers (Mahouts) still come here, bringing offerings and asking for success in taming their animals. A number of graves display peacocks upon tusks, which are seen as distinguished offerings for the next life.

Lak Lake

Also worth a trip is the 500ha/1.9 sq mi Lak Lake (Ho Dak Lak), which lies 50km/31mi south of Buon Ma Thuot. Its location at the foot of the Annamite range is very pretty, and it is worth a short climb to enjoy the view of the lake and its surroundings.

The lake is well known for its high fish count and wide variety of bird life (including cranes and storks). On the banks of the lake are the remains of the small palace of the former emperor Bao Dai (▶Famous People). Many Vietnamese come here, particularly in spring, to watch **boat and elephant races**. Also of interest is a visit to the neighbouring village of the Mnong. Visitors can make trips onto the shallow lake in rowing boats or even on the back of an elephant.

❶ Homestays with minority families and elephant rides are possible here (a tour costs roughly 700,000 VND per hour, or depending on the season and negotiation skills, prices may start at 300,000 VND without transportation to the starting point.

✳ Can Tho

✦ C 7

Province: Can Tho (capital)
Region: Mekong Delta
Population: 500,000

Can Tho, the largest city in the Mekong Delta, is a good base for excursions into the amphibious everyday life of the region. From here it is possible – early in the morning is best – to visit the delta's floating markets, take a trip into the mangrove swamps in the far south of the country, and in the evening go for a stroll down the promenade of the Can Tho River.

WHAT TO SEE IN CAN THO

Munirangsyaram Pagoda (36 Hoa Binh Street) was built in 1946. It serves as a temple for the Khmer community of Can Tho (approximately 2000 members). Because the Khmer practice Theravada Buddhism, there are no depictions of Bodhisattvas, gods or patron saints,

*Munirang-
syaram
Pagoda

It is worth making an early start to the floating markets, they are at their busiest in the morning

Can Tho and the surrounding area

INFORMATION
Can Tho Tourist
20 Hai Ba Trung, Ninh Kieu, Ca Tho
tel. 0710/382 18 52 and 382 2719
Mon-Sat 7am-11am
www.canthotourist.info

TRANSPORT
Can Tho International Airport
To the northwest of the city, opened in
2011. Flights thus far to Saigon, Hanoi,
Phu Quoc and Con Dao.

EXCURSIONS
Cai Be Princess
The elegant, traditional wooden ship departs from Cai Be Floating Market (maximum of 35 passengers) chugs along to
Vinh Long to visit the fruit orchard and
stops for lunch in Sa Dec before passengers return to Saigon by road.
www.caibeprincessmekong.com

Mekong Eyes Cruise
9/150 KDC no.9, Road 30/4 (i.e. in
»30 Thang 4« street, Ninh Kieu,
Can Tho
tel. 0710/378 35 86
Hotline: 093/336 07 86
www.mekongeyes.com
This tour operator offers tours on a converted rice barge with 30 attractive double rooms.

Sinhbalo Adventure Travel
283/20 Pham Ngu Lao, 1st district,
Saigon
tel. 08/38 37 67 66
http://sinhbalo.com
www.cyclinvietnam.net
Bike tours under coconut palms, for example fro Ben Tre via Mo Cay and the

picturesque town of Tra Vinh to Can
Tho.

EVENTS
Each year from the 13th to 15th day of
the fourth lunar month (April/May) the
Khmer new year's celebration is held in
the Mekong Delta. Also in the middle of
the tenth lunar month (October/Novem-
ber) in Soc Trang, the Khmer stages the
Ghe Ngo Festival featuring famous races
with traditional boats.

GOING OUT
Party boats
Sadly, the Ninh Kieu folkore boats are
dying out, replaced by loud and garish
restaurant and disco boats, three or four
decks high, draped in blinking fairy
lights. The nightlife in the Mekong Delta
has become bright and gaudy, Las Vegas
style as the Vietnamese like it (boats between 6pm-8pm).

❶ *Xe Loi Club*
(Cyclo Club) ££
Hau Giang Promenade (Hau Riverside
Park) approx. 2km/1mi north of the
centre), Can Tho
tel. 0710/346 03 62
Popular with young Vietnamese, this
sprawling al fresco bar even has a
»beach« on the riverbank: either a DJ or
live bands often play in the rustic western style bar, or guests try their luck at
karaoke (daily from 5pm).

❷ *Roof Top Bar* £
(roof terrace at the Xoai budget hotel)
3 Mau Than, Ninh Kieu district, Can Tho
Mobile tel. 090/765 29 27
http://hotelxoai.com

Travellers' meeting point with panoramic open air views: when almost everything else has closed, the dance goes on over the rooftops of Can Tho. A German-Vietnamese couple preside over occasional parties, or guests can check their mails (Wi-Fi) and chill out to cool music in hammocks. Drinks are served down below in the lobby. The location is, however, 20 minutes walk from the river.

SHOPPING

The lively, colourful and loud Can Tho market takes up the middle section of Hai Ba Trung Street, which is completely closed to traffic. Every kind of food that the heart desires is available here from fish and seafood, vegetables, fruit to rice and bakery goods.

WHERE TO EAT
❶ *Sao Hom* ££

50 Hai Ba Trung (Ninh Khieu Pier on the promenade, close to the night market). Can Tho
tel. 0710/381 56 16
This establishment, housed in the old market hall on the riverbank, is always full: vast selection of seafood and Vietnamese classics such as spring rolls and hot pots, extensive range of ice creams.

❷ *Nam Bo* ££

50 Hai Ba Trung, Can Tho
tel. 0710/382 39 08
http://nambocantho.com
Panorama bar: enjoy Can Tho's evening activity along the riverside promenade from the balcony, where western and Vietnamese dishes are served. A number of attractive rooms and suites are also available (**£££**).

Phuong Thuy Restaurant £

Vinh Long, Vinh Long province (approx. 35km/22mi northwest of Can Tho)
1/5 Street (i.e. in »1 Thang 5« street)
tel. 070/382 47 86
Located directly on the riverbank, this destination boasts lovely views across the Mekong Delta, Vietnamese and international cuisine (daily 8am-11pm).

WHERE TO STAY
❶ *Victoria Can Tho* £££–££££

283 Tran Van Khoe Cai Khe Ward Can Tho
tel. 0710/381 01 11
www.victoriahotels.asia
Accommodation on the riverbank with colonial flair: splendid rooms with parquet floors and every luxury. Two pools, good patio bar.

❷ *Kim Tho Hotel* ££

1A Ngo Gia Tu
tel. 0710/381 75 17
www.kimtho.com
Views of the Mekong come as standard from the 8th floor upwards: this three star, twelve-storey hotel close to the river boasts 51 chic parquet rooms, large and spacious bathrooms, Wi-Fi and rooftop bar. Fruit in the rooms is part of the service.

Mekong Lodge ££   Insider Tip

An Hoa, Dong Hoa Hiep, Cai Be (approx. 80km/50mi outside Can Tho, halfway to My Tho)
Mobile tel. 093/344 93 91 (Mr. Quang), tel. in Saigon: 08/39 48 21 75
(ext. 115, 107)
www.mekonglodge.com

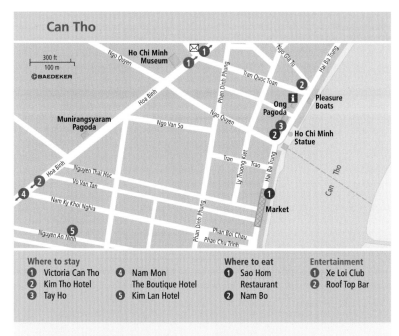

Can Tho

300 ft
100 m
©BAEDEKER

Ngo Quyen

Ho Chi Minh Museum

Ngo Gia Tu

Hai Ba Trung

Phan Dinh Phung

Tran Quoc Toan

Hoa Binh

Ong Pagoda

Pleasure Boats

Munirangsyaram Pagoda

Ngo Van So

Ngo Quyen

Ho Chi Minh Statue

Hoa Binh

Nguyen Thai Hoc

Vo Van Tan

Tran Trao

Ly Thuong Kiet

Hai Ba Trung

Can Tho

Nam Ky Khoi Nghia

Market

Nguyen An Ninh

Phan Dinh Phung

Phan Boi Chau

Phan Chu Trinh

Where to stay
1 Victoria Can Tho
2 Kim Tho Hotel
3 Tay Ho
4 Nam Mon The Boutique Hotel
5 Kim Lan Hotel

Where to eat
1 Sao Hom Restaurant
2 Nam Bo

Entertainment
1 Xe Loi Club
2 Roof Top Bar

A jaunt into the countryside: reside in one of 30 rustic but clean little houses with palm roof, terracotta tiles, bamboo beds, mosquito nets and open air bath, some with small, private pools for a quick dip – a small oasis on a river island where evenings can be savoured on the terrace, listening to the chirping crickets. Bar, cycle tours, cookery classes.

3 *Tay Ho* £
36 Hai Ba Trung, Can Tho
tel. 0710/82 33 92
This mini hotel for families offers some fine river views. An inexpensive alternative to the top of the range hotels in Can Tho.

4 *Nam Mon The Boutique Hotel* £
C 233/4 Nguyen Van Linh, Hung Loi ward, Can Tho
tel. 0710/625 08 66
www.nammonhotel.com
Colourful, yet simple rooms with air conditioning and Wi-Fi, TV, free bicycles and moped tours – Bryan and his wife Truc's hostel is a hit with young and thrifty guests. Attractive roof terrace, albeit some distance from the tourist track, some 3km/2mi further along the river promenade.

5 *Kim Lan Hotel* £
138A Nguyen An Ninh, Tan An ward, Can Tho
tel. 0710/381 70 49
http://kimlanhotelcantho.com

Small guest house with 30 rooms (plus balcony), modern furnishings and friendly staff. VIP accommodation in the penthouse. Breakfast on the roof terrace.

Best CM Hotel £
463 Nguyen Trai, ward 9
Ca Mau (170km/106mi southwest of Can Tho)
tel. 0780/382 98 28
The name says it all –
with good reason: the three star highrise hotel on the edge of town is the best in Ca Mau, offering 69 rooms at unbeatable prices, a fine breakfast buffet and free Wi-Fi. The American/Viet-

namese owners have even built a pool on the roof.

Cuu Long Tourist
01 Road 1/5 in Vinh Long (approx. 35km/22mi northeast of Can Tho)
tel. 070/382 36 16
http://cuulongtourist.com/en/homepage
Homestays on the island of An Binh, for example. Sleep in stilt houses beneath mosquito nets, bathe in the Mekong and explore the region by bike (all included for approx. £30 per day). Advance booking is recommended as Homestays cannot necessarily accommodate an additional driver or travel guide.

only likenesses of the historical Buddha Sakyamuni. The main court of the pagoda is reached through a mighty, richly decorated portal. On the upper floor is a 1.5m/5ft-high Buddha statue beneath a holy Bodhi tree. The resident monks are usually happy to welcome visitors, but the doors tend to be closed during lunchtime.

An impressive silver statue of Ho Chi Minh (▶MARCO POLO Insight p.265) marks the beginning of the pretty esplanade, which is decorated with flowers and trees and offers a number of nice cafés.

Esplanade

Nearby is Quang Thanh De Pagoda, which was built by the city's once-populous Chinese community. On the main alter is Quan Cong with his sentinels, to the left is Thien Hau (the sea goddess) and on the right is the god of luck, Ong Bon. At the table where incense sticks are sold there is usually a **calligrapher** writing Chinese characters into red prayer scrolls.

Quang Thanh De pagoda

❶ daily 5am–8pm

AROUND CAN THO

Many travellers visit Can Tho for the various boat tours that are offered from here. It is possible to rent a small rowing boat, take trips through orange and mango plantations, or navigate the Mekong in large motorboats. A visit to one of the so-called **floating markets** is definitely worthwhile; all kinds of fruit and vegetables as well as drinks and kitchen appliances are sold here, and it is even possible to

*Boat tours on the Mekong

get a haircut. The little barges are often so heavily loaded that it seems they are just about to sink; many houseboats have crooked frames, scantly covered in an attempt to conceal the family's »living quarters«. More often than not, women strain at the overlapping oars of some of the sampans.

*Floating markets

Two of the three larger floating markets in the area lie to the west of Can Tho, the larger, busier market at Cai Rang (7km/4mi from Can Tho) and the smaller, quieter one in Phong Dien(a further 10km/6mi away). The locality of **Phung Hiep**, 25km/15mi southeast of Can Tho, is a transport hub where several canals meet, the longest of which leads to the remote province of Minh Hai. Upon one of these waterways, the Yang Canal, a large floating market is also held early each morning. It is very popular with tourists due to the fact that, from a bridge, the activity of the market can be well observed – and photographed of course. Because Phung Hiep lies directly on the N 1, it is easily reached using public transport.

Insider Tip

My Phuoc

By boat, it is also possible to reach the island of My Phuoc in the Hau River, a branch of the Mekong. When travelling through the narrow canals, it is sometimes necessary to duck to avoid the mighty fronds of the coconut palms, which grow far beyond the banks. The route drifts past gardens and pretty houses. It is like a visit to the **Garden of Eden**, with stops at the many orchards where jackfruit, bananas, pineapples, mangos, papayas etc. can be sampled.

*Soc Trang

Soc Trang, the main locality in the province of the same name, is located 30km/19mi southeast of Phung Hiep. The main attraction is the nearby Khmer Matoc Pagoda (also: Chua Doi, »bat temple«), ornately decorated with depictions of dancers and animals. The large **bats**, which live in the trees around the sanctuary, are a peculiarity of the place. In the late afternoon they can be observed gradually awakening as the temperature drops, preparing themselves before flitting away on the evening's hunting trip. Some of them have a wingspan of 1.5m/5ft! The interior walls of the pagoda list the names of other Khmer congregations and depict scenes from the life of Buddha. The life-like portrayal of a monk, who even wears glasses, is quite astonishing.

?

Concerns over mangrove forests

MARCO POLO INSIGHT

Did you know that the mangrove forests of the Mekong Delta are the third largest in the world, according to the WWF? Only Cuba and Bangladesh can claim to have larger forests. In recent years a programme of reforestation has sought to counter the adverse development which is severely endangering reserves, as the trees play an important role in protecting the Vietnamese coastline.

Boat trips in the Mekong Delta. Negotiate a labyrinth of waterways, floating villages and mangrove forests

MINH HAI PROVINCE

As the economic centre of Minh Hai province, the most sparsely populated province of the Mekong Delta, the town of Ca Mau – like all the other Mekong towns – has experienced rapid development in recent years. Because Minh Hai is the only province in the Mekong Delta without any of the major estuary creeks flowing through it, it is the site of much standing water, with swamps and moors. The countryside is covered with dense **mangrove and bog forests**. There are hoards of mosquitoes buzzing about. The place itself doesn't offer much worth seeing, but botanists and ornithologists are sure to have a field day in the area's wetlands. Alongside a Catholic and a Protestant church, Ca Mau is also home to a large Cao Dai temple, which was built in the 1960s. At Ca Mau's market, fish, tortoises and snakes are sold. The latter are still alive – connoisseurs agree that snake meat is best enjoyed freshly slaughtered. A large portion of the reptiles from the market in Ca Mau are brought to Saigon to be prepared in the finest restaurants.

Ca Mau

They are called »monkey bridges« as they are traversed by swinging across

*U Minh Forest

U Minh Forest lies directly north of Ca Mau. This approximately 1000 sq km/386 sq mi primeval forest numbers among the largest self-contained mangrove forests on Earth. It is a habitat for birds and reptiles, which find ideal living conditions in this marshland. Because the area provided a very good hideout for the Vietcong, it long served as a retreating ground and field of operations against the Americans, who sprayed defoliants to deprive their invisible enemy of their natural cover. The trees are gradually recovering from this destruction, yet today the forest faces the new **danger of deforestation**, firstly to exploit the lumber, secondly to reclaim expanses of water for fish and shrimp harvesting. Measures taken by the government to limit deforestation have so far had little effect. The area can be reached by boat from Ca Mau.

Bird sanctuaries

Around 50km/31mi south of Ca Mau are two bird sanctuaries: Hiep Hung and Than Khanh. It is possible to take a boat tour there from Ca Mau, but the timid birds can only rarely be observed at close range.

VINH LONG PROVINCE

Vinh Long

Surrounded by water, encircled by boats and stilt houses, the island on which the centre of Vinh Long lies seems like a medieval fortress. The first impression is of rather hectic and loud streets, yet the esplanades, with their cafés and restaurants, provide a place to relax and take in life on the edge of the Tien Giang. Vinh Long is also known by the name Cuu Long (Nine Dragons), after which the entire ▶Mekong Delta is named. The My Thuan suspension bridge over the Cho Chien which resembles the Golden Gate Bridge in San Francisco, was built with Australian assistance in the year 2000. Vinh Long is a good base for excursions into the marvellous surrounding areas.

Thick, semicircular barques full of coconuts, rambutans and rice; delicate female ferryboat pilots, in cone hats, who row powerfully; fishing barges and sampans with watchful eyes painted onto the bows – everything flows, glides and chugs along with the Mekong River. Every ten minutes, the fishermen pull nets hanging with octopuses' spindly tentacles out of the canals. Peculiar bamboo frames (»monkey bridges«) protrude across a thousand waterways. A sleepy, dreamlike water-world exists beyond the markets and tourist spots. Do not miss the chance to visit the little islands of **Binh Hoa Phuoc** and **An Binh**, which can only be reached by boat. The tourist trail here includes a visit to experience the everyday world of Vietnam's industry, including for example a visit to a rice paper and puffed rice factory, an incense manufacturer or lychee farmers. Cai Be Market, with its »swimming« stands, is also worth a visit.

**Trips to the river islands

Insider Tip

The former capital of Dong Thap Province, Sa Dec (23km/14mi west of Vinh Long), has become known as the location for the film of **Marguerite Duras'** novel *The Lover*. But it is also the original site of the story, drawing readers of the author, many of them French, to this small town not otherwise known as a tourist destination. The French writer lived in Sa Dec as a young girl, a teacher's daughter, between 1928 and 1932, playing out a love story with a young man thirteen years her senior, the son of a rich Chinese merchant family. Built in 1895, the colonial house of her lover Huynh Thuy Le, who died in 1972, stands by the river where it was used as a government building for many years, housing the anti-drug authority.
Since 2007 the elegant villa with its sweeping tiled roof in North Vietnamese pagoda style, beautiful blue façade and balustrade, has been open as a **museum**. Eastern and western styles are unified in its architecture. Inside, Chinese décor dominates in red and gold with shrines and antiquities. The town's many nurseries are remarkable: throughout Vietnam, cut flowers are particularly sought after, and those from Sa Dec are transported daily to Saigon.

Sa Dec

Museum: 225A Nguyen Hue, admission approx. 12,000 VND; ideal for those who have always wanted to spend the night in a museum rich in history: there are two simple guest rooms. Tours and bookings through the Dong Thap Tourist Company in Cao Lanh, tel. 067/387 30 25, www.dongthaptourist.com (Vietnamese)

Most tourists come to Tra Vinh (67km/42mi southeast of Vinh Long) to admire the Khmer temple or to watch storks. The thousand-year-

Tra Vinh

old **Sam Rong Ek Temple** (4km/2.5mi south of the town centre) could have been brought here directly from Thailand or Cambodia, as it displays all the hallmarks of the temple architecture common there. These include the stacked roofs, the stylized Nagas on the roof ridges and the horns on the gables, which symbolize the fire bird Garuda. Inside, as is normal for Hinayana Buddhism, are depictions only of the historic Buddha. There are so many of them that no one can name the actual figure.

*An Vuong Pagoda — A couple of miles outside Tra Vinh, beyond a lotus pond and stupas and surrounded by frangipani trees, is An Vuong Pagoda (photo ►p.76). The site of the temple is said to be 1200 years old, though the existing building is considerably newer. Within the sanctuary are wall and ceiling paintings depicting scenes from the life of Buddha. The pictures that were added when the building was last renovated in 1939 can be recognized by the inclusion of uniforms worn by the French colonialists. After the harvest, rice from surrounding fields is piled up next to the altar, where it is guarded by an impressive golden Sakyamuni figure.

? MARCO POLO INSIGHT

Thanks for the monks' influence

The monks of the Sam Rong Ek temple beg for their food in a procession twice a day. Donors come to the temple to fill their begging bowls, hoping for a better reincarnation in their next life as a result of their actions.

Stork watching — Over 100 storks live on the grounds of Hang Pagoda (6km/3.5mi south of Tra Vinh). They are best seen early in the mornings, when they circle above the treetops, or before sunset. An even larger group of around 300 storks can be seen near Giong Lon Pagoda (43km/27mi southeast of Tra Vinh).

* Chau Doc

✦ C 7

Province: An Giang
Region: Mekong Delta
Population: 200,000

The Mekong town of Chau Doc is home to many fish farmers: down in the »cellar« beneath the floating buildings and the houseboats flap tons of thriving fish. Visitors can venture deep into life along the Mekong River on boat tours. The broad ethnic diversity of the region means there are many different temples, mosques and churches, and Cambodia is just a stone's throw away.

WHAT TO SEE IN CHAU DOC

Fish farmers

Chau Doc is home to the most fish farmers in Vietnam. Their houses float upon empty oil barrels on the Hau Giang River (aka: Bassac), one of the Mekong's eight arms. It is mainly **catfish** that throng in the nets beneath the houses. When the water becomes shallower during the dry season, the houses move to the middle of the river, where the piscine lodgers have enough air to breath.

Boat trips

North of Quan Cong Temple is a ferry which brings visitors to the island of Con Tien and its pile-dwelling settlements, but the river journey is more enjoyable in a small boat, from which it is also possible to view the fish farming houseboats.

Quan Cong Temple

Between the market stands of Gia Long Street towers the imposing portal of Quan Cong Temple. The courtyard is usually very lively, as many children come here to play. Two dragon-figures watch over the site, and inside two tortoises wander around, said to look after the temple's well-being (in Buddhism, the tortoise is a symbol of immortality). On the main altar stands a bust of the red-faced General Quan Cong, clothed in a green robe and wearing a richly decorated crown.

About 80% of Vietnam's Cham are Muslims today

Chau Doc

INFORMATION
An Giang Tourist
An Giang Tourist
563/29 Tran Hung Dao, in Long Yuyen
tel. 076/395 44 32
http:/angiangtourist.vn (Vietnamese)
Also in hotels

DAY TRIP
There are daily excurstions from Chau
Doc to Phnom Penh in Cambodia (public
services or a faster boat from the Victoria Hotel), approx. 4 hours.
A cheaper way to cross the border from
Chau Doc is to catch an early morning
Blue Cruiser express boat (www.blue-
cruiser.com), a Hang Chau express boat
or the Tu Trang speedboat which crosses
the Mekong several times a day (www.
tutrangtravel.com). Entry visas for Cambodia can be completed at the border:
US$25 (passport photograph required).
Many public service boats only go as far
as the border for around US$10, the
journey to Phnom Penh then continues
by bus – those who wish to make the
entire trip by boat should specifically ask
for such an itinerary, expecting to pay
more for the privilege.

EVENTS
Via Ba (Ba Chua Xu) Pilgrims festival at Nui Sam (Sam mountain)

Insider Tip

For Chinese New Year and the annual
Via Ba festival (April/May), thousands of
believers and tourists climb the
230m/750ft high mountain at midnight
– Taoists and Caodaists, Christians, Buddhists and Muslim Cham, many from
abroad, arriving from Hong Kong, Taiwan or the USA.

WHERE TO EAT
Bassac Restaurant £££–££££
1 Le Loi Street Chau Doc
tel. 076/386 50 10
www.victoriahotels.asia
daily 6am-11pm
The magnificent riverside terrace of the
colonially tinged Victoria Hotel (p.179) is
a great place to enjoy a meal. French
and Vietnamese dishes are accompanied
by wines and cocktails.

Lam Hung Ky £
71 Chi Lang Chau Doc
tel. 076/386 67 45
Restaurant near the market, serving the
best Chinese and Vietnamese cuisine in
town.

Mekong ££
41 D De Loi (opposite the Victoria Hotel),
Chau Doc
tel. 076/386 73 81
A family-run establishment serving good
food in pleasant surroundings, namely
the courtyard of a small colonial villa.
Classics such as noodle soup and spring
rolls or squid in garlic (penny pinchers
should note: peanuts and refreshing tis-
sues brought to the table will appear on
the bill, as in most place in Vietnam).
There is also a similarly named »Floating
Restaurant Mekong« (£).

Xuan Thanh Restaurant £
Corner of Ben Tran Hau/Tham Tuong
Sam
(at the market) Ha Tien
tel. 077/385 21 97
Best address in Ha Tien, be sure to
try one of the many local coconut
specialities!

WHERE TO STAY

Victoria Chau Doc £££–££££
1 Le Loi Street, Chau Doc
www.victoriahotels.asia
resa.chaudoc@victoriahotels.asia
Luxury in a colonial atmosphere: convincing replica of a colonial palace with Franco-Vietnamese flair. Located right on the bank of the Hau River.

Green Island Hotel ££
Tran Hau Business Center
in Ha Tien
Tel 077/395 58 88
www.greenislandhotel.com.vn
Modern, comfortable hotel resembling a spaceship. River views, tiny pool, good (and more reasonably priced restaurants) in the vicinity.

Sea Light Hotel £–££
A11 3/2 Street
(i.e. in »3 Thang 2« street)
Vinh Bao ward in Rach Gia
tel. 077/625 59 99
www.sealighthotel.vn
Now even the little fishing settlement has its own polished glass tower hotel. Superlative view from 19 floors of modern rooms and suites, bathed in light. Small pool, fitness area, cycles for hire. Breakfast could be better.

Thuan Loi £
18 Tran Hung Dao Street
Chau Doc
tel. 076/386 61 34
hotelhuanloi@hcm.vnn.vn
Hovering on stilts over the Mekong. Mini hotel with 26 air-conditioned rooms, small restaurant, free Wi-Fi.

Trung Nguyen £
86 Bach Dang, Chau Doc

Pilgrims' most important destination in South Vietnam: Sam mountain

tel. 076/356 15 61
www.trungnguyenhotel.com.vn
Popular mini hotel offers exceptionally fair deals on four floors (some rooms with balcony). Situated right next to the market so it can be noisy in the early morning (ear plugs recommended), but the 15 rooms represent the best value for money in the province. Flat-screen televisions, DW-TV, air-conditioning, Wi-Fi.

Mosques	Chau Doc also has several mosques for the Muslim Cham community, including Chau Giang Mosque on the other side of the river and Mubarak Mosque, which houses a Koran school for children and young people. Visitors should not enter during prayers, held five times per day.

✳ SAM MOUNTAIN (NUI SAM)

In the northwest of An Giang province rise a number of hilltops, the very last foothills of the Cambodian Phnom Damrei range. Among these, 5km/3mi south of Chau Doc, is Sam Mountain. In Vietnamese, »Sam« means something like **»prawn«** – which the hill does actually resemble from a distance. Only 230m/755ft in height, it is not particularly imposing, but the peak offers an extensive view over the Mekong Delta, which is flat and just barely above sea level, all the way to Cambodia in the distance. Over the course of the year, the area around the hill presents an **enchanting display of colours**: between August and December the land is covered with water as far as the horizon, with only the embankments, densely built over with wooden huts, rising up from this shimmering watery world, as if drawn with a ruler. From the beginning of the year until April the wet rice paddies finally glow a magnificent lime-green, and in May and June the ears are ripe for harvesting – an expansive, undulating sea of gold. In the evenings, the setting sun bathes everything in a fiery red light, until the sky itself appears to be in flames.

Ba Chua Xu Temple	Ba Chua Xu Temple was built in the first half of the 19th century and was continually altered until the 1970, to the point where not much of the original construction remains. The story of the person of Chua Xu and of the building of the temple is not quite clear. The most important **celebration** takes place from the 23rd to the 26th day of the fourth lunar month of each year (April/May), when pilgrims from across the land come and spend the night near the temple. On display in glass cases inside the building to the left are countless offerings in honour of Chua Xu: finely embroidered sequined clothes, head-high mother-of-pearl vases, strings of pearls, crowns and gold bars.
Chua Hang (cave pagoda)	Monks live in the lower part of the cave pagoda on the west side of Sam Mountain. The founder of the pagoda was the **seamstress Le Thi Tha**, who retreated here around 50 years ago to lead a cloistered life. The legend has it that upon her arrival, she came upon two snakes, which she tamed and then converted to a life of meditation. Upon her death, the two snakes disappeared. The grave of Le Thi Tha, as well as that of a high-ranking monk, can be found in the lower part of the pagoda. In the upper part are statues of A Di Da, the Buddha

of the Past, and of the historical Buddha Sakyamuni; behind them, in a grotto, is a shrine dedicated to the Goddess of Compassion.

Very near to the border with Cambodia, approximately 55km/34mi southwest of Chau Doc on the road to Ha Tien, a pagoda commemorates the raids on Vietnamese soil by the Khmer Rouge between 1975 and 1978. The official justification thereof was Cambodia's historic claim on the provinces of the Mekong Delta. Within just two weeks in April 1978, a total of 3157 civilians were routinely murdered. Today horrific photographs and a memorial recall the massacre. As at Choeung Ek Pagoda at the Killing Fields outside the gates of Phnom Penh, the bones of the murdered are laid out at Ba Chuc.   **Ba Chuc**

In the middle of an attractive landscape in the province of Kien Giang, Ha Tien (population 40,000) is located on the Gulf of Siam just 8km/5mi from the border with Cambodia. Unlike other parts of the Mekong Delta, in addition to long sandy beaches, the area around Ha Tien features limestone formations with an extended system of **caves**, in which temples have been built. The town possesses old colonial buildings and its inhabitants live from agriculture and fish farming. Due to its proximity to Cambodia, it has become a distribution hub for smuggled goods from the neighbouring country over the   **Ha Tien**

A Buddha watches over the Mac family graves

recent years, whilst an increasing number of tourists spend a night in the small provincial town (having entered via a border crossing which opened in 2007 around 8km/5mi from Ha Tien). Hydrofoils leave Ha Tien harbour on a daily basis for the offshore island of Phu Quoc (also from Rach Gia, p.182; several boats per day, trips lasting for 2 and a half hours). To be on the safe side, the older ferries and barges between Ha Tien and Phu Quoc are better avoided.

*Tombs of the Mac family Northeast of Ha Tien, on a chain of hills known as Nui Lang (the hill of the tombs), is the final resting place of the Mac family. On the initiative of the first emperor of the Nguyen dynasty, Gia Long, the Mac family tombs were built in 1809 in thanks for their providing him with shelter during the Tay Son uprising. The tombs are in the traditional Chinese style, horseshoe shaped with depictions of dragons, lions, tigers and phoenixes. The largest tomb belongs to the **first ancestor, Mac Cuu** himself.

Thach Dong The »stone cave« 3km/2mi outside of Ha Tien, holds an underground temple. At the entrance stands a memorial to 130 people who lost their lives in a massacre by the Khmer Rouge in 1979. Inside are tablets dedicated to the Jade Emperor and the Goddess of Compassion.
➊ daily 7am– 5pm

Mui Nai The beaches near Ha Tien, with their clear, warm water and fine sand, are the only ones in the entire Mekong Delta. Due to their remote location and proximity to the Cambodian border, they have hardly been developed. Around 4km/2.5mi south of the city, the rocky range of Mui Nai forms a promontory, on both sides of which are beaches.

Hon Chon Also very beautiful is Duong Beach on the Hon Chong peninsula, 20km/12mi south of Ha Tien. Here, there are long, sandy beaches with palms and clear but often very shallow water, alongside rocks that extend into the sea, the end of a limestone range which runs to the south from Ha Tien. A number of caves have formed here. One of them, the **Hang Tien Grotto**, is where the later emperor Gia Long is said to have hid during the Tay Son uprising in 1784. Close by – unfortunately unmissable – is a cement factory.

Duong Beach Just a few miles further on, the road ends at a Buddhist cave-temple, Chua Hang. From here, it is possible to walk to Duong Beach, a real gem with fish restaurants and boats. The Father and Son Island (Hon Phu Tu), a few hundred metres from the coast, resembles a column with a pedestal that has been eroded by the waves.

Rach Gia The centre of Rach Gia, on the Gulf of Siam in the far west of the Mekong Delta, stretches between two canalized arms of the Cai Lon

River. Rach Gia and Long Xuyen are joined by a system of canals that resembles a rope ladder, with the main canal being the Thoai Ha. Alongside the cultivation and processing of tropical fruit, fishing also plays an important role in this port town. A walk through the streets of Rach Gia presents a chance to see splendid villas from the colonial era as well as pretty cafés, numerous shops and colourful markets. All in all, the city makes a very pleasant and prosperous impression.

The **Rach Gia Museum** (27 Nguyen Van Troi Street) displays archaeological finds from the historic town of Oc Eo, the ruins of which can be visited 12km/7.5mi east of Rach Gia. North of the city centre, in Quang Trung Street, stands the 200 year-old **Phat Lon Pagoda** (Big Buddha Pagoda), which was built by the Khmer in the Theravada Buddhist style. The carved roofs and the wall paintings depicting scenes from the life of Buddha are particularly impressive. The large park, with a lotus pond and a stupa field, is a nice place to linger. Around 30 monks live in the buildings at the back of the monastery. Boats depart from the little harbour town for Phu Quoc on a daily basis, along with flights which stop over here en route from Saigon to Phu Quoc.

Insider Tip

Museum: Mon-Fri 7.30am-11.30am, 1.30pm-4.30pm, Sat mornings only

** Cu Chi

✦ D 7

Province: Ho Chi Minh City (city state)
Region: South

For the Vietnamese, the notorious Cu Chi tunnels are a reminder of the resistance against the South Vietnamese government and of the citizens who died in this tunnel system during the Vietnam War. School classes, former guerrillas and guests of the state come and go here, especially in Ben Duoc, the larger complex.

First of all, visitors are shown a **film on the history** of the Vietnam War and the building of the tunnel – from the point of view of those in power now, naturally. A map illustrates the magnitude of the tunnel complex and points out the positions of the Americans, the South Vietnamese Army and the Vietcong. Drawings and cross-section diagrams illustrate the construction of the tunnels, in three levels, each up to 10m/33ft deep. Through the system of tunnels, the Vietcong soldiers could get as far as Cholon in the South Vietnamese metropolis. The brief occupation of the US Embassy (or its garden) in Saigon by Vietcong guerrillas during the Tet Festival of 1968 was

**Tunnel complex

** *Tunnel Networks of Cu Chi*

In the 1930s and 1940s underground chambers and trenches served as hiding places and weaponry stores for guerillas fighting the French. Over time, they were connected by corridors and further extended in the fight against the Americans.

❶ daily 7.30am–5.30pm

Extent
This concealed network ultimately extended from the Cambodian-Vietnamese border, following the Ho Chi Minh Trail (►DMZ) all the way to Saigon's Chinese quarter of Cholon.

Shots from nowhere
In 1966, unaware of the subterranean enemy, American troops of the 25th Infantry Division set up their headquarters close to the tunnels. At first, they were unable to explain where these nightly attacks on the heavily fortified military camp were coming from – until they discovered the tunnels. Some 50,000 US soldiers combed the terrain in search of the well-camouflaged entrances.

❶ An underground city
The partisans lived on three levels up to 10m/32ft under the ground. Narrow shafts broadened out into a subterranean labyrinth of sleeping quarters and muster stations, sick bays, kitchens, prayer rooms with shrines, workshops, stores and bomb shelters. Babies were even born in the tunnels, only seeing the light of day some years later.

❷ Entrances
Tiny trapdoors, overgrown with grass and foliage, led up into the outside world. They were all protected by primitive, yet effective, traps. Some tunnels are thought to have ended in rivers, thus improving the chances of escape in the event of pursuit or bombardment.

❸ Perfect camouflage
Ventilation was ensured through inconspicuous bamboo canes, where pepper and chili were grown to throw tracker dogs off the scent. In time, the dogs were no longer able to distinguish between Vietnamese and Americans as the Vietcong had begun using American soap, after-shave and clothing they had taken from their prisoners.

❹ Deadly traps
Attempts to flush the Vietcong out of the tunnels were thwarted by a variety of tricks. Trapdoors over pits, for example, in which bamboo cane had been filed into spikes, sometimes tipped in poison – booby traps, as they were called. Dummy tunnels and entrances were deployed to lure intruders into explosive traps, with bombs and mines laid beneath the turf.

Entrances were hidden all over the jungle, measuring just 33cm/12in x 25cm/10in. They were covered in grass and foliage.

Villages ar
forcibly ev
»free fire z
gallons of
carpets we
region, wh
ultimately
almost con
deforestat

All rooms
connected
80cm/2.6f
has been c
western t
80cm/2.6f

Cu Chi

GETTING THERE
The tunnel complex can be reached via the N22 (approx. 60km/40mi northwest of Saigon): upon reaching Cu Chi, turn right and follow the blue signs along the paddy fields for a few miles.

MARCO ⊕ POLO TIP

Insider Tip
Stifling and cramped

Some places in the tunnels are so narrow that the only way forward is to crawl along on one's front. Claustrophobics shoud steer clear of the tunnel system, as should anyone carrying too much weight.

ADMISSION
approx. 80,000 VND (with or without tunnel crawls)
The trip to Cu Chi is also available as a 3 to 5 hour tour from Saigon (about US$6-10 per person, individual tours roughly US$30 per person), usually combined with a visit to the Cao Dai Temple in Tay Ninh (p.412).
Shooting range: US$17 for ten shots with an AK47

WHERE TO STAY
Canh Sang Guesthouse (A) is a simple establishment close to the tunnels in Benh Dinh (tel. 08/37 94 21 75, http://hochiminhcookingclass.com).
Chef Tan is a passionate cook.

possible only because of this tunnel. It is possible to tour the complex only with a guide or in a group. Visitors pass barely perceptible tunnel entrances, around 20 x 40cm/8 x 16in in size, into which the guides disappear as a demonstration. Field kitchens and base hospitals, trap doors, captured tanks and oversized bomb craters can be seen above ground. The tourist trail finally leads through »minefields« armed with blanks.

Wooden Vietcong figures can be seen in all manner of poses around the site, some of them moving mechanically, writing letters home to their families, for example, or manufacturing explosives. The Vietnamese know how to commercialise the war to the very last shell casing. Popular among Asian guests in particular is the **shooting range** – one shot, one dollar. According to information from a military expert, it is better to abstain from this questionable pastime: the weapons (AK 47s and M 16s) are thought to be old and not particularly well maintained, presenting a high risk for the user.

❶ daily 7am–5pm

Ben Duoc Temple
On the expansive grounds of Ben Douc, visitors can also visit Ben Duoc Temple with its 40m/131ft high, nine-storey tower, which was built on the banks of the Saigon River in 1995. Inside, the names of around 50,000 of the fallen from this region are engraved in stone.

AROUND CU CHI

»Mot Thoang Viet Nam« (»a glimpse of Vietnam«) is the motto of this tourist project near Cu Chi. On a park-like area of 22ha/54ac with a small lake in the middle, visitors are given demonstrations of old Vietnamese handicrafts and traditional art. A kind of **miniature Vietnam** with famous buildings can be viewed from a platform. Buildings characteristic of ethnic minorities and various regions – for example the clay houses in Central Vietnam – are displayed in their actual size. Also on the grounds is a small zoo housing numerous plants and animals native to Vietnam, a sugar factory, a rice wine distillery and a rice mill, an open-air restaurant, various workshops, and exhibition rooms with musical instruments and traditional clothing, as well as souvenir stands. The village is intended as both a classic tourist attraction and a training centre for typical and traditional professions. The grounds are around 5km/3mi from the Ben Duoc tunnels, in the vicinity of the village of Phu Binh.

Handicraft village Phu Binh

✶ Da Lat

✦ E 7

Province: Lam Dong (capital)
Region: Central Highlands
Population: 200,000

Da Lat nestles between the terraced vegetable fields and the green hills of the plateau at the foot of mountains rising up to 2163m/7096ft. Even in French colonial times, this attractive mountain landscape was chosen as a holiday and resort destination, with Da Lat referred to as the »city of eternal spring«.

In past years, the Central Highlands have seen recurring guerrilla battles against the central government, as hill tribes fight for their independence in the Vietnamese, Cambodian and Laotian highlands. As increasing numbers of Vietnamese were relocated to the **»economic development zones«** around Da Lat after 1975, FULRO (»United Front for the Liberation of Oppressed Races«) came into being. With the support of western countries, the resistance movement opposed »Vietnamization« by the communist regime in Hanoi. The entire highland region was closed to tourism at short notice in 2001 and 2004, when demonstrations by the hill tribes turned violent.

FULRO

Since then, the situation has calmed down considerably. The residents of Da Lat live from the cultivation of vegetables, fruit and flowers (especially orchids for export), as well as from cattle farming and from handcrafts (silk weaving, embroidery and wood carving). The sweet, syrupy strawberry jam and strawberry wine from Da Lat are famous throughout the country.

WHAT TO SEE IN DA LAT

Picturesque villas and dilapidated houses, which look like the witch's house from a fairy tale, ascend the hill above Xuan Huong Lake – the architectural mix in Da Lat lies somewhere between palace and tower block. The **French colonial era** has left a number of traces, for example the cathedral, the university and the Pasteur Institute, and the streets bore French names until 1975. Old, arcaded villas with terraces or country houses built with rough stone bricks are still to be found, especially along Tran Hung Dao Street – many houses have been renovated and today serve as guesthouses.

Da Lat provides an exotic atmosphere for Vietnamese: cool temperatures, hilly woodlands, roses and strawberries

Phan Boi Chau Street and Lu Tu Trong Street lead to the loftily situated Lam Dong Museum, which focuses on the history and culture of the province. Above all, the artisan handicrafts (ceramics, weaving, jewellery and traditional costumes) of the hill tribes, the Montagnards, is exhibited; among other pieces, visitors can marvel at the cigar case of Emperor Bao Dai. The **view** of the city and its surroundings is especially pretty from here.

Lam Dong Museum

● Tue–Sat 7.30am–11.30am and 1.30pm–4.30pm, admission: 6,000 VND

On the south side of the city centre stretches Xuan Huong Lake, surrounded by villas. It takes its name from a Vietnamese authoress from the 17th century. The lake, with a surface area of approximately 4ha/10ac (7km/4.3mi in circumference) was artificially dammed in 1919. Sadly, both the lake and the waterfalls nearby are suffering as a consequence of the vast Da Nhim reservoir to the west, particularly in the dry season. If there is enough water in the lake after the rainy

Xuan Huong Lake

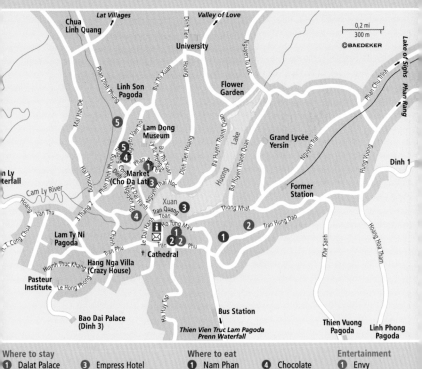

Da Lat

Chua Linh Quang
Lat Villages
Valley of Love
Dinh Tien
University
Phan Dinh Phung
Mai Hac De
Linh Son Pagoda
Bui Thi Xuan
Hoang
Flower Garden
Nguyen Tu Lu
Lake of Sights
Phan Rang
0,2 mi
300 m
©BAEDEKER
Phan Chu Trinh
Hung Vuong
Lam Dong Museum
Ly Tu Trong
Dinh Tien Hoang
Ba Huyen Thanh Quan
Huong
Lake
Ba Huyen Thanh Quan
Grand Lycée Yersin
Nguyen Trai
Dinh 1
Cam Ly Waterfall
Hai Thuong
Phan Dinh Phung
Dinh
Nguyen Van Troi
Market (Cho Da Lat)
Bui Thi Xuan
Dinh Tien Hoang
Nguyen Thai Hoc
Former Station
Cam Ly River
Van Thu
3 Thang 2
Chanh Phu
Tran Phu
Nguyen Du
Le Dai Hanh
Nguyen Tri
Xuan
Tran Quang Toan
Ao Tung Mau
Thong Nhat
Tran Hung Dao
Khe Sanh
Hoang Hoa Tham
N.T. Cong Chua
Hoang Van Thu
Lam Ty Ni Pagoda
Huynh Thuc Khang
Hang Nga Villa (Crazy House)
Le Hong Phong
† Cathedral
Tran Phu
Phu
Pasteur Institute
Ha Huy Tap
Bao Dai Palace (Dinh 3)
Bus Station
Thien Vien Truc Lam Pagoda
Prenn Waterfall
Thien Vuong Pagoda
Linh Phong Pagoda

Da Lat

INFORMATION
Da Lat Trip
1/17 Tran Nhan Tong, Da Lat
tel. 063/355 57 68
www.dalattrip.com

Phat Tire Ventures:
109 Nguyen Van Troi, Da Lat
tel. 063/382 94 22
Mobile tel. 098/661 88 61
www.phattireventures.com
(hiking, action adventure etc)

TRANSPORT
Lien Khuong Airport
approx. 30km/20 mi south of Da Lat
tel. 063/384 33 73
Vietnam Airline Shuttlebus: 063/382 28 95 (approx. 40,000 VND)
daily flights from Saigon

Easy Riders
When the »Easy Riders«, an organized group of moped taxi riders from Da Lat, began ferrying adventurous backpacker tourists around the highlands some years back, a new trend was born. Typically, copycat operations popped up throughout the country – so that today's Da Lat tourists are inundated with such offers.
Pillion passengers should make sure of the following: an English speaking driver / guide, a roadworthy moped, a solid helmet and suitable prices (not too high, not too low) in the region of US$15-20 in the region, longer tours from around US$50, fuel included and depending on route and desired hotel standard.

EVENTS
Da Lat Flower Festival
Insider Tip
Every two years (2015, 2017), between 10 and 18 December, Da Lat is transformed into a sea of blossoms: orchids, roses, tulips as far as the eye can see. Flower arranging competitions are held, along with music and fashion shows, with the climax of the festival being a parade of colourfully decorated wagons throughout the city.

Sa Ropu
(Buffalo Feast of Sacrifice)
After a bountiful harvest, the Buffalo Feast of Sacrifice Sa Ropu is celebrated in honour of the rice god Ndu. The »can« flows freely: revelers suck the high-proof rice wine through bamboo straws from large clay mugs.

LEISURE
Golf
Swing clubs on the scenic 18-hole golf course (roughly US$100, book at the Dalat Palace Golf Club in the Dalat Palace Hotel, see below: tel. 063/382 54 44 and 063/382 12 01).

SHOPPING
Cho Da Lat Market
Mountains of flowers, vegetable and fruit can be found in the alleys and on the steps in front of the market hall. Inside, customers rummage through lacquerware and typical household goods, as well as handicrafts made by the hill tribes.

GOING OUT
❶ Envy Lounge Bar ££
tel. 063/382 26 24
1 Nguyen Thi Minh Khai
Lounge around in the corner seating arrangements of this flashy, chic establishment and listen to local bands. Salsa, tango and cha-cha dances sometimes ensue.

② *Larry's Bar*
Sofitel Da Lat Palace
Daily 4pm–midnight
Atmospheric little bar with large selection of wines, beer and cocktails, as well as very good pizza.

WHERE TO EAT
① *Nam Phan* **££££**
7 Trang Hung Dao, Da Lat
tel. 063/381 38 16
Beautifully situated fine dining locale in the villa quarter with lake views and garden. The best of Vietnamese cuisine, elegant atmosphere and attentive service, albeit rather expensive.

② *Le Rabelais* **£££**
12 Tran Phu
(in Da Lat Palace, see below)
tel. 063/382 54 44
daily noon–10pm
Elegant French restaurant with panoramic lake view.
High tea served 4pm–5pm.
Piano accompaniment from 7pm.

③ *Thuy Ta,*
»La Grenouillère« **££–£££**
1 Yersin
(on the shore of Xuan Huong Lake)
tel. 063/382 22 88
Unsightly exterior, comfortable inside: Vietnamese dishes with lakeside view and piano accompaniment or traditional folk music.

④ *Chocolate Café* **£–££**
Tang Bat Ho
tel. 063/351 09 79
Seafood in the highlands – no problem at all here! A café restaurant serving fine Vietnamese cuisine, but not to worry, spaghetti, pizza and burgers are also on the menu – usually full as a result.

⑤ *Café Tung* **£**
Hoa Binh, tel. 063/382 13 90
Time appears to have stood still some 50 years ago inside this narrow, inconspicuous café in the centre of town. Savour ca phe sua nong whilst sitting on thick leather sofas beneath oil paintings. Mona Lisa smiles down on diners. The homemade yoghurt is a must.

WHERE TO STAY
① *Dalat Palace* **££££**
12 Tran Phu
tel. 063/382 54 44
www.dalatresorts.com
In a class of its own: restored, colonial hotel, 43 rooms with beautiful nostalgic furnishings – the bathroom alone is worth staying here for! Cookery courses available on request.

② *Ana Mandara Villas Dalat & Spa* **£££**
Insider Tip
Le Lai
tel. 063/355 58 88
www.anamandara-resort.com
A journey into the past: 17 restored French colonial villas from the 1920s spread across a park. The 57 rooms are arranged with elegant, old »granny« furniture and décor, the bathtub stands on lions' paws. »In-villa dining service« in the room's own kitchen. Heated pool. Wine cellar, exclusive restaurant.

Forest Floor Lodge **£££**
In the Cat Tien National Park, Tan Phu
Dong Nai
tel. 061/366 98 90
www.vietnamforesthotel.com
At the heart of nature inside Cat Tien National Park, above the rapids. A chic, yet rustic, Forest Floor Lodge comprising bungalows and comfortable tents, plus restaurant. Treks and night safaris on offer.

❸ *Empress Hotel ££*
5 Nguyen Thai Hoc
tel. 063/383 38 88
www.empresshotel.vn.com
Located on a hill, ten of the 19 elegant rooms at this restored villa have a view of the lake. Some are beautifully furnished with parquet floors, Italian terracotta and antique telephones. Italian restaurant, although breakfast is rather underwhelming.

❹ *Ngoc Lan Hotel ££*
42 Nguyen Chi Thanh, Da Lat
tel. 063/383 88 38
An erstwhile cinema in the centre of town has been given a new lease of life as a mid-range hotel with 91 stylish rooms, some particularly spacious with parquet and lovely views across the lake from the balcony. Good value for money.

❺ *Dream's Hotel 1 and 2 £*
151 and 164 Phan Dinh Phung
tel. o63/383 37 48
dreams@hcm.vnn.vn
Centrally located, these two mini hotels feature large beds, pleasant shower facilities, TV, minibar, some rooms with balcony) and a large breakfast buffet in the kitchen with the family is included.

The Dalat Palace Hotel is graced with the charms of the 1920s and enjoys a wonderful location on the Xuan Huong lake

season, **paddleboats** can be rented near the Thanh Thuy restaurant. On the north side lies a 50ha/124ac golf course, on which Bao Dai (▶Famous People) played, and beautiful flower gardens (full of roses, orchids and hydrangeas).

❶ daily 6am-6pm

The railway line between Saigon/Phan Rang and Da Lat was built   **Train station** around 1930. Today, most of the route is disused. From the station (approx. 500m/550yd east of the lake) an old train runs to Linh Phuoc Pagoda in Trai Mat (approx. 8km/5mi further on). The Linh Phuoc Pagoda presents a popular photo opportunity for tourists, keen to capture the towering dragon crafted from 50,000 beer bottle shards and pieces of pottery. During the half-hour nostalgic journey, passengers can get to know the hill landscape and pine forests of the area. From Trai Mat an approximately 7km/4.5mi-long signposted trail runs to **Tiger Waterfall** (Thac Hang Cop). Visitors are greeted by a tiger statue – whose wide-open mouth they often climb into. It is possible to climb down the stairs that run alongside the impressive waterfall to the foot of the cascade, or relax above in one of two restaurants.

Trains run from 7.45am-4pm roughly every two hours, minimum 15 passengers, tickets 120,000 VND; **waterfall:** admission approx. 6000 VND

South of Tran Hung Dao Street, the main street in the south of Da   **Linh Phong** Lat, two holy sites await. Heading along Hoanh Goa Tham, visitors   **Pagoda** reach the colourful Linh Phong Pagoda, the doorway of which is adorned with a baying dragon's head with threatening, protruding eyes.

The previous junction, on Khe San Street, leads to Thien Vuong Pa-   **Thien Vuong** goda, which is visited primarily for the huge Buddha statue that sits   **Pagoda** on a throne on the hill above. Stands sell candied strawberries and artichoke tea.

On the other side of the street stands the city's cathedral, which was   **Cathedral** built in the 1930s and dedicated to St Nicholas. The 70 colourful **glass windows** from Grenoble are noteworthy, as is an otherwise inconspicuous collage next to the altar. This was made, in honour of the Catholic martyrs of Vietnam, out of recycled paper, symbolizing the renewal of Catholicism in the country.

The Dinh 3 Palace, belonging to Bao Dai (1913–97, Famous people)   ***Bao Dai** in the city's southwest was built between 1933 and 1938, and bears a   **Palace** certain similarity to Art Deco architecture. The **last Emperor of**   **(Dinh 3)** **Vietnam**, from the Nguyen dynasty, lived here with his family in the 1940s, and later only with his concubine, after the Empress Nam

Phuong and the children had gone into exile in France. The two-floored, ochre-coloured palace houses 26 rooms and a large garden. The emperor also finally went into exile in France in the mid-1950s, and President Ngo Dinh Diem used the palace from then on. On the ground floor is Bao Dai's working area, with the private chambers of the imperial family on the top floor. The reception hall is furnished with a piano, seating and hunting trophies.

To the right of the entrance is a simple office with a bust of the emperor and a photo of his father, Khai Dinh. Hanging in the assembly room on the ground floor are a number of photos from his time in office. At the end of the hallway, the visitor enters a rather modest throne room with some antique objects (including hunting lances). Here also stands the wooden bathtub of the emperor's mother. A narrow spiral staircase leads to the first floor, where rooms were once rented out to tourists. The first room was used by Princess Phuong Mai and the princes Phuong Dung and Bao Long as a living area. Adjoining it are the imperial chambers, which do not exactly leave an impression of any particular pomp. Also of note is an old wooden box by the large stairs, in which Bao Dai liked to take his steam baths.

❶ daily 7am-5.30pm; admission approx. 12,000 VND

Mere mortals may also have their photograph taken in the Emperor's clothes (around 40,000 VND).

*Hang Nga Villa (Crazy House) The much vaunted Hang Nga Villa – also known as the »Crazy House« – in Huynh Thuc Khang Street is another regular attraction for groups of tourists. Under the motto »back to nature«, the Vietnamese architect and president's daughter Hang Nga created a garden out of quirky treehouses and huts without angles and corners, sometimes shaped like animals, with fantastical statues, Russian puppets, spiders' webs, stalactites and »bamboo« bridges – all made of concrete. The rather peculiarly arranged rooms are intended for various animals, and elaborately furnished with decorations and mirrors. Attached to the guesthouse are a café and an art gallery.

❶ admission: approx. 30,000 VND

Utterly mad: Crazy House

The area around Da Lat boasts a number of waterfalls, the nearest being **Cam Ly Falls** near Hoang Van Thu Street. It has been a tourist attraction for many years, also for Vietnamese visitors. Bustling on the lawns are **ponies and cowboys**, to create an exotic atmosphere – for the Vietnamese.

● 7am–6pm, approx. 30,000 VND

AROUND DA LAT – TO THE NORTH

Those who want to get an impression of how the Vietnamese most like to spend their weekends should pay a visit to the »Valley of Love«. Around 5km/3mi north of the city centre lies this well attended getaway, where Emperor Bao Dai used to go hunting. Here, visitors enjoy extensive hiking in pine forests and paddling in the manmade Ho Da Thien Lake, pony rides with Vietnamese dressed as cowboys, picnics and souvenir frenzies. There is also a campsite on the grounds. In good weather, there is a wonderful **panoramic view** of the countryside around Da Lat, and particularly of the two peaks of the legendary Langbiang Mountain.

*Valley of Love

● daily 8am–6pm, admission: 30,000 VND

MARCO POLO INSIGHT

? *Why the Lake of Sighs?*

When listening closely to the lake, it is possible to hear the sighs of Hoang Tung and Mai Nuong. The happy couple lived here more than 200 years ago, until Hoang Tung was called up to the war, where he is said to have fallen in battle. Overcome with grief, Mai Nuong threw herself into the lake. Yet some years later her lover returned home after all, searching for his bride – to no avail. In despair, he followed her to a watery grave.

This small Lake of Sighs is also a popular and typically Vietnamese destination for day-trippers. It lies around 6km/4mi outside the city centre, to the east, and is surrounded by pine forests. Pony rides, hiking trails around the lake and copious souvenir stands and pubs are part of the variety of attractions on offer here. The lake is the source of many sad tales and legends.

*Lake of Sighs

In the area around Da Lat are nine villages, which form the **Lat Community**, within which indeed even different dialects are spoken. Visitors require a permit in the form of a ticket. Tourists should only visit as part of a tour organized by a travel agency. The ethnic Lats (pronounced Lak) themselves live in six villages and number around 3000 citizens. They are mainly Catholics and live from cultivating vegetables (e.g. rice, sweet potatoes, manioc, beans), still practising slash-and-burn methods to clear the land. They also produce charcoal, which is sold at the market in Da Lat. In a Lat village at the foot of the Langbiang Mountain, 12km/7.5mi north of the city, it is possible to see a number of private pile dwell-

Colourfully woven fabrics

ings, the church and a tiny weaving mill with a souvenir shop. The Lat were once a **matriarchal society** and, even to this day, a man moves into the house of his wife, or that of her parents, until a couple can afford to build one of their own. Children take on their mother's family name. The everyday life of the Lat who live here otherwise largely conforms to that of most Vietnamese: children go to Vietnamese schools; in church the hymns vary between Latin, Vietnamese and the Lat language. The **traditional clothing** – a kind of two-piece Sarong – is only worn by the elderly or on very special occasions. Filed teeth or ears pierced with pegs are now rarely found and only among the oldest in the village.

Langbiang Mountain (Nui Ba)

Close to the Lat village is the gateway to Langbiang Mountain. Accompanied by a guide from Da Lat Tourist, **walking groups** and bird lovers can climb the 2000m/6562ft peaks in around three hours. The route passes through red rhododendrons and wild orchids, and countless butterflies, rare indigenous birds and perhaps even a wild boar are to be seen. Part of the forest has already fallen victim to clearance for charcoal production, especially on the lower slopes. Evergreen forests still grow around the two highest peaks. Depending on the weather, there can be a magnificent view of Dat Lat and its surroundings. One section of the marked hiking path initially follows the tarmac road for two kilometres/just over a mile, complete with tourist busses and jeeps – these only drive as far as a radar station with cafeteria, not all the way to the summit! The trail continues on foot along a beautiful path into the rain forest and through pine trees (not recommended if it is raining).

❶ admission: approx. 40,000 VND

AROUND DA LAT – TO THE SOUTH

Thien Vien Truc Lam Pagoda

Above **Tuyen Lam Lake** (also Quang Trung) lies the popular Thien Vien Truc Lam Pagoda with a beautiful bonsai garden. The Buddhist place of worship offers a fantastic view of the neighbouring mountain and the reservoir (built in 1982). It is also possible to take the **funicular** from Robin Hill, a couple of miles south of the city. Many Vietnamese take a motorboat trip across to the other shore, where there is a camp site and bungalows. Those who wish to can **take a ride on an elephant**. The meditation monastery (1993) houses a gilded Buddha as well as many woodcarvings of scenes from his life. Interested foreigners can get individual instruction on the art of meditation here – in exchange for a small donation and with prior booking. The monastery and reservoir are around 5km/3mi southwest of Da Lat.

Pagoda: daily 7am–5pm.
Funicular return ticket: approx. 70,000 VND
Monastery: daily 6am–5pm

Prenn Waterfall lies in the middle of a sort of amusement park. Visitors can walk behind the approximately 10m/33ft-high waterfall as if behind a huge, spraying curtain. At weekends there is a jostling throng of people here. It is possible to spend the night in a tent or ride a paddleboat in the forest-like park. A small zoo is also among the attractions. It seems unthinkable that even into the 1970s the tigers roaming here kept tourists away. Prenn Waterfall can be reached via the N 20, around 10km/6mi outside Da Lat.admission: approx. €0.35 (there is a small charge for all of the waterfalls)

Prenn
Waterfall

The silk factories in Cu Xa can be reached via National Highways 20 and 27b (approximately 25km/15mi from Da Lat). The drive into the valley first passes coffee plantations, pineapple and vegetable fields. The many strange straw huts on the edge of the road are used to grow mushrooms, which thrive in the moist climate. Seen all around the area are mulberry trees, the leaves of which are a favourite food of silkworms. Interested visitors can get a demonstration of the individual phases of silk production at the family-run businesses based here: for example the cultivation of the worms, the manufacturing of the threads and the winding by machine. The worms produce the silk fibres, wrapping themselves around in them as they pupate. The thumb-sized cocoons are boiled in a kettle until the fibres come loose and can be wound onto spools. The worms are then fried and enjoyed as a delicacy.

*The silk-
weaving
village of
Cu Xa

Insider
Tip

After around 30km/19mi, National Highway 20 (toward Saigon) runs past Lien Khuong Waterfall. During the rainy season, the approximately 100m/330ft-wide waterfall is among the most beautiful in the area: the water of the Da Nhim River rushes over the rocks to cascade 20m/66ft downwards. It is nicely viewed from patio of the simple **Ngoc Hoa street café**, from where steps lead down to the riverbed. Less frequented but just as spectacular are the Elephant Falls (N20 heading towards Buon Ma Thuot at the village of Nam Ban), where physically fit visitors can clamber down slippery rocks beside the thundering cascades, an impressive 30m/100ft high – a soggy, yet thrilling, pursuit.

**Lien
Khuong
Waterfall

*Dambri Waterfall The road also leads to Dambri Waterfall (110km/68mi southwest of Da Lat, near Bao Loc; follow the signs along the bumpy, only partially paved country road). The enormously loud roaring of the 50m/164ft-high waterfall can already be heard from the car park of the small amusement park. The masses of water thunder steeply down several levels of rock in a mighty cascade, spraying mist far and wide – a deafening natural spectacle!

»Chicken Village« On the road leading toward ▶Nha Trang, only 18km/11mi from Da Lat, lies the place known to travellers as »Chicken Village« (actually called Lang Con Ga), which takes its name from the 5m/16ft-high **chicken statue** on the village square. The reason for its being there is no longer really known – perhaps it was for political or religious reasons; a love story is sometimes mentioned. The inhabitants of the village are very poor and belong to the Koho ethnic minority.

*Bao Loc pass If time allows, it is best to drive from Da Lat to Saigon in a car, rather than flying – the trip over the Bao Loc pass is accompanied by breathtaking landscapes: the road meanders through valleys and deep ravines, with waterfalls and giant trees shrouded in fog. Spread out across the Bao Loc plateau are vast tea plantationsand mulberry fields – an almost Tuscan, gently rolling hill-landscape with white-blossomed, intensely scented frangipani trees. Fruit stands with durian, red dragon fruit and rambutans are set up right by the side of the road. The conspicuous bricked chimneys along the road are overgrown with pepper plants.

*Cat Tien National Park With an area of around 80,000ha/309 sq mi, Cat Tien National Park (160km/100mi northeast of Saigon) is one of the largest in Vietnam, and is now a UNESCO Biosphere Reserve. For a long time, the National Park was famous for its rhinoceros population. The WWF has now confirmed that the Javan rhinoceros is extinct in Vietnam, the last specimen having been shot by poachers in 2010. Alongside elephants, crocodiles, gibbons and buffaloes, there are at least 100 other mammalian species (apparently some leopards still among them), around 350 bird species, 120 reptile and amphibian species, as well as 460 types of butterfly. Added to that are around 1600 plant species, including 170 medicinal herbs and 52 types of orchid.. The landscape is made up of many lakes, rivers, waterfalls, lagoons and extensive swamp areas. The terrain descends from the Truong Son Mountains in a step-like pattern southwards to the plain. Water birds and crocodiles can be seen at the many lakes and watering holes. There are around 9000 members of ethnic groups living in the national park, the Chau Ma (Maa) and Stieng. They live from rice and fruit cultivation, as well as income from the harvest of coffee

Da Lat and the waterfalls are popular destinations for loving couples

and cashew nuts. Relatively good places to stay can be found at **Dong Nai River**. To get to the park from Saigon, it takes around four or five hours by car (N 20 to Madagui, then a further 23km/14mi).

❶ Admission: approx. 50,000 VND, simple overnight accommodation at the entrance to the park or at the Forest Floor Lodge (▶p.191). Guides cost roughly 250,000 VND per day.
www.namcattien.org

The special thing about La Nga Lake is that there is a settlement on it. Along with houseboats, it consists of wooden huts built upon empty oil barrels. As in ▶Chau Doc, fish are farmed here beneath the floors of the boats and huts. The boats with which the inhabitants travel from house to house, which are rowed by foot, are a local oddity.

La Nga Lake

✳ Da Nang

✦ E 4

Province: Quang Nam–Da Nang (capital)
Region: Southern Central Coast
Population: Approx. 1.1 million

Da Nang is considered the gateway to the three UNESCO cities of Central Vietnam (►Hue, ►Hoi An and ►My Son). The city itself has little in the way of outstanding attractions, but the Cham Museum is worth seeing as is the magnificent China Beach, which is steeped in history.

History
From the 4th until into the 14th century, the area around Da Nang belonged to the kingdom of the Cham. It wasn't until the end of the 15th century that the Vietnamese founded a settlement here. Due to its ideal location, the city was often beset with invaders, which is why it has a reputation as traditional **centre of resistance**. In the 16th and 17th centuries, Da Nang began to establish itself as a port town, as trade ships often had to wait here at harbour before being discharged of their cargo in Faifo (today Hoi An). From 1802, when Hue became the Vietnamese capital, all visitors to the court went ashore in Da Nang. The new Nguyen emperor Gia Long promised the French a concession for Da Nang (French: Tourane) in exchange for the help that put him on the throne. This however was granted only in 1888, after the French had shelled the harbour several times.

The city grew steadily as the base of the **South Vietnamese Air Force**, but growth accelerated when US troops landed here on 8 March 1965. No doubt many remember the television pictures of the advance guard of Marines wading ashore at Da Nang Bay with amphibious vehicles and helicopters, to be greeted with garlands of flowers by young Vietnamese women. In no time at all, Da Nang was practically transformed into an American small town, with hospitals, cinemas, bowling alleys, parks and most of all, a whole load of bars – many GIs spent their weekends and vacations in Da Nang or at China Beach (see below). Refugees from the so-called free-fire zones flooded into service jobs, working as washers, labourers, prostitutes and drug dealers. Yet Da Nang's role as a US military base brought not only benefits. The area surrounding the »City of War« suffered terribly from the ravages of battle: 33,000 tons of bombs were dropped, and tens of thousands died. From 1967 to 1972, the German hospital ship »Helgoland« was anchored in Da Nang's harbour, and, despite protests from the US, cared for the wounded from either side. In March 1975, the North Vietnamese finally began a large-scale offensive, the South Vietnamese troops fled, leaving the Vietcong to take the city without resistance.

** CHAM MUSEUM

❶ daily: 7am–5pm; admission 30,000 VND, two hour guided tours at 8am and 2pm; http://chammuseum.vn/en

The most important attraction in Da Nang is unquestionably the Cham Museum, with a collection of Cham art that is unparalleled worldwide. It is under no circumstances to be missed, especially for those also planning to visit ►My Son. It is found on the southerly Vuong Street, near the banks of the Han. The museum is planning to expand in the near future, with further exhibition rooms. There are 1700 smaller and larger sculptures in storage, awaiting their presentation.On the initiative of the École Française de l'Extrême Orient, the building of a museum began in 1915. Another 24 years would pass before it is actually completed. The building itself and the meticulous presentation of the exhibits alone make a visit worthwhile. The garden, with blossoming frangipani trees and a row of superb sculptures, creates an **exceptional mood** and an impression of the epoch and reign of the Cham, who ruled for over a thousand years in southern Vietnam. Unfortunately the individual exhibits are not sufficiently explained, and the catalogue on sale at the entrance gives only a general overview and does not refer to the pieces on display.

For the most part, the art of the Cham is religious art; here, as in their general system of beliefs, Buddhist, Hindu and Islamic elements, as well as local influences, can be found. Recurring themes are depictions of lions, elephants and Hindu deities. Above all, Shiva, the Hindu god of destruction and reconstruction, was honoured by the Cham as the defender of their kingdom. Shiva is portrayed either as a strong man or symbolically as a lingam (phallus). Indonesian and Khmer influences can be recognized in the Buddha sculptures from the 9th century (Indrapura). The best known and most individual form of expression in Cham art is the Uroja, a kind of universal mother of the Cham kings, exemplified in the form of a breast or a nipple (►photo p.332).

Religious art

Around 475 exhibits (altars, friezes, reliefs and statues) from the 4th to the 14th centuries are spread across ten rooms and in the garden.
My Son Room: A tour begins with the sculptures from the temple valley of My Son (4th–11th century). The Cham kingdoms were consolidated at the beginning of the 8th century and their own artistic style emerged. The different styles brought to light by excavations are named in accordance with the sites at which they were found. The altar, with its magnificent frieze, is considered a masterpiece of early sculptural art. The unfinished gable with the depiction of the birth of Brahma from the navel of Vishnu is especially interesting.
Tra Kieu Room: The archaeological site of Sinhapura is near Tra Kieu. The splendid **capital of the Cham kingdom** of the 4th to the 8th century lies 40km/25mi southwest of present-day Da Nang. A monumental altar with scenes from the Indian epic Ramayana is very impressive. The portrayal of the marriage of Princess Sita from the 7th century displays a strong Indian influence, not just in content, but also in form.
Dong Duong Room: Under the rule of King Indravarnam II, who moved the capital to the north (Indrapura), there was a move towards Buddhism. A monastery was built there at the end of the 9th century, later named Dong Duong. Scenes from the life of Buddha can be seen on the altar reliefs.
Thap Mam Room: From the beginning of the 11th century, the Cham had to retreat ever further south in response to the advances of the Viet. In the Thap Mam Room, the **stylistic changes** between the 12th and 14th centuries

A Davarapala, palace or temple guard (9th/10th century)

are easy to comprehend from the exhibits. The mythical creatures and the Shiva statues seem rougher, and not as finely and elegantly worked as the examples from earlier epochs.

FURTHER ATTRACTIONS IN DA NANG

Cao Dai Temple in Da Nang (35 Hai Phong Street) is the second largest in Vietnam ▶Tay Ninh. Here, too, the interior is ruled by the all-seeing-eye of the highest entity, and the walls are graced with pictures of religious leaders, including Laozi, Confucius, Jesus Christ and Buddha. The place of worship was closed from 1975 to 1986, but services are now held four times per day. Around 50,000 believers are said to live in Da Nang.

Cao Dai
Temple

❶ Services: 6am, noon, 6pm and midnight

Da Nang • Cham Museum

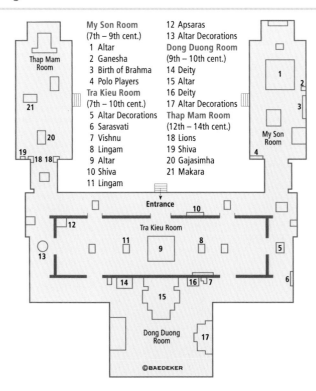

My Son Room
(7th – 9th cent.)
1 Altar
2 Ganesha
3 Birth of Brahma
4 Polo Players
Tra Kieu Room
(7th – 10th cent.)
5 Altar Decorations
6 Sarasvati
7 Vishnu
8 Lingam
9 Altar
10 Shiva
11 Lingam
12 Apsaras
13 Altar Decorations
Dong Duong Room
(9th – 10th cent.)
14 Deity
15 Altar
16 Deity
17 Altar Decorations
Thap Mam Room
(12th – 14th cent.)
18 Lions
19 Shiva
20 Gajasimha
21 Makara

Thap Mam Room
My Son Room
Entrance
Tra Kieu Room
Dong Duong Room

©BAEDEKER

Da Nang

INFORMATION
Saigon Tourist
357 Phan Chu Trinh, Da Nang City
tel. 05 11/389 72 29
info@saigontouristdanang.com

TRANSPORT
International Airport Da Nang
5km/3mi southwest
tel. 0511/382 33 91 and 381 10 41

Railway station
Tran Cao Van, Da Nang
tel. 0511/382 38 10

EVENTS
Liberation Day
Each year on 29 March, »Liberation Day« is celebrated with traditional boat races on the Han River.

Cau Ngu Festival (Ca Ong)
The »Whale Festival« is celebrated every year (February, March) by the fishermen of the surrounding villages to honour the whales – believed to protect them and considered gods – with decorated boats, sacrifices, traditional singing and music, regattas and other sporting competitions.

SHOPPING
Da Nang has various markets worth strolling through: the market hall on the corner of Tran Phu/Hung Vuong or the Cho Con on the corner of Hung Vuong/ Ong Ich Khiem, with shops offering handicrafts, especially basketwork. In addition, a lively street market is located in Hai Phong Street, east of the railway station.

Non Nuoc Fine Art Village Insider Tip
At the foot of the Marble Mountains

(Hoa Hai, Ngu Hanh Son district) it is possible to watch the stone masons and sculptors at work, then purchase their pottery and marble figures, animals and countless Buddhas in all sizes, for example – or how about a life-sized Ho Chi Minh for the living room?

WHERE TO EAT
A wealth of opportunities to sample fine seafood at fair prices at My Khe Beach (China Beach) with panoramic views of the sea.

❶ **Waterfront ££–££££**
150-152 Bach Dang, Da Nang
tel. 0511/384 33 73
Bar and restaurant with panoramic views alongside the Han River: international (tender steaks, tapas, crêpes) and Vietnamese dishes, excellent seafood, a winelist for connoisseurs and tasty cocktails.

❷ **Babylon View £–££**
Truong Sa, corner of Ho Xuan Huong (beachside, close to the Furama Resort), Da Nang
tel. 0511/398 79 89
From delicious Asian appetizers via light, vegetarian fare, all the way to steaks, spicy kim chi, Japanese and barbecues, there are dishes galore to try on the rooftop terrace. Even spaghetti, pasta and fries are on the menu and there is a play area for kids.

❸ **Truc Lam Vien (Garden View Café) £**
8 Tran Quy Cap, Da Nang
tel. 0511/358 24 28
www.truclamvien.com.vn
Imperially inspired garden oasis: Vietnamese and Chinese specialities, hotpot

and other classics, tasty seafood, week-end buffet, good cappuccino.

❹ *Cool Spot £*
112 Tran Phu
tel. 0511/382 40 40
daily 10am-11pm
Small bar on two levels: the food is a mix of Vietnamese-Japanese-western dishes.

WHERE TO STAY
❶ *Furama Resort £££££*
68 Ho Xuan Huong, China Beach (Bac My Anh Beach)
tel. 0511/384 73 33
www.furamavietnam.com
An oasis of luxury: this attractive complex was the first – and still the best - five-star accommodation on a Vietnamese beach. The three-storey buildings are spread out across a vast landscape of gardens and lagoons, rooms with plenty of fine wood and rattan, a veranda and every comfort. Diving school, golf and an extensive array of pools and canals.

❷ *Da Nang Sun Peninsula Resort (InterContinental) £££££*
Bai Bac, Son Tra Peninsula (approx. 20km/12mi northeast of Da Nang)
tel. 0511/393 88 88
www.ichotelsgroup.com
Stylishly designed beach residence on remote stretch of coast below Monkey Mountain: around 200 rooms and suites with all mod cons are arranged steeply above the dreamy bay. Champagne brunch on Sundays (also for non-residents), three restaurants, two pools.

❸ *Banyan Tree Lang Co £££££*
In the village of Cu Du
Loc Vinh (Lang Co Peninsula), Phu Loc.
tel. 054/369 58 88

www.banyantree.com
Now the dreamlike Lang Co has its own dream resort: the trusted world class standard of the Banvan Tree chain opened in one of Vietnam's newest resorts at the end of 2012. Hue style pool villas, 49 in number, fulfil virtually every desire from home movie selections to spa facilities and five restaurants.

❹ *Lifestyle Resort (Accor) £££-£££££*
Truong Sa Street (Bac My An Beach), Ngu Hanh Son district, Da Nang
tel. 0511/395 88 88
www.accorhotels.com/
Five-star service: 187 very spacious rooms (although not so well soundproofed) in a five storey building plus some really attractive villas. Pool at the infinite beach. Kids club, spa, fitness, golf and cookery classes.

❺ *Lang Co Beach Resort £-££*
Loc Hai, Phu Loc (approx. 35km/22mi from Da Nang International Airport)
Lang Co Beach Resort
tel. 054/387 35 55

Insider Tip

www.langcobeachresort.com.vn
Too good to be true: a marvelously located complex has architecture in the imperial stlye of Hue. 84 rooms in bungalow villas with TV, minibar and sea vies, simpler rooms up on a hill. Mostly indigenous holidaymakers who take advantage of internet deals. Prices may be negotiable, but do not expect four-star service.
On the other hand, the wonderful beach is sparsely populated. Just take care in the water – dangerous currents are not uncommon!

❻ Dai A Hotel £
51 Yen Bai, Da Nang
tel. 0511/382 75 32
www.daiahotel.com.vn
Centrally located near the railway station, this mini hotel offers 34 clean, tiled rooms (minibar, TV, some rooms without windows). Simple, but with huge beds and internet connection. Five floors with an elevator and helpful staff. Shuttle service from the airport.

❼ Hoa's Place £
2q5 Huyen Trang Cong Chua
(China Beach close to the Melia Resort and Marble Mountains)
Da Nang
tel. 0511/396 92 16
Backpackers love Hoa's »take it easy« atmosphere. Everyone gets together for dinner and a cheap, chilled beer – just a stone's throw from the empty beach. Hoa and family are a great source of information. Their simple little guesthouse may be in the second row – but the view is slowly becoming obscured by first-class hotels (some rooms with air conditioning).

AROUND DA NANG

Monkey Mountain
The long Son Tra peninsula with the Monkey Mountain protects Da Nang from the winter monsoon. There really are quite a few monkeys living here. But only a small section of Son Tra can be visited, as much of it has been declared a military restricted area; a huge, white Quan Am Buddha statue stands at the top.

My Khe (China Beach) and Bac My An Beach
On the side of the peninsula facing the South China Sea lies My Khe (7km/4mi southeast of central Da Nang), the legendary China Beach, where American soldiers went for recreation while away from the fighting. The beach is popular among young people and families in the evening. There are numerous hotels, beach restaurants and stands serving fresh seafood.

*Marble Mountains
Around 12km/7mi southeast of Da Nang, the Marble Mountains (Ngu Hanh Son) rise up quite unexpectedly. They were named by Emperor Minh Mang (1820–40); the five individual mountains are named after the elements of fire, water, earth, metal and wood. Their peaks and caves, in which **sanctuaries** are located, were used during the war by the guerrillas as observation posts due to the optimal view afforded of the US airbase. The view of the coast is also impressive. Members of the Cham people came here to worship their Hindu deities, and later built Buddhist altars in the caves, which in time became significant places of pilgrimage. After the death of Ho Chi Minh, marble from the local quarries was used to build his mausoleum. The most visited mountain is **Thuy Son** (water). Tam Thai Pagoda, originally a Cham sanctuary, can be reached via stairs carved into the rock. Under Minh Mang, the pagoda was built on this site in

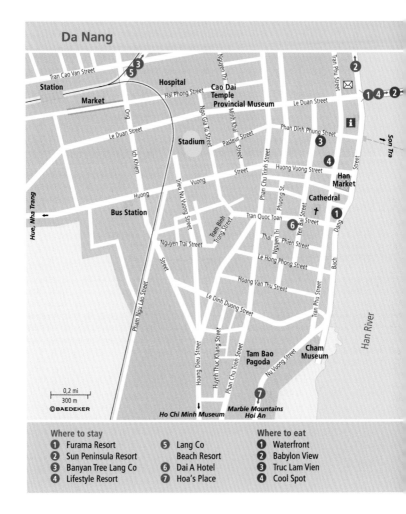

Da Nang

Tran Cao Van Street

Station

Market

Hospital

Nguyen Thi

Hai Phong Street

Cao Dai Temple

Provincial Museum

Le Duan Street

Le Duan Street

Ong

Ich Khiem

Ngo Gia Tu Street

Minh Khai Street

Pasteur Street

Stadium

Tran Phu Street

Phan Dinh Phung Street

Huong Vuong Street

Vuong

Tran Quoc Toan

Street

Tran Phu Street

Son Tra

Phan Chu Trinh Street

Phuong St.

Yen Bai Street

Dang

Han Market

Cathedral †

Hue, Nha Trang

Huong

Bus Station

Trieu Nu Vuong Street

Tam Binh Trong Street

Nguyen Trai Street

Tran Quoc Toan Street

Thai Phien Street

Nguyen Tri

Le Hong Phong Street

Bach

Hoang Van Thu Street

Le Dinh Duong Street

Tran Phu Street

Pham Ngu Lao Street

Han River

Street

Hoang Dieu Street

Huynh Thuc Khang Street

Phan Chu Trinh Street

Nu Vuong Street

Tam Bao Pagoda

Cham Museum

0,2 mi
300 m
©BAEDEKER

Ho Chi Minh Museum

Marble Mountains
Hoi An

Where to stay
1. Furama Resort
2. Sun Peninsula Resort
3. Banyan Tree Lang Co
4. Lifestyle Resort
5. Lang Co Beach Resort
6. Dai A Hotel
7. Hoa's Place

Where to eat
1. Waterfront
2. Babylon View
3. Truc Lam Vien
4. Cool Spot

1825, where statues of the Buddha Sakyamuni (past), the Bodhisattva Quan Am (future and Goddess of Mercy) and Van Thu (wisdom) can be worshipped. Branching off from the main path to the left, a stone arch leads to a grotto, within which stands a very beautiful Quan Am statue. Adjoined to this grotto is **Huyen Khong Cave**. Originally a site of animistic worship, it later became a **Buddhist place of pilgrimage**. To the left, past the Quan Am, comes a dark, somewhat slippery corridor. It takes a while until it becomes possible to make

?

How the Marble Mountains were created

According to legend, a dragon laid an egg on the coast. When it disappeared into the sea the Tortoise God appeared and told an old man to watch over the egg. When the shell broke into five pieces, a nymph came ot of the egg.

out the imposing Buddha statue carved out of the stone at the other end of the enormous hall. Four brightly painted guards watch over the entrance; holes have been broken into the high ceiling, through which shines a diffuse daylight, brilliantly illuminating the Buddha at midday. Around him are a number of altars and sanctuaries honouring Hindu, Buddhist, Taoist and Confucian gods. In addition, there are some wonderful rock formations, which can be interpreted as a stork, or a fish or an elephant. A plaque commemorates the fact that the Vietcong also used this cave as a dugout. From here, a women's unit shot down 19 US planes with only 22 rockets. The nearby vantage point offers a magnificent view of the other mountains, Non Nuoc Beach, the Cham Islands and Monkey Mountain. An elevator now transports those unable or unwilling to climb the mountain.

Insider Tip

❶ Admission: 15,000 VND

Non Nuoc   Only about 500m/550yd from Thuy Son Mountain lies the so-called new China Beach, Non Nuoc Beach, which challenges My Khe for the name and the »fame«. There are already quite a few hotels and restaurants – and further touristic development is underway here, too.

Ocean Cloud   About 30km/19mi north of Da Nang lies Ai Van Son (1176m/3858ft),
Pass (Deo Hai   the first of three peaks of the Truong Son Mountains, which mark Viet-
Van)   nam's »narrow waist« in the middle of the country. This is where the country's weather divide is found. The sun may still be shining on one side while black clouds hover on the other side and the rain lashes down. Over these mountain foothills runs the Hai Van Pass, which means something like »pass of the ocean clouds«. From there, National Highway 1 leads to the pass, at an elevation of 496m/1627ft; a **winding drive** up to the peak then follows, along with some fascinating views. Cyclists and mountain-bikers sweat their way through the challenging ascent, and there are clapped-out old buses that have broken down along the way. The Hai Van Tunnel is probably the longest tunnel in southeast Asia (at 6.3km/3.9mi) and, since 2005, has shortened the journey between Da Nang and Hue by an hour. But it is still possible to take the steep, now pleasantly empty route over the Cloud Pass.

*Lang Co   Driving down the other side of the pass, it gradually gets warmer again, and after a while, the aquamarine glow of Lang Co Lagoon comes into view (approximately 40km/25mi north of Da Nang). A number of huge fishing nets hang over the water from poles. **Oysters** are also farmed in the lagoon, and Vietnamese artists use the mother-of-pearl from them to create their inlays. From between the palms emerges the village of Lang Co, which lies on a small promontory. Remains can still be seen of the bridge which spanned the lagoon until Vietminh destroyed it in 1947. Many travellers make a stop here to get something to eat, or to swim at the nearby beach. Beware of the treacherous current!

Dien Bien Phu

�֎ B 2

Province: Dien Bien (capital)
Region: Northern Mountains
Population: approx. 70,000

The journey to Dien Bien Phu is its own reward. A delightful drive over the mountains leads to the provincial capital near the Laotian border. Despite its remote location, Dien Bien Phu turns out to be a surprisingly large, but not particularly attractive city. A remarkable number of French tourists throng here, for the end of the French colonial era was sealed in Dien Bien Phu.

The small town lies in an 18km/11mi-long and 6–8km/4–5mi-wide high mountain valley, through which flows the Nam Rom River. The region, whose inhabitants live from rice cultivation, is very fertile and densely populated. Mild winters and warm summers are typical of the climate of this **mountain region**. Mainly Thai and Muong people live here, along with some Vietnamese who were encouraged to do so by the government. Although the landscape has been defaced by slash-and-burn land clearance and the damage of war, there are still quite a number of very beautiful spots, particularly at higher elevations.

Fertile and densely populated

Dien Bien Phu was founded in 1841 and was continually the target of foreign invasions. The French developed the strategically located town into an important bastion. After the Second World War, however, with the strengthening of the left in France, public opinion regarding the colonial war in Indochina shifted. Although the **Geneva Conference** was already scheduled for May 1954, the French military continued to secure the plateau around Dien Bien Phu from the air. The position was meant to be invulnerable, with over 16,000 soldiers stationed here, especially the Foreign Legion. Yet the Vietnamese opposition proved to be particularly tenacious. Despite great dif-

History

ficulty, they were able to transport weapons into this difficult-to-access region, and gradually captured the land piece by piece. Both sides suffered thousands of casualties in these battles. On the day before the peace conference, 7 May, after a long siege, the commandant finally gave the order – contrary to the instructions from Paris – to fight to the last man. Victory was attributed to General Vo Nguyen Giap, a legendary figure ever since. This battle spelt the end of the First Indochina War.

WHAT TO SEE IN AND AROUND DIEN BIEN PHU

Museum   Today at the site of the battle is a small museum. Visitors can view charts and photographs that make it possible to grasp the events of the time. Diagonally across from the museum, the **strategic Hill A1** with the bunker can be viewed. A memorial is dedicated to the fallen: between 3000 and 10,000 on the French side and 20,000 and 40,000 on the Vietnamese side. The Cemetery of Dien Bien Phu across from the museum can be entered through a large archway. A white marble wall panel lists the names of the fallen Vietminh. A stairway can be climbed at the entry way, giving a good view onto the seemingly endless rows of graves with the red and black star.

❶ daily: 7am-6pm

Bunker de   Around 1.5km/1mi away, on the way to the airport, lies the bunker
Castries   of the French commandant, Colonel de Castries, who surrendered on

Child playing in a tank on the former battlefield

the afternoon of 7 May 1954. The rooms have been painstakingly restored, whilst old French tanks and artillery may be found nearby.

AROUND DIEN BIEN PHU

110km/68mi northeast of Tuan Chau, on the way from Dien Bien   Tuan Chau
Phu to ▶Hanoi, is a larger market town for the Black Thai and White
Thai of the area. They can be seen in their beautifully worked **traditional clothing**, particularly in the early morning. Those who appreciate this kind of handiwork can find especially nice cloth here.

After another 40km/25mi, at an altitude of 660m/2165ft, comes the   Son La
lofty provincial capital, Son La. Visible from afar, the former French
fortification is home to a small museum today. South of Son La are a
number of hot springs, ideal for bathing and relaxing. A small zoo,
home to, amongst others, bears, porcupines and tortoises, can be visited at the forestry centre (6km/4mi west of Son La).

Further along the way to Hanoi, it is worth stopping in Hoa Binh and   Note
Mai Chau (▶Hanoi, Surroundings).

Dien Bien Phu

INFORMATION
Dien Bien Tourism
7A-7/5 Road,
Tan Thanhm Dien Bien Phu
tel. 023/382 48 41
Also in the hotels

TRANSPORT
Airport: tel. 023/382 49 48,
daily flights from Hanoi: 45 min

SHOPPING
Members of the hill tribes meet at the
daily market to offer their goods, mainly
on the weekends.

WHERE TO EAT
Lien Tuoi Restaurant £
Hoang Van Thai Street on the N 42, approx. 500m north of the army museum
tel. 0230/382 49 19

The only recommendable restaurant in
Dien Bien Phu, menu in English and
French

WHERE TO STAY
Muong Thanh Hotel £
Him Lam (to the east of the roundabout)
tel. 0230/382 67 19
The best hotel in town, with 70 different
rooms in an old and a new building.
Pool, good large restaurant with bar,
many tourist groups.

Him Lam Hotel £
6 Him Lam, Dien Bien Phu
tel. 0230/381 16 66 (-999)
Provincial hotel on a lake, outside the
centre. Some rooms rather dingy (but
with balcony), Wi-Fi included. Loud karaoke evenings sometimes.

DMZ (Demilitarized Zone)

✴ **D 4**

Province: Quang Tri
Region: Northern Central Coast

Nowhere else in Vietnam is it possible to see traces of the war so impressively as in the Demilitarized Zone along the Ben Hai River. Ruins full of holes, bunkers, military cemeteries, memorials, overgrown trenches and a range of rusting junk bear witness to the terrible battles that were once fought here.

The unfittingly named Demilitarized Zone was one of the most bitterly embattled locations of the Vietnam War (▶MARCO POLO Insight p.58). Between 1954 and 1975, the Ben Hai River, directly on the 17th parallel, was deemed the **Line of Demarcation** between North and South Vietnam. The DMZ covered an area of 5km/3mi on either side. This separation into two provisional spheres of influence was a product of the Geneva Conference in 1954. It was created under the proviso that elections would be held in the near future, but this never came to pass. As in Germany, the Line of Demarcation then became a political border between a Communist and a capitalist state.

PLACES TO VISIT IN THE DMZ

The »Street without Joy« is the name by which the 60km/37mi-long section of the N 1 between Hue and Quang Tri is known. During the French colonial era there was especially heavy fighting with the Vietminh in the area, and the French subsequently called the road the »route sans joie«. In 1960 **Bernard Fall**, an American historian, wrote a book named after the street about the First Indochina War. He met his death seven years later, as a war correspondent, exactly here.

The city of **Quang Tri** (59km/37mi north of Hue) was almost totally levelled in 1972, having been captured by North Vietnamese divisions. After a battle lasting four months, South Vietnamese troops and American B-52 bombers left only more rubble. It is said that in 82 days, bombs with **seven times the explosive power of the atom bomb in Hiroshima** were dropped on the 4 sq km/1.5 sq mi city centre. Today there is a memorial, the remains of the once mighty citadel of Emperor Minh Mang with a small war museum, and the ruins of the La Vang Basilica, riddled with bullet holes, which all create an impression of the gravity of the battle for Quang Tri.

HO CHI MINH TRAIL TOUR

Heading west, the journey on the N 9 runs from Dong Ha to Khe Sanh (also Huang Hoa), the site of one of the most infamous battles. Passing through an idyllic landscape of jackfruit trees, pepper plants, tea plantations and caoutchouc fields, visitors reach the battlefield of Cam Lo. A side trip to the north leads to the **Truong Son Cemetery**. Here, there are more than 10,000 gravestones and chapels (with lists of names) dedicated to ten thousand »martyrs« – women and men who lost their lives in the construction, transportation and defence of the Ho Chi Minh Trail. Many of the graves are purely symbolic and

Past battle-fields and bases

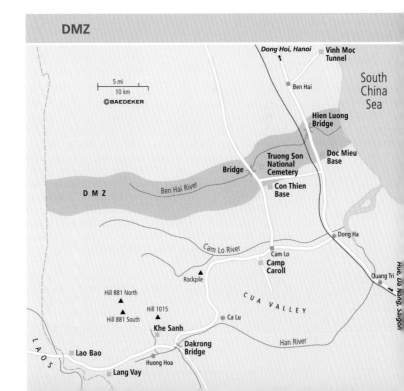

MARCO ⏚ POLO INSIGHT

Ho Chi Minh Trail

According to estimates by American experts, in its heyday some 5000 tons of material were transported on the Ho Chi Minh Trail on foot, by bike, truck etc. to the guerrillas in South Vietnam. This enabled the preparation of the Tet Offensive against the Americans.

empty, as the mortal remains were never found after the inferno. Back on the N 9, turn after 10km/6mi to get to the former **US Base Camp Carroll**, of which little more remains than overgrown trenches with some rusty war machinery lying around. Continue on the N 9, and after crossing the Dau Mau Bridge, it is possible to see the 230m/755ft-high Rock Pile, which was used by the Americans as a sentinel, and was heavily fought. After a further 20km/12mi comes **Dakrong Bridge**, which was rebuilt in 1975–76 with support from Cuba. The Cubans also helped with the repair of the narrow road to Aluoi (15km/9mi southwest), which was part of the legendary **Ho Chi Minh Trail**, a hidden network of routes through the jungle with a total length of 16,000km/9940mi. On these concealed paths, the North Vietnamese army and the Vietcong brought supplies to the guerrillas in the south. The Ho Chi Minh Trail is the best example of how the Vietnamese were able to overcome the supremacy of the US Army during the Vietnam War. The high-tech warfare of the American forces was met with simple means, perfect organization and flexibility. Further south is the legendary Hamburger Hill (Ap Bia Mountain), where one of the heaviest battles took place in May 1969.

HCM Highway

Since the year 2000 work has been underway on the Ho Chi Minh Highway (also Truong Son Highway). With a total length of 3129km/1944mi, this road from Cao Bang on the Chinese border to Ca Mau in the Mekong Delta is meant as an alternative to the N 1, which due to its proximity to the coast is constantly under threat of flooding and typhoons. The project is still a work in progress, costing billions. It includes 314 bridges and also runs through several national parks, following the old, legendary Ho Chi Minh Trail on some stretches. The two-lane section between Khe Co (Ha Tinh province) and Ngoc Hoi (Kontum) is complete – already an extremely attractive scenic route compared to the traffic chaos on the N 1; 350km/215mi of dense jungle and barely a soul await travellers.

Khe Sanh

In early 1968, the mountain fortress of Khe Sanh (65km/40mi west of Dong Ha) was the site of one of the most infamous battles of the Vietnam War. As early as 1967, there was fighting here between US troops and the North Vietnamese infantry, who were posted in the surrounding hills. Around the end of the year, American reconnaissance noticed that tens of thousands of soldiers and masses of weap-

Memorial on the 17th parallel

ons had been transported here. Fearing a second ▶Dien Bien Phu, where the French were devastatingly beaten, General Westmoreland dropped 100,000 tons of explosives, napalm and phosphorus bombs in the area around the base in only a few days – never before had a place been bombed so vehemently. Thousands, if not tens of thousands of Vietnamese died in these clashes; around 400 GIs are said to have died. But what the Americans didn't realize is that Khe San was just a **diversionary tactic** to distract from the real strike, the Tet Offensive. While the military and the media were occupied with Khe San, troops from the North Vietnamese People's Army and the National Liberation Front of South Vietnam were able to capture Hue and Quang Tri and even advance to the US Embassy in Saigon. Today Khe San lies on a barren hill in the middle of an idyllic mountain landscape. Most of all, metal scavengers are a reminder of the events of the war; the contours of the former landing field can be readily identified, as to this day nothing will grow on the ground there. A small museum and a number of bunkers are open to visitors, displaying photos and a guest book including some poignant contributions from American veterans.
❶ daily 7am–5pm

Turn eastwards near Ho Xa and after 13km/8mi comes a former supply depot and hideout. The Vinh Moc tunnels were very similar to those at ▶Cu Chi, as they originated when families dug shelters near their villages in order to shelter themselves from the bombing raids. Later, the Vietcong took over the approximately 3km/2mi-long tunnel system to use as a base. A small museum shows the living conditions at the time. Many visitors find these tunnels more authentic than those at Cu Chi.
❶ daily 7am–5pm, admission approx. 25,000 VND

Vinh Moc tunnels

Dong Hoi

 D 4

Province: Quang Binh (capital)
Region: Northern Central Coast
Population: Approx. 130,000

This constantly growing port city on the Nhat Le River is the best base for a visit to the UNESCO-listed caves of Phong Nha. In the north and south of the city, beautiful beaches beckon with new and attractive hotel complexes. It is only 40km/25mi over the Truong Son Mountains to Laos.

✷✷ PHONG NHA - KE BANG NATIONAL PARK

Due to its mile-long passageways full of stalactites and stalagmites, the Phong Nha Cave, around 50km/31mi northwest of Dong Hoi, was added to the list of **UNESCO World (Natural) Heritage Sites** in 2003. In the 9th and 10th centuries, the Cham considered it to be an important shrine; inscriptions and remains of altars can be recognized in the grottoes. The 1.5km/1mi-long main path leads through 15 grottoes inside the cave, and can be seen either on foot or by boat on the underground river. The part of the cave explored so far is around 19km/12mi in extent. Around 85 mammalian species live in the **Ke Bang National Park** adjoined to the cave complex (e.g. a total of ten ape species, some indigenous, including langurs and gibbons, of which four species are in danger of extinction).

❶ daily 7am-4pm, may be closed in November and December if the caves are flooded. Admission: both caves approx. 160,000 VND (i.e. 120,000 VND and the Dark Cave (Hang Toi): 40,000 VND extra (plus boat or kayak rental: approx. 100,000 VND pp or 320,000 VND per boat, remember to take bathing gear).

*Paradise Cave (Thien Duong) The breathtaking and 31km/19mi long Paradise Cave (Thien Duong) was only discovered in 2005 by a local inhabitant and also belongs to the Phong Nha – Ke Bang National Park. Thus far, it has resisted commercialization and is less overwhelmed by throngs of tourists than the larger main cave of Phong Na at Son Trach (where domestic groups of up to 100 are common, accompanied by constantly flashing cameras). The Paradise entrance is hidden away in a narrow, jungle-like valley. First there are 524 steps to be climbed before descending a further 200 steps into the abyss. A well-lit walkway, roughly 1km/ half a mile long, leads through this mysterious, stark world of stalagmites and stalactites. Those who choose to book a more challenging caving tour (approx. US$130) can crawl and climb their way through

Dong Hoi

INFORMATION
Quang Binh Tourism
Quang Binh Tourism
1 Me Suot Street, Dong Hoi
tel. 052/382 20 18
www.quangbinhtourism.vn

TRANSPORT
Dong Hoi Airport
in Loc Ninh,
approx. 6km/4mi outside Dong Hoi
tel. 052/381 08 78
Several flights a week to Hanoi and
Saigon

WHERE TO EAT
Opposite the Huu Nghi Hotel on Quach
Xuan Ky, beer gardens and food stalls
open in the evening.
A number of inexpensive restaurants
can be found close to the market at the
end of Quach Xuan Ky (the southern
extension of Truong Phao, which leads
northwards to Nhat Le Beach and the
mouth of the river).

Anh Dao £
Tieu Khu 4
Hai Dinh Ward
Dong Hoi
(near the N1 at the bus station in the
southwest)
tel. 052/382 22 34
Vietnamese dishes and some snacks

WHERE TO STAY
Saigon Quang Binh Hotel ££
20 Kach Xuan Ky, Dong Hoi
tel. 052/382 22 76
www.sgquangbinhtourist.com.vn
Pleasant business hotel in a nice spot
(alongside the market on the river promenade). 95 tidy rooms (if a little overpriced) with river views from the balcony
and Wi-Fi. There is also a pool in the
garden and a tennis court.

Sun Spa Resort ££
My Canh Beach
Bao Ninh
tel. 052/384 29 99
www.sunsparesortvietnam.com
Marvellous beach complex with 234
comfortable rooms with balconies
around a gigantic pool. Watersports
(jet skis!), spa with massage pavilion
on the beach, whirlpool and tennis
court.

Luxe Hotel £
Truong Phap, Dong Hoi
tel. 052/384 59 59
www.luxehotel.vn
Seven-storey mini hotel on the Nhat Le
River: 29 especially good rooms with all
mod cons. Moonlight restaurant and sky
bar on the rooftop terrace.

Phong Nha Farmstay £
Cu Nam
(35km/22mi northwest of Dong Hoi)
tel. 52/367 51 35
Mobile tel. 094/475 98 64
http://phong-nha-cave.com
The Farmstay created by Australian Ben
and his wife Bich is a small and friendly
oasis with extended family and pool at
the heart of the paddy fields. Ten rooms,
no air conditioning, one dormitory. Book
well in advance!
Caving tours to the Phong Nha Cave
(rather expensive) are also on offer,
along with motorbike / Jeep excursions
to the old Ho Chi Minh Trail.

another 6km/4mi or so of narrow passages and muddy streams, kitted out with headlamps and sturdy footwear, of course! It goes without saying that the shiny dripstones are not to be touched, as this would impede the growth of these natural wonders.

The Phong Nha cave in Son Trach is some 45km/28mi from Dong Hoi, the Paradise Cave another 25km/15mi – it is possible to explore both on the same day. Between the two lies the Nooc Mooc Spring Eco Trail, following the river at times over bamboo bridges.

Trail: admission 50,000 VND;

Paradise Cave: admission 120,000 VND incl. guide. Restaurants on site.

✱✱ Dry Ha Long Bay

✦ C/D 2

Region: Red River Delta
Population: approx. 53,000

The fairytale landscape of Tam Coc is anything but dry. Like dark guardsmen, karst mountains and rocky outcrops watch over the charming region around the provincial capital of Ninh Binh and the village of Tam Coc. They rise up from the paddy fields and are only described as dry because they do not stand directly in the sea, in contrast to their geological cousins further north in Ha Long Bay.

Tam Coc   Boats depart from a landing stage at Tam Coc into the incomparable landscape. They make their way past high cliffs and paddy fields before finally gliding into the dark world of the **Three Grottoes** (Tam Coc, 2-3 hours), sadly no longer alone, as word of the area's beauty has travelled. At times it resembles an Asian fairground, complete with hordes of hawkers, rowing boat convoys on the riger and a queue in front of the caves. There may even be amusing »water battles« among youths. Boat, horse and carriage or bicycle are the main means of transport for tourist explorers from Hanoi and the world.

It can get really cold in winter, but then it is also less busy, which is also true of weekdays. For those who find Tam Coc too much of a tourist village, Trang (also pretty, many caves, temple) and the Van Long Nature Reserve (▶ p.226) provide alternatives.

Just 2.5km/1.5mi from the jetty stands **Bich Dong Pagoda**, hewn into the rock of the cliff on two levels. At its foot lies the

MARCO ⊕ POLO TIP

!

Pack sunscreen!   Insider Tip

Sunlovers take note as well: a sun hat or parasol is an essential accessory on a boat trip through Dry Ha Long Bay, as the sun beats down mercilessly between the limestone mountains.

main hall, whilst a second room higher up contains some wooden statues of Buddha. Steep steps lead up to the Green Grotto with the three Buddhas of the Past, Present and Future, as well as representations of the Goddess of Mercy (Quan Am). The sound of the bells and the aroma of incense in the temple transport visitors into the spiritual world of Buddhism. From the summit of the mountain, unparalleled views of the Dry Ha Long Bay may be savoured.

HOA LU

At the heart of Dry Ha Long Bay is Hoa Lu, once the capital of imperial Vietnam. Idyllic minor roads lead the way there, across dams between paddy fields, past lotus and palm trees and via overgrown, green limestone rocks – a fine journey to undertake by bicycle. After the yoke of Chinese central government had been cast off in the year 939, the country initially fragmented into a mass of small principalities. In the year 968, the Governor Dinh Bo Linh shifted the capital from Co Loa to his home town of Hoa Lu, which was better protected against possible attacks by the Chinese, due to its »hidden« location at the heart of the limestone mountains and karst cliffs. As Emperor Dinh Tien Hoang he seized power and established his royal household in Hoa Lu. During two short-lived dynasties, Hoa Lu maintained its

Relics of an ancient imperial capital

Wooded karst hills rise up from the paddy fields

Dry Ha Long Bay

INFORMATION
Ninh Binh Tourist
Dinh Tien Hoang, Dong Thanh district,
Ninh Binh City
tel. 030/384 41 01
www.dulichninhbinh.com.vn/en/

Boat Trips
in Tam Coc/Van Long/Trang An:
Tickets: 40,000 –
100,000 VND per person   *Insider Tip*
Rowing boats: for up to four persons,
approx. 100,000 VND per person for a
90 minute to 3 hour tour along the river
and to various caves (bamboo boats at
the Van Long Nature Reserve and metal
ones in Tam Coc. The tours from Tam
Coc and Trang An are spectacular, taking
in caves and temple grottoes, but tend
to be busier. From Van Long, the chance
of seeing rare animals, langurs, kingfish-
ers, is greater. Tour buses arrive here
from 10am onwards.

SHOPPING
Several handicrafts villages await customers: Van Lan close to Tam Coc offers
embroidered goods such as tablecloths
and serviettes.

WHERE TO EAT
On Le Hong Phong in Ninh Binh City
(before the bridge over the River Van)
al fresco establishments serve fresh Vietnamese beer on draught and light
snacks.

The Emeralda Resort is close to a number of cultural site worth seeing

Trung Tuyet £
14 Hoang Hoa Tham, close to the railway station, Ninh Binh City
no telephone
A small family restaurant serving flavourful Vietnamese fare, even vegetarian and tofu dishes.

WHERE TO STAY
Emeralda Ninh Binh £££££–££

Van Long Reserve, Gia Van
Ninh Binh province
tel. 030/365 83 33
www.emeraldaresort.com
Luxury hotel and oasis of the highest order. The Emeralda resembles a temple site, with brick monastic buildings, some in the shadow of swaying palms, in a beautiful landscape between paddy fields. The rustic, ancient feel to the place is complemented by much use of wood, terracotta and brass. Some rooms have a private pool. Two expensive restaurants, one of which serves organic food, a wine bar, spa and two pools, the indoor one is heated. A bargain during the off-season, with online discounts of up to 40%. The Van Long jetty is roughly 500m/1640ft from here.

Cuc Phuong Resort & Spa £££££ – ££
Dong Tam, Ninh Binh province (approx. 7km/4mi from the entrance to the Cuc Phuong National Park)
tel. 030/384 88 88
Rustic double bungalows with wooden bathtub in the room (flatscreen TV), two pools (one indoors with heated spring water), predominantly Vietnamese guests. It can get a little cold in winter. Prices double at weekends! Golf course.

New Queen Mini Hotel £
(not to be confused with the Queen Hotel!)
256 Ngo Gia Tu
(100m/110yd from the railway station)
Ninh Binh City
tel. 030/389 31 18 and
091/258 02 95
queenminihotel@gmail.com
Family hotel run by three siblings with the charm of a western youth hostel: typical backpacker haunt with dormitory and pleasantly cheap rooms. Not the best place to rent a moped (or check their condition thoroughly), earplugs a boon due to the proximity of the station.

Thuy Anh Hotel £
55 A Truong Han Sieu
Ninh Binh City
tel. 030/387 16 02
www.thuyanhhotel.com
Modern hotel in town with friendly staff and 37 bright, reasonable rooms. Bar on the 5th floor, rooftop restaurant on the 7th floor. Travel agency. Car and bicycle hire. Small eatery next door: Thao Son Tuu (the menu features rather amusing »translations«).

The Long Hotel £
Tam Coc
(approx. 10km/6mi west of Ninh Binh)
tel. 030/359 55 95
This little hotel stands right on the jetty and car park at Tam Coc, offering small, air-conditioned rooms with communal terraces. The views are no longer quite so open, but the karst hills can still be seen (ideally from the 5th floor of the newer adjacent building). Large restaurant, popular with groups.

new status. In 1009 the rulers of the Ly dynasty seized power and relocated the capital to Thang Long (Hanoi). Not a great deal remains of the old capital's Citadel, which housed its temples, shrines and the emperor's seat of government. **Two temples** have survived, however, to serve as a reminder of the two main rulers of Hoa Lu. The Bai Dinh Pagoda is a must for temple fans – 700 hectares/2.7 sq mi amount to the largest temple complex in Vietnam: the Bai Dinh Spiritual and Cultural Complex. The old Bai Dinh Pagoda, under a conservation order, can look back on around one thousand years of history. It is situated in a copse on the slopes of Dinh Mountain, along with numerous atmospheric shrines in the temple grottoes. Since 2003 hundreds of construction workers and artisans from the area have been involved in extending the monastery (work is expected to continue into 2015 at least). The eleven-storey pagoda tower can be seen from afar across the paddy fields – a touch of gigantism in a remote province. Entering through a vast temple gate, a covered staircase of some 300 steps, flanked by 500 outsized, incredibly lifelike Arhat monks (all in different poses) sculpted in marble, leads up to the vast area containing the main pagoda on the summit. From here, the 360° panorama over the temple rooftops is magnificent. The spacious grounds feature four impressive temple buildings with valuable woodcarvings, lacquer work and sweeping three-pointed roofs reaching heavenwards. They are dedicated to the Sakyamuni Buddha, Avalokitesvara Bodhisattva and Quan Am – the 16m/52ft high bronze statue of Sakyamuni, the largest in the land, is believed to weigh 100 tons. There must be thousands of Buddha statues here – in different sizes, materials and colours. Further attractions include the bells, weighing in at 36 tons, and the bronze drums in the bell tower. The place is almost deserted in the afternoons, but busy and crowded on holidays. .

Insider Tip

❶ Gia Sinh, Gia Vien District (approx. 20 km/12 mi northwest of ninh binh, 95 km/59 mi south of Hanoi), daily 8am-5pm. Combine a visit with an excursion to Hoa Lu

Den Dinh Tien Hoang

Dinh Temple (11th century) was erected in honour of Emperor Dinh Tien Hoang. The room to the front is adorned with beautiful carvings and inscriptions celebrating the glory of the king. In the hall behind this room stands one of the oldest statues of a Vietnamese ruler. It represents Dinh Tien Hoang, accompanied by his three sons: the eldest son, Dinh Lien, is on his left, whilst the two younger sons, Hang Lang and Dinh Tue, are on his right.

Le Dai Hanh Temple

Le Dai Hanh Temple is very similar to the neighbouring Den Dinh, although of a more simple design. It is around 600 years younger and was built in honour of Le Dai Hanh, the first emperor of the early Le dynasty. Statues of the emperor and his wife Duong Van Nga, who had already been married to his predecessor Dinh Tien Hoang, can be found in the hall to the rear of the temple. Alongside stands the statue of his son Le Ngoa Trieu, who became emperor in the year 1005 whilst his father was still alive. The tombs of both rulers can be found behind the temples at Ma Yen Mountain: Le Dai Hanh's tomb is the lower of the two, with that of Dinh Tien Hoang on the knoll. From the top, there is a splendid view of the landscape of Dry Ha Long Bay.

CUC PHUONG NATIONAL PARK

❶ daily 8am-6pm; admission (with guide for the Primate Center and Turtle Conservation Center): approx. 70,000 VND, tel. 030/84 80 02/06, dulichcucphuong@hn.vnn.vn, www.primatecenter.org

Cuc Phuong National Park (25,000ha/61,775ac) is situated in the far northwest of Ninh Binh province (approx. 50km/31mi from Ninh Binh City, approx. 120km/87mi, 3 hours ride, from Hanoi). Established in 1962, it is the oldest national park in Vietnam. The region boasts impressive karst mountains and **primary forest**, one of the last surviving in North Vietnam. Some of the giant trees, up to 50m/164ft high, with buttress roots as tall as a man, are centuries old, forming a dense roof of leaves which allows little light to penetrate through to the climbing plants and moss on the forest floor (one of the colossi has a circumference of a phenomenal 25m/82ft).

Vietnam's oldest national park

The park is a lovely place to wander and, with luck, see one or two animals

MARCO ● POLO TIP

Hiking in the National Park ^{Insider Tip}

Well-signposted hiking trails lead to the attractions that have been made accessible (max. 18km/ 10mi). The excursions take one to four days (overnight stays in a Muong village). Wild cats can be seen on a night time hike with a little luck. Bikes can be rented too. Some of the guides speak English. The best time to visit is October to December and March/ April. Anyone looking for peace and quiet should stay away on weekends, Vietnamese holidays and school holidays.
For more information see tourism.com.vn.

The national park is home to over 2000 species of tree alone and a wealth of fauna, 125 varieties of mammal (including clouded leopard and Asian black bear), 110 species of reptile and amphibian and more than 300 bird species. Delacour's langur, endemic to Vietnam, is a rare breed of ape which was rediscovered in the national park in 1987, having previously been considered extinct. To aid their conservation, in 1993 the **Endangered Primate Rescue Center** (www.primatecenter.org) was opened, a nonprofit organization in which some 140 animals live in 15 groups, subsequently to be released into the wild (including six unique to this institution, namely the greyshanked douc). Visitors can »adopt« a primate and/or get involved as volunteers. Almost wiped out in the wild, the Vietnamese sika deer (axis deer) are kept in enclosures. Other residents of the Cuc Phuong National Park include the Asian black bear, clouded and common leopard, serow and muntjac – although these are not likely to be spotted on a tourist excursion. Countless butterflies can be seen, however, especially in April/May. There are many caves, such as the Nguoi Xua, inside the karst mountains, which are up to 600m/1960ft high. Prehistoric stone tools, bone remnants and ceramics at least 7000 years old have been discovered in the grottoes. Sadly, there are repeated incidents of poaching and illegal felling in the national park. The onrush of some 80,000 tourists each year (mostly Vietnamese) also has adverse effects on the park and its ecological balance: the access road has been tarmacked and an artificial lake created with hotels and bungalows, some comfortable (US$14-27), a campsite and restaurant. Moreover, the new N 2 (the so-called Ho Chi Minh Highway, a second connecting route between Hanoi and Saigon) in the valley of the Buoi River cuts right through the national park.

∗ KEO PAGODA

Traditionally carved wooden building
Standing on the bank of a lake, in the shade of trees, is the Buddhist Keo Pagoda (approx. 50km/31mi east of Ninh Binh), a remarkable example of traditional Vietnamese timber construction and wood

carving. It was established in the 12th century and dedicated to the monk Khong Minh Khong, who cured Emperor Ly Than Tho of leprosy. Under the rulers of the Ly dynasty (11th and 12th centuries) Buddhism received its greatest support from the state. As this waned, many of the temples fell into disrepair, as did the original buildings of Keo Pagoda. It was only in the 16th and 17th centuries that Buddhism experienced a renaissance, and most of the buildings of the Keo Pagoda complex visible today date back to this era. At the same time, a new architectural style emerged, which became known as **Tam Quan** (named after the entrance portal with its three wings) and also found favour in China. This is a 17th-century original, adorned with carved clouds, suns and dragons.

The bell tower is a masterpiece of Vietnamese carving

The temple site: the low-lying roof of the vestibule gives the room the impression of being very wide and squat; statues of guards and the Earth God can be seen here. The central hall is almost square and features altars for sacrificial offerings and incense sticks. Finally, the main hall is broad in appearance, a **pantheon** with Buddhas and Bodhisattvas. Almost all of the statues date from the 19th century, with the exception of the Goddess of Mercy, a 17th-century figure.

Minh Khong

Keo Pagoda departs from the usual trinity of structures, with an additional hall behind the main one dedicated to the monk Minh Khong. His sanctuary is only opened for the temple festival (see below). The final structure on the north-south axis is a three-storey bell tower with two bronze bells dating back to 1687 and 1796. The columns and beams display a fantastic variety of unique. The heavy construction is supported by massive pillars.

Temple festival

Every three years, on the 15th day of the 9th lunar month, a widely-renowned **temple festival** is staged. **Boat races** form a part of the festivities. The boats are stored in the courtyard's covered galleries.

FURTHER PLACES TO VISIT IN THE REGION

Van Long Nature Reserve An **idyllic boat trip** through the reeds of the canals of Van Long Nature Reserve (approx. 23km/14mi northwest of Ninh Binh) offers the opportunity to glide between the limestone mountains, listening to birdsong as the boatsmen stand and punt their vessels through green waters. Vietnam's last great population of Delacour's langurs lives here and, with luck, they may be spotted (the chances are higher in the early morning or late evening, when the tourist groups have left).

Phat Diem / Kim Son The area to the south of Ninh Binh was traditionally a bastion of Catholicism in Vietnam. Although over 100,000 Christians fled to South Vietnam when the Communists seized power in 1954, around half of the inhabitants today are still Catholic, as demonstrated by the fact that almost every community has a church, the spires rising between the paddy fields. *Phat Diem cathedral (28km/17mi south of Ninh Binh) is particularly impressive. Having been badly destroyed in the war, it was reconstructed thereafter. It was built in the 1880s and 1890s under the guidance of the Vietnamese priest Tran Luc, also known by the name Père Six, whose grave can be found in the courtyard between the nave and bell tower. In 1933, the **first Vietnamese Bishop** was ordained here. The persecution of the Catholics (1954–75) led to the arrest of the priests and closure of the seminary, yet as a result of the Doi Moi policy, the situation grew more relaxed in the mid-1980s. Today, the imposing complex of buildings is again the centre of Catholicism in Vietnam. The complex consists of several buildings which unify eastern and western styles of construction, as well as featuring both Buddhist and Christian elements.

Hence the free-standing bell tower, which plays a role in a war scene in Graham Greene's *The Quiet American*, not only contains a huge bell, but also a Buddhist drum. Statues of the Four Evangelists surround the bell tower. Alongside, two large stone slabs served as seats for the mandarins of the region from which to observe the church services. Perhaps this was their way of dismantling reservations with regard to Christianity. The interior is dominated by gold lacquered ironwood columns and a number of altars. Most impressive of all is the **high altar at the back**, fashioned from a single block of granite. Representations of six martyrs serve as a reminder of the persecution of Christians during the Nguyen dynasty in the 19th century. Alongside the main building are several small chapels – the most spectacular being that of St Peter, with splendid carvings – and behind them three artificial caves and another bell tower. Living accommodation and seminary buildings for the aspiring priests completing their training here stand among the gardens.

● daily 7.30am–11.30am, 2.30pm-5pm; services Mon-Fri 5am and 5pm, Sat/Sun 5am, 10am and 4pm

At the excavation site of **Dong Son**, some 8km/5mi northwest of Thanh Hoa (50km/31mi south of Ninh Binh), **bronze ritual drum**s were unearthed, thereby lending their name to the Dong Son culture (8th–13th centuries). Some fine examples can be inspected in the history museums of Saigon and Hanoi. The meaning of the stellar inscriptions in the centre of the drum skin remains a mystery until today. Images of ships and seabirds on the bronze drums suggest that their owners travelled overseas from the Malayan-Indonesian islands and intermingled with the Sino-Tibetan inhabitants of North Vietnam. As

One of the finest collections of Dong Son drums (History Museum, Hanoi)

well as these unique relics, other items found at the dig included axes, daggers and belt buckles. Dong Son culture is now perceived as the **cradle of Vietnamese civilization**. It stretched across the Song Ma and Song Hong regions and, for the Vietnamese, is on a level with the mythological Hung kings (▶Hung Temple p.274) and their kingdom of Van Lang.

The rest of the Ho dynasty citadel was granted UNESCO World Heritage Site status in 2011. The former imperial city was only briefly Vietnam's capital – then called Dai Ngu – from 1398-1407, one of the shortest periods of rule in Vietnam's chequered history. The Tay Do stands close to the banks of the Ma River near what is now the town of Thanh Hoa. It was completed in 1397 using heavy sandstone blocks to an almost square plan according to feng shui and geomantic principles – a symbol of so-called Neo-Confucianism. The impressive gates can still be seen today, such as the 10m/32ft high South Gate with three passageways, the buttress arch of the East Gate, remnants of the stone »Dragon Gate« within the open grounds between paddy fields and perimeter walls, each roughly 800m/2624ft in length, having held fast for six centuries.
❶ Tai Giai village, Vinh Loc, admission: approx. 10,000 VND

Tay Do fortress

The white sandy beaches of Sam Son (16km/10mi southeast of Thanh Hoa) are some of North Vietnam's finest places to bathe. The French held these beaches in high regard, building their colonial villas here. Subsequently, an increasing number of tourists found their way here from the countries of the Eastern Bloc. Today, there are many west-

Sam Son

ern visitors here as well. Sam Son is also a favourite destination of the wealthy Hanoi crowd. The range of accommodation on offer is suitably broad, from old French colonial villas to hotel blocks dating back to the socialist era and on to modern bungalows.

Kim Lien   The village of Kim Lien, where Ho Chi Minh grew up as a child, lies a mere 14km/8.5mi northwest of Vinh. He was born on 19 May 1890 in Hoang Tru, just 1km/0.6mi away, where his mother came from. After his family moved out, the simple house increasingly fell into disrepair. In 1955, however, the villagers began to rebuild it and today the attractive renovated home is open to visitors, with writing desk, books and toys which belonged to little Ho. Nearby, a museum has photographs of Ho Chi Minh's many travels on display.

✶✶   Ha Long Bay

✦ **D 2**

Region: North
Area: 1500 sq km/580 sq mi

This is a landscape in which legends come true: the approximately 2000 islands of Ha Long Bay inspire the imagination of every visitor, who might expect to come across dragons, sleeping giants or a caravan of camels here. The magnificent scenery of wildly overrun limestone mountains, where junks with rose-red sails float by, was created over the course of millions of years.

In recent years, the UNESCO World Heritage Site has been inundated by tourists – sadly with all the negative side effects. Between six and seven million sightseers per year (in 2012 alone) and 400 boats leave their mark, so visitors who spend the night in the erstwhile isolated bay at the common anchoring ground are no longer safe from off-kilter karaoke singing and the thrum of diesel engines.

Formation   Ha Long means »descending dragon«, in contrast to Than Long (»ascending dragon«), the old name of the capital, Hanoi. As the **first legend** would have it, aeons ago a huge dragon came down from the mountains into the valley, in order to assist the Vietnamese in the fight against their enemies. He furiously smashed around with his tail, and in doing so, split the mountains and cut huge notches and valleys into the landscape. When he finally disappeared into the sea, he displaced so much water that the land was flooded, leaving only the steep crags jutting out. A **second legend** tells of the heavenly dragon mother and her children, who lived here and protected the

Dreamy landscape for holidaymakers on Titop Island beach. Junks and pleasure boats float between the limestone collossi

fishermen. When one day pirates attacked the bay and its inhabitants, the dragons spat fire at the invaders. The fireballs fell back into the sea as grey clumps of ash, and so created the jagged islands of rock that stand today. Exhausted, the baby dragons lay down in the easterly Bai Tu Long Bay, which is therefore named after them.

** PLACES TO VISIT IN HA LONG BAY

Most tourists begin their exploration of the spectacular Ha Long Bay in Ha Long City (population 40,000) – previously two idyllic fishing villages, today an emerging holiday destination with an amusement centre (including an overpriced water-puppet show), dolphin shows, casino, luxury resorts and dingy karaoke bars. In the **Bai Chay district** to the west lies the pier for the approximately 400 tourist boats, barges, junks and paddle-steamers that navigate Ha Long Bay. Among the boats are some real eye-catchers with bright red ribbed sails and

Ha Long City

Lighting effects in the Hang Sung Sot »Cave of Surprises«

temple-like superstructures on the upper deck (e.g. the Annam Junk, www.annamjunk.com; the Huong Hai Junk, www.huonghaicruise.com; or the Jewel of the Bay). The two districts of Ha Long City, the more tourist-oriented Bai Chay with its hulking hotels towering into the sky and **Hon Gai** with its coal-loading harbour, were only recently joined by a bridge. Neither district is particularly well suited to bathing, even though Bai Chay recently received a light sandy beach and the sun chairs with colourful umbrellas stand in rank and file on the promenade – the water here is not especially appealing.

Limestone giants
Instead, Ha Long Bay and Lan Ha Bay have earned a reputation as Vietnam's favourite climbing destinations – not so surprising, considering the magnificent views from the limestone giants and great fun may be had deep water soloing here.

Canoe trip
In a canoe, it is possible to paddle into a number of the caves through their small entrances and explore the emerald-green lagoons behind (e.g. in Hang Luon). Alternatively, row over to the **floating fishing villages**, e.g. Van Gia, where even the school floats. Sometimes there is an opportunity for a chat with the villagers and an invitation for tea on the veranda of a rickety little floating house. Most inhabitants live from fishing and fish farming: beneath the planks of the veranda, the

fish flap noisily in their cages when the lady of the house feeds them – with leftover food and fellow members of their own species, finely chopped.

The excursion boats chug past the magnificently green oversized limestone giants, many of which take their name from the similarity of their characteristic form to animals (tortoise, elephant, buffalo), or have simple names such as »nose«, because the island resembles the human profile. It is not only the limestone rocks leave plenty to the imagination; so too do the **stalactites and stalagmites** in the caves, which can be interpreted as fairies, ghosts and goblins. It is possible to be dropped off on some of the islands to view one of the many caves there. **Hang Dau Go,** the »Grotto of Wooden Stakes« on the French-named Ile des Merveilles takes its name from the bamboo stakes that aided the commander Tran Hung Dao in sinking the Mongolian fleet (▶p.50) at the **Battle of Bach Dang** in 1288. Some of them are preserved in a dripstone cave which is reachable by way of 90 steps and consists of three domes, one behind the other.

**Journey through the wondrous limestone scenery

! *Sleeping on the water*   Insider Tip

MARCO ⊕ POLO TIP

A night on board a boat is the ultimate experience, offering the chance to enjoy the light playing on the striking rocky islands without having to contend with masses of tourists. In the evening the scenery is bathed in a soft pink light, and later on the moonlight illuminates the limestone giants surrounding the boat like ghostly sentinels.

From the ***Hang Thien Cung** (Thien Cung Cave), a very pretty cave full of unusual stalagmites and stalactites, from which there is a good view of the calm bay, strewn with small islands and jagged coral reefs. Colourful light reflections enhance the wondrous impression.

In the **Hang Trinh Nu** (Trinh Nu Cave) all kinds of interestingly formed dripstones are to be seen. Some of them are said to resemble the face of a young girl, and as the story goes, a Mandarin kidnapped a young maiden from a poor fisher family and made her his mistress. Because any attempt to flee would put her family in danger, the maiden decided to end her own life. Since then, the isle has been known as the **Virgin Island**. After ***Hang Dong Tien/ Dong Me Cung** squeezing through the sometimes narrow corridors of the Hang Dong Tien/Done Me Cung caves, there comes a larger hall full of stalagmites and stalactites from which a path leads into the open. Suddenly a wonderfully calm, turquoise-blue sea appears, surrounded by a few shrubs and bushes. The little visited Me Cung Cave is just as enchanting. The **Hang Sung Sot** is effectively illuminated with electric light, which is not actually necessary. The vault is massive, and even entire tourist groups can spread out within the three extremely impressive rooms. The circular path reveals almost mystical views of the dripstone in the shimmering haze.

Ha Long Bay

INFORMATION
Tourist Service Center
Tourist Service Center
Bai Chay Pier (new tourist pier)
Ha Long City
tel. 033/384 74 81
www.halong.org.vn

TRANSPORT
Getting there: travel to Ha Long City by tourist bus or public bus (approx. 3½ hours), train or ferry from Hai Phong (or by hydrofoil from China); Cat Ba Island and Bai Tu Long Bay served by (fast) boats from Hai Phong or (tourist) boats from Ha Long City (Hong Gai).
In Ha Long City: bicycle, moped or taxi.

EXCURSIONS
Tickets and boats for trips on the bay and to Cat Ba Island can be found at the new tourist pier (from around £20 per boat per day, depending on the type of boat). Ha Long tours also start out from Cat Ba.
Those travelling on their own should steer clear of the characters on the pier, street and beach touting extremely cheap excursions around Ha Long Bay. This is not money well spent, even if the price seems attractive. Tours including transportation, overnight stay and refreshments on a boat can be booked in the Tourist Information Travel Center in the old town of Hanoi (approx. US$35)

Boat trip to explore the caves

– there is the risk of ending up in an overcrowded, barely seaworthy vessel with poor food and unfriendly guides, but there is also a chance that one is virtually alone on board. If an overnight stay is part of the plan, it is advised to book with the more renowned operators, whose 2 day tours begin at around US$100 (e.g. Indochina Junk: www.in-dochina-junk.com).
Access to the caves costs extra: 40,000VND

SHOPPING

Night market in Bai Chay (Ha Long City, daily 6pm-11pm): wander amongst the souvenir stalls between the esplanade and beach, where chopsticks, bathing costumes, shoes, toys and bric-a-brac are piled up high and a little funfair magically attracts children.
Gold Hand Silk (Ha Long Road, Bai Chay): boutique on the promenade with stylish silk dresses and shirts, pillowcases, ties, embroidered bags.
Hong Ngoc Humanity Center *Insider Tip* (halfway between Hanoi and Ha Long City, Sao Dao, Hai Duong, tel. 0320/388 29 11): a huge handicrafts centre offering shoes, ties and silk garments, tea sets, vases, jewellery, sculptures, books, paintings etc. Customers can wait in the cafeteria for half an hour or so for smaller made-to-measure goods. Decent quality, but still worth haggling a little over the price. Proceeds go to an educational project for the disabled.

ENTERTAINMENT
Ever tried karaoke?
In all of Ha Long City, karaoke is the definitive form of entertainment of an evening, and has been for years. Everyone should have a go at this typically Asian amusement at least once. There are karaoke machines in all mini hotels and the huge, open-air restaurants on the promenade – join in the fun …

Trung Nguyen £
Ha Long Road, Bai Chay, Ha Long City
tel. 033/384 43 38
daily 10am–11pm
Vietnamese coffeehouse chain, whose outdoor patio restaurants on the promenade are meeting places for well-heeled young people and tourists: fairy lights, disco music, fruit juices, beer, whisky, ice cream and iced coffee, snacks.

Blue Note £
Nui Ngoc Street, Cat Ba City
(cross street behind the post office and Sunflower Hotel)
tel. 031/388 89 67
daily 5pm–2am
Small bar with dirt cheap, really good cocktails, beer and other alcoholic beverages.

Flightless Bird £
Promenade, Cat Ba City
tel. 031/388 85 17
Daily 6pm-open end
Nice micro bar on two floors with games, darts, newspapers and books – run by a New Zealander.

WHERE TO EAT
Green Mango ££
1/4 Road (near the Holiday View Hotel on the eastern promenade), Cat Ba City
tel. 031/388 71 51
daily 6.30am-open end
Modern restaurant and bar with »fusion« food: variations on tapas and salads, vegetarian and seafood dishes, Vi-

etnamese classics and pasta, as well as sweets.

Kim Hang Restaurant £–££
Ha Long Road, Bai Chay (approx. 4km/2.5mi outside Ha Long City)
tel. 033/384 68 09
https://www.facebook.com/pages/Kim-Do-Restaurant/319808461394929
daily noon-10pm
A five-storey building with a restaurant on each floor. **Insider Tip** Excellent Vietnamese cuisine at bargain prices. Speciality of the house is a delicious seafood menu selection with crab, fish filet, prawns and fried squid.

Phuong Oanh Restaurant £
Bai Chay (opposite the post office and Thong Nhat Hotel)
tel. 033/384 61 45
daily 6am-10pm
Small restaurant with good Vietnamese food (rare, English menu with prices!), lots of seafood, also breakfast.

Asia Restaurant £
Vuon Dao (up aboe the promenade, Ha Long City
tel. 033/384 69 27
Simple, universally popular mini restaurant serving Vietnamese fare (tasty seafood in particular). A few western dishes as well.

Duc Tuan £
Promenade (roughly halfway along)
Cat Ba City
tel. 031/388 87 83
daily 6am-11pm
Vietnamese restaurant with a sunset balcony on the first floor, large selection of seafood, chicken and pork dishes, hotpots and breakfasts. There are also several large dormitories with panoramic views of the harbour (£).

WHERE TO STAY
Tuan Chau Holiday Villa Halong Bay (ehemals Au Lac Resort) £££–££££
Tuan Chau peninsula, Ha Long (approx. 5km/3mi beyond Ha Long City)
tel. 033/384 29 99
www.holidayvillahalongbay.com
Beautifully decorated villas and hotel rooms on a private beach or hillside (spacious bathrooms, some with Jacuzzi, pool, karaoke, fitness room, golf course, helicopter tours across the bay, many Asian guests.

Sunrise Resort £££
Cat Co 3 Beach, Cat Ba
Ha Long Bay
tel. 0317388 73 60
www.catbasunriseresort.com
There are worse places to spend a week (ideally between May and November – from December on, it can be cold and wet) than at the best beach hotel in Ha Long Bay! This marvellous small villa-like complex is situated on a tiny 100m/110yd-wide bay. Jacuzzi, pool, three restaurants, water sports. 15 minutes walk to the centre.

Novotel Halong (Accor) ££–£££
Ha Long Road (close to the water puppet theatre in the Royal Amusement Park)
Ha Long City
tel. 033/384 81 08
For genuine service and a high class experience in Ha Long City, this is the place to stay: 214 attractive rooms with

Asian flair, Wi-Fi, ocean view balcony (surcharge), pool alongside the (noisy) street.

Thang Long Hotel ££
Bai Chay, Ha Long City
tel. 033/384 64 58
Hulking new building across from the new tourist boat pier, with nicely decorated rooms.

Ocean Beach Resort ££
Bai Chay, Ha Long City
Cat Ong Island (approx. 5km/3mi southeast of Cat Ba, 20 minutes by boat, included in the price)
Reservation hotline in Hanoi: 04/39 26 04 63
Moblie tel. 098/323 46 28 and 090/323 46 28
www.oceanbeachresort.com.vn
www.oceantours.com.vn
Live like Robinson Crusoe on a deserted jungle island in one of 20 rustic bamboo huts with palm leaf roofing on two mini beaches or on the hillside. Fall straight from the hammock on the veranda straight into the sea.
There are three larger family bungaloes (deluxe, suite, panorama) and even a brand new pool villa, beach barbecue, kayak tours and beach volleyball.

Minh Chau Beach Resort ££
Minh Chau Beach, Quan Lan Island
Bai Tu Long Bay, Ha Long
tel. 033/399 50 16
Mobile tel. 090/408 18 68
www.minhchauresort.vn
A small, modern three-star hotel offering 50 decent rooms near the beach. Mini pool and rooftop bar – and even a congress hall.

Viethouse Lodge £–££ *Insider Tip*
Tuan Chau peninsula, Ha Long
(approx. 5km/3mi outside Ha Long City)
tel. 033/384 22 07

Loving attention to detail: the Sunrise Resort

www.viethouselodge.com
One of the most original guesthouses in Vietnam: a rustic brick building on a slope with a great view, 23 rooms with old roof beams and pillars, nice old-fashioned style folding doors, lots of rattan, terracotta and wood. Satellite TV and internet, patio restaurant, sauna, friendly stagg, tours.

Sea Pearl Cat Ba £–££
219 Road 11///4 (shore promenade)
Cat Ba City, Ha Long Bay
tel. 031/368 85 67
www.seapearlcatbahotel.com.vn
Eleven-storey hotel in the centre with 85 pleasant rooms, excellent views and Wi-Fi included. It is possible to strike a fine bargain, not only in the off-season. Rooftop eatery and a boisterous disco on the first floor.

Thuy Duong £
20 Ha Long Road, Ha Long City
tel. 033/384 61 37
www.thuyduonghotelhalong.com
No frills, dirt cheap mini hotel near the night market. Some rooms have nice balcony views of the lake. Lots of young guests (not the right place for those sensitive to noise). Two dining options, one on the roof. Bicycles for hire.

Sunset Hotel £
Cat Ba promenade (=1 Thang 4 Street No. 180, opposite the pier)
Cat Ba
tel. 031/388 83 70
Clean, extremely cheap rooms (satellite TV, air conditioning), harbour views. A wealth of information and tips from the amiable Mr. Tung and his wife.

Villa Song Chau £
In the main village on Quan Lan Island (Van Don province)
Bai Tu Long Bay, Ha Long
tel. 033/387 75 66
Mobile tel. 098/955 18 07 (Mrs. Hanh)
www.songchauguanlan.com
Twelve different rooms in a striking three-storey new building topped with a tower which offers excellent panoramic views.

Ha Long Bay

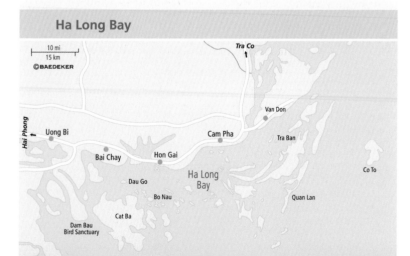

✳ CAT BA ISLAND AND NATIONAL PARK

Cat Ba is the largest island of an archipelago that has been a nature reserve since 1986. Cat Ba National Park takes up approximately half of the mostly rocky island (around 28,000ha/69,200ac). Most of the approximately 7000 islanders live in **Cat Ba City** in the south, which has transformed itself into a small Asian version of St Tropez. There are regular traffic jams in the overflowing town, especially in summer and at weekends. An esplanade runs around the bay and the harbour with high-rise hotels, discotheques and puny little trees.

Asian St Tropez

> ### ❓ Chopstick Trees
>
> MARCO ⊕ POLO INSIGHT
>
> In Cat Ba National Park there are trees which are commonly known as »chopstick trees«. Apparently, the wood reacts to poisonous substances by becoming darker in colour, which is why the emperor had his chopsticks made from this wood.

The old town in the west is somewhat calmer, and here colourful little houses still crouch along the promenade, a small Taoist temple awaits visitors, and a market hall offers fresh goods all day long. From the eastern end of the esplanade in Cat Ba City it is possible to walk, partly along the cliffs, to the three numbered **Cat Co Beaches**. Day trips set out from Cat Ba to islands and caves in the nearby Lan Ha Bay, e.g. to »Monkey Island«.

A drive across the island gives an impression of its wild karst landscape. The road snakes along through the rice fields or the rugged coastline with its shrimp farming ponds. The **limestone formations** typical of the area are remarkable, and they are covered with sub-tropical evergreen trees which hold on to the jagged rocks as if with tentacles. As late as 1893, seafarers gave reports of **pirates** who retreated to this at-the-time wild island after their forays. Among the ecosystems deserving protection are swamps and mangrove forests, small freshwater lakes, beaches and the coral reefs off the coast.

The karstified limestone walls and their caves (e.g. the Trung Trang Cave) offer shelter to various types of macaque and gibbon, as well as mountain goats and bats. A rare subspecies of langur, the golden-headed langur, has also been found here.

Flora and fauna

On archaeological digs, traces of the primitive **Cai Beo culture**, which thrived here around 5600 years ago, as well as of the **Ha Long culture** (2000 BC) have been found. On the coast the karst is surrounded by mangrove forests, forming a unique habitat: migratory birds from the north gather here in winter. In addition, an unusually high number of reptiles (including geckos, water snakes, pythons) congregate in the area of the national park, as well as dol-

Tower Karst • Formation

Surface water seeps into the porous subsoil. Dissolution creates hollow areas.

Progressive karst formation causes these hollow areas to cave in. Star-shaped sinkholes form between the karst cones.

The forces of erosion lead to the sink-holes expanding not only sideways but also downwards. Kars towers are created.

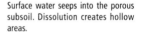

▢ Vegetation cover ▢ Water-permeable limestone ▮ Water-permeable rock layer

phins. Around 700 plant species, many of pharmaceutical use, can be found on Cat Ba.

Trung Trang Cave: admission approx. 30,000 VND

Bai Tu Long Bay
The neighbouring Bai Tu Long Bay is much quieter than Ha Long Bay. The caves here are less spectacular, but the beaches larger. On the sleepy little island of **Quan Lan**, tiger prawns and fish are farmed. The people here still enjoy ancient traditions such as the boat race during the village festival. A regional speciality is xa sung, a sand worm from the sea, which is put in some noodle soups. The ferries from Cam Pha on the mainland run several times daily to Quan Lan, as they also do from Hon Gai (Ha Long City).

From Quan Lan there is a ferry running twice per day to the north-ern-lying island of **Van Don** (or take the hydrofoil from Ha Long City) – a larger island, marvellously located between two limestone giants. At Dai Beach, at the eastern end, Van Don still seems sleepy and rural. Beyond the beach and the magnificent setting of hunched, rocky islands runs an endless stream of freighters, ships, old boats and ferries – around 1000 years ago Van Don was the first commercial fishing harbour under the rule of the Ly dynasty. Since 2004, Van Don has been connected to the mainland by means of a bridge at Cam Pha. Solar energy played an important role in the Ha Long Bay, when the James Bond movie »The Man With The Golden Gun« was filmed here: the villain Scaramanga threatened the world with his solar-powered super-weapon stationed on one of the is-lands.

* Hai Phong

─── ⟡ D 2

Province: Hai Phong (city state)
Region: Red River Delta
Population: approx. 900,000

Vietnam's fourth-largest city, the industrial centre of Hai Phong surprises visitors with a pretty, old colonial centre, where wide avenues are lined with flame trees and surrounded by canals and streams. Some travellers use the town as a base for the boat trip to Cat Ba Island or Ha Long City.

Close to Hai Phong, Bach Dang has repeatedly been the site of battles against the Chinese and Mongols since the second century before Christ: in the year 938 the Vietnamese general Ngo Quyen found himself confronted with the overpowering Chinese fleet, whereupon he ordered that stakes fortified with iron points be anchored in the riverbed. When the Chinese appeared at the estuary of Bach Dang, he sent a small fleet of agile boats out as a lure. The enemy launched their attack, but when they reached the ebb, their heavy ships were pierced by the stakes (▶see also p.50). More than half of the Chinese drowned in this battle. This strategy was similarly repeated in 1288, when 400 Mongolian ships approached with the intention of invading Vietnam. In both cases the victories were so overwhelming and the losses of the enemy so immense that any further plans for inva-   History

Ornate carvings decorate Nghe Temple

Hai Phong's wonderful carpets are crafted here

sion by the Chinese and the Mongols were put to rest. During the 17th century there were first attempts to turn the small fishing village and military post into a **port city** – yet the natural conditions were not the best: the village lay in a swamp area around 20km/12mi from the sea. It was not until 1874, when the French took over Hai Phong, that the area could be drained and a city built. Just a few years later, the colonial rulers set up a supply base, creating the foundation for the important role of the harbour, still in use today.

WHAT TO SEE IN HAI PHONG

Cathedral   Somewhat to the south is the recently restored cathedral, which was built at the end of 19th century.

Theatre   On the same street a few blocks further south, across from a lavish avenue, stands the salmon-coloured theatre, the materials for which were shipped over from France at the beginning of the 20th century. The broad square in front is where 40 Vietminh died in a skirmish with the French in November 1946.

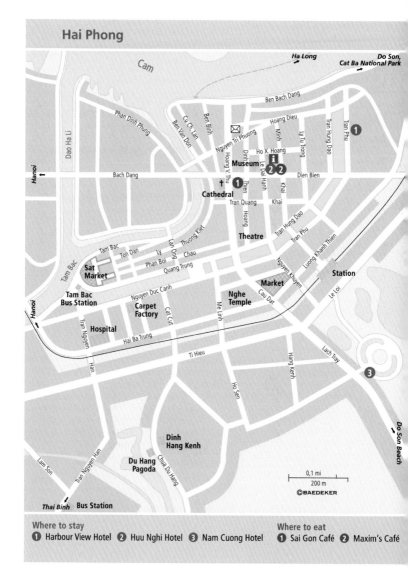

Hai Phong

Cam

Ha Long

Do Son,
Cat Ba National Park

Ben Bach Dang

Phan Dinh Phung

Cu Chi Lan

Ben Van Don

Ben Binh

Hoang Dieu

Tran Hung Dao

Tran Phu

Nguyen Tri Phuong

Minh

Ly Tu Trong

❶

Hoang V Thu

Dinh

Ho X. Hoang

Museum ❶

Le Dai Hanh

Khai

❷ ❷

Dao Ha Li

Bach Dang

Dien Bien

Hanoi

✝ ❶

Thien

Cathedral

Tran Quang

Khai

Hoang

Tran Hung Dao

Theatre

Tran Phu

Thuong Kiet

Lan Ong

Luong Khanh Thien

Tam Bac

Ton Dan

Ly

Chau

Phan Boi

Nguyen Khuyen

Quang Trung

Tam Bac

**Sat
Market**

Market

Station

Le Loi

**Tam Bac
Bus Station**

Nguyen Duc Canh

Cat Cut

**Nghe
Temple**

Cau Dat

**Carpet
Factory**

Me Linh

Hanoi

Tran Nguyen

Han

Hospital

Hai Ba Trung

Ti Hieu

Hang Kenh

Lach Tray

❸

Ho Sen

Do Son Beach

**Dinh
Hang Kenh**

**Du Hang
Pagoda**

Lam Son

Tran Nguyen Han

Chua Du Hang

0,1 mi

200 m

©BAEDEKER

Thai Binh **Bus Station**

Where to stay
❶ Harbour View Hotel ❷ Huu Nghi Hotel ❸ Nam Cuong Hotel

Where to eat
❶ Sai Gon Café ❷ Maxim's Café

The Den Nghe, around 10 minutes on foot to the east, is also par- **Den Nghe**
ticularly impressive. The small, somewhat hemmed-in temple was
built at the beginning of the 20th century and dedicated to Le Chan,

Hai Phong

INFORMATION
Haiphong Tourism
18 Minh Khai, tel. 031/382 26 16
www.haiphongtourism.gov.vn

TRANSPORT
Cat Bi International Airport
Cat Bi International Airport
(regional airport, approx. 7km/4mi outside the centre, scheduled to open as International Airport in 2015, a number of
flights to and from Saigon, Da Nang and
(from 2015) Macao, for example.

Railway Station
Luong Khanh Thien, Hai Phong
tel. 031/392 13 33 and 392 02 25

Boats
Daily hydrofoils to Ha Long City and
Cat Ba

EVENTS
Do Son Buffalo Festival Insider Tip
Every year, in the middle of September, a

bullfight festival is held in Do Son in
honour of the resistance fighter Huu
Cao. However, these bear little resem-
blance to those held in Spain: the first to
run away loses. Afterwards, the bulls are
blessed and distributed among the par-
ticipating villages as Loc, a gift of the
spirits.

SHOPPING
Commercial centre
North of Tam Bac Lake, between Tran
Thinh Street and Cho Sat, is the commercial centre of Hai Phong, full of
street markets, flower stalls, grocers and
hardware stores. Siamese fighting fish
are a local feature, sold on many street
corners!

WHERE TO EAT
❶ *Sai Gon Café £*
107 Dien Bien Phu/corner of Dinh Tien
Hoang
tel. 031/382 21 95
daily 7am–11pm

a comrade of the Trung sisters (▶Famous People). Sacrifices are offered at the main altar, especially on the 8th day of the 2nd lunar
month, the annual **temple festival**, when plates of shrimp with rice
noodles are laid here. The Den Nghe is also known for its pretty
woodcarvings.

Dinh Hanh Kenh
The origin of the Le Chan district was the village of Kenh, the old
Dinh of which is found on Duong Hang Kenh Street. In general, the
village gods are usually honoured in these congregation houses, but
this one is dedicated to King Ngo Quyen, the conqueror of South
China (938). The short building with the curved roof was built opposite an artificial lake, in the shape of a boat. Great attention to detail was put into the façade and the astonishing **carvings**. More than
500 wooden reliefs, portraying scenes from everyday life, are found
here. Despite being over 200 years old, most of them are still in their
original condition.

Beef steak and fried rice, spaghetti, sandwiches and other snacks, »bia«, whisky and cocktails are served in this large, air-conditioned restaurant and bar with a TV projector on the main street. Live bands sometimes perform.

❷ Maxim's Café £
51 Dien Bien Phu
Hai Phong
tel. 031/382 29 34
Young locals gather here of an evening to enjoy the nice atmosphere in the bar, decent food and live music (from 9pm). Western breakfast served from 7am.

WHERE TO STAY
❶ Harbour View Hotel £££–££££
4 Tran Phu
Tel 031/382 78 27
This luxury hotel with colonial flair is located at the harbour, of all places. Pool, vintage car tours through town – almost like travelling back in time … Regular

barbecue parties with live music and a pleasant spa.

❷ Huu Nghi Hotel ££
60 Dien Bien Phu
tel. 031/382 32 44
www.huunghihotel.vn
Modern city hotel with pool and comfortable, sometimes elegant four-star rooms with balcony. Evening piano accompaniment in the tenth-floor bar (open 24 hours).

❸ Nam Cuong Hai Phong Hotel ££
47 Lach Tray, Ngo Quyen district
tel. 031/382 85 55
www.namcuonghaiphonghotel.com.vn
Modern hotel in the business district with all amenities (the upper floor rooms facing the park are quieter) plus pool, sauna and fitness room. Professional service and attention to detail: fresh fruit and flowers every day. Three good restaurants: 24/7 »Light House Café« lobby bar, a rooftop grill with international cuisine and an Asian diner.

AROUND HAI PHONG

Around 20km/12mi south of Hai Phong, surrounded by lush green forests and palm-lined beaches, the Do Son peninsula juts out into the Gulf of Tonkin. The approximately 4km/2.5mi-long sandy beach is divided into three sections and protected by a chain of hills. Daytrippers from Hanoi or Hai Phong like to flee from the heat of the city to the peninsula to enjoy the cool sea breeze beneath the palms and casuarinas. For the many visitors, 40 more or less confidence-inspiring hotels line the 4km/2.5mi beach. Since 1994 there has also been a gaming house, the first in Vietnam, at the discerning Do Son Casino & Resort Hotel (www.dosonresorthotel.com.vn). A walk to the **Spring of the Dragon** can be recommended, and to the **Ba Da Temple** at the northern end of the peninsula, interwoven with a romantic tale: Ba Da Temple was dedicated to a young maiden who killed herself after a night of love with a courtier.

Do Son

** Hanoi

⬥ C 2

Province: Ha Noi (city state)
Region: Red River Delta
Population: approx. 3 million

»The city between the rivers« – that is what the Vietnamese call their capital. The Red River delta, where dragons and Mongols once ruled, is today home to one of the most beautiful cities in Asia – with French charm and typical Vietnamese chaos. In the historic old town beats the somewhat lived-in heart of Hanoi – increasingly between chic boutiques and cafés.

The area around Hanoi is referred to as the cradle of Vietnamese culture. Even if, in the consciousness of the Western world, Saigon played the lead role in colonial history and the wars of the 19th and 20th centuries, Hanoi, with its 4000 years of history, is undoubtedly the more important city. Here, in the Red River delta and the nearby mountains, is the source of the early **ancestral legends** of the Viet-

Cradle of Vietnamese culture

Highlights Hanoi

▶ **Tai chi, jogging and aerobics at Hoan Kiem Lake**
Get up early to witness this huge sporting spectacle. The best thing to do is join in!
▶page 254

▶ **Water Puppet Theatre**
Drama in the damp: where the Vietnamese get their puppets to dance.
▶page 254

▶ **Stroll through the old town**
Wander through the tangle of streets, follow the scents or buy something exotic.
▶page 257

▶ **Temple of Literature**
The highest official of the land were once trained at this important Confucian sanctuary.
▶page 261

▶ **Ho Chi Minh Mausoleum**
Expect to wait in line for quite a while before paying respects to the father of the country.
▶page 264

▶ **Ethnological Museum**
The place to visit for those keen to learn about Vietnam's people, history and culture, their customs and traditions.
▶page 272

The bridge to the Jade Mountain Temple is also known as »the place where the morning sun rests«

namese people. There are numerous mythological tales, too, about the city itself and its foundation. Like no other place in Vietnam, Hanoi's atmosphere is characterized by the various epochs and their representative figures. Kings and Confucius, colonial rulers and military recruits, and, more recently, even capitalists have made their mark on the cityscape: hundreds of temples and pagodas alternate with colonial era façades and Art Deco villas, socialist prestigious buildings, mirror-glassed high-rises and department stores. The highly modern Hanoi can best be seen in the **West Lake district**: villas, mini hotels and luxury accommodation have appeared on the banks. The many parks, lakes and tamarind-shaded avenues lend Hanoi a pleasantly green countenance. Close to Hanoi, archaeological finds have revealed traces of significant early cultures such as the Dong Son epoch 2500 years ago or the prehistoric Hoa Binh culture. Under various names over the last two millennia, Hanoi has served as the **residence of princes and kings** and the centre of the administration and the military, of Confucian teachings and science, but the city was also often the setting for power struggles between competing dynasties. Particularly in the 18th and 19th centuries, many palaces were razed to the ground, while remnants of old fortresses such as Co Loa (3rd century BC) and Dai La (9th century) remained intact.

History		
	7th century	The Chinese construct the Dai La fortress.
	1010	The Ly dynasty moves its seat to Dai La.
	18th century	The Chinese are finally expelled from the city.
	around 1882	French occupy Hanoi.
	1945	In Hanoi, Ho Chi Minh declares the Democratic Republic in the north.
	1976	Hanoi becomes the national capital of the unified Vietnam.
	1986	Economic reforms, enacted at the National Party Congress in Hanoi, mark the turning point in Vietnamese politics.
	1996	US Embassy opens in Hanoi.
	2010	Hanoi celebrates its 1000th anniversary on 10.10.10 with a spectacular pageant and fireworks.

The year 1010, when the Vietnamese **Ly dynasty** moved their residence to the fortress of Dai La, is considered the time at which Hanoi was founded. Under the rule of the Ly dynasty in the 11th century, the One Pillar Pagoda and the Temple of Literature, the first academy in Vietnam, were built and the civil service established. Over the course of the following centuries, Hanoi was repeatedly conquered by invaders (China, the Nguyen dynasty), from time to time lost its function as capital and was renamed several times. Only since the beginning of the 19th century has the city been called Hanoi. Beginning in 1862/1863, the French wereable to bring large portions of

The Temple of Literature is where the highest officials of the land were trained from 1076 to 1915

Vietnam under their influence, starting from the south and moving up. Eventually, in 1882, they captured Hanoi. They declared the city the capital of their northern protectorate of Tonkin and of the entire **colony of Indochina**. After the Second World War, on 2 September 1945, Ho Chi Minh declared independence from Ba Dinh Square and proclaimed the Democratic Republic of Vietnam (DRV) in the north. The French colonial power initially recognized this independence in a treaty, but shortly afterwards reoccupied Hanoi and Saigon. It was not until 1954, after eight years of the Indochina War, that the Communist Vietminh was able to emerge from the underground to re-enter Hanoi and take over power in the north of the now partitioned country – around one million people fled to the southern republic in the time that followed. After the end of the **Vietnam War** – the bombs fell on Hanoi until December 1972 – Vietnam was reunited as the Socialist Republic of Vietnam (SRV) on 2 July 1976, with Hanoi the capital of the unified nation for the first time. The turning point in Vietnamese politics came at the Sixth National Party Congress of the Communist Party in Hanoi (1986), at which, amongst other motions, far reaching economic reforms were enacted. A further decade passed before the US Embassy was opened in Hanoi in 1996. Finally, in 2000, President Clinton visited Hanoi. Today, national leaders from across the world come and go regularly, as Vietnam ranks high on the list of countries attracting **foreign investment**, and trade with the Americans in particular has doubled several times in a row over recent years. Tourists no longer neglect Hanoi either. The Vietnamese capital is just as much a part of the Vietnam sightseeing itinerary as its southern sister metropolis, Saigon.

Hanoi

INFORMATION
Vietnam Tourism Hanoi
30A Ly Thuong Kiet, Hoan Kiem, Hanoi
tel. 04/38 26 41 54 and 38 26 40 89
www.vn-tourism.com
www.vietnamtourism.com

TIC (Tourist Information Center)
7 Dinh Tien Hoang (near Hoan Kiem
Lake), Hanoi old town.
tel. 04/39 26 33 66

TOUR OPERATORS
Asiatica Travel
A1203, Building M3-M4,
91 Nguyen Chi Thanh, Hanoi
tel. 04/62 66 28 16
www.asiatica-travel.com
City tours, walking tours, excursions to
Ha Long Bay, kayak tours etc. English
and French-speaking guides.

TRANSPORT
Noi Bai International Airport
tel. 04/38 84 35 63 and
38 86 50 02
www.hanoiairportonline.com
approx. 40km/25mi north of Hanoi (currency exchange counter only upon until
10pm): tel. 04/8 86 65 27; Vietnam Airlines shuttle buses starting in the old
town, public bus lines 7 and 17.
Taxi – set fares (depending on type of
vehicle): approx. 300,000 VND (incl. all
fees, exact change recommended!):
minibus shared taxis depart when they
are full (approx. US$1-2 per person).
Public buses 7 and 17 go to the centre
(5000 VND, every quarter hour from
5am to 10pm). Vietnam Airlines mini-
buses also an option.

Main railway station
tel. 04/38 25 39 49
(for tourists: desk 2 – beware: in the past,
not all trains have departed from here).
There is another desk on Tran Quy Cap
Street which is less busy (English spoken).
www.seat61.com/Vietnam.htm#.
UQqnRo50AtF
(good private train website)

In the city
The best way to get around is on foot,
on the back of a moped taxi or by Cyclo
(also negotiate beforehand!) or the inexpensive taxameter taxis (around 30 cents
per km).
Only the new, very good public buses
are cheaper, there is a map for sale
showing the bus routes.

EVENTS
National Holiday
On 2 September independence is celebrated extremely elaborately with a military parade (traditionally clad men and
women march along), fireworks display
at Hoan Kiem Lake and boat races.

SHOPPING
In the **old town**, the best streets for
shopping are Hang Gai, Hang Bong,
Hang Trong (silk goods, tailors), the chic
and pricey Pho Na Tho, Bao Hung and
Hai Van (Ho Chi Minh T-shirts) and Hang
Bong (handicrafts).
Shop until midnight: the **Dong Xuan
market hall**, the largest market in Hanoi, offers fresh fish, sweets, lacquerware, karaoke machines and much more
(Hang Khoai, corner of Dong Xuan, old
town).

Craft Link (43 Van Mieu) and **Hoa Sen Gallery** (51 Van Mieu and 42 Cau Go): both of these handicraft shops at the Temple of Litera- ture funnel their profits into projects for street children or ethnic minorities in the mountains.

Hanoi Gallery

62 Hang Buom, Hanoi old town
A potpourri of galleries on every corner in the old town, this one specializes in propaganda posters, which are very much in vogue.

CULINARY SPECIALITIES

Nom bo kho is the name of a tasty beef salad with green (unripe) papaya strips and peanuts, attracting locals to the cookshops next to the Thang Long The- atre at Hoan Kiem Lake.

Bun cha, the North Vietnamese special- ity with grilled meat and rice noodles, fresh herbs, chilli and cabbage, is best enjoyed in the old town street of Hang Manh.

ENTERTAINMENT

❶ Funky Buddha £

2 Ta Hien, old town
tel. 04/32 92 76 14
from 11pm on
Long after everything else is closed in the original bar street the base tones still make the floor of this salon-sized bar shake; filled to bursting on weekends.

❷ Bar & Jazzclub Minh's ££

65 Quan Su (2. St. Hot Live Café), south of Hoan Kiem district,Hanoi
Daily from 10am, live music every even- ing from 9pm
www.minhijazzvietnam.com
The old classic has finally found a wor-

thy home again after a veritable reloca- tion odyssey. Owned by the Vietnamese »Godfather of Jazz« Quyen Vanh Minh.

WHERE TO EAT

❶ La Verticale ££££

19 Ngo Van So, Hanoi
tel. 04/39 44 63 17
www.verticale-hanoi.com
Closed Sun lunchtime
Five-star chef Didier Corlou works his magic on fusion haute cuisine, serving his coveted creations in a beautiful old colonial villa – five to ten courses. Herbs on sale on the ground floor.

❷ Nam Phuong ££–£££

19 Phan Chu Trinh
tel. 04/38 24 09 26
Elegant restaurant in a wonderfully re- stored French villa. South Vietnamese dishes, traditional music performances, eight course dinners (from US$30). The lobster is, however, definitely over- priced!

❸ Khai Brothers ££–£££

26 Nguyen Thai Hoc
tel. 04/37 33 38 66
Mon-Sat 11.30am-2pm, daily 6.30pm- 10.30pm
Lovely old temple masonry with pillars and peaceful courtyard oasis, Vietnam- ese buffet, bar in the evenings. The lunchtime buffet (approx. US$13) tends to be very busy and noisy, quieter in the evening – but also more expensive (around US$23 incl. wine).

❹ Green Mango ££

18 Hang Quat, Hanoi old town
tel. 04/39 28 99 16,-18
http://greenmangohanoi.com/
Ever tried Nouvelle Asian? The place for

Hanoi

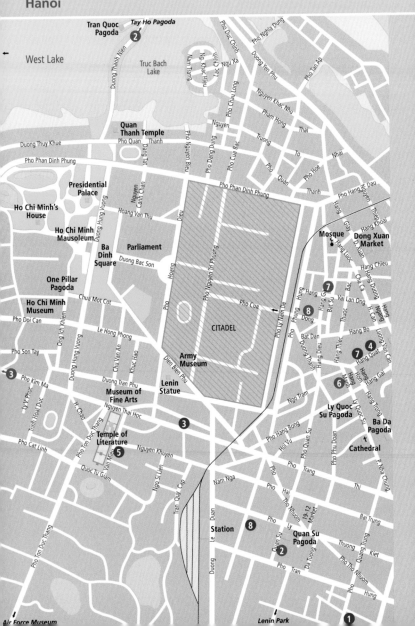

West Lake

Tran Quoc Pagoda

Tay Ho Pagoda ❷

Truc Bach Lake

Pho Duc Chinh

Pho Nghia Dung

Duong Yen Phu

Pho Tan Ap

Ng. Khac Hieu

Ngu Xa

Nam Trang

Pho Chau Long

Nguyen Khac Nhu

Pham Hong

Thai

Duong Thanh Nien

Quan Thanh Temple

Pho Quan Thanh

Duong Tat

Pho Nguyen Bieu

Pho Dang Dung

Pho Cua Bac

Nguyen

Truong

To

Nhat

Pho Hoe

Thanh

Duong Thuy Khue

Pho Phan Dinh Phung

Pho Phan Dinh Phung

Pho Hang Dau

Presidential Palace

Nguyen Canh Chan

Hoang Van Thu

Dieu

Hang

Giay

Hang Khoai

Ho Chi Minh's House

Duong Hung Vuong

Hang Than

Hang Luoc

Mosque ❖

Dong Xuan Market

Ho Chi Minh Mausoleum

Ba Dinh Square

Parliament

Duong Bac Son

Hoang

Pho Nguyen Tri Phuong

Pho Cua

Hang Chieu

Cha Ca

Hang Duong

One Pillar Pagoda

Chua Mot Cot

Hang Hung ❼

Hang Ga

Bat Su

Vai Lan Ong

Hang Ma

Ho Chi Minh Museum

Pho Doi Can

Ong Ich Khiem

Le Hong Phong

CITADEL

Dong ❽

Phung

Pho Ly Nam De

Bat Dan

Duong Thanh

Thuoc

Hang Bo

Pho Son Tay

Pho Kim Ma ❸

Duong Hung Vuong

Chu Van An

Khuc Hao

Duong Tran Phu

Dien Bien Phu

Army Museum

Hang Dieu

Hang Thiec

Hang Quat ❼ ❹

Luong Van Can

Ly Y Phuc

Tinh Hoai Duc

H. Chao

Nguyen Thai Hoc

Lenin Statue

Ngo Tram

Mam ❻

Hang Hom

Hang Gai

Hang Trong

Museum of Fine Arts

❸

Pho Cat Linh

Pho Ton Duc Thang

Van Mieu

Temple of Literature ❺

Nguyen Khuyen

Pho Hang Bong

Ho Vu

Pho Quan Su

Ly Quoc Su Pagoda

Ba Da Pagoda

Quoc Tu Giam

Ngo Si Lien

Pho Phu Doan

Cathedral ✝

P. Nha Chung

Nam Nga

Pho Trang

Pho

Thi

Pho Ton Duc Thang

Tran Quy Cap

Le Duan

Pho Hai

Tho Nhuom

Pho

19-12 Market

Bai Trung

Station ❽

Nguyen Khuyen

Pho Su

Ly

Quan Su Pagoda ❷

Da Tuong

Pho Tho Nhuom

Thuong

Quang Trung

Trung Kiet

Le Duan

Duong

Pho Tran

Hung

Air Force Museum

Lenin Park

❶

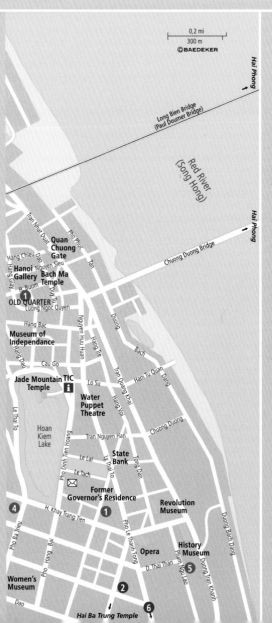

0,2 mi
300 m
©BAEDEKER

Hai Phong

Long Bien Bridge
(Paul Doumer Bridge)

Red River
(Song Hong)

Hai Phong

Chuong Duong Bridge

Tran Nhat Duat

Quan
Chuong
Gate

Pho Phuc

Nguyen Sieu

Hang Chieu Dao

Hanoi
Gallery

Bach Ma
Temple

H. Buom

Tan

Hang Giay

Duong

OLD QUARTER

Luong Ngoc Quyen

Hang Bac

Museum of
Independance

Hang Dao

Nguyen Huu Huan

Cau Go

Hang Tre

Bach

Jade Mountain
Temple

TIC

Lo Su

Tran Quang Khai

Ham Tu Quan

Water
Puppet
Theatre

Hang Vai

Chuong Duong

Le Thai To

Hoan
Kiem
Lake

Dinh Tien Hoang

Tran Nguyen Han

Le Lai

Ly Thai To

State
Bank

Long Dan

Le Tach

Former
Governor's Residence

Revolution
Museum

Duong Bach Dang

4

H. Khay Trang Tien

Pho Le Thanh Tong

1

Pho Ba Trieu

Pho Hang Bai

Opera

History
Museum

5

Duong Tran Khanh

Pho Ngu Lao

Women's
Museum

D. Thai Than

Dao

2

6

Hai Ba Trung Temple

Where to stay

1. Sofitel Legend Metropole
2. InterContinental
   Hanoi Westlake
3. Daewoo Hotel
4. Zephyr Hotel
5. Army Hotel
6. Hong Ngoc Dynastie
7. Hanoi Charming 2 Hotel
8. Hanoi Serenity Hotel

Where to eat

1. La Verticale
2. Nam Phuong
3. Khai Brothers
4. Green Mango
5. KOTO
6. Au Lac
7. Bar Restaurant 96
8. Quan An Ngon

Entertainment

1. Funky Buddha
2. Bar & Jazzclub Minh's

a romantic dinner with tasteful musical accompaniment. Vietnames and Thai dishes, beautifully presented with a touch of French influence, some western classics (steak, pasta, pizza). Also 15 stylish parquet rooms available (**££**).

❺ *KOTO (Know one, teach one)* **££**

daily 8am–11pm
Tiny restaurant belonging to an Australian project for street children who are trained as cooks, barkeepers and waiters here. Small Asian, western and vegetarian dishes, sandwiches, fruit juices, milkshakes, cocktails etc. are served on two floors.

Street children can demonstrate their cookery skills at KOTO

❻ *Au Lac House* **£–£££**

3 Tran Hung Dao, Hanoi
tel. 04/39 33 35 33
Especially beautiful colonial building with terrace and elegant dining rooms on two levels, good Vietnamese dishes in spite of numerous tourists, service sadly not the fastest.

❼ *Bar Restaurant 96* **£**

34 Gia Ngu, Hanoi old town
(close to Hoan Kiem Lake)
tel. 04/39 35 23 96
Small old town restaurant on two floors, bun cha Hanoi style is the house speciality, thin rice noodles with grilled pork skewer, or pork in bamboo. One lovely place on the balcony.
Be sure to sample the ginger ice cream!

❽ *Quan An Ngon* **£**

18 Phan Boi Chau
tel. 04/39 42 81 62
www.ngonhanoi.com.vn
A vast array of freshly prepared dishes are presented at different stands and eaten in the large courtyard beneath potted trees and canvas marquees or in the rooms of the adjacent villa.

WHERE TO STAY
❶ *Sofitel Legend Metropole* **££££**

15 Ngo Quyen, Hoan Kiem
tel. 04/38 26 69 19
www.sofitel.com
sofitelhanoi@hn.vnn.vn
Hanoi's time-honoured hotel dating back to 1901, praised by authors like Graham Greene and Somerset Maugham. Comfortable rooms and exceptionally good service, French restaurant, bar, swim-

ming pool and conference rooms
(▶MARCO POLO Insight p.104)

❷ InterContinental Hanoi Westlake £££–££££
Insider Tip

1A Nghi Tam
(right on West Lake)
Tay Ho district, Hanoi
tel. 04/62 70 88 88
www.ichotelsgroup.com
Luxury residence in a fantastic, idyllic location (albeit at some distance from most of the sights): classy hotel suites with parquet and wood furnishings, three-storey villas reached via footbridges. Balconies overlooking the water (butler service for some). Massages in the spa are an absolute bargain. Three restaurants.

❸ Daewoo Hotel £££
Daeha Centre, 360 Kim Ma Street, Ba Dinh district (West Lake)
tel. 04/38 31 50 00
www.hanoidaewoohotel.com.vn
This modern, 15-storey hotel in the west of the city is a joint venture with South Korea. The many extras include: swimming pool, night club, fitness centre, restaurants and conference rooms.

❹ Zephyr Hotel ££—£££
4 Ba True, Hoan Kiem
tel. 04/39 34 12 56
www.zephyrhotel.com.vn
Elegant hotel with 40 rather overpriced rooms, centrally located and quiet (quieter to the rear), some with large balconies and panoramic views of Hoan Kiem Lake. Good breakfast buffet.

❺ Army Hotel ££
33c Pham Ngu Lao
tel. 04/38 25 28 96

armyhotel@fpt.vn
Don't be put off by the name! This hotel (84 rooms) is central yet quietly located in a side street near the Historical Museum. The décor – in a former military guesthouse – is plain but quite acceptable. Good service, large pool.

❻ Hong Ngoc Dynastie ££
34 Hang Manh
Hoan Kiem
tel. 04/38 28 50 53
www.hongngochotel.com
Mini hotel with large rooms, beautiful furniture with woodcarvings and mother-of-pearl inlays. TV, air conditioning, some rooms with balcony (meanwhile, nearly every district in Hanoi has a hotel from this very good chain).

❼ Hanoi Charming 2 Hotel £–££
31 Hang Ga, Hanoi old town
tel. 04/39 23 40 31
www.hanoicharminghotel.com
40 spacious parquet rooms on eight floors, nicely decorated, even with laptops (and Wi-Fi) in the rooms. Fresh fruit or flowers daily, balcony or (quieter) no windows at all. Very friendly and attentive service. Free transfers from airport (for stays of three nights or more).

❽ Hanoi Serenity Hotel £
1B Cua Dong
(old town to the west)
Hanoi
tel. 04/39 23 35 49
Central, comfortable, good value: 17 rooms with Wi-Fi, satellite TV and minibar, helpful team. Early booking advised! (Belongs to the same popular chain as the Hanoi Phoenix at 43 Bat Su.)

AROUND HOAN KIEM LAKE

**Hoan Kiem Lake

At first sight, Hoan Kiem Lake in the centre of Hanoi seems rather small – it is possible to walk around it in a hour without hurrying. Yet it is still the soul of Hanoi. Even early in the morning, there is already plenty going on. Joggers do their laps, walkers stroll around, and aerobic dancers move to disco rhythms. In the northwestern corner of the lake a small community of mostly older people practise **tai chi**. At midday, many who work in the nearby offices and shops take their breaks in the park at the lake. In the afternoons, old men play Chinese chess and children scramble around. There is also plenty going on in the evenings: couples meet, families enjoy a stroll and many tourists head from here to the streets of the old town again. In the middle of Hoan Kiem Lake, which means »lake of the restored sword«, a three-level pavilion, the **Tortoise Tower**, stands on a little island. An old legend tells of Le Loi, the national hero who led the uprising against the Chinese occupiers in the 15th century. It is said that while fishing in this lake, Le Loi caught a shining sword, with whose help he was able to defeat the Chinese after ten years of battle. When he returned, he wished to thank the spirit of the lake, but while he was preparing his offering there was a loud roll of thunder and the sword flew out of its sheath directly into the mouth of a golden tortoise, who brought it back to the gods. The story is one of the most popular in Vietnam to this day, and it is often presented at water puppet theatre performances (►MARCO POLO Insight p.78 and p.368).

Huc Bridge and Jade Mountain Temple

Across the red-lacquered The Huc Bridge is another small island on which stands Jade Mountain Temple. The pretty setting makes the bridge seem very romantic, so it is called »the place where the rising sun rests«. Next to the crossing is a 9m/30ft-high obelisk with Chinese ideographs which label it as »a pen to write on the blue sky«. Jade Mountain Temple (Den Ngoc Son, opening times: daily 8am–5pm) is beautifully situated between two ancient trees. It was built here in the 14th century and dedicated to a very select group: General Tran Hung Dao, who defeated the Mongols in 1288, the God of Literature Van Xuong, the physicist La To and the warrior Quan Vu. The building that stands today dates from the 19th century and displays a number of elements typical of the Nguyen dynasty, such as the remarkable **dragons' heads**. The real highlight, and the reason most tourists come here, is not found in the main altar room, but in another room outside: it is the shell of a gigantic tortoise, caught in 1968.

Jade Mountain Temple: daily 8am – 5pm, admission approx. 20,000 VND

** Kim Dong Water Puppet Theatre (Thang Long Ensemble)

For more than 1000 years, an art form that is unique worldwide has held its own in Vietnam in the face of MTV, soap operas, Gameboys and the rest: in water puppet theatre (mua roi nuoc), people and sto-

Morning exercises at Hoan Kiem Lake

ries from everyday life in Vietnam play the lead role. The colourful wooden puppets and figures rise from the water as in a real water ballet. To this day, the puppeteers stand behind a curtain, up to their hips in water and, by means of metre-long, invisible bamboo poles and strings, they get the puppets to glide across the water as if by magic (►MARCO POLO Insight p.78 and p.368).

Insider Tip

❶ 57B Dinh Tien Hoang, tel. 04/39 36 43 35,www.thanglongwaterpuppet. org daily shows, 4pm, 6pm and 8pm (hourly from 4pm in peak season), 60,000 – 100,000 VND (buy tickets early!).

When walking around the southern part of the lake, there is the chance to take a detour to the cathedral in Nha Tho Street. On the way is Ba Da Pagoda, its entrance decorated with arcades. The pagoda contains an impressive collection of Buddha figures. **Cathedral** In order to build the Cathedral of St Joseph in the 1880s, the French colonial rulers sacrificed the most significant pagoda in Hanoi (Chua Bao Thien) with its ten-floor tower. Particularly notable are the colourful glass windows and the many votive tablets in the Lady Chapel in the northern nave. A black marble grave lies on the opposite side

Ba Da Pagoda

– this is where the last Vietnamese cardinal was laid to rest after his death in 1990. The main entrance to the cathedral is only used during Mass, otherwise it is possible to enter through the side door in Nha Chung Street.

🕐 closed 1pm–2pm

Ly Quoc Su Pagoda   Follow Ly Quoc Su Street heading north to reach the little Ly Quoc Su Pagoda (13th century), named after a Buddhist healer, teacher and royal adviser. He is said to have cured the hallucinating king Ly Thanh Tong of his mad belief that he was a tiger. The healer's likeness crowns the altar, with three Buddhas behind it. He is flanked by a number of interesting statues: four female figures on one side and three mandarins on the other. Walking around the various altars, a number of old stone figures, which date from around 1500, can be seen opposite the rear wall.

Paper goods and devotional objects on sale in Hang Ma Street

✴✴ OLD QUARTER

The narrow streets of the old commercial district of Hanoi call to mind a beehive. The shops are overgrown with climbing plants and bird cages are hung outside, their occupants tweeting and chirping away. The pavements are crowded with street stands and food stalls, from which pleasant-smelling soups are offered. Any space left over is filled with bicycles and mopeds, or populated with playing children and gossiping neighbours. Still pottering about are the scattered descendants of the **earlier trades people**, like in the street for bamboo goods (Hang Tre) or Hang Quat, in which religious devotional objects are sold. Anything to do with paper is found in Hang Ma, and jewellery can be purchased in Hang Bac. Those interested in tin objects should head for Hang Thiec, and enthusiasts of traditional healing methods will find what they need in Lan Ong. In recent years, designer boutiques and souvenir shops, galleries, travel agencies and smart restaurants have been competing for space with the stores belonging to long-term residents, who often live on the premises and just pull down a metal lattice in the evenings. Visitors can explore the streets confidently – getting lost is almost impossible, as train tracks border the district to the north, as do the large streets Phung Hung and Tran Nhat Duat to the east and west. The many cafés are ideal for watching the hustle and bustle in peace. By 5pm at the latest, rush hour arrives in the form of two-wheeled, rattling chaos. What might have been a pleasant stroll is now transformed into an obstacle course, indeed often it becomes impossible to continue on foot – pavements are mercilessly blocked by parked conveyances and the traffic jams on hopelessly overrun streets is exacerbated by hundreds of buzzing and honking »Tiger« two-wheelers zipping through.

Among all the distractions that present themselves in these streets, it is easy to overlook one of the architectural features of the quarter, which, alongside ▶Hoi An, boasts Vietnam's only trading houses from the 15th century. These buildings in the Old Quarter are, however, not so exquisitely decorated, but are nevertheless striking, primarily for their form. They are known as »tube houses« because from the street only a small

Atmospheric quarter with narrow, noisy streets

> **MARCO POLO TIP**
>
> *A typical tube house* **Insider Tip**
>
> … can be viewed at number 87 Ma May Street (put slippers on!). The former inhabitants were members of the bamboo-makers' guild and three generations of them lived in this marvelously restored wooden house. Note the finely carved folding doors and windows with the four mythological animals and the real gem on the second floor in the form of a bed with mother-of-pearl decoration (daily 8am-5pm: approx. 10,000 VND). Within these historic walls, »House Singing« performances take place on Tuesdays, Thursdays and Saturdays at 8pm (www.catruthanglong.com).

shop can be seen, often only 2m/7ft wide, but this is attached to a workshop and then several living, sleeping and storage rooms, so that in the end the buildings often reach lengths of 60–80m/200–260ft! This kind of house arose because **taxes** were once calculated based on the size of the shop front, and businesses were divided accordingly upon inheritance. The entire building features courtyards at regular intervals, letting in light and air, and where rain water can be collected and vegetables planted; there are also often pens for small animals. The outer façades of some of the »tube houses« were changed during the colonial era, and received balconies when the streets were widened to build walkways. Yet some of the owners were wealthy or influential enough that exceptions were made for their houses, and to this day they stand out in the streetscape, as can be seen in Hang Ba and Ma May Street.

Museum of Indepen- dence

The building at 48 Hang Ngang is where Ho Chi Minh drafted the Declaration of Independence of the Democratic Republic of Vietnam of 1945. The building, in which he lived at the time, today houses the Museum of Independence. In the upper rooms, the original furnishings can be seen, while downstairs there is a small photo exhibition.
❶ Tue-Sun 8am–5pm

*Bach Ma Temple

Bach Ma Temple on Hang Buom Street is the oldest and most visited sanctuary in this district. Founded in the 9th century, it was later dedicated to the White Horse (Bach Ma), the guardian spirit of Thang Long. The building that stands today dates from the 11th century, and its most valuable possession is the **copper Bach Ma statue**, represented here in its original form as the earth god, Long Do. On either side of the altar a replica of a horse and two guard figures, which are blessed with gold-painted rows of teeth, catch the eye.
❶ Tue–Sun 7.30am–11am, 2pm–6pm

* FRENCH QUARTER

Colonial legacy on broad boulevards

A stark contrast to the busy bustle in the narrow streets of the Old Quarter can be found in the generously proportioned boulevards of the French Quarter, south and east of Hoan Kiem Lake. The first French settlement was established in 1874, close to the site of the Opera today. Many unique Vietnamese buildings were razed to the ground at this time. The attractions in this area are not as close to one another as they are near Hoan Kiem Lake and in the Old Quarter.

*Opera

It is easy, even at the first glimpse, to see that the Hanoi Opera is modelled on an important building, namely the Paris Opera. For its construction, the land near the Red River was first reclaimed; after

Modelled on the Paris original

ten years of construction, it was finally inaugurated in 1911. For many years, the Opera was the pride of French Hanoi, its cultural and commercial heart – until 1945, when the Vietminh proclaimed the **August Revolution** from its balcony. It is located on the corner of Trang Tien and Le Thai To. Unfortunately, it is not possible to visit its interior.

❶ access only possible in conjunction with a performance, tickets from approx. 100,000 VND, www.hanoioperahouse.org.vn

The History Museum is located only one block further east (1 Pham Ngu Lao Street). The building can be found a little hidden behind trees, a mixture of a Vietnamese palace and a French villa. The first room wastes no time in teaching about the Dong Son culture (1200 to 200 BC). The most significant relics from this time are the large **bronze drums** (photo ▶p.227), which were beaten at ceremonies, at funerals, to summon the monsoon or to perform fertility rituals. An especially beautiful piece with finely worked figures (game, people, ships) is found in the next room: the Ngoc Lu Drum. Further important exhibits on this level are the meditating Buddha from Phat Tich Pagoda (11th century), a gold-inscribed lacquered tablet (11th century) with a poem by King Ly Thuong Kiet, which is considered to be Vietnam's first declaration of independence, and a group of five wooden posts (photo ▶p.50) originating from the glorious battle at Bach Dang River (1288). The upper floor is dominated by the 3m/10ft-high **steles in praise of Le Loi**, who led the resistance movement against Chinese occupation (15th century). Some interesting exhibits refer to the Nguyen dynasty and their life at the court of Hue as well as the time of French colonial rule. The last section of

*History Museum

the room is dedicated to the struggle for independence under the leadership of Ho Chi Minh.

❶ Tue–Sun 8am–12am and 1.30pm-5pm; admission: approx. 20,000 VND

Revolution Museum

Those wishing to learn more about the Vietnamese independence movement should pay a visit to the Revolution Museum, one block further north (216 Tran Quang Khai Street). The colonial building was once the headquarters of the customs supervision.

❶ 216 Tran Quang Khai Street; Tue–Sun 8am–12am, 1.30pm–5pm; admission approx. 20,000 VND

*Residence of the Governor of Tonkin

The **prettiest colonial building in Hanoi** was built in 1918 and is used today by the government as a guesthouse for high-ranking visitors of state. Unfortunately, it is not possible to visit this impressive estate on Ngo Quyen Street. The terrace my seem familiar to film buffs, as a number of scenes from the film *Indochine* were shot here.

*Trang Tien Street

Trang Tien Street, the main street of the French Quarter, runs south of Hoan Kiem Lake directly to the Opera. On this lively commercial street are all kinds of book shops and galleries, cafés and hotels. On the corner of Hang Bai stands the eight-storey »Hanoi Plaza« with shops, apartments and offices. South of Trang Tien is the start of the actual **villa district** of the French Quarter, through which run cool, shady boulevards. As in the Old Quarter, these genteel buildings have survived primarily due to a lack of money. There are many European influences from the early 20th century exhibited here, from the elegant neoclassicism of the 1920s to Art Deco with a particularly oriental note.

*Women's Museum

36 Ly Thuong Kiet Street is home to the Women's Museum, opened in 1994. The exhibits are very nicely presented on three floors and also explained in English. The purpose of the collection is to present the role of women in Vietnamese society, including the wartime phenomenon of Vietnamese women in combat. Also depicted are the world of the gods and ethnic minorities. Of particular interest are the handcrafted works by women of the, Khmer, Hmong, Ede, Cham and Dao peoples.

Insider Tip

❶ Tue–Sun 8am–5pm, admission approx. 25,000 VND

*Hanoi Hilton / Hoa Lo Prison

The legendary »Hanoi Hilton«, which attained worldwide notoriety in the 1960s, stood just one block further west at the crossing of Hai Ba Trung and Hoa Lu. This was under no circumstances luxury accommodation; rather it was a prison in which American soldiers were held and also tortured, US Senator John McCain among them (p.271). Since 1997, an exclusive hotel and conference centre has been here, a modern high-rise has jutting skywards (»Hanoi Tower«).

A **museum** was established in a remaining part of the old building to commemorate the prisoners – both Americans and also Vietnamese, who were held here under French colonial rule.

❶ daily 8am–11.30am, 12.30pm–5pm; admission approx. 20,000 VND

Turn left at the next crossing into Quan Su Street to reach the Ambassador's Pagoda. As the name suggests, it was built in the 15th century to provide accommodation for ambassadors from neighbouring Buddhist countries. However, the building which stands today is not so old, having been constructed in 1942. To this day, Quan Su Pagoda is one of the most significant and **most-visited cult sites** of the city. In the large prayer room, old ladies sit beneath the smoky lanterns, reciting sutras. On the 1st and 15th days of the 5th lunar month, pilgrims and beggars crowd the forecourt, while inside a huge iron lamp seems to hover over the believers, lighting the crimson Buddhas through a misty shroud of incense smoke.

*Amba-
ssador's
Pagoda (Chua
Quan Su)

❶ daily except Sat 8.30am-11.30am, 1.30pm-4pm

★★ TEMPLE OF LITERATURE (VAN MIEU)

❶ daily 8am–6pm; admission: 20,000 VND;
www.templeofliterature.com

Van Mieu Pagoda is not only the most lavish and beautiful temple complex in the city, but primarily the main sanctuary of Confucian-

Statue of a student of Confucius

Temple of Literature

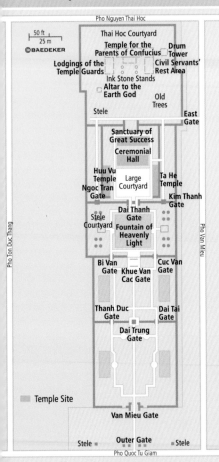

Pho Nguyen Thai Hoc

50 ft
25 m
©BAEDEKER

Thai Hoc Courtyard

Temple for the
Parents of Confucius

Drum
Tower

Lodgings of the
Temple Guards

Civil Servants'
Rest Area

Ink Stone Stands

Altar to the
Earth God

Old
Trees

Stele

East
Gate

Sanctuary of
Great Success

Ceremonial
Hall

Huu Vu
Temple

Large
Courtyard

Ta He
Temple

Ngoc Tran
Gate

Kim Thanh
Gate

Dai Thanh
Gate

Stele
Courtyard

Fountain of
Heavenly
Light

Bi Van
Gate

Cuc Van
Gate

Khue Van
Cac Gate

Thanh Duc
Gate

Dai Tai
Gate

Dai Trung
Gate

Pho Ton Duc Thang

Pho Van Mieu

Temple Site

Van Mieu Gate

Stele

Outer Gate

Stele

Pho Quoc Tu Giam

ism and the first university in Vietnam. The Temple of Literature was built in 1070 under Emperor Ly Thanh Tong, and the National Gallery was founded six years later by King Ly Nhan Tong and dedicated in honour of Confucius, who had a large and wealthy legion of followers in Vietnam. It is said that the design of the temple complex is based upon a sanctuary at Confucius's birthplace in Qufu (China). Today the Temple of Literature is interpreted as a symbol of the diminishing status of Buddhism during the Ly dynasty, which the religious teachings of Confucius began to supersede. In time, Van Mieu became the intellectual and spiritual centre of the kingdom, whereby education took on a new status at the court, under the Mandarins and also among the people. But the place serves not only as a venue for exams; as at other pagodas, the poor and the sick are fed. The complex, aligned from north to south, built as a series of walled courtyards, is entered from Quoc Tu Giam Street.

On both sides of the outer gate, an inscription on the **stelae**, »ha ma«, orders the visitor to descend from his horse. This is to remind even the highest of dignitaries that they must continue along the path on foot from here. It leads to the large **Van Mieu Gate** (15th century), which is decorated with dragons and only opened on special holidays. Pass through it to arrive at a small, meticulously laid out park with lawns and trees. Through the plainer **Dai Trung Gate** is a second, similarly designed garden and the Khue Van Cac Gate (1805), the two-storied pavilion, which leads to the third courtyard. Its upper section is decorated with four shining suns; the roof is covered with yin-yang tiles.

The Stelae Courtyardstelae courtyard comes next. In the middle is a pond bordered by walls: the Fountain of Heavenly Light. It is flanked on both sides by rows of stone tortoises, which carry stone stelae. These are the **most valuable pieces in the sanctuary**, for they record the results of the examinations of the Confucian academy as well as the names of 1037 successful graduates. In 2012 the stelae were designated a UNESCO World Heritage Site. The 82 remaining tablets – 30 are no longer there – originate from the years 1442 to 1779. Each one stands vertically on the back of a tortoise, the symbol of strength and long life. There is no recognizably consistent order, but the

Stelae carried by tortoises

two oldest stelae (1442 and 1448) are each found in the middle of the first row. The 14 smallest, dating from the 15th and 16th centuries, carry floral motifs and yin-yang symbols, but no stately dragons. The portrayal of dragons was first allowed in the 17th century, as can be seen on the 25 stelae from this period. The remaining 43 were made in the 18th century. They are the largest and most imposing, decorated with two stylized dragons and flames.

The fourth yard is entered through the Gate of Great Success (Dai Thanh Gate)and leads to the actual temple buildings. The pavilions on both sides once held altars and statues, which were dedicated to the 72 mostly venerated students of Confucius. Today books and souvenirs can be purchased here, and an exhibition can be viewed.

*Gate of Great Success (Dai Thanh Gate)

The Ceremony Hall, a low building with a curved roof, is crowned by two dragons supporting a full moon. The red-gold altar room is where the king and his mandarins made their offerings to the sound of drums and gongs. Two bronze cranes, standing on tortoises, guard the genealogical table of Confucius. The beautiful carvings showing dragons, phoenixes, lotus flowers, fruit, clouds and yin yang symbols are striking. These portrayals stand for the Confucian concept of the order of the universe and for the god-given hierarchy of society – both principles which the Communist rulers hardly welcomed, but did tolerate. Sometimes there is an opportunity to attend traditional concerts.

*Ceremony Hall

Insider Tip

*Sanctuary of Great Success

Directly behind the Ceremony Hall lies the sanctum that was once even forbidden to the king. In the middle of the darkened room stands a statue of Confucius, surrounded by his four most important students. To the side on two altars are the genealogical tables of a total of ten further important students.

Fifth courtyard / Thai Hoc Courtyard

The fifth and last courtyard (Thai Hoc Courtyard) was once the seat of the National Academy, the first university in the land. It was founded in 1076, originally to educate the heirs to the throne, and later also the sons of the mandarins and high officials. This procedure was practiced almost without interruption until 1802, when Emperor Gia Long moved the capital to Hue. Then a temple to the parents of Confucius was established. However, in 1947 French bombs destroyed the building, which was restored some years ago. In the former National Academy, a small **museum** on the ground floor shows a model of the Temple of Literature, historic garments, wooden printing plates and old writings, as well as writing utensils belonging to the former students. On the second floor are three altars in honour of the kings Ly Nhan Tong, Ly Thanh Tong and Le Thanh Tong.

> **?**
> MARCO POLO INSIGHT
>
> *Civil service examinations*
>
> The examinations held in the National Academy to qualify for civil service of the ruling administration were particularly difficult. In 300 years, only 1307 applicants were successful. The chances for the exclusively male candidates improved if they were born into a rich family or were well connected.

HO CHI MINH MAUSOLEUM AND ITS SURROUNDINGS

Ba Dinh Square

The lavishly arranged Ba Dinh Square is the political and ceremonial centre of the Vietnamese capital. The mausoleum of Ho Chi Minh dominates the west side of the square, and the National Assembly stands opposite. This is where, on 2 September 1945, Ho Chi Minh read the **declaration of independence** in front of half a million people, and a military parade has been held here every year in commemoration ever since.

**Ho Chi Minh Mausoleum

As is traditional for all great communist leaders, the corpse of Ho Chi Minh was embalmed – against his will, however. The instructions he left were as follows: »Divide my ashes into three parts and keep them in three ceramic urns, representing the north, the centre and the south«. The body was not displayed publicly until 1975, but today the mausoleum is one of Hanoi's main attractions – for Vietnamese and tourists alike. The masses throng here, especially at weekends and on

Uncle Ho

Faithfully referred to by most Vietnamese to this day as Bac Ho (Uncle Ho), little is actually known of Ho Chi Minh's private life. He is inseparable from the history of his country and its struggle for independence.

He left almost no personal notes and used around 50 different names in his lifetime, mostly aliases. What do we know about him as a person? Only that he was a highly cultured man – an aesthete. He never married, dedicating himself unreservedly to his family, the entire Vietnamese people.

Early Career

He was born with the name Nguyen Sinh Cung on 19 May 1890 in a small village near Vinh, the son of a lowly official. His father was a great believer in education, sending his son to the **French Lycée** in Hue in 1905, although he rejected French colonial supremacy and their local Mandarins – a stance his son would also adopt. Ho left the country in 1911, travelling as a cabin boy to America and Europe, working at the docks in Brooklyn and as a pastry chef for Escoffier in London's Carlton Hotel. In 1917 he finally arrived in Paris, assuming the name of Nguyen Ai Quoc (Nguyen the patriot) to reflect his nationalist spirit. He soon drew attention to himself by publishing a **petition** at the time of the Paris Peace Conference, calling for a democratically elected govern-

Visitors wait in line outside the Ho Chi Minh Mausoleum

ment in Indochina. For a while he joined up with the French socialists, but when this group dissolved he became a founder member of the French Communist Party – emboldened by Lenin's outright dismissal of Imperialism. Thus began Ho Chi Minh's career as a revolutionary.

Freedom Movement

In 1923 he was summoned to **Moscow** by the Communist International (Komintern) and installed as secretary for colonial affairs. On behalf of the Komintern Ho travelled to China, Western Europe, Thailand and Hong Kong in the years that followed. The first Vietnamese freedom movement he organized in 1924 attracted primarily young people. But the leader of the Chinese Nationalists, Chiang Kai-Shek, turned on the Communists three years later, forcing Ho to flee the country. He hid for a while in Thailand, disguised as a Buddhist monk, before returning to Hong Kong where in 1930 he founded the Vietnamese Communist Party, which was renamed the »Communist Party of Indochina« shortly afterwards, on the insistence of the Komintern. The French passed a **death sentence** on him for instigating an uprising. Ho was arrested on trumped up charges and taken to a hospital on account of his poor condition of health. With the aid of hospital staff, who were able to convince French police that he had died, he was able to escape. He lived in the underground for a number of years, for the most part in Moscow, only resurfacing at the end of the 1930s

on the Southern China border, from where he organized anti-colonial resistance.

Founding the Vietminh

After thirty years on foreign soil, he finally set foot back in Vietnam in early 1941, with nothing more than the clothes and sandals he wore, a bamboo stick and his old typewriter. He was 51 years old, suffering from dysentery, malaria and tuberculosis. Home again, he took on the now famous name of Ho Chi Minh **(he who strives for enlightenment)**, which he would use until his death. In the mountains of North Vietnam he was joined by Vo Nguyen Giap, Pham Van Dong and other young soldiers, establishing the League for the Independence of Vietnam (Vietminh), an alliance of anti-colonial groups under the leadership of the Vietnamese Communist Party. Their aim was to fight for the country's independence, liberating it from French colonial power and Japanese occupation. Alas, events conspired against Ho once more. On a trip to China in 1942, he was arrested on suspicion of being a **Franco-Japanese spy**. He spent over a year in various prisons – during which time he wrote his legendary prison diaries, effectively a poetry collection.

Partisan Struggle

The situation in Vietnam had grown more precarious in the meantime. When Japanese occupation ended in August 1945, a political vacuum ensued. The Vietminh were now in a position, for a short period at least, to govern the country, but the French wrested back power in 1946 as the government fled to the jungle of Cao Bang. From here, Ho Chi Minh led the partisan struggle which endured until 1954 at **Dien Bien Phu**. The Geneva Conference designated the 17th parallel at Dong Ha as a provisional line of demarcation. This »provisional« division would remain in place for more than 20 years. Over the next fifteen years, Uncle Ho led his nation as President of the Democratic Republic of Vietnam down a somewhat stony path of socialism, always striving for reunification. His struggle with South Vietnam, supported by the USA, made him into a symbolic figure of the protest movement in America and Europe against American intervention in Vietnam. He would not live to see Vietnam reunited, passing away on 2 September 1969, Vietnam's national holiday. The anniversary of his death was thus transferred to 3 September. The legend of Ho has since become indistinguishable from his own life, transformed into a cult of sorts with him as the ultimate Vietnamese national hero – something he would no doubt have neither wished for nor approved of.

Still omnipresent after his death – Ho Chi Minh himself rejected the cult of personality

holidays, to pay their respects to »Uncle Ho«. Even if the building seems gloomy and hulking, a visit is not to be missed. The escort by soldiers in white uniforms, the ceremonial silence and the effective lighting of Ho Chi Minh's face and hands make the passage through the hall a unique experience. Foreign visitors must leave their bags and cameras at reception in Hung Vuong Street before proceeding to the assembly point. From here, visitors are escorted into the mausoleum. There is no admission for those in shorts, miniskirts or spaghetti tops.

❶ April-Sept daily except Mon and Fri 8am–17am, Dec–March daily except Mon and Fri 8am–11am, from beginning of Sept to beginning of Dec usually closed

Presidential Palace

After leaving the mausoleum, the path continues to the former Presidential Palace and the house of Ho Chi Minh, which is also located on this premises. The Residence of the Governor General of Indochina was built from 1900 to 1908; today guests of state are received here. The palace is closed to the public.

*Ho Chi Minh House

After independence in 1954, Ho Chi Minh officially moved into the former royal residence, but said that it was now the property of the people. He had a more modest house built nearby. When it got too hot for him in summer, he designed a small **stilted hut**, which was built at an idyllic site on a small lake. The rooms on ground level are furnished with a desk, telephone and table; his study and bedroom upstairs are kept just as he left them. Ho Chi Minh lived here for the last 11 years of his life (from 1958), as well as during the Vietnam War. What looks like a guest room to the left is the entrance to his bunker. It is said that Ho was very attached to his garden and carp pond.

❶ daily 8am–11am, 1.30pm-4pm; admission: approx. 25,000 VND

**One Pillar Pagoda

In the immediate vicinity is the One Pillar Pagoda (Chua Mot Cot). Like the Tortoise Tower at Hoan Kiem Lake, it is an emblem of Hanoi. Among the hundreds of pagodas that the Ly kings donated in the 11th century, this one is surely the most unusual. The wooden Quan Am sanctuary has an area of only around 3 sq m/32 sq ft and is supported only by a single pillar, which juts out from the middle of the lake. The form is intended to represent a lotus flower, the Buddhist symbol of enlightenment. As can easily be seen, the structure in question is not actually the original, and the concrete pillar, poured in 1954, detracts from the scene immensely. Little is known about the origins of the pagoda, but a **folk legend** says that it was built in 1049 under King Ly Thai Tong. Quan Am appeared to him in a dream, sitting on her lotus throne and holding a baby boy out toward him. Shortly thereafter the queen gave birth to a boy, and Ly

Thai Tong had the pagoda built in thanks. In actual fact, he had already had a son in 1022, six years before he ascended the throne, making a less romantic version of the story slightly more believable: the king dreamed that Quan Am had invited him to sit with her on the lotus throne. The royal advisor saw this as a bad omen and persuaded him to build a pagoda in the form of a lotus in order to obtain a long life. Behind the pagoda is a Bodhi tree, a cutting from the tree under which Buddha found enlightenment. Ho Chi Minh was presented with the sapling in 1958 during a trip to India.

One of Hanoi's landmarks: the One Pillar Pagoda

❶ daily except Mon 8am-6pm

The large, modern building around 100m/110yd west of the One Pillar Pagoda was built with Soviet help for the 100th birthday of Ho Chi Minh on 19 May 1990. The museum honours the man and the special role he played for the country. Small exhibits describe his life, the Vietnamese revolution and the development of socialism throughout the world. Also to be seen are personal objects such as documents and photographs, as well as the clothes he wore when he fled Hong Kong.

*Ho Chi Minh Museum

❶ Tue–Sun 8am–12am, 2pm–4.30pm

Heading east of the Ho Chi Minh Museum via Ba Dinh Square, visitors reach Dien Bien Phu Street, a road with gnarled old trees and pretty colonial buildings. Around 500m/550yd from the square, a statue of Lenin stands in front of the white, arcaded Army Museum. It is worth a visit, even for those who are not especially interested in all things military, as it gives an informative overview of the history of Vietnam – also in the English language. The yard of the museum is full of weapons, including a Russian MiG 21, artillery from Dien Bien Phu, antiaircraft guns from the Vietnam War and wreckage from American planes, among them a B52 bomber. The exhibition begins on the second floor. A feature is the **diorama of the Battle of Dien Bien Phu**. In addition, a video in English can be viewed. In comparison, the exhibition on the war is relatively drab, with mostly medals on display.

*Army Museum

❶ daily 8am-11.30am, 1pm-4.30pm, closed Mon and Fri

Cot Co Flag Tower	In the grounds of the Army Museum stands the 33m/108ft-high Cot Co Flag Tower, one of the few remnants of the citadel built by Emperor Gia Long in the early 19th century. There is a nice view over the city from the top, though climbing the tower is not always permitted.
Thang Long Citadel	Since 2010 the centre of the Imperial »Citadel of the Rising Dragon« has enjoyed UNESCO World Heritage status. The wide reaching site at the heart of the city had previously been a restricted military zone for half a century. Originally built by the Ly Dynasty in the 11th century, only a few historical structures remain, among them the Cot Co Flag Tower (erected in 1805), marking the southern boundary of the citadel. Most of the palace has been destroyed and the temple has fared no better. The fortress, commissioned by Emperor Gia Long and constructed between 1805 and 1812, was conquered by French soldiers in 1872, then serving as a barracks for colonial troops. Since 2002, archaeologists have been working on the vast site, unearthing relics from the first Chinese fortress in the 7th century and from the Ly Dynasty.

Along with the entrance gates, the attractive Princesses Palace is well worth seeing. It was also destroyed by the French but later reconstructed. It was in the simple concrete building named »D 67« that plans were hatched for the North Vietnamese army to overthrow the south. General Vo Nguyen Giap's seat is marked – a kind of North Vietnamese Pentagon with Soviet equipment in a nondescript, prefabricated building, with bunkers and tunnels underneath.

Access to the sprawling citadel is possible via the imposing Doan Mon main gate (near the Ho Chi Minh Mausoleum), through the Cua Bac north gate (with beautiful reliefs) and the west gate in Phung Hung Street.

❶ Wed-Sun 8am-5pm;
admission: 20,000 VND

WEST LAKE AND SURROUNDING AREA

The district around West Lake, also known as »Hanoi's Beverly Hills«, recently came into fashion as a villa district. Around the lake there are nice hotel buildings and conference centres, parks and clubs. This is also the site of **Chua Tran Quoc**, Hanoi's oldest pagoda. In the 17th century the village inhabitants built a dam at the southeastern end of the lake, creating a small lake that was rich with fish (Truc Bach). The attractions of West Lake are on the south side, only around 500m/550yd away from Binh Dinh Square, making it easy to combine seeing the sights there with a detour to the lake (or vice versa).

The name Truc Bach refers back to a summer palace, which was built in the 18th century under the Trinh rulers and later served as a kind of asylum for concubines and other »fallen« women, who were employed here for the weaving of fine white silk (truc bach). It is splendid to ride around Truc Bach Lake on a bike, as there is barely any traffic on the very quiet, narrow streets here. **Truc Bach Lake**

The palace no longer exists, but on the southeast bank of the lake stands Quan Thanh Temple, which was built under King Ly Thai To and dedicated to the Guardian of the North (Tran Vo). The 3m/10ft-high statue of Tran Vo on the main altar is made out of black bronze (1677) and shows the Taoist god with his two animal symbols: a snake and a tortoise. In the altar room are tablets with poems and parallel sentences (words of wisdom written in pairs hanging on neighbouring columns). Some of them are decorated with elaborate mother-of-pearl inlays. On the way back to the main street, a large bronze bell, also from the year 1677, makes itself noticeable at the gate. ***Quan Thanh Temple**

❶ daily 8am-4.30pm; admission: approx. 10,000 VND

> **? MARCO POLO INSIGHT**
>
> *How was West Lake created?*
>
> A long time ago, a monk had a bell cast in bronze from the imperial Chinese treasury, in which there lived a golden calf. The calf heard the bright ringing and followed it, believing it to be his mother calling. When the ringing stopped, the calf became disoriented and in his despair he turned around and around on his own axis. This created a trough, which filled with water. It is said that the golden calf still lives at the bottom of the lake.

Directly opposite lies a small park with a monument to the anti-aircraft gun assistants who were stationed here during the Vietnam War. In particular, **the landing of US Officer John McCain** comes to mind here. When his plane was shot down, he landed with a parachute in Truc Bach Lake in October 1967 and was held prisoner at the notorious »Hanoi Hilton« (▶p.260) for more than five years. Afterwards he returned to the United States of America, where he became a Senator for Arizona, and did much to normalize relations between Vietnam and the USA. He was defeated by Barack Obama in the presidential election of 2008. This little park is today a popular meeting point, where families picnic and many drinks sellers and Cyclo drivers await their customers. **Monument**

The street along the shore (Thanh Nien Street) is lined with Royal Poincianas and leads to Hanoi's oldest sanctuary, Tran Quoc Pagoda, which lies upon a small island in West Lake. It is believed to have been founded as early as the 6th century during the early Ly dynasty, which for a short time interrupted the 1000-year rule of the ***Tran Quoc Pagoda**

A group of sculptures in Tran Quoc Pagoda

Chinese. On a stone stele (1639) at the entrance is an inscription saying that the pagoda was brought here from the Red River in the early 17th century, when Buddhism regained prominence. The temple complex is reached via a dam. The interior of the temple appears very grandiose, with many Buddhas and various sentinel figures between red-gold columns. The garden and the yards, especially the stupa garden and the eleven-floored pagoda tower, are very impressive.

❶ Mon–Sat 7am–11.30am and 1.30pm–6pm, Sun, holidays 7am–6pm

**Museum of Ethnology The Museum of Ethnology in Nguyen Van Huyen Street was opened in April 1998. It impresses with its lavish premises – the building's design is based upon a bronze drum. With the help of good, explanatory plaques, charts and overviews (also in English), much is explained about the life and diverse culture of the ethnic minorities, who are often still seen as underdeveloped in Vietnam itself. The first section is concerned with the largest and dominant group of the Viet, the actual Vietnamese. Further along is the section on the Muong, Tho and Chut, in which scenes (e.g. a burial) and tools from everyday life are shown. The first room on the upper floor focuses on the Thai, Tay and Nung peoples, mainly upon various models of buildings and traditional garments. Particularly vivid is the open-air section with many house replicas to inspect. Not to be forgotten are the water puppet theatre and cult of ancestral spirits (Viet department), the Dao frames that were used to keep special wedding hairstyles in place, the batik and dying work of the Hmong women and Khmer calabashes.

❶ Tue-Sun 8.30am-5pm; admission 40,000 VND; www.vme.org.vn

The futuristic Hanoi Museum – an inverted pyramid, so to speak – was inaugurated by the Hamburg architects' firm of Gerkan, Marg and Partner (GMP) in honour of Hanoi's 1000 year anniversary. Covering more than 50,000 sq m/59,000 sq yd and four floors of exhibition space, including a spiral ramp to the top (or take the elevator), the most modern museum in the country documents the 1000 year history of the city and of the Vietnamese nation. Pride of place goes to a bronze drum (on the second floor) from the Dong Son era, whilst there are a number of ancient ceramics, pots and jewellery on

Hanoi
Museum

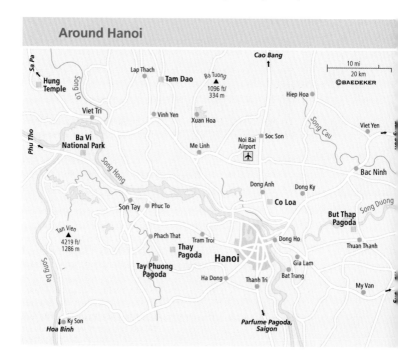

Around Hanoi

display. Sadly, many of the exhibists are either unmarked or, if there are descriptions, they are written in poor English. Hence the journey to this remote district is of most interest to architecture fans.

❶ Pham Hung St. (next to the National Convention Center), Tu Liem district, Hanoi; Tue–Sun 8am–11.30am, 1.30pm–5pm; free admission

AROUND HANOI – NEAR VICINITY

Even if Hanoi itself does have so much to offer, it is still worth taking at least one **excursion** out of the city. The pretty delta landscape of the ▶Red River is strewn with dykes, villages with old community houses, and tomb groups in the rice fields, as well as temples and other sanctuaries. Some of the most beautiful pagodas in the country are actually found in the near vicinity of the capital. Those interested in handicrafts also have an opportunity to visit a number of handicraft villages and observe how carvings or pottery are made there. All of the following destinations can be visited on a day trip. The best solution is to book the appropriate tour directly from Hanoi or to rent a car and a driver.

HUNG TEMPLE AND CO LOA CITADEL

History and mythology seem to intertwine here – the very **origins of Vietnam** can be found at the temples of the legendary Hung kings. For it is said that the capital of Van Lang, the legendary first kingdom of Vietnam, was founded not far from the intersection where the Red,

the Black and the Clear rivers meet. Just 12km/7mi west of the industrial city of Viet Tri, near the village of Phong Chau, an almost conical hill rises straight up from the plain of the Red River. At its foot lie two idyllic little lakes. The special beauty of this place alone explains why a temple to the Hung kings was built here. Although the actual existence of the Hung dynasty remains disputed by scientists to this day, most Vietnamese still consider the kings to be the creators of their country. **Ho Chi Minh** even assembled his troops here before the liberation of Hanoi to recall these forebears and to defend their legacy. The simple temple complex is spread over three levels. There are nearly 500 steps to be climbed in order to reach the highest temple, where once stood the assembly hall of the rulers, who made offerings to the earth god here. Approaching from the car park, visitors first reach a small **museum**, in which finds (13th–10th century BC) from the area such as arrow heads, ceramics and jewellery can be seen, as well as bronze drums from the Dong Son epoch (3rd–5th century BC).

Just as Ho Chi Minh would have wished, pilgrims come to the temple all year round to remember their forebears. But it is especially lively here during the temple festival on the 10th day of the 3rd lunar month. Hawkers, jugglers, stalls and snack bars offer every kind of diversion. **Boat races** are held on the swan lake.

Temple festival

The northern hill country of the province is characterized by tea plantations, bamboo groves and fan palms. At the beginning of the 20th century the French built their first holiday resort here at Tam Dao (930m/3050ft, approximately 35km/22mi east of Hung Temple), with a backdrop of up to 1400m/4600ft-high mountains. The place was badly damaged during the various wars, leaving only few colonial era buildings intact. In the meantime, work has begun on restoration and the building of new spa and leisure facilities.

*Tam Dao

The earliest Vietnamese kingdoms had their origins in the plain of the Red River – the legendary Van Lang of the Hung kings, as well as Au Lac (258–207 BC), which was ruled by King An Duong from the imposing Co Loa Citadel (»snail-shaped citadel«, 16km/10m north of Hanoi). Little of its former splendour remains today, but if passing through is worth a stop to see two temples and a 1000-year-old banyan tree. At the entrance stand statues of King An Duong and his daughter. The pond in front is said to have magical powers. There are plans to build a National Tourism Park next to Co Loa Citadel. The three fortification rings, canals and the grave of Princess My Chau are to be restored. The park is scheduled to open in 2015 at the earliest.

Co Loa Citadel

✷✷ BUT THAP PAGODA (CHUA BUT THAP)

The most beautiful temple statue in Vietnam stands inside the pagoda of the small village of Dinh To, around 25km/16mi east of Hanoi. Founded by monks in 1647, the pagoda lies in the middle of the fields, right behind a dyke.

Home to the most beautiful Quan Am figure

The altar room contains an abundance of ornate statues, but one overshadows all the others: the portrayal of the **Goddess of Com-**

**Quan Am statue

Chua But Thap

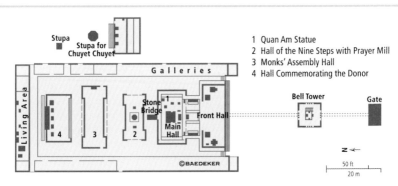

Stupa
Stupa for
Chuyet Chuyet

G a l l e r i e s

Living Area

4 3 2

Stone
Bridge

1

Front Hall

Main
Hall

©BAEDEKER

1 Quan Am Statue
2 Hall of the Nine Steps with Prayer Mill
3 Monks' Assembly Hall
4 Hall Commemorating the Donor

Bell Tower

Gate

50 ft
20 m

passion (3.7m/12ft high, photo ▶p.73, left) decorated with gold and lacquer. Springing from the richly ornamented pedestal is a monster with a lotus flower, from which Quan Am rises up in a meditation position. One pair of arms rests in her lap, the other is crossed in front of her chest; the 16 others growing from her back once held her attributes. Further, smaller-scale arms – each with an eye in the palm of the hand – surround the figure like a fan. It is said that Buddha gave them to her in order to defeat the monster at her feet. On her head Quan Am wears a crown of Buddha heads with an Amitabha in the middle. She is accompanied by Kim Dong, the Golden Child, and Ngoc Nu, the Jade Daughter. Uncharacteristically, there is an inscription on the pedestal of the statue giving the name of the donor and the year (1656). Through the interplay of light and shadow, it seems as if the hands of the figure are moving. Also remarkable are the depiction of the Fasting Buddha on the left side of the altar and the figures of the 18 arhats (protectors, La Han) along the side walls.

Hall of the Nine Steps — The passageway to the three following buildings , which are not otherwise common in the design of Vietnamese pagodas, is made up of a richly decorated stone bridge. The first is the Hall of the Nine Steps, in which a 6m/20ft-high 13th-century wooden prayer mill stands. During the pagoda festival on the 24th day of the 3rd lunar month, the mill is put into motion in a festive ceremony through which all of the prayers written on slips of paper inside are considered to have been spoken.

Tip — It is a good idea to combine the trip to Chua But Thap with a visit to the handicraft villages (▶p.280). Dong Ky is close to the N 1a, while Bat Trang and Dong Ho are not far from the N 5.

Pilgrim boats on the way to the Perfume Pagoda

★★ PERFUME PAGODA (CHUA HUONG)

There are two other interesting stops along Highway 6 on the way to the Perfume Pagoda: around 10km/6mi southwest of Hanoi is the **silk village of Van Phuc**, where of course visitors can also purchase silk clothes and fabric. About 13km/8mi southwest of Hanoi is the **Ho Chi Minh Trail Museum**, which offers an impressive overview of the network of jungle paths in the border regions of three countries. The trail played a decisive role in the outcome of the war. On the road to the Perfume Pagoda is another specialized handicraft village, **Chuong** (also Phuong Trung), where the famous conical hats are made and sold in all variations.

Sights along the way

Hardly any other attraction in Vietnam is so idyllically and mysteriously hidden away as the Perfume Pagoda, the most famous pilgrimage site in northern Vietnam. Huong Tich Son, the »Mountain of the Fragrant Traces« (60km/37mi southwest of Hanoi), home to the sanctuary dedicated to Quan Am, can only be reached by boat. The trip runs through a flooded valley between karst mountains, where fishermen and farmers work in the flooded fields. Visible on the shore and a little further into the valley are little temples, which are also related to the legend surrounding the Perfume Pagoda (crowded on summer weekends).

Pilgrimage site at the »Mountain of the Fragrant Traces«

Legend Once upon a time there was a king with a beautiful daughter. She did not wish to marry any of the suitors her father had presented, but instead wished to devote her entire life to Buddha. She hid herself away in a temple, and when threats and promises would not change her mind, the king ordered his soldiers to kill her. A white tiger rescued the princess and brought her to a secluded mountain cave. But then her father became sick with leprosy, went blind and lost his hands. None of the doctors or healers could help him. However, a Buddhist sage told him that he could be saved if one of his subjects would give him his hands and eyes. Yet no one came forward. When the news finally reached the princess in her cave, she decided to make the sacrifice. After he was saved, the king wished to visit the donor with a reward. He was brought to the cave, where he saw his daughter, who had in the meantime become a Buddha and regained her eyes and hands. The king subsequently realized the error of his ways and also devoted his life to Buddhism.

Thien Tru Pagoda After leaving the boat, the difficult part of the journey begins, unless the choice is made to take the funicular (approx. €4). A steep, only

Guarding the temples and shrines carved into caves and rock ledges

occasionally shaded path leads up to Chua Thien Tru, a 15th-century sanctuary (approximately 2 hours). There is a **stone statue of Quan Am** here, made in 1793 after the Tay Son rebels stole its bronze predecessor and melted it down to make cannon balls.

A path leads further on into a wide open cave, which the Vietnamese see as a giant dragon's mouth. It is found on the edge of a large hollow, which is grown over with trees and bushes. A member of the Trinh family had this inscription chiselled into the rock: **»The most beautiful grotto under the southern sky.«** Steps lead downward to the interior of the over 50m/164ft-high cave. The gilded Buddha can be glimpsed in the darkness, shrouded in billows of incense smoke; pilgrims mumble the magical greeting »Nam mo A Di Da Phat« (»Praise Amitabha Buddha«). In addition to pilgrims, ever since its foundation in the 17th century, the pagoda has attracted poets and scholars, whose verses are engraved in the stelae. The scenery is very impressive here, even despite the masses of visitors and peddlers. The Vietnamese pilgrims visit the sanctuary in March and April in particular. The peak provides a stunning view.

**Perfume Pagoda

TAY PHUONG PAGODA (CHUA TAY PHUONG)

Located in the village of Thac Xa (42km/26mi west of Hanoi), Chua Tay Phuong (Pagoda of the West) is one of the oldest pagodas in Vietnam (8th century). Moss-covered steps lead up the hill to the temple complex, built in the Tam Quan style. The pagoda has been destroyed and rebuilt several times since its establishment, but today the basic structure of the building mostly dates back to the 16th century.

Simple building in Tam Quan style

The pagoda is famous for its unique collection of more than 70 man-sized sculptures, made from the wood of jackfruit trees. Today some of them can be marvelled at in the Museum of Fine Arts in Hanoi. Particularly worth seeing are the **18 Arhat figures** (18th century), extremely lifelike portrayals of monks and ascetics, which can be found behind the main altar. Their realistic, individualized features are meant to emphasize the status of Arhats, who are about to enter nirvana, as human beings and students of Buddhism. Also known throughout the land are the imposing guard figures.

*Collection of unusual wooden sculptures

** THAY PAGODA (CHUA THAY)

The long Thay Pagoda (6km/4mi east of Tay Phuong Pagoda) looks as if it is snuggled up against the limestone rocks, before which

Ideal setting for water puppet theatre

The pagoda at Dragon Lake is the setting for one of the nicest water puppet theatres in the land

spreads the picturesque Dragon Lake. The 11th-century sanctuary lies in the village of Sai Son, just 40km/25mi southwest of Hanoi. The name of the pagoda means »Pagoda of the Master«, though it is also called Thien Phuc Tu, or »Pagoda of the Heavenly Blessing«. It was built in honour of the **healer Tu Dao Hanh**, the master who lived here in the village and is said to have performed many miracles. Yet he was not just a monk, he was also a declared lover of water puppet theatre (►MARCO POLO Insight p.78 and p.368), for which he had an attractive lake pavilion built. According to legend, the healer Tu Dao Hanh had three incarnations: as a master, as King Ly Nhan Tong and as a Buddha.

The dark prayer halls are full of statues – nearly 100 of them. The oldest ones date back to the establishment of the pagoda, but the most striking are the two huge guard figures from the 15th century, made out of clay and papier maché. Each of them weighs 1000kg/1.1 tons, and they are said to be the **largest of their kind in Vietnam**. On the first altar stand a Buddha and a likeness of the master in a yellow robe. To the right, the tomb of the master is held inside a shrine, which is only opened for viewing during the temple festival (5th to 7th day of the 3rd lunar month). A water puppet festival is also held at this time.

❶ admission: approx. 12,000 VND

HANDICRAFT VILLAGES

Dong Ho   Dong Ho is known in North Vietnam as the »village of the new year's pictures« (►also p.85). The new year's Tet Festival is the most important festivals of the year, the time when the kitchen god Tao Quan goes up to heaven to report on how the family has behaved (►MARCO POLO Insight p.114). The colourful **wood carvings** that are hung up on the day, depicting old stories and legends or showing good-luck motifs such as well-fed children, pigs, fish or chickens, are made here. Dong Ho lies on the right bank of the Song Duong, just a few miles from the centre of Hanoi.

On the other side of the Red River in the Gia Lam district (approximately 7km/4mi east of Hanoi) lies Bat Trang, which specializes in ceramics and pottery. Bricks and stoneware were manufactured here as early as the 15th century. Today about 2000 families live in Bat Trang, predominately producing the traditional blue and white ceramics. Everything can be found at the street stands and in the showrooms here, from small figurines and chopstick holders to huge animal sculptures and cachepots (photo p.87).

Bat Trang

Insider Tip

AROUND HANOI – FURTHER AFIELD

It is possible to get to know other facets of Vietnam on excursions of two or three days. Nature lovers will appreciate the wonderful landscape of ►Dry Ha Long Bay, with the old capital of Hoa Lu and Cuc Phuong National Park (►photo p.223), as well as Ba Vi National Park (see below). Those interested in art should pay a visit to Keo Pagoda (►photo p.225), a masterpiece of woodcraft. To get a sense of the mountainous region of the north and the various ethnic sections of the population (►MARCO POLO Insight pp.26 – 30), it is worth a making a trip to Hoa Binh, ►Sa Pa or ►Dien Bien Phu. Excursions to all of these destinations are available from Hanoi. It is recommended to book a tour or rent a car with a driver from here.

Countless lakes, streams, waterfalls and grottos are the attractions of the area where the Black River converges with the Red River (65km/40mi west of Hanoi). Including the surrounding nature reserves, Ba Vi Park has a total area of around 7000ha/27 sq mi. The highest elevation is the **Dinh Vua Mountain** (1296m/4252ft). Daytrippers from Hanoi like to visit the three pagodas at heights of up to 1200m/3937ft. 38 mammalian species are said to live here: easiest to spot are gibbons and macaques, mountain goats and bats. There were nearly 5000 subtropical plant species counted here at the end of the 19th century, only half of which probably exist today. This has to do with the slash-and-burn land clearance practiced by the Muong and Dao who live here. The national park is also famous for its **myths**, which tell of earth and water spirits and play a big role in the perception of the hill tribes. There are a number of simple guesthouses for tourists here (bring a passport!). From Hanoi, the national park can be reached on the N 11 via Son Tay.

Ba Vi National Park

❶ www.vietnamnationalparks.org

Dinh Tay Dang
When visiting the park, a trip to the cult house of Tay Dang at the foot of the Ba Vi is a must. The wood carvings inside depicting scenes from country life are particularly worth seeing.

Dong Mo Lake
The nearby Dong Mo Lake and its surroundings has become a popular bathing and hiking area, even featuring an 18-hole golf course.
❶ King's Island Golf Resort and Country Club, tel. 04/33 68 65 55
http://brgkingsislandgolf.vn, £££

HOA BINH AND ITS SURROUNDINGS

Hoa Binh
The landscape around Hoa Binh (74km/46mi southwest of Hanoi, 2½ hours) is like a prehistoric Garden of Eden with its karst cones rising suddenly from the plain and expansive bamboo thickets. The scenery and the atmosphere seem symbolic of Vietnam. Hoa Binh is known as the location of Vietnam's largest hydroelectric power station, which was built with Soviet help and to this day is still not in service.

Villages in the area
From Hoa Binh it is possible to visit a number of Muong villages (►MARCO POLO Insight, pp.26 – 30), including Xom Mo, Ban Dam and Giang, all of which are less than 10km/6mi away. Here the families live in large pile dwellings (longhouses) and small farm animals and poultry amble around the lanes. The inhabitants live mainly from rice and vegetable cultivation.
Boats run from Hoa Binh roughly 25km/16mi upstream to the **Daovillages of Duong and Phu**.

Mai Chau
The village and the valley of Mai Chau, located around 40km/25mi south of Hoa Binh, are well known for their marvellous setting of rice fields and distant mountain ranges. This is where the White Thai live in their beautifully decorated stilt houses, in which families also offer accommodation to tourists. The village market sells all kinds of products from the area.

Moc Chau
In order to visit the Thai, it is worth travelling further west to the plateau of Moc Chau (approximately 70km/43mi southwest of Hoa Binh). The Thai villages are beautifully located in an enchanting mountain landscape.

Ho Chi Minh City

►Saigon

✳✳ Hoi An

◈ E 5

Province: Quang Nam – Da Nang
Region: Southern Central Coast
Population: Approx. 80,000

A hint of China is perceptible in the old harbour town of Hoi An, with its narrow streets and low houses that seem to crouch beneath their curious tiled roofs. The area around Tran Phu Street in particular, where the pretty trading houses, temples and pagodas are found, seems like an Asian open-air museum.

The one-time Cham harbour of Hoi An had long been situated on the trade routes between east and west before, in the 16th and 17th centuries, the Chinese from Fujian – and later also Japanese, Dutch and Indians – set up bases here, making the place an important **centre of commerce**. Ships from around the world headed into this harbour to participate in the important fairs and exchanges held here. The trade with China led to a decrease in influence for the city, then called »Hai Pho« (place on the sea), and then the mouth of the Thu Bon

History

The old town of Hoi An was the only one to survive intact during the Vietnam War. In 1999 it was designated a UNESCO World Heritage Site

silted up. During the Tay Son uprising (1771–88), the city of foreign merchants was nearly destroyed. Unlike the Japanese, the Chinese rebuilt their quarter. Under the Nguyen emperors and French colonial rulers, who gave Hoi An the name »Faifo«, Da Nang was favoured for its better transport conditions. This led to the remote and neglected Hoi An becoming a **hideout for resistance movements** against the French and later also against the Americans, which led to heavy attacks on the city.

Old Town The old town of Hoi An is relatively small and easy to get to grips with. Because the centre has been preserved, with its unique concentration of residential and trading houses, assembly halls, pagodas, shrines and temples, the fountain, the central market and the wharf, it vividly recreates the image of a Southeast Asian town of the past. The historic centre is for the most part made up of three streets, which extend parallel to the riverbank, with sections closed to cars and motorcycles. To this day **Tran Phu Street, the oldest of these

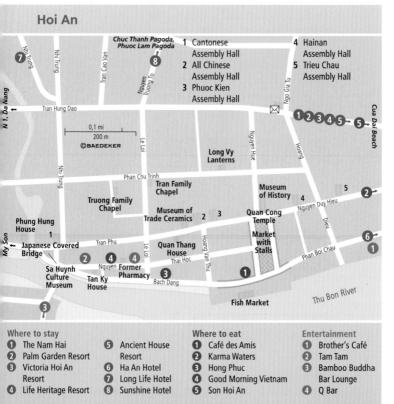

Hoi An

Chuc Thanh Pagoda, Phuoc Lam Pagoda
8

1 Cantonese Assembly Hall
2 All Chinese Assembly Hall
3 Phuoc Kien Assembly Hall
4 Hainan Assembly Hall
5 Trieu Chau Assembly Hall

0,1 mi
200 m
©BAEDEKER

Nhi Trung
Nhi Trung
Tran Cao Van
Nguyen Truong To
Ngo Gia Tu
Cua Dai Beach
Tran Hung Dao
N 1, Da Nang
Le Loi
Long Vy Lanterns
Nguyen Hue
Hoang
Phan Chu Trinh
Tran Family Chapel
Museum of History
5
Nguyen Duy Hieu
Truong Family Chapel
Museum of Trade Ceramics
Quan Cong Temple
Dieu
Phung Hung House
My Son
Japanese Covered Bridge
Tran Phu
Quan Thang House
Market with Stalls
Phan Boi Chau
Sa Huynh Culture Museum
Tan Ky House
Nguyen Former Pharmacy
Thai Hoc
Bach Dang
Hoang Van Thu
Fish Market
Thu Bon River

Where to stay
1 The Nam Hai
2 Palm Garden Resort
3 Victoria Hoi An Resort
4 Life Heritage Resort
5 Ancient House Resort
6 Ha An Hotel
7 Long Life Hotel
8 Sunshine Hotel

Where to eat
1 Café des Amis
2 Karma Waters
3 Hong Phuc
4 Good Morning Vietnam
5 Son Hoi An

Entertainment
1 Brother's Café
2 Tam Tam
3 Bamboo Buddha Bar Lounge
4 Q Bar

streets, is the main thoroughfare of Hoi An boasting the main points of interest as well as a whole host of shops, galleries and restaurants. One block further south is **Nguyen Thai Hoc Street** with its pretty shops and traditional pharmacies. Running directly along the river-side is the lively **Bach Dang Street**; here there are a number of pleasant cafés and restaurants, from which the comings and goings on the river and the street can be watched in peace. The old town of Hoi An was declared a UNESCO World Heritage Site in 1999. East of the three streets is the market, with a large hall and many street stalls. When following Phan Boi Chau Street in the same direction, there are numerous relics of French colonial architecture. The following highlights are worth noting: an interesting system of interlocking **roof tiles**. This style of tiling is known as »yin-yang« after the way the alternating concave and convex-shaped tiles are slotted into one another. The rows are usually then closed off with decorative, often colourfully glazed Chinese coins. Another detail typical of Hoi An are the **»eyes«** (mat cua) that guard the entrances to houses or religious buildings. In addition to this are two thick wooden spikes with a diameter of 20cm/8in hammered like nails into the door lintels in order to protect residents and visitors from dark forces. At the Phuoc Kien Assembly Hall they are found in form of yin-yang symbols with two dragons who pay homage to the sun; alternatively, at the Tan Ky House they take the form of flowers or often simply an octagonal amulet. Seen again and again during a visit to Hoi An, on weather vanes, lantern holders or roof beams, is a mythical creature with the body of a fish and the head of a dragon. The **carp** (cá chép) is a symbol for wealth and success, and in this form, showing its transformation into a dragon, is meant to remind that nothing in this life happens all by itself. In order to become a dragon, thereby attaining immortality, the fish must pass through three gates, much like a scholar must pass three examinations before becoming a mandarin, requiring a great deal of patience and hard work.

Transformation of a carp into a dragon

Hoi An

INFORMATION
The Sinh Tourist
(formerly Sinh Café)
587 Hai Ba Trung, Hoi An
tel. 510/386 39 48
www.thesinhtourist.vn

TVH Travel
72b Nguyen Phuc Tan, An Hoi Island
tel. 0510/3916732, 0905/19 68 02
www.tvh-travel.de

TRANSPORT
Da Nang International Airport (approx.
25km/16mi north of Hoi An):
tel. 0511/381 1811
www.danangairportonline.com

COMBINATION TICKET
Combination tickets are sold for the
main attractions of the city, which are
valid for one museum, one assembly
hall, one old house and the Japanese
Bridge or Quan Cong Temple (120,000
VND), alternatively also for a handicrafts
workshop or theatre performance.

EVENT
Hoi An Legendary Night
Insider Tip
Each month on the evening before the
full moon (14th day of the lunar calendar) the old town is illuminated by silken
lanterns and fairy lights,
light balloons ascend into the evening
sky, traditional music and theatre are
performed in the lanes and old houses.

SHOPPING
Hoi An – Shopping Paradise
The many **souvenir shops in the centre** invite customers to browse and buy
their wares, ranging from inlayed ornaments, carvings, embroidery to T-shirts
and puppets, opium pipes, Vietnamese
ceramics and beautifully decorated
chopsticks, indeed virtually everything
imaginable (don't forget to haggle!).

Tran Phu Street Market
Inside the market hall and the numerous
surrounding stands everything from fruit
and vegetables, poultry and fish, basketry and medicimal herbs to kitchen appliances and ceramics can be found.

Hoi An Handicraft Workshop
(9 Nguyen Thai Hoc, daily 8am to
around 7pm): large selection of nice
souvenirs and handicrafts, traditional
music performances daily.

Somewhat further on: **Reaching Out**
(103 Nguyen Thai Hoc, Mon–Fri
8.30am–9pm, Sat and Sun 9.30am-
8pm, www.reachingoutvietnam.com).

Tailors offer their services in Le Loi
Street (▶p.128). It is possible to have
suits, pyjamas, kimonos, blouses and
skirts clothes made overnight at low
prices, in western or Asian designs.

Buying silk: »Vietnamese silk« is synthetic. »Thai silk« is the real deal, genuine raw silk. In order to be certain, set fire to a thread: if it melts, it's polyester. Real silk smells like burnt hair.

LEISURE
Lantern workshops
Long Vy Lanterns
6 Phan Chu Trinh, Hoi An
tel. 0510/360 66 11 and
Mobile tel. 090/86 46 47 31
www.hoianlantern.com.vn
(from around 60,000 VNC/US$3)
Or at
Life Start Foundation
77 Phan Chu Trinh, Hoi An
Mobile tel. 0167/35 59 44
(halfdays US$25)

Cookery courses Insider Tip
Those wishing to enjoy typical Vietnamese flavours and dishes such as Cao Lau or hotpot at home, using herbs correctly and avoiding overcooking the vegetables, can take part in a Vietnamese cookery course – the latest trend in Hoi An. Many restaurants offer more or less complicated taster courses, e.g. **Vy's Cooking School** at the Morning Glory restaurant (107 Nguyen Thai Hoc, tel. 0510/91 04 89) or **Red Bridge Cooking School**, Thon 4, Cam Thanh, tel. 0510/393 32 22, www.visithoian.com, 5 hours, US$29 per head, attractively located river restaurant (▶p.45). It is well worth it to visit the market with an English-speaking guide, boat trip to the restaurant, cooking with a view of the river. On the idyllic stream island of **Thuan Tinh**, cookery courses are also offered as part of a half-day excursion (market, boat trip, herb garden and open air course with Mrs. Hoa, around US$30

per person, mobile tel. 090/647 77 70, www.cooking-tour.com, ▶p.45).

ENTERTAINMENT
❶ *Brother's Café*
27 Phan Boi Chau
tel. 0510/391 41 50
daily 10am-10pm
Excellent Vietnamese dining at a colonial villa in a tropical garden, right on the riverbank, also cocktails, wines and beer.

❷ *Tam Tam*
110 Nguyen Thai Hoc
tel. 0510/386 22 12
daily 10am-1am
Popular café-restaurant and bar in the old town, on two floors with a narrow balcony from where activity on the street below may be observed, otherwise comfy sofas in the corner, Vietnamese and international dishes (from tapas to steak to pasta), good selection of wines, cocktails.

❸ *Bamboo Buddha Bar Lounge*
40 Nguyen Phuc Tan, An Hoi Islet (close to the night market on the river islet) Hoi An
tel. 0510/392 50 00
www.bb-hoian.com
daily from 2pm
Stylish yet earthy establishment, see and be seen on three floors: inventively prepared, predominantly French and Vietnamese dishes, but also tapas, three-course menus (£8.20!), good selection of drinks, 2 for 1 Happy Hour 5pm-6.30pm.

❹ *Q Bar*
94 Nguyen Thai Hoc, Hoi An
tel. 0510/391 19 64
The place to be! Finally the Q Bar Saigon

has a funky branch in the hitherto rather sleepy Hoi An (in one of the town's oldest chop houses): hip music, cool cocktails, chilled atmosphere. Even the toilets are an attraction here. Snacks and Asian food on offer. Happy Hour 4pm–8pm.

WHERE TO EAT
Banh Bao snacks are a must, small, round pastry buns filled with pork and egg sold by bicycle vendors from the afternoon onwards. They should not cost more than 5000 VND each.

❶ *Café des Amis* £
52 Rue Bach Dang
tel. 0510/386 16 16
No menu, but guests can decide between seafood or vegetarian and be surprised with a tasty five-course meal. Nice location with a view onto the water.

❷ *Karma Waters* £
213 Nguyen Duy Hieu, Hoi An
tel. 0510/392 76 32
www.karmawaters.com
At long last, Hoi An has its own vegan restaurant! Western, Indian and Vietnamese dishes, imaginative and tasty, from tofu burgers to vegan ice cream, curries

---

and hotpots. Wide range of fruit juices, but no alcohol! Small, a little loud on the streetside, but very friendly. Cookery courses and ecotours also on offer.

❸ *Hong Phuc* £—££
86 Bach Dang
tel. 0510/386 25 67
Magnificently situated on the esplanade, this restaurant in an old trading house offers many fish specialities (wrapped in banana leaves, for example) and the regional delicacy: Cao Lau noodle soup.

❹ *Good Morning Vietnam* £
34 Le Loi
tel. 0510/391 02 27
Tasty Italian dishes and wines are served at this pizzeria, now found in many tourist areas.

❺ *Son Hoi An* £—££
177 Cua Dai (close to the beach of the same name), Hoi An
Mobile tel. 098/50 14 00
Rustic, romantic al fresco diner on the river between palms and paddy fields (midges, fireflies at dusk!), lovingly presented slow food (mostly Vietnamese, but pizzas and burgers also available) with gentle jazz accompaniment. Neighbouring river cafés provide an alternative if it gets too busy.

WHERE TO STAY
❶ *The Nam Hai* ££££
in Dien Duong village, Dien Ban district (approx. 8km/5mi north of Hoi An)
tel. 0510/394 00 00
www.thenamhai.com
When money is no object: ultra chic, luxury minimalist design hotel, earning the reputation of being Vietnam's best by some distance. 100 dream villas with

---

! *Culinary speciality* **Insider Tip**

MARCO ⊕ POLO TIP

The noodles found in the culinary speciality known as Cao Lau do not seem typically Asian at all. They are combined with soybean sprouts and a few slices of pork in a light soup, flavoured with star anise and mint and topped with rice-flour crackers and fried onions. To be truly authentic, Cao Lau must only be prepared using water from a particular spring.

Restaurant in the old town of Hoi An

sea views, some with large private pool and butler, perfectly subtle service and an endlessly flowing pool and waterfall landscape.

❷ *Palm Garden Resort* ££££
Lac Long Quan, Cua Dai Beach (the northern stretch is also known as An Bang Beach), Hoi An
tel. 0510/392 79 27
www.palmgardenresort.com.vn
At the northern end of the Cua Dai Beach (An Bang Beach), where it is still quiet, 20 bungalows and 168 hotel rooms are spread around a huge garden. Some outdoor pools, a pool landscape, Italian restaurant, good internet offers and shuttle bus to Hoi An.

❸ *Victoria Hoi An Resort* £££–££££
Cua Dai Beach
tel. 05107392 70 40
www.victoriahotels-asia.com
Pure elegance at Hoi An's best beach hotel (10 minutes from the centre): 4-star luxury under French management, with gorgeous bungalows and rooms with balcony. Views of the sea or the estuary, the resort is arranged in the style of a fishing village.

❹ *Life Heritage Resort* £££–££££
1 Pham Hong Thai
tel. 0510/391 45 55
Highly praised hotel on the riverbank: stylish colonial replica with 94 spacious, smart rooms (walls are a little thin) on two floors, small patios, pool, spa, good internet offers.

➎ *Ancient House Resort £££*
377 Cua Dai (beach road, approx. 1km/
half a mile outside Hoi An on the road
to the beach)
tel. 0510/392 33 77
www.ancienthouseresort.com
Pretty, somewhat convoluted two-storey
complex with tile-roofed houses
grouped around a traditional villa with
42 mid-range rooms. Veranda provides
river or garden views. Large pool.

➏ *Ha An Hotel ££*
6 Phan Boi Chau, Cua Dai Beach
tel. 0510/386 31 26
www.haanhotel.com
A calm oasis with a pretty garden, lovingly furnished rooms (rose petals, CD
player), courteous service. Complimen-
tary bicycle rental.

Le Domaine de Tam Hai ££
Tam Hai, Nui Thanh (island approximately 45km/28mi from Hoi An, 15 minutes
by boat)
Tel 0510/354 51 03
A small island paradise: twelve quaint
bungalows shaded by palm leaves and
decorated in Vietnamese style (air-condi-

tioned, minibar, telephone) on the
beach, some with large, airy baths. Pool,
French restaurant and cocktail bar.

➐ *Long Life Hotel £-££*
30 Bat Trieu, Hoi An
tel. 0510/391 66 96
http://longliferiverside.com
20 bargain rooms in an attractive mini
hotel a little way away from the old
town (10 minutes walkt), the rooms are
equipped with satellite TV, minibar and
some with balconies over the garden,
looking towards paddy fields. Breakfast
is served in the garden, where there is
also a pool.

➑ *Sunshine Hotel £*
2 Phan Dinh Phung, Hoi An
tel. 0510/393 78 99
www.sunshinehoianhotel.com.vn
New hotel with 45 really lovely, very
cheap rooms with Wi-Fi on four floors.
Some of those under the roof have balconies. In a rather quiet residential hinterland, but the old town and beach are
only five minutes away by bike, available
free from the hotel.

PLACES TO VISIT IN CENTRAL HOI AN

*Japanese
Covered
Bridge

The modest Japanese Covered Bridge at the west end of Tran Phu
Street once joined the Japanese quarter of the city with the Chinese
quarter. At the western exit are two simple dog statues; on the eastern
side, two monkeys can be seen. It is therefore assumed that the construction of the bridge took two years, beginning in the year of the
monkey and ending in the year of the dog. According to legend, the
bridge was built following heavy **earthquakes** in Japan, which geo-
mancers(▶(p.69) attributed to a huge dragon. His head was said to
be located in India, his tail in Japan and his heart in Hoi An. Because
of this, the crossing was built on stone abutments meant to symbolically pierce his heart – and at the same time provide a protective,

The Japanese Covered Bridge once connected the Chinese and Japanese Quarters

covered bridge over the muddy current. The first bridge was built crossing the small arm of the Thu Bon at the end of the 16th century. It was destroyed and rebuilt several times. It is assumed that during the work in 1763, the **bridge pagoda** (Chua Cau) was also built, attached to the north side and dedicated to the Taoist god Tran Vo Bac De (the Emperor of the North), to whom power over the wind, rain and other bad influences is ascribed. A few hundred yards north of the bridge, at the western end of Phan Dinh Phung Street, is a mysterious shrine beneath an old banyan tree. The Emperor of the North is also honoured here, in order that he protect the bridge from harm. ❶ The bridge is open day and night to everyone. Between 8am and 6pm, however, admission is controlled. Ticket information ▶p.286, as a small temple shrine may also be visited.

At the western end of the bridge stands the nearly 200-year-old Phung Hung Old House (4 Nguyen Thi Minh Khai Street), which has been in the same family for eight generations. The carved shutters and the free-floating ancestral altar on the upper floor are particularly pretty. The book shop is a nice place to browse around, and there is a ceramics exhibition here to admire.
❶ daily 8am–6pm

Phung Hung Old House

The Sa Huynh Culture Museum (149 Tran Phu) located diagonally across from the eastern exit of the bridge, houses a number of archaeological finds, giving an impression of the time before the Cham rulers.

Sa Huynh Culture Museum

*Cantonese Assembly Hall

Just a bit further on is the impressive portal of the Cantonese Assembly Hall (176 Tran Phu). The Chinese immigrants organized themselves according to their region of origin and built five assembly halls, which serve as a meeting point as well as a **religious centre**. Even today it is quite clear that the atmosphere here is not one of a museum, but of everyday life. The halls are all similar from the basic set up, with the main buildings and the altars all arranged on one axis. However from the entrance the view of the godly figures is blocked, as walls or »blind« doors have been built in between to mislead evil spirits and keep them out. First comes a small forecourt, which leads to a gatehouse with just such a door, as well as memorial plaques and inscriptions. Next is a courtyard, usually adorned with a miniature stone landscape, trees and other plants. It is adjoined on either side by assembly and business rooms.

Next comes the **temple area**, the size and features of which correspond with the wealth of the community. In general the rooms are characterized by lacquered and painted wooden columns and finely carved altars with figures of gods and ancestral charts. The roof ridges also stand out, embellished with almost excessive reliefs and mosaics made with shards of porcelain. The Cantonese hall, built in 1884, has nothing to show in the way of old, valuable treasures, but has a particularly nice courtyard with plants. The elaborate fountain immediately catches the eye, with its colourful dragons and carp decorated with ceramics. The red-faced Quan Cong, a Chinese general of the Han dynasty is honoured at the main altar.
● daily 7am–6pm

*Quan Thang House

The Old House of Quan Thang (no. 77) is among the oldest and best preserved buildings in the city (from 1690). The layout of the house – actually two buildings joined by a courtyardand a covered passageway – is **characteristic of southern China** and Hoi An. From the street, all that is visible is a dark, wooden-panelled shop front. There follows a light and airy courtyard, and finally the living quarters, with the furthest end housing the kitchen, toilet and fountain. The fine wood carvings and green ceramic tiles at the roof ridge are marvellous, particularly the various home altars.
● daily 9.30am–6pm

Ceramics Museum

Diagonally opposite is the Museum of Trade Ceramics (80 Tran Phu). It holds a small collection of ceramics from various places with which Hoi An had trading relations during the 16th and 17th centuries. In addition, it is possible to learn more about the **typical roofing techniques** (yin-yang) in Hoi An. At least as interesting as the exhibition itself is the chance to stroll around the building and enjoy the view across the town and the rooftops.
● daily 8am–5pm.

To visitors to the Phuoc Kien Assembly Hall (46 Tran Phu) it is soon ****Phuoc Kien Assembly Hall** apparent that this facility belongs to the largest and most influential Chinese community of Hoi An. A relatively new gateway leads into the impressive complex with its green yards and exuberantly decorated halls. The origins of this sanctuary are said to date back to the late 17th century, when a valuable Buddha statue was found on the riverbank, and a pagoda was built in its honour. But over time it was neglected, so the Chinese from Phuoc Kien rededicated the temple to Thien Hau. At the main altar is a 200-year-old gilded **papier maché statue**. It is flanked by two helpers, the green-faced Thien Ly Nhan (who can hear from over a thousand miles away) and the red-faced Thuan Phong Nhi (who can see for over a thousand miles). A striking wall painting at the entrance shows the goddess in a storm, as she watches protectively over a junk. The altar room behind the **main sanctuary** is a destination for many childless couples and pregnant women. This is where three heavenly women are honoured who are believed to have a great influence over the fate of children. It is said that the middle one decides if a woman is to become pregnant, the right one influences the gender of the child, and the left one watches over the birth itself. They are flanked by twelve mid-wives, each of whom teaches the newborn something during its first year, for example to feed, to smile or to roll over. To the left stands the actual main altar of the room, paying homage to six ancestors who left Phuoc Kien in the 17th century to settle in Hoi An (then called Faifo). Standing in a small display case is a figure of the famous Vietnamese doctor Le Huu Trac.

Insider Tip

❶ daily 8am–5pm

Those wishing to get to know an entirely different facet of Hoi An should pay a visit to **Phan Boi Chau Street**. This was once the site of the French Quarter, with town houses decorated with plaster work, colonnades and balconies. The private house of Tran Duong is open to visitors (no. 25). **French Quarter**

Back in Tran Phu Street, opposite the entrance to the market is the eye-catching colourful façade of Quan Cong Temple (Chua Ong) from the 17th century. Originally built as the religious centre for the immigrants from the Chinese province of Quang Nam, it is now dedicated in honour of Ong Quan Cong, a legendary general (3rd century). To his right and left are the military mandarin Chau Xuong and the administrative mandarin Quang Binh. His red and white horses are also standing guard. The carp, a symbol of patience commonly seen in Hoi An's Chinese buildings, is found here in a particularly appealing form: as colourfully glazed dragon figures and water spouts. **Quan Cong Temple (Chua Ong)**

❶ daily 6.30am–6pm

Museum of History Through the rear exit of the temple or via the entrance in Nguyen Hue Street is Hoi An's Museum of History, which is also housed in a former pagoda. A number of old maps showing details of the previous city of Faifo are very interesting. The **tranquil courtyard** with its many plants and wooden ornamentation is also particularly pretty.
❶ daily 7.30am–5pm

*Trieu Chau Assembly Hall Further along the road (from the market onwards it is no longer called Tran Phu Street, but Nguyen Duy Hieu) is the Trieu Chau Assembly Hall, which was built by merchants from Chaozhou or Trieu Chau in 1776. For those who have not already seen enough beautiful ornaments and decorations, there are some very special **wood carvings** to discover here. Ong Bon, a Chinese marine general who is said to have power over the wind and waves, is honoured here. Running alongside his statue is a frieze full of birds, insects and small animals – so realistic that it almost seems as if chirping and rustling should be audible. The altar itself depicts scenes from life on land and at sea, and at the doors before it are two Chinese ladies who are trying out the latest Japanese hair fashions.
❶ daily 6.30am–6pm

Tran Family Chapel On the return trip, the cross street Le Loi is slightly more than halfway back; follow it to the right for one block further to reach Phan Chu Trinh Street. At exactly this corner stands the 200-year-old Tran Family Chapel. Like those of the other Chinese clans, the chapel was originally built as a **merchant's house** (see below), but over time the religious meaning of the place became more significant for the family. The focal point here is the large altar room honouring the ancestors. The Tran, who once became rich and influential through trade and whose ancestors include mandarins, still meet here once per year to this day. On these occasions, family matters are discussed and the ancestors are remembered.

Truong Family Chapel The small but also very pretty chapel of the Truong family is slightly hidden next to the Pho Hoi Restaurant at 69 Phan Chu Trinh. A visit here is not included on the ticket (▶p.286), but it is possible to enter and look around on request. The house is full of family mementos and carvings.

Old House of Tan Ky The prettiest and most-visited of the old merchant's houses is the Old House of Tan Ky (101 Nguyen Thai Hoc). The English and French-speaking guides at this two storey house relate quite a bit about its architecture and history, which makes it popular among tour groups. The nearly 200-year-old building with its exquisite carvings and inlay work is very well preserved and is viewed by the city as a showpiece. It was built by a member of the second generation of the Tan Ky family, who fled China for political reasons in the late 16th century. Through a narrow, slightly spooky store and the richly decorated living room is the courtyard. From here it is possible to continue to the rear section with the kitchen and an exit to the river. It was possible to bring goods directly into the warehouse on the upper floor from here, protecting the goods from flooding. The use of the dark **jackfruit wood for the main pillars, which is resistant against termites, is an interesting feature. The filigreed carvings are imaginative and playful, and the abundance of mother-of-pearl inlays is especially elegant.

❶ daily 8.30am–7.45pm

OUTSIDE THE CITY CENTRE

Following Nguyen Truong To Street (the northern extension of Le   Tiger Temple
Loi) and passing numerous market stalls leads directly to the gate of

In front of Quan Cong Pagoda

the Tiger Temple, which is easily recognized by its brightly coloured statues. The sanctuary itself is decorated only with Chinese calligraphy.

CHUC THANH PAGODA

*Chuc Thanh Pagoda

Turn left before the Tiger Temple onto a rather dusty road, bordered by small houses with attractive gardens and burial sites, to reach two pagodas in idyllic surroundings. This perfectly tranquil, isolated spot is a pleasant contrast to the hustle and bustle in the centre of Hoi An. Some 700m/770yd further on stands Chuc Thanh Pagoda. It was founded as early as 1454 by Minh Hia, the first Buddhist monk of Hoi An. The present building is somewhat younger, but some of the older cult objects, including bells and a gong in the form of a carp, can still be seen. Trees, bougainvillea and other flowers decorate the pagoda grounds. To the left is a small area with coloured stupas and mossy tombs (photo ►p.73, bottom right).

*Phuoc Lam Pagoda

Follow the well-worn path another 500m/545yd (crossing a small canal) to Phuoc Lam Pagoda, erected in the mid-seventeenth century. According to legend, the young monk An Thiem reported for military duty instead of his brothers at the end of the century and rapidly rose to the rank of general. After the war he returned to the monastery, where, in order to be cleansed of his sins, he would sweep the market of Hoi An for the next twenty years. On completing this penance, he was nominated as the highest figure of Phuoc Lam Pagoda, the holy ground of which is surrounded by frangipani trees and flowerbeds. To one side, moss-covered memorial stones, adorned with ceramic mosaics, stand in a small field.

AROUND HOI AN

Cua Dai Beach

Following a healthy round of sightseeing, some time to relax on the beach is in order. Follow Tran Hung Dao Street eastwards, cycling for some 20 minutes through paddy fields and a residential area before arriving at the white Cua Dai Beach. The broad expanses of the beach are spotlessly clean, dotted with refreshments stalls and traders. Here, sun and sea can be savoured in peace. The presence of numerous new hotels and restaurants is indicative of efforts to **develop the area further as a tourist centre**. **Excursions by boat** along the Thu Bon lead to islands on the river and artisan settlements, such as the potters' village of Thanh Ha or the woodcarvers' Cam Kim Island, where boats and furniture are manufactured. Somewhat further in from the coast lie the Cham Islands: the Cu Lao Cham archipelago has been sustained for centuries by trade in swallows' nests.

** Hue

D 4

Province: Thua Thien–Hue
Region: North Central Coast
Population: 400,000

The former imperial city of Hue nestles between the foothills of the Annamite mountain range and the sea. As early as the 18th century, poets paid romantic tribute to its gardens, lakes and canals and its charming location on the »Perfume River«. Today, the complex of Hue monuments is on the UNESCO World Cultural Heritage list. The city retains a certain courtly flair and a hint of the Francophile lifestyle.

Essentially, the town can be divided into three parts, each with its own distinctive character. The Citadel complex with the Imperial Enclosure on the north bank of the Perfume River really is a must-see. To the east of the Dong Ba Canal lies Phu Cat, an erstwhile trading post, now an overcrowded district packed with shops, pagodas and Chinese union halls; on the south bank of the Perfume River the European town has developed, the modern administrative centre of Hue and home to many of the town's hotels and restaurants, graced with beautiful streets and villas. The landscape to the south of the town is marked by pine forest hills interspersed with tombs and pagodas. This is where the Nguyen emperors built their mausoleums. The Perfume River winds its way through the scenery, its name a legacy of the blossoms and tree gum it carries with it. An excursion with a **dragon boat** through the romantic river valley is an unforgettable experience. The famous Thien Mu Pagoda and Thuan An Beach are just a bicycle ride or boat trip away.

A town in three parts

MARCO ⊕ POLO TIP ❗

Culinary specialities Insider Tip

The most famous delicacy in Hue is banh khoai, small, crispy pancakes with shrimps, pork and bean sprouts, served with peanut-sesame sauce and star fruit, green bananas, salad and mint leaves. Noodles are also very popular in Hue, above all as a specially spiced rice noodle soup called bun bo, bun ga or bun bo gio heo – depending on whether beef, chicken or beef and pork is used.

Until 1306 Hue belonged to the Cham dynasty, before the land north of Da Nang was handed over to the Vietnamese as a condition of a peace treaty. However it was **Emperor Gia Long** (1802–20), founder of the Nguyen dynasty, who bestowed such significance on Hue as the capital of his empire. His reign not only witnessed the construction of the Citadel, but also of dykes, bridges and canals, as well as the

History

Mandarin Road, which connects Hue to Saigon and Hanoi. Hue would subsequently become an important centre for Buddhism, the arts and scholarship. In 1885, the **French** conquered Hue. The colonial rulers allowed the Nguyen to continue as masters by name, but without the corresponding influence. So it was that Hue was stripped of its status as capital city and fell into a slumber of almost Sleeping Beauty proportions, which lasted for almost 20 years. When the Geneva Conference of 1954 split Vietnam in two, Hue was allocated to the south. Thousands died on both sides in the **Vietnam War** and the Citadel was almost completely reduced to rubble and ash. Meanwhile, the gargantuan task of rebuilding Hue has spanned a period of over 20 years. Thanks to UNESCO, which designated the Imperial Enclosure and Royal Tombs as **World Heritage Sites** in 1993, these initiatives have gained immense support, proving not only beneficial to the historical buildings, but also helping to revive the traditional craftsmanship required.

Offical guests of the Hue Palace entered through the Noon Gate

☀ CITADEL

❶ Summer: 6.30am–5.30pm, winter: 7am–5pm; admission approx. 80,000
VND (be sure to count your change!); www.hueworldheritage.org.vn
There are various combination tickets available; palace museum approx.
25,000 VND (video illustrates how the Imperial Enclosure once looked).
Photographs in royal costume: approx. 50,000 VND, 20 minutes elephant
ride: approx. 150,000 VND. Daily 9am Change of the Guard ceremony at
the Noon Gate.

The glorious days of Hue began when Emperor Gia Long ordered
the construction of the Citadel in the year 1802. It was to be more
than just a fortress; it would be a home for the imperial family and
the officials, a kind of idyllic »**town within a town**«. What remained of the former Imperial Enclosure with small villages, paddy
fields, artificial hills, temples, gardens, lakes and alleys. It was con-
ceived as a square in shape, with three concentric defences behind a
Flag Tower rising high into the sky. Behind the walls lay the Imperial Enclosure with its administrative buildings, gardens, and dynastic temples, yet the imperial palaces of the Forbidden Purple City

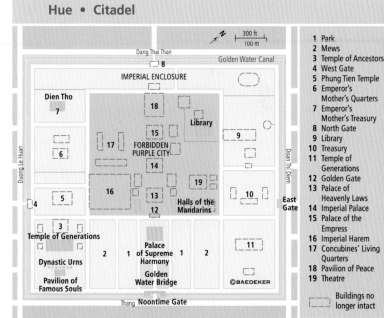

Hue • Citadel

1 Park
2 Mews
3 Temple of Ancestors
4 West Gate
5 Phung Tien Temple
6 Emperor's
   Mother's Quarters
7 Emperor's
   Mother's Treasury
8 North Gate
9 Library
10 Treasury
11 Temple of
   Generations
12 Golden Gate
13 Palace of
   Heavenly Laws
14 Imperial Palace
15 Palace of the
   Empress
16 Imperial Harem
17 Concubines' Living
   Quarters
18 Pavilion of Peace
19 Theatre

⬜ Buildings no
   longer intact

Hue

INFORMATION
Vietnam Tourism
14 Nguyen Van Cu, Hue
tel. 054/382 83 16
In the Huong Giang Hotel and in a small
tourist information office opposite the
Saigon Morin Hotel

TRANSPORT
Airports
Phue Bai Hue Airport: (approx.
15km/9mi southeast of Hue)
tel. 054/382 32 49, 386 11 31
Saigon, Hanoi flights; shuttle bus (approx. 100,000 VND) and taxi to the city
(approx. 200,000 VND)
International Airport Da Nang:
tel. 05 11/381 18 11 and 383 33 91
Seaport at Thuan An Beach and pier at
Hotel Huong Giang

Hue Railway Station
2 Bui Thi Xuan, Hue
tel. 054/382 21 75

EVENTS
Hue Festival   Insider Tip
Held over several days in even-numbered
years (2016, 2018…), Hue Festival's highlights include classical court music and
dances, exhibitions, fashion show, folklore,
kite-flying competitions and fireworks.

Wrestling Festival
In the village of Sinh on the south bank
of the Huong (Perfume River), thousands
of young men congregate in January
and February for the traditional wres-
tling championships.

Hon Chen Temple Festival
Twice a year in the third and seventh lunar months (February/March and July/
August): on the Perfume River, west of
Hue and in the village of Cat Hai, wor-
shippers gather to perform plays and
take part in processions, with lighted
rafts and boats illuminating the river.

SHOPPING
Dong Ba Market is several storeys high
and it is said that the finest conical straw
hats in all of Vietnam can be found here.
They are decorated with delicate silhouettes which shine through the virtually
transparent hats in the light. The usual
market wares of fruit, vegetables, meat
and fish are also on offer, not forgetting
typically Asian fake goods such as Louis
Vuitton handbags at dumping prices.

ENTERTAINMENT
❶ Why Not £
21 Vo Thi Sau
tel. 054/382 47 93
Enjoy a game of pool or darts in this
small bar offering western and Vietnamese classics, pizza, snacks, fresh fruit
juices and cocktails, wine or beer.

❷ Brown Eyes Bar £
56 Chu Van An, Hue
Proven nightlife classic with small garden, still going strong when the rest of
Hue has gone to bed: mostly youthful
crowd on the dancefloor. Pool also
played here.

WHERE TO EAT
❶ Ancient Hue £££
4/4/8 Lane 35, Pham Thi Lien (close to
Thien Mu Pagoda), Hue
tel. 054/359 03 56
www.ancienthue.com.vn

Tourists can dine in style like emperors in this (replica) temple (try the nine-course Royal Dinner, for example) – and afterwards wander through the enchanting garden and watch vegetable carvers – or have a go themselves (cooking courses available).

❷ *Tropical Garden* ££
27 Chu Van An, Hue
tel. 054/384 71 43
Popular garden restaurant in tourist district with daily folklore shows and universally loved Vietnamese classics such as banh khoai pancakes and a range of noodle dishes.

❸ *Song Huong Floating Restaurant* ££   Insider Tip
3 Thang 2 Park, Le Loi Street
tel. 054/382 11 97
http://nhahangnoisonghuong.com/
daily 8am–9pm
Built on stilts on the riverbank next to

the Trang Tien Bridge. Hue cuisine can be sampled here, along with international dishes. The location in a stylized, illuminated lotus blossom on the river is wonderful, the food rather average. Better to drink a cocktail elsewhere after dinner.

❹ *Family Home Restaurant* £
11/34 Nguyen Tri Phuong, Hue
tel. 054/382 06 68
Tiny backpacker restaurant, family-run, more like a living room. Pancakes and »musli« for late breakfast, noodle soup, fried noodles, curries, chips, fresh fruit juices and cheap Huda beer – tours can also be booked here.

❺ *Banh Khoai Lac Tien* £
6 Dinh Thien Hoang (at the citadel's Thuong Tu Gate), Hue
tel. 054/352 73 48
Banh Khoai are the house specialty: pancakes with shrimps, meat, soy bean

The colonial Saigon Morin Hotel

sprouts and nuoc leo, a peanut-sesame sauce. There are several good places to eat banh khoai on this street.

WHERE TO STAY

❶ *Pilgrimage Village* ££££

130 Minh Mang Road (approx. 3km/2mi in the direction of the Royal Tombs)
tel. 054/388 54 61
www.pilgrimagevillage.com
info@pilgrimagevillage.com
A village for pilgrims. Designed in traditional style, rustic yet elegant: two-tier brick houses with 50 rooms, each with two balconies, peaceful exotic garden, pool with a small waterfall and bar.

❷ *Ana Mandara Hue* ££££

Thuan An Beach (approx. 15km/9mi outside Hue)
tel. 054/398 33 33
https://anamandarahue-resort.com
Splendid luxury hotel with stylish pool villas on a lengthy palm beach: excellent wine selection and exclusive restaurant (expensive, naturally, but there are some private restaurants close by). Shuttle bus to Hue.

❸ *Best Western Premier Indochine Palace (formerly Celadon Palace)* £££–££££

105A Hung Vuong, Hue
tel. 054/382 35 26
www.bwp-indochinepalace.com
Luxurious tower hotel visible from afar with a hint of colonial flair, elegant rooms and club suites. A little further away from the tourist district (approx. 2km/1mi) but very good value for money. Fancy bathroom is separated from the room either by just an artistically carved sliding door or glass. Lovely palm pool, bars and restaurants.

❹ *La Residence* £££

Insider Tip

5 Le Loi, Hue
tel. 054/383 74 75
www.la-residence-hue.com
The old governor's residence on the river was converted into a first class hotel with 122 luxurious rooms and suites – a colonial touch of Art déco, four-poster beds and parquet floors have remained. Pool, spa, several chic bars and restaurants.

❺ *Saigon Morin* ££–£££

30 Le Loi
tel. 054/382 35 26
www.morinhotel.com.vn
sgmorin@dng.vnn.vn
Splendidly ostentatious colonial construction from the year 1901: 130 restored rooms (»extended« in some cases) with balcony (facing a main street, unfortunately), whilst the courtyard is a veritable oasis with a fountain, a beautiful café by a mini-pool, three restaurants and rooftop bar. Following the Royal Cemetery marathon, relax with a foot massage (good offers available via the internet)..

❻ *Orchid Hotel* £–££

30A Chu Van An
Phu Hoi District, Hue
tel. 054/383 11 77
www.orchidhotel.com.vn
Very reasonably priced, central mini hotel in the traveller area with 19 well equipped rooms (kingsize beds, TV, DVD, nice bathrooms, fruit bowl, even an ironing board and computer!). Good breakfast buffet. Collection service. Book well in advance!

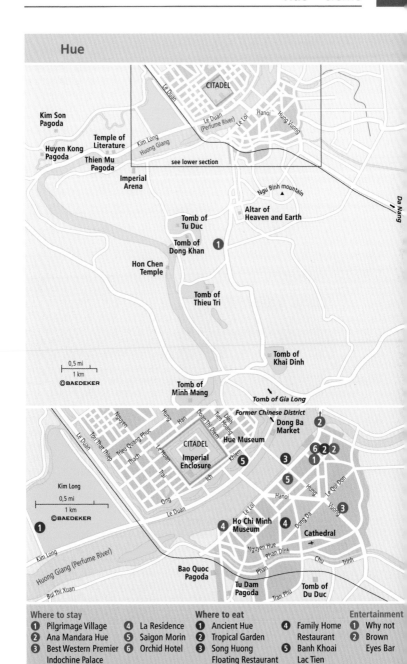

Hue

Kim Son Pagoda

Huyen Kong Pagoda

Temple of Literature

Thien Mu Pagoda

CITADEL

Le Duan

Le Duan (Perfume River)

Kim Long

Huong Giang

Hanoi

Le Loi

Hung Vuong

see lower section

Imperial Arena

Ngu Binh mountain

Da Nang

Altar of Heaven and Earth

Tomb of Tu Duc

Tomb of Dong Khan

❶

Hon Chen Temple

Tomb of Thieu Tri

Tomb of Khai Dinh

0,5 mi
1 km
©BAEDEKER

Tomb of Minh Mang

Tomb of Gia Long

Former Chinese District

Nguyen

Hung

Ham

Dinh

Trieu Hương

Doan Thi Diem

CITADEL

Dong Ba Market

❷

Le Thai Thien

Trieu Quang Phuc

Thach

Le Huan

Thai

Hue Museum

Khiem

❻❷❷

Ich

Ong

❺

❸

❶

❺

Kim Long

0,5 mi
1 km
©BAEDEKER

Le Duan

Hanoi

Hung

Le Qui Don

Vuong

❸

❶

Le Loi

Ho Chi Minh Museum

❹

❹

Dong Da

Cathedral

Kim Long

Huong Giang (Perfume River)

Nguyen Hue

Phan Dinh

Chu

Trinh

Bui Thi Xuan

Bao Quoc Pagoda

Tu Dam Pagoda

Phan

Tran Phu

Tomb of Du Duc

Where to stay
❶ Pilgrimage Village
❷ Ana Mandara Hue
❸ Best Western Premier Indochine Palace
❹ La Residence
❺ Saigon Morin
❻ Orchid Hotel

Where to eat
❶ Ancient Hue
❷ Tropical Garden
❸ Song Huong Floating Restaurant
❹ Family Home Restaurant
❺ Banh Khoai Lac Tien

Entertainment
❶ Why not
❷ Brown Eyes Bar

were the actual heart of the Citadel. The English traveller George Finlayson was utterly fascinated by what he saw. He wrote in 1821/1822 that the Imperial Enclosure was of such sheer elegance, grandeur and perfection, that all other Asian cities seemed in comparison to be the work of children.

Today, only around 80 of the original 300 buildings can be seen – and these too are in ruins. Battles, fire, typhoons and floods have all played their part, but it was primarily the **bombing attacks** during the Vietnam War (Tet Offensive, 1968) that left the complex, completed in 1833, in its present state. The ancient magic can still (or again) be sensed here and there, but, for the most part, Hue's most important landmark is a disconsolate place.

Geomantic guidelines
Inspired by Peking, Hue was destined to become the most magnificent city of the region. Geomancy was the defining rule for even the smallest of planning details. A long time was spent looking for the ideal place to build, to establish the crucial harmony between emperor and his subjects, man and nature. Hence the entire complex would face southeast, towards the mountain of **Nui Ngu Binh** (the »emperor's shade«), which would repel evil spirits. Two small islands in the Perfume River symbolize the benign spirit of the Blue Dragon in opposition to the aggression of the White Tiger. If this were not protection enough, the 520ha/1285ac complex is surrounded by a 7m/23ft-high and 20m/65ft-wide wall and a 23m/75ft-wide, 4m/13ft-deep moat. In accordance with geomantic principles of construction, the Citadel's ground plan is almost square, as this was the symbol of authority over the earth – the perception of earth itself was that of a quadratic plane.

Symbols of the emperors of the Nguyen dynasty

Flag Tower and Holy Cannons
Before entering the Imperial Enclosure, small pavilions can be seen on the river. In former times, edicts were read out here. Behind them, the 21m/69ft-high, three-storey Flag Tower rises upwards. For 25 years during the Tet Offensive the yellow star of the Vietcong flag fluttered here. To either side stand the Nine Holy Cannons, representing the four seasons and the five elements (earth, fire, metal,

wood and water). Like the Dynasty Urns outside the Pavilion of Famous Souls, they also symbolize the empire.

Of the four gates that lead into the Imperial Enclosure, the most impressive is the Noontime Gate. At the zenith of the Nguyen dynasty visitors must have been overwhelmed as they cast their gaze over the yellow and green tiled rooftops, entered the pavilions, resplendent in red and gold, and wandered amongst the lotus pools. After 1945, however, the entire complex was neglected and the acts of war contributed further to its state of disrepair. Nevertheless, the buildings that remain standing have been carefully restored and are deeply impressive, particularly the Palace of Supreme Harmony and the Temple of Generations.

Imperial Enclosure

The majestic Noontime Gate (Ngo Mon), built under Minh Mang in 1833, leads into the Imperial Enclosure. The portal has five entrances, with only the emperor permitted entry through the central one. The smaller two on each side were for the military and official mandarins, whilst the two giant openings in the wings were intended for the **imperial elephants**. The lower part of the Noontime Gate was built out of vast blocks of ashlar stone. An elegant pavilion stands regally on top of it, scene of important ceremonies held in the presence of the emperor. It was here that the last Nguyen ruler Bao Dai (▶Famous People) announced his abdication in 1945. The middle section of the roof is decorated with painted tiles in royal yellow; the sides are in green – the colour of the nobility. The wonderfully ornate roof ridges also catch the eye, featuring symbols of good fortune such as dragons, bats, gold coins, orchids and chrysanthemums.

*Noontime Gate

Countless lotus blossoms float on the two pools bisected by the Golden Water Bridge (Cau Trung Dao), which was also exclusively for the use of the emperor, and leads to the Great Rites Court.

Golden Water Bridge

This broad courtyard is where the mandarins would assemble for official events. 18 stone stelae mark the exact points according to the nine ranks, divided into civilians (on the left) and military (on the right).

Great Rites Court

Miraculously, the Palace of Supreme Harmony (Dien Thai Hoa, 1805) has survived all military onslaughts. It has been restored several times and stands glittering in all its former glory today. In the red and gold finery of the **Throne Room** the emperor would receive envoys and attend important festivities. His elevated seat was placed beneath a heavy golden canopy and he wore a golden tunic and crown, decorated with nine dragons. Events of this nature were, however, extremely few and far between and the ruler seldom showed

**Palace of Supreme Harmony

Dragon boats on the Perfume River bring passengers to the Thien Mu Pagoda and the Royal Tombs

himself to his officials, thus feeding the aura of mystery so closely associated with imperial power. The emperor would get ready for his grand appearances in the room behind the throne, where nowadays people come to purchase souvenirs.

Royal Theatre The Duyet Thi Dhong Royal Theatre stages traditional performances with music and dance, tea and Hue pastries – if there is a large enough audience.

❶ daily 9am, 10am, 2.30pm and 3.30pm; show: approx. 120,000 VND

Forbidden Purple City The crumbling walls to the north of the Palace of Supreme Harmony surrounded the Forbidden Purple City (Tu Cam Thanh) with the palaces of the emperors and empresses. The only persons allowed to reside here, apart from the imperial family, were concubines and eunuchs – and, of course, the many members of staff whose job it was to maintain their well-being and the estate's splendour. A great effort of the imagination is required to conjure up an image of life in days gone by when confronted with the barren field of dry grass and rubble visible today.

Only a few buildings have survived here, the Halls of the Mandarins, for example, where imperial robes may be hired out for a photographic pose. In the centre once stood the **Palace of Heavenly Laws**, to which the emperor would retreat to consider political decisions. The right-hand hall is now a souvenir shop.

*Library The Imperial Library, an attractive building with a garden and pond, has been lovingly restored. It was constructed during the reign of Minh Mang and redesigned on the orders of Khai Dinh, who had it decorated with mosaics. Inside, historic scenes of Hue can be viewed, souvenirs purchased and a flautist's music admired.

❶ Currently undergoing renovation.

The Octagonal Pavilion close by is the only other remaining building (reconstructed) of the Forbidden Purple City. It was originally one of two such buildings and a favourite retreat of emperors, who are said to have come here to listen to music.

Octagonal Pavilion

At the southwest perimeter of the Imperial Enclosure there are more buildings that are worth seeing, collectively known as Trieu Temple (Temple of the Ancestors). The easiest way to reach them is by returning through the Noon Gate and then turning right.

Trieu Temple

The three-storied Famous Soul Porch (Hien Lam Cac, 1821), with its interesting carvings, leads onto the courtyard where the momentous Nine Dynastic Urns (Cuu Dinh) stand.

Famous Soul Porch

Some 2m/6ft high, these bronze urns represent the finest examples of local craftsmanship and were cast at the behest of Minh Mang between 1835 and 1837. Each of them features intricately engraved details (mostly landscape scenes), eulogizing the beauty and uniqueness of Vietnam. Traces of bullet impact can still be seen on some of them. The largest and **most ornate urn** (approx. 2600kg/5730lbs heavy) stands in the middle of the line. It is dedicated to the founder of the Nguyen dynasty, Gia Long.

**Nine Dynastic Urns

Across the courtyard stands the Temple of Generations (The Mieu), built on the orders of Minh Mang in 1821 to honour his father. A row of **ten altars** bearing the genealogical trees of the rulers and their wives can be found inside the memorial. Officially, there were 13 emperors between the years of 1802 and 1945, but some are neither recognized nor represented in the temple. On each Holy Table lie a sleeping mat, blankets and other personal belongings and images of the sovereign. On the anniversary of each one's death, a small ceremony is held in The Mieu Temple. To the north is the **Temple of the Resurrection** (Hung Mieu, 1804) dedicated to the worship of the parents of Gia Long.

* Temple of Generations

In the northwest corner of the Forbidden Purple City stand the restored chambers of the emperor's mother, latterly the residence of the last emperor, Bao Dai. Today the palace houses antique furniture and valuable royal robes, whilst an exhibition of photographs in the reception hall helps visitors to visualize the courtly life of the past.

Dien Tho

ON THE BANKS OF THE PERFUME RIVER

A trip on one of the colourful dragon boats on the Perfume River is not to be missed. It is not only a lovely way to enjoy the idyllic land-

*Dragon boat cruises

scape, but also an opportunity to take in some of the unique sights away from the main streets. As a rule, organized boat trips stop at Thien Mu Pagoda, Hon Chen Temple or one of the more interesting mausoleums, usually Tu Duc, Khai Dainh or Minh Mang (►Royal Mausoleums, see below).

❶ around 200,000–300,000 VND per boat (depending on the season, for example, two and a half to five hours for two people). Longer excursions lasting half a day can be arranged, to Minh Mang's tomb perhaps and the boat proprietor might even agree to throw in lunch on board.

*Thien Mu Pagoda The history of Thien Mu Pagoda (Linh Mu Pagoda or the Pagoda of the Heavenly Lady) is closely associated with two legends. In one, an old woman appears before Prince Nguyen Hoang at Song Huong, telling him to light a torch and follow the river eastwards until the flame goes out. At this point he should build his town. He later had a pagoda constructed in honour of the old woman, believing her to be a messenger of God. The second legend has the old lady appearing on a mountain in the form of a dragon's head and prophesying that one will come and build a pagoda here, bringing eternal prosperity to the land. Either way – it was, indeed, Nguyen Hoang who ordered the construction of the pagoda in 1601, making it the **oldest pagoda in Hue**. The pagoda's tower can be seen from a great distance, standing on a bank above the river, around 4km/2mi upstream on the former site of a Cham sanctuary. The Phuoc Duyen Tower (1844) has seven storeys, each representing an incarnation of Buddha ; at its peak a basin collects rainwater, as water is seen as the source of happiness. Pavilions stand on both sides, housing a large bell (1710) and a turtle (1715) carrying a stele. The stone tablet relates the tale of the pagoda and the history of Buddhism in Hue.

> **? MARCO ⊕ POLO INSIGHT**
>
> *Unusual exhibit*
>
> The old Austin in the garden of Thien Mu Pagoda is the vehicle that the monk Thich Quang Duc (Famous People) drove to Saigon in June 1963, where he burned himself to death in protest against the persecution of Buddhists under the Ngo regime.

Insider Tip A platform provides a wonderful panoramic view of the romantic river valley. An archway, protected by six colourfully painted guards, leads to the **main sanctum**, with a laughing bronze Buddha in front.

** ROYAL MAUSOLEUMS

❶ Opening times for all tombs: summer: 7am–5.30pm; admission: approx. 80,000 VND (count your change). At present, the tombs of Thieu Tri and Dong Khanh are closed for restoration.

Along with the Citadel, the tombs of the emperors, which lie south of the city in the vicinity of the river, are Hue's main attraction. The acclaimed resting places of seven of the thirteen Nguyen rulers are all similar in design, yet each has something of the taste and preferences of each individual emperor. They were built whilst their future oc-cupants were still alive; Tu Duc (1847–83) actually spent several years of his life here. It could sometimes take years to find the right loca-tion, as the courtly geomants and astrologers also had their say in the matter. The ideal scenario entailed sheltering mountains to the north, if possible to the east and west as well, and an opening southwards down to the water. If these conditions were not naturally available, the terrain was landscaped accordingly. Artificial lakes, waterfalls and hills were added to meet the geomantic requirements on the one hand, and to create the most picturesque park environment possible on the other, as can be seen at the **tombs of Tu Duc and Minh**

Park of Death

The Minh Mang tombs are inspired by Chinese design

Mang. They may differ in some respects, but each mausoleum comprises the following three elements: a temple dedicated to emperor and empress, containing the reliquary of the imperial family, a stele pavilion as an encomium of the ruler, watched over by stone elephants, horses, soldiers and officials, and finally – on a hilltop, ideally – the tomb itself, enclosed by thick walls. It was customary to keep the actual location of the tomb a secret to guard against grave robbers and enemies of the state; in extreme cases, for this reason, all those who attended the burial were subsequently executed. The best way to reach the tombs is by car or bicycle. Alternatively, the mausoleums of Tu Duc, Dong Khanh and Minh Mang can also be reached on foot from the boat jetties.

Tomb of Minh Mang (Lang Hieu) The tomb of Minh Mang (1820–41) is the only one situated to the west of the Perfume River (12km/7.5mi from Hue). Many consider it to be the most beautiful, inspired by Chinese design and blending harmoniously into the landscape. Architecture was a passion of the second Nguyen emperor Ming Manh. He also completed the Citadel in Hue after the death of Gia Long, and planned his mausoleum on a symmetrical axis running east to west. The tomb was built between 1841 and 1843 under his successor. The tall main gate leads onto the Honour Courtyard where stone mandarins and elephants stand guard and on to the Stele Pavilion with the eulogy written by his son Thieu Tri. Beyond several more courtyards stands the red and golden **Sung An Temple, dedicated to Minh Mang and the empress. The

Hue • Tomb of Minh Mang

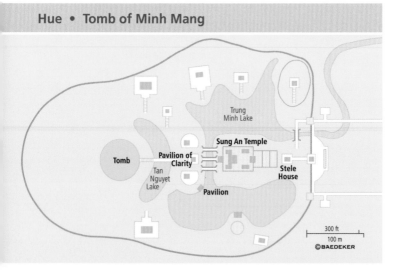

columns and beams are intoxicatingly beautiful, as are the many antique pieces decorating the room. Three bridges span Trung Minh Lake, the central one reserved for the emperor's use alone. On the other side stands the elegant **Minh Lau Pavilion** (Bright Pavilion), offering a wonderful view across the crescent-shaped Tan Nguyet Lake. Adjacent is a small garden where the flowerbeds were once painstakingly planted to spell out the Chinese characters for a long life. Past sweet-smelling frangipani trees, steps bordered by dragon pillars point the way to the actual tomb of Minh Mang on a pine-covered hill, surrounded by a round wall.

Lang Khiem attracts the most visitors and is an especially beautiful site (7km/4mi from Hue), built from 1864 to 1867. Tu Duc (1847–83) was not only emperor during a period in which the independence of Vietnam was greatly threatened, but also, indeed above all, a **Romantic poet**, who liked nothing better than to hide away from the world in his garden. Thus he lived for 16 years in this artificially created landscape protected by a wall, spending his time in a boat, fishing, meditating, writing poetry and drinking tea. On entering through the southern gate, a path leads the way past a pond filled with water lilies and lotus flowers to a prettily decorated pavilion. Across the lake stands the **Xung Khiem Pavilion**, restored courtesy of UNESCO. Where once Tu Duc would retire to write, Vietnamese families come today to enjoy a picnic. The steps leading up from the lake end at a portal with three entrances. The central one, painted yellow, was re-

**Tomb of Tu Duc (Lang Khiem)

Hue • Tomb of Tu Duc

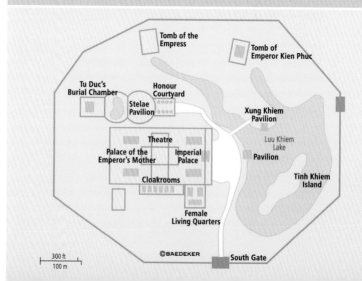

- Tomb of the Empress
- Tomb of Emperor Kien Phuc
- Tu Duc's Burial Chamber
- Honour Courtyard
- Stelae Pavilion
- Xung Khiem Pavilion
- Theatre
- Palace of the Emperor's Mother
- Imperial Palace
- Luu Khiem Lake
- Pavilion
- Cloakrooms
- Tinh Khiem Island
- Female Living Quarters
- South Gate
- ©BAEDEKER

300 ft / 100 m

Statues of mandarins, elephants and horses in the Court of Honour in the tomb of Khai Dinh

served for the emperor. Continuing onwards through an enclosure, **Hoa Khiem Temple** is reached, used by Tu Ducas as the imperial palace. Following his death, the funerary tablets were displayed here, with Tu Duc's being noticeably smaller than that of the empress. A theatre stood behind the temple to the left, with the clothing stores opposite and the living quarters of the emperor's wives and concubines close by. Continue along Luu Khiem Lake to reach the emperor's tomb. Before entering, however, visitors must pass the stone elephants, horses and guards standing watch on the Court of Honour. The military mandarins can be identified, on closer inspection, by their swords, whilst each of the mandarin officials holds a sceptre. Moving on to the **Stelae Pavilion**, this is a chance to see the largest stele in Vietnam (weighing 20 tons and inscribed with almost 5000 characters). Traditionally the sons of the emperor would write their father's epitaph, yet the childless Tu Duc had no option but sorrowfully to compose his own. A small crescent lake is situated immediately behind the pavilion, and behind the lake lies the walled tomb of the emperor. In actual fact, however, Tu Duc is said to be buried elsewhere. His adopted son Khien Phuc, who reigned for a mere seven months, and the empress are buried in a small pine wood on the opposite side of the lake. The tomb of Tu Duc is pervaded with the faintly morbid atmosphere of a place which has been in thrall to decay for decades. Until German conservationists arrived in 2009 to take up the challenge of heavy rainfall, damp, rootage and rampant moss, striving to protect this »aeruginous beauty«. In 2009/10, the German Conservation Restoration & Education Project (GCREP) worked together with Vietnamese experts to restore the tomb of Tu Duc, in particular the main gate and spirit screen (behind a short, parallel wall, with a »hidden« opening in the temple wall designed to lead spirits astray).

The magnificent resting place of Emperor Khai Dinh (1916–25) is the last mausoleum of the Nguyen dynasty to have been built and serves as an example of the downfall of Vietnamese culture in the colonial era. Khai Dinh was a **puppet of the French**, dazzled by the French lifestyle and its architecture. Instead of bricks, the European-influenced structure was built with concrete. Even the faces of the mandarins in the Court of Honour reveal a mixture of Vietnamese and European traits. The mausoleum sits majestically on Chau Chu Mountain (10km/6mi from Hue) looking towards a white Quan Am statue. Before construction commenced, Khai Dinh had the graves of Chinese nobility removed. The Chinese nobles had selected the place for its exceptionally beautiful and geomantically favourable location. Steep, broad steps, bordered by imposing concrete dragons, lead the way up to the Court of Honour, with its obligatory statues of mandarins, elephants and horses, and on to the octagonal Stele Pavilion. Higher still is the **actual tomb**, consisting of three connecting rooms. Mosaics of coloured glass and ceramic chips decorate the walls and ceilings, depicting, amongst other scenes, the four seasons. The actual tomb is situated approximately 9m/30ft beneath the throne where the bronze statue of the emperor sits, a jade sceptre in his hand. In the third and final room stands the altar dedicated to Khai Dinh.

*Tomb of Khai Dinh (Lang Ung)

The tomb of Dong Khanh (1885–89) lies just 500m/550yd from that of Tu Duc. Constructed in 1889, it is the smallest of the royal mausoleums, but has its own individual note. Although Dong Khanh was the first Nguyen ruler to be installed by the French, the rumour persists that he was also disposed of by them. The mausoleum is notable for its »double architecture«, with a walled-in part containing temples, pavilions and courtyards, and a second part some 100m/110yd away, an open arrangement of terraces featuring the Guard of Honour, Stele Pavilion and tomb.

Tomb of Dong Khanh (Lang Dong Khanh)

❶ currently closed for restoration

Thieu Tri 's tomb is a smaller version of the resting place of his predecessor Minh Mang. Unusually, it faces northwest, considered unfavourable then as now, indeed seen by many as the reason that Vietnam fell under French rule just a few years after its construction (1847/48). Few visitors venture this far, although the temples and pagodas are well worth inspecting.

Tomb of Thieu Tri (Lang Xuong)

❶ currently closed for restoration

FURTHER PLACES TO VISIT IN HUE

Hue Museum

The museum also goes by the name of Museum of Royal Antiques or Royal Fine Arts Museum. It presents a variety of exhibits from the collection of the Nguyen emperors, including furniture, robes, porcelain and much more besides. The building itself, the beautiful Long An Palace, is certainly worth a look. It was originally built inside the Imperial Enclosure in 1845 and later moved to its present location. In 1923, Emperor Khai Dinh had the palace converted into a museum.

❶ east of the Citadel, 3 Le Truc; daily 8am–5pm; admission: approx. 40,000 VND

Provincial Museum

Directly opposite stands the Provincial Museum. It is housed in the Di Luan Pavilion (1808), formerly a school for princes and the sons of senior mandarins. Three different exhibitions can be witnessed here: in the central portion, archaeological and ethnological collections with impressive burial statues of the Ede are on display. In the western building there is an interesting section dealing with regional architecture, industry and agriculture, whilst the eastern building is dedicated to more recent history, particularly the war against the USA.

❶ daily except Thu 7.30am–11am and 1.30pm–5pm

Cung An Dinh

The Cung An Dinh (built between 1916-18 under Kha Dinh) or An Dinh Palace once served as a restaurant. It was closed until 2008 for renovation work by the German Conservation Restoration & Education Project (GCREP). With a little bit of luck and powers of persuasion, the guard may allow a glimpse into the two floors of this stately, ochre building with its splendid stucco, wall and ceiling paintings, garden and lotus pond. It was not until mid-2012 that antique furniture and furnishings were reintroduced to the palace. The wall paintings in particular (imitating typical Vietnamese silks) reveal a unique »culture fusion« of the period, integrating Vietnamese and European baroque motifs. Emperor Khai Dinh used the palace as his private retreat outside the Imperial City, indulging in opium and cognac whilst playing cards. His son, the last Vietnamese Emperor Bao Dai, lived here from 1945 (Famous People) with his family until he was forced to give way to a Communist government office (the Palais is also called Khai Tuong Lau).

❶ entrance in Nguyen Hue or 97 Phan Dinh Phung Street; admission: 40,000 VND

European quarter

The main street of the French quarter is Le Loi Street, running parallel to Song Huong. This is also where the Quoc Hoc High School can be found, its illustrious pupils including not only Ho Chi Minh, but also General Vo Nguyen Giap, victorious at Dien Bien Phu, and the

former president Ngo Dinh Diem. A few steps further on is the **Ho Chi Minh Museum**, with the obligatory photographs and souvenirs. The **Cathedral** of Notre Dame on Nguyen Hue Street looks like a cross between a church and a pagoda. It was erected in 1962–63 at the instigation of the Archbishop of Hue, Ngo Dinh Thuc, brother of President Diem.
Museum: Tue-Sun 7.30am–11.30am, 1.30pm–4.30pm

At the western perimeter of the European quarter, there are two pagodas worth visiting: **Chua Bao Quoc** is up on Ham Long Hill and can be reached by taking Dien Bien Phu Street away from the town and turning right immediately after the railway tracks. Just 500m/550yd further south, on the corner of Dien Bien Phu and Tu Dam Street, stands **Tu Dam Pagoda** (1690–95).

The Cathedral of Nottre dame is situated in the south of the European quarter

Phu Cat district (also known as: Gia Hoi) lies on the small stream island between Dong Ba Canal and the Huong River and, with its little cafés, bric-a-brac shops and internet cafés, beauty salons or greengrocers in faded old shop houses and rickety wooden shacks along Chi Lang Street, appears a relatively authentic Chinese-influenced part of town. Dragons and other mythological animals often sit atop the roof ridges. Assembly halls (like Phuc Kien or Trieu Chau) and pagodas, inside which the immigration of Fujian-Chinese and Cantonese as traders in the 18th century is documented, are unfortunately only open to the public on holidays, as a rule. At 7 Nguyen Binh Khiem, the eponymous Madame Ba Do serves up Hue specialities such as banh beo, banh khoai and banh nam to predominantly local guests in her Ba Do restaurant – simple, good and hearty good fare.
Phu Cat district

Just a short distance from the centre, some 3km/2mi further north, close to the old North Gate, Bao Vinh district is reminiscent of an old fishing village with its market and street traders – much like Hoi An today, but almost completely free of tourists.
Bao Vinh district

AROUND HUE

Thuan An Beach Roughly 13km/8mi northwest of Hue (4km/2.5mi from the road to Da Nang), the Perfume River opens out into a vast lagoon, protected by a long sandbank. Across the lagoon lies the village of Thuan An and beyond the village is the beach. Past the refreshments stalls and small seafood establishments, the sunloungers and parasols peter out after a few hundred yards and the atmosphere becomes appreciably more peaceful.

The route to the beach is dotted with countless tombs and formidable burial temples of Vietnamese families who fled into exile as »boat people«. Approximately 6km/4mi further on, the **village of Duong No** is reached, where Ho Chi Minh (▶MARCO POLO Insight p.265) lived for some years as a child. The simple wooden house with a grass roof is open to visitors.

Bach Ma National Park Bach Ma (Hai Van) National Park (22,000ha/54,000ac) extends from the Central Highlands to the coastal region and is the wettest of Vietnam's rainforests with over 8000mm/315in of precipitation per annum, most of which falls between September and December (leeches included). On a clear day, the mountains of Bach Ma (1450m/4750ft) and Noc (1259m/4130ft) offer a spectacular panorama towards the coast. Streams and rivers flow through steep and narrow gorges, numerous waterfalls plunge from a height into idyllic bathing pools, such as Do Quyen Waterfall, whose cascades total 300m/985ft in height. The scenery is especially impressive in February when the red rhododendrons are in bloom. The park's fauna includes over 330 species of bird and at least 55 different mammals.

In 1992, a **breed of antelope named saola**, thought to be extinct, was discovered here. Another rare and exotic inhabitant is the muntjac, a deer species. A few tigers, and perhaps some leopards as well, move back and forth in the dense borderlands between Vietnam and Laos. Automatic cameras are positioned at locations where the deer pass is at its busiest, as natural scientists seek to plot their movements. One thing seems certain: the local herd of elephants has retreated to Laos. Illegal felling and poaching have taken their toll on the national park. A kilogramme (two pounds) of rhinoceros

> **!**
> MARCO ● POLO TIP
>
> *Walking in the National Park* **Insider Tip**
>
> Six not especially long walking trails lead through the rainforest of the national park, none of them particularly long. The best time to visit the park is after the rainy season from March to June. Six rustic, restored brick villas from the colonial period are to-day again in service as guesthouses. There is also a campsite and jeeps are available for hire (information: Phu Loc, Hue, tel. 054/87 13 30, www.bachma.vnn.vn).

horn can fetch as much as 60,000 US dollars according to the WWF, and the antlers of a particular species of deer around 3000 US dollars. The national park lies approximately 45km/28mi southwest of Hue (N 1, exit at Truoi).

❶ admission: approx. 45,000 VND; simple accommodation at the main base

The hat-making village of Phu Cam lies on the south bank of the An Cuu River. For several hundred years and many generations, the women here have been painstakingly making the intricate conical hats for which the region is so famous from (ironed) palm leaves. Their dexterity is essential in fashioning the wafer-thin hats, decorated with silk threads, painted landscapes or poetry, although these Non Bai Tho can also be found at the market in Hue and almost every souvenir shop. | Phu Cam (Phuoc Vinh)

The hot springs of Thanh Tan (approx. 30km/18mi northwest of Hue) are a popular destination at weekends for the Vietnamese, although women will only enter the 60°C/140°F hot, bubbling water in shorts and T-shirts. The thermal baths consist of several basins, private areas and a restaurant (towel required). | Thanh Tan

Lang Son

✴ D 2

Province: Lang Son (capital)
Region: Northern Highlands
Population: 70,000

Lang Son, the provincial capital, is an excellent base from which to tour the mountainous north, e.g. ▶Dien Bien Phu, ▶Sa Pa or the Ba Be National Park. The town itself has been thriving since the resumption of border traffic to China (1992), but can hardly be termed attractive.

Following the Vietnamese invasion of Cambodia, China retaliated in 1979 with a form of **punitive campaign** which had a severe impact on Lang Son, which along with Lao Cai (▶Sa Pa) is the most important border crossing to China. | Frontier town to China

Since the border was reopened in 1992, trade has flourished – both legally and illegally – as Lang Son enjoys good road and rail connections to Hanoi. A train runs from Hanoi to Lang Son (approx. 150km/95mi, roughly 8 hours), or a bus (about 6 hours), although the poor state of the roads make this something of an ordeal. At least the beautiful mountain scenery offers a compensatory distraction.

Lang Son

INFORMATION
Lang Son Tourist Service
9 Tran Hung Dao, Chi Lang
Lang Son
tel. 025/387 20 36

SHOPPING
Close to town, on a rocky granite out-crop visible from some distance, the dai-ly market of Kya Lu is held. Tay, Nung and Dao womenfolk can be seen here selling fruit, vegetables and craftwork from the early hours of the morning.

WHERE TO EAT
In Lang Son, the inns of the Le Loi and Tran Dang Ninh Street serve good food, but the hot food stalls and market stands are not to be dismissed, with noodle dishes, suckling pig and duck all especially worth sampling.

New Dynasty Restaurant £
at Phai Loan Lake, Lang Son
tel. 025/389 80 00
Views of the lake, predominantly Viet-namese dishes, a few western classics (spaghetti, sausage) and German beer on draught.

WHERE TO STAY
Muong Thanh Lang Son Hotel £
68 Ngo Quyen, Vinh Trai Ward
Lang Son
tel. 025/386 66 68
(Vietnamese only)
Typically modern mid-range hotel in the province, more suited to large Asian groups, but fine for an overnight stay. Actually has a pool (a little on the cold side) and tennis court. Minh Quang Restaurant is close by.

AROUND LANG SON

Ky Cung Temple
Roughly 1km/1100yd down from the market at Kya Lu, by the river, stands the small **Ky Cung Temple**, tucked under the bridge on the north bank. It was dedicated to Quan Tuan Tranh, who fought brave-ly against the Chinese, over 500 years ago. Inside the temple is a pic-ture of Ho Chi Minh, who paid a visit to Lang Son in 1960.

Tam Tanh Cave
Around 2km/1mi further north, two beautiful caves wait to be ex-plored. The **Tam Tanh Cave** boasts a deep pool and an impressive vantage point in the form of a natural window in the rock offering a vista of the neighbouring paddy fields. The enchanting features of **Nhi Thanh Cave** include beautiful stalactites and stalagmites and a small cave stream.

Dong Dang
Dong Dang Market, at the border gate some 14km/8.5mi away, is also frequented by Tay and Thai people. The most popular items on sale here are water buffalo, groceries, Russian motorbikes and cheap goods from China. On the hills between Lang Son and Dong Dang some **Japanese fortifications** from the Second World War can be looked over.

BA BE NATIONAL PARK

Vietnam's largest natural lake, the Ho Ba Be, forms the heart of the eponymous national park to the north of Lang Son in the province of Cao Bang. At the heart of evergreen rainforest and karst limestone mountains, which seem to grow out of the lowlands and reach up to 1800m/5900ft high, the 9km/5.5mi-long lake extends across three valleys. The hills, the habitat of apes, flying squirrels, Asiatic mountain goats and bats, are awash with orchids in bloom, flamboyants and palms. The flora encompasses around 450 species, including many varieties of bamboo and rattan. There are probably still tigers and leopards in the region, as well as some macaque troops. Boat trips can be undertaken to the neighbouring villages of Tay and Hmong and the Puong Cave (north bank of the lake). The imposing **Dau Dang Waterfall**, crashing down from a height of 45m/145ft, is also close by. The entrance to the park is between and, where guesthouses offer overnight accommodation, such as the Ba Be Guesthouse, the Nha Nghi Guesthouse and other Homestays.

❶ admission: approx. 12,000 VND; overnight stay, all inclusive, around 600,000 VND

Bamboo is a foodstuff, construction material and garden ornament all in one

Cao Bang, the capital of the province of the same name, lies some 40km/25mi northeast of the national park, on the border to China. Almost completely destroyed by the Chinese in 1979, Cao Bang now profits from the border traffic with its great neighbour. It is also a common point of departure for jaunts to the Ban Gioc Waterfall (also known as Ban Doc).

Cao Bang

★★ Mekong Delta

✦ C/D 7/8

Region: South
Area: 70,000 sq km/27,000 sq mi

The Mekong Delta is Southeast Asia at its most authentic: few large towns but a deeply rich, rural terrain. Its warm, sultry climate and lush vegetation make the Mekong Delta the ultimate example of a tropical landscape. A certain somnolence pervades the region, inspiring a veritable holiday feeling in visitors, perhaps more so than in other regions of Vietnam.

»Nine Dragon River«

The Mekong is one of the largest rivers in Asia, its final 200km/125mi of a total of 4800km/2980mi coursing through South Vietnam. It rises in the highlands of Tibet, flows as Lancang Jiang through Southwest China, forms the border between Burma and Laos, continues through Laos and demarcates a further frontier between two states, namely Laos and Thailand. Thereafter it enters the lowlands of Cambodia, dividing into two currents at Phnom Penh, the Tien Giang (Upper Mekong) and the Hau Giang (Lower Mekong, Bassac). In Vietnam these two rivers fan out into **eight main tributaries**, one canal and numerous other distributaries, forming a vast delta as they progress to the sea at different points. Although it only has eight estuaries, the Mekong is also called the Song Cuu Long in Vietnam: »Nine Dragon River«, due to the Chinese mythological attachment to the number nine.

What to see in the delta

From ▶My Tho a **boat trip** along the northernmost branch of the Mekong, the Tien Giang, to the lush fruit orchards at Ben Tre is recommended. Cau Lanh is the perfect destination for ornithologists. It can be reached via Vinh Long (▶Can Tho), where those interested can venture to the Khmer pagodas at Tra Vinh. Pleasant hotels and restaurants await in ▶Can Tho, along with floating markets and fruit plantations. To the south lies the **primeval swampland** of Ca Mau (▶Can Tho). Boats depart from the coastal town of Rach Gia(▶Chau Doc) to Phu Quoc Island and its unique beaches. Those wishing to penetrate deeper into the western area of the delta should visit Ha Tien (▶Chau Doc) and ▶Chau Doc close to the Cambodian border.

Flooding

Every 2–5 years, the delta is subject to serious flooding. Thanks to the sand and mud which is swept along by the Mekong and its tributaries, the **fertility of the soil** is maintained. Furthermore, the Mekong Delta is advancing at an annual rate of some 80m/87yd into the sea. Thus the remains of the ancient port of Oc Eo, which belonged to the Funan Empire, and surrendered in the 7th century, today lies 30km/18mi inland.

As the delta region in the north runs seamlessly into the Cambodian lowlands, it is virtually the only area of Vietnam to which neighbouring peoples had unhindered access. This is the reason for the influx of diverse ethnic groups in the past and the high contingent of **ethnic minorities** in the Mekong Delta today. From the 1st century it formed part of the Funan Empire, and following that regime's demise (7th century) it fell to the various Khmer dynasties over the next 1000 years. In the 17th century it ultimately became a catch basin for Chinese refugees who had been forced out of their homeland under the Qing dynasty. The Cham also retreated here, taking flight from the Vietnamese. The latter did not assume control of the region until the 18th century as they ventured south and integrated the area into the empire of the Nguyen dynasty. As Cambodia offered ample opportunities for rice cultivation, the Mekong Delta was, at this time,

Colonization

South Vietnam's rice bowl: around 16 million tons of rice are gleaned from three harvests per year in the Mekong Delta

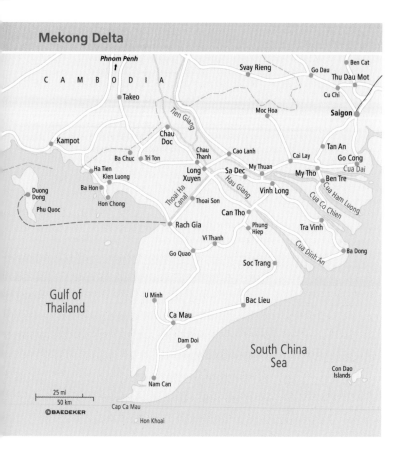

Mekong Delta

an overgrown swampland, rife with malaria. It was not until the French took possession of the Mekong Delta from 1861 and added Cochinchina to their colonial empire that the land was reclaimed and drained to create the **largest »rice bowl« in the country**. With approximately 20 million inhabitants, the Mekong Delta is now one of the most densely populated and economically successful regions in Vietnam. Both the Cambodians and the Vietnamese live in villages in the middle of their agricultural areas. In contrast to the otherwise compact huddles of villages in the rest of Vietnam, **more loosely scattered settlements** dominate the picture here. The houses are often built on stilts. Homes of this type, commonly found in Laos, Cambodia and Thailand, feature a living area mounted on twelve round supports accessed by a ladder with five, seven or nine rungs

– an even number is considered unlucky. The room below is reserved for pets. This design improves air circulation and serves as protection against floodwater.

With the exception of the mangrove swamps near the coast, the region is intensively farmed and is, along with the Red River delta, one of the two largest rice bowls in the country. Although the Mekong Delta covers less than 10% of the surface area of Vietnam, approximately half of the country's rice harvest is yielded here. This is a major contributing factor to Vietnam's status as the **second largest exporter of rice in the world** after India. Even so, the monoculture of rice, as propagated primarily by the French, has given way to a wider variety of tropical fruit crops, including sugar cane and coconut palms. Recent years have also seen a significant increase in shrimp and fish farms.

Economy

The Mekong Delta has a relatively good road transport system and a number of huge, new bridges. Progress can be slow, nevertheless, as larger and smaller ferries criss-cross the tributaries and estuaries of the Mekong. Variations in water level mean that not all rivers are navigable throughout the year, whilst the dry months of March and April present the boats with their own problems of sandbanks. A **network of canals** with an aggregate length of 5000km/3100mi is therefore used to transport goods independently of the river levels.

Transport

The Mekong Delta is one of the regions most severely afflicted in the war. Dense primeval forest provided ideal cover for the Vietcong, enabling them to overrun enemy troops in jungle warfare. It comes as little surprise that this area was uncompromisingly targeted in the **Americans' deforestation strategy**, depriving the Vietcong of their natural hideouts. The devastating consequences for the tropical forests can still be seen today – the decimated natural woodland is compounded by the deformities in the growth of trees and leaves. Today, however, the greatest threat to the woods is the economy, as ever increasing areas of forest stand and mangroves are cleared to make way for fresh arable land or, over the past decade, to create gigantic shrimp farms and aquacultures (e.g. shark catfish). In recent years, a reforestation programme with mangroves has sought to arrest this dangerous development. Mangroves (►MARCO POLO Insight p.172) protect the coast from erosion and storm floods.

Consequences of war

> **! MARCO POLO TIP**
>
> *Organized tours*   Insider Tip
>
> Those booking a dirt cheap day trip from Saigon through the delta should be prepared for the hard sell, i.e. including visits to various farms and production facilities offering everything from puffed rice to coconut sweets and honey.

Nourishing Sweet Grass

Vietnam may only be the fifth largest producer of rice in the world, with some 7.5 million tons per annum, but it is the third largest }exporter. The main production region is the fertile Mekong Delta, where several harvests are possible each year.

▶ **Over 1600 varieties of rice are grown in Vietnam. The most commonly known are:**

Fragrant rice: this type of grain is also known as »Jasmine rice« and is also cultivated in Thailand. Characteristics: white, jasmine fragrance, slightly sweet.

Apati: »green rice« is a Vietnamese speciality. It is usually gathered in before the main harvest. Cooked to a porridge-like consistency, it tastes slightly sweet.

Glutinous rice: in spite of its name, this »sweet rice« has a rather neutral taste. As it sticks together when cooked, it can easily be formed into little balls which can be dipped in sauce.

Deep water rice: »floating rice« is a specialty of the Mekong Delta. The rice plant stands in 50cm/20in to 100cm/39in of water and can grow up to 25cm/10in a day. The stems can grow several yards high.

▶ **Traditional techniques for wet rice cultivation**

A field surrounded by waist-high dams is prepared for planting with simple ploughs, usually drawn by water buffalo.

Produced in vast seedbeds, the rice grains are removed after around three weeks.

▶ **Rice cultivation regions and harvest quantities in Asia** in millions of tons, 2013

Bangladesh
51

Myanmar
28

India
159

China
205

Vietnam
44

Philippines
18

Thailand
36

Indonesia
71

▶ **The largest rice exporters** in millions of tons, 2013

India	10
Thailand	8.5
Vietnam	**7.5**

After roughly a month, the young rice plants are replanted by hand in the fields, flooded to knee height.

After three to four months, the fields are drained and the ears cut off in clumps.

* My Lai

✦ E 5

Province: Quang Ngai
Region: South Central Coast

The name of My Lai is surely familiar even to those whose knowledge of Vietnam is otherwise limited. Located 12km/7.5mi north of the provincial capital Quang Ngai, the village gained tragic notoriety through the brutal actions of the US Army on 16 March 1968, going down in history as the My Lai Massacre.

My Lai Massacre The district of Son My was known as the Vietcong stronghold. Some American soldiers were injured and killed in the area in March 1968, stinging the US Army into an **act of reprisal**. During the course of a so-called Search and Destroy operation the village was razed to the ground and the entire population – more than 500 people, the majority of them women, children and the elderly – abused and slaughtered in the most gruesome manner imaginable. A year later, one »traitor« in the American ranks found himself unable to keep his memories to himself any longer and the atrocities were made public. He told the press what had really happened and presented photographic evidence to back up his statement. In this way the world came to learn that defenceless people had been herded together and gunned down with automatic weapons into ditches. Women and girls had been mutilated and gang-raped, babies and children butchered. America was deeply shaken. Nobody could fathom that the young men sent to Vietnam as protectors of peace and human rights had revealed themselves to be murderers of babies and the elderly. Media pressure did lead to an **investigation**, but the commission seemed intent on perpetuating the cover-up – especially when it became apparent that My Lai was not an isolated incident. Only one single participant, Lieutenant William Calley, was tried in court. Initially sentenced to life imprisonment, he found vehement support from one element of the public and was portrayed as a martyr. Ulti-

My Lai

GETTING THERE
Located approx. 170km/105mi north of Quy Nhon and approx. 120km/87mi south of Hoi An
To reach the memorial, take the N 1 eastbound from the provincial capital Quang Ngai and cross the Tra Khuc River. A signposted path branches off eastwards after the bridge.

mately, he was given an early reprieve by President Nixon, tantamount to an illegal interference in the jurisdiction of the United States. More than 40 years after the massacre, in August 2009 in Georgia, Calley publicly expressed regret over the act for the first time. Since 2007 Oliver Stone has been planning to make a film about the events. It would be his fourth Vietnam picture, but for various reasons, including funding, the project has been subject to repeated delays.

✴ MEMORIAL

My Lai was only one of four villages in the Son My region where massacres occurred simultaneously. Today the hamlets again nestle idyllically between paddy fields and palm groves. Dedicated to the victims of the events on 16 March 1968, the Son My Memorial stands on the original site of the massacre. The first impression of a peaceful park landscape is challenged by the **monumental war memorial** in its midst. On the few remaining palm trees, notices inform visitors where particular families' huts once stood in their shade, still scorched and riddled with bullet holes. Small pathways wind through the meadows past the gravestones, with incense sticks in memory of the dead. On each an inscription notes whose house stood at this point and how many members of the family (with names and ages) lost their lives in the massacre. Nearly all of them were either children or old people. Mass graves are also noted.

Lest we forget

Memorial for victims of the massacre

Immediately at the entrance to the museum, a US pilot and two US soldiers, who refused to shoot locls from a helicopter, ultimately saving thirteen people, are honoured. The **museum** shows images captured by an American military photographer, Ronald L. Haeberle, 27 years of age at the time, and presents detailed information about the war and the events that unfolded at My Lai in particular. Personal effects of the victims, found in the rubble, can also be seen. A documentary filmed by Dutch television for the 30th anniversary of the massacre can be viewed on request in the adjacent building. It is worth considering the gruesome nature of the images on display here, not suitable for children.

➊ daily 7am-5pm, admission: approx. 12,000 VND

** My Son

✦ E 5

Province: Quang Nam–Da Nang
Region: South Central Coast

Standing before the temple ruins of My Son in the hills of Song Thu Bon, the erstwhile grandeur of the religious and cultural centre of the Cham (4th–13th centuries) can only be imagined. The transient nature of an ancient civilization is strikingly apparent – and provides a vivid contrast to the sprawl of vegetation, forcing its way into every nook and cranny.

History A good 20km/12.5mi from the capital Tra Kieu, in a basin almost entirely surrounded by mountains, the Cham king Bhadravarman (4th century) built a sanctum dedicated to **Shiva**, the Hindu god. Around three hundred years later, the original wooden temples were replaced with brick constructions. Ensuing generations extended the site continuously and added further sacral buildings. Today it is thought that the temple complex was considered to be the realm of gods and divine kings, populated by many priests, dancers and servants. French scientists divided the buildings into groups based on their findings and ordered them alphabetically. Within these groups, the individual buildings were sorted numerically. When the Vietcong used My Son as their hideout in the late 1960s, the US Air Force **carpet bombed** the area. Most of the unique temple towers were destroyed, including the legendary Kalan A1, declared by the French to be the most beautiful **brick construction** in Asia. Bomb craters can still be seen here today, especially in groups E and F, where they have evolved into harmless looking pools filled with water lilies. Since 1981, this unique historical site has been restored. In 1999 the sanctuary was added to the UNESCO World Heritage list, and UNESCO along with the World Monuments Fund and other sponsors provide funds to protect the site.

** RELICS OF THE TEMPLE SITE
🕐 daily 6.30am–4.30pm; dance and musical performances daily except Mon 9.30am and 10.30am

Although the site of My Son was built upon over centuries, the only temple buildings grouped here consist of a tower (kalan), library, meditation hall (mandapa) and auxiliary buildings – none of the three-tower sanctuaries typical of later Cham architecture. The temple towers symbolize the **Hindu mountain realm of Mehru**, home

It is advisable to set off for My Son as early as possible in the day, as there will be fewer tourists and more bearable temperatures

of the gods. Inside, the sanctum is plain and simple, with an iconic image of the revered god at its centre. Usually this was the phallic symbol of Shiva, a lingam. South of the kalan stood the library, housing objects of ritual. The mandapa, a rectangular hall to which the priests would retreat in preparation for ceremonies, was located outside the temple walls. Temple dances were also held here. It remains a mystery just how the highest towers on site could be built with fired bricks, **yet without mortar**. One theory suggests that the Cham used a kind of resin instead of mortar, mixed with ground shells and brick dust. A contrasting theory posits the idea that unfired bricks were first built up, the building was covered with earth and then completely fired.

The entrance leads directly onto the B, C and D groups, still relatively intact and offering an idea of how the site may once have looked. The religious centre is thought to have been located in Kalan B1, of which only the foundations have survived. A few years ago, the **lingam** was discovered in the earth below and now stands in front of the building.

Group B

My Son

GETTING THERE
Located approx. 40km/25mi southwest of Hoi An. As the heat tends to accumulate in the temple valley, it is advisable to set off to My Son early in the morning, or visit in the afternoon.
This is the only way to explore the terrain at a bearable temperature.

ADMISSION
100,000 VND
There are reasonably priced bus tours in large groups from Hoi An (from US$5, 6 hours, only 1 hour of which is on site – those with a keener interest in Champa history should plan to visit for at least two hours).

SECURITY NOTICE
It is strongly recommended that visitors keep to the marked pathways as a number of (live) mines and bombs are still thought to be in the area.

Stone inscriptions found close by reveal that this lingam was erected in the 11th century in honour of the god Bhadresvara, a descendant of Shiva and King Bhadravarman. The two smaller temples (B3 and B4) on the south side of B1 were dedicated to Shiva's offspring, Skanda and Ganesha. Fortunately, B5, with its roof in the form of a boat, is better preserved. Ritual objects and sacred scriptures were kept here in former times. The outer walls feature not only ornate stonemasonry, but also bullet holes resulting from Vietcong skirmishes with the Americans. Above the entrances on both sides, reliefs of two elephants can be admired, their trunks wrapped around a palm. The interior of B6 contains a basin where **holy water** was collected and poured over the lingam in sacral ceremonies. It is particularly noteworthy, being the only one in existence in Cham culture. Between B5 and B6, a ruined gate listed as B2 leads to the D1 group, a prayer hall in which the priests would meditate prior to services.

Group C   Group C (8th century) was designed in similar fashion, originally separated from B by a wall. The main tower, C1, is still fairly well preserved. Small statues of the gods and an ornate lintel can be marvelled at here. The statue of Shiva in human form, however, which once stood inside the sanctum, has long since been relocated to the Cham Museum in Na Dang. Outside, a Garuda, a mythological birdlike creature with human and feline features, can be seen.

Group D   In the former meditation halls D1 and D2, **exhibition rooms** house Cham sculptures. French archaeologists were the first to name the space between the buildings the Stelae Court. As time has passed, the most beautiful stelae, altar relics, divine statues, rods and columns have been placed here.

Heading further east, a path crosses a stream to the completely de-   Group A
stroyed Group A, once the pride of the entire temple site. Judging by
what can be seen today, the magnificent **Kalan A1** (10th century)
must have folded like a house of cards when attacked. Unusually, it is
the only Cham construction to have an eastern and western gate. The

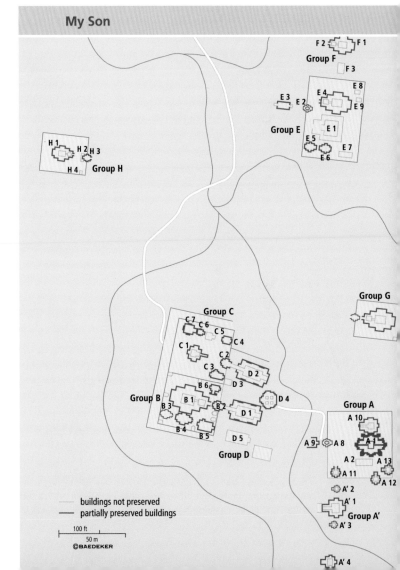

My Son

F 2   F 1
Group F
F 3
E 8
E 4
E 3   E 2   E 9
Group E   E 1
E 5
E 7
E 6

H 1   H 2 H 3
H 4   **Group H**

Group G

Group C
C 7 C 6
C 5
C 1   C 4
C 2
C 3   D 2
B 6   D 3
Group B   B 1   D 4
B 3   B 2   D 1
B 4   B 5   **Group A**
D 5   A 10
Group D   A-1
A 9   A 8
A 2   A 13
A 11
A 12
A' 2

buildings not preserved
partially preserved buildings   A' 1
100 ft   **Group A'**
50 m   A' 3
©BAEDEKER
A' 4

Uroja symbol, the Earth-Mother and Goddess of Fertility worshipped by the Cham

ruins of Group A are completely overgrown.

Leaving the remains of group A behind, the neighbouring hill is the site of **Group G**. The main kalan is no longer in good condition but some interesting figures with devilish expressions can still be seen. At its southeastern corner is a bizarre character resembling a gargoyle. At the front of the site is a plinth, its foundation bordered with breasts, the symbol of the Earth-Mother Uroja.

Groups E and F (7th century) lie at the end of a small trail to the north. This area was almost completely destroyed. The pools on the terrain are, in actual fact, bomb craters. A few stelae and lingams are dotted around the temple remains, along with a circular lingam base, a Nandi and a decapitated statue.

* My Tho

 D 7

Province: Tien Giang (capital)
Region: Mekong Delta
Population: 180,000

The upcoming commercial town of My Tho on the Tien Giang River is surrounded on three sides by water. What better way to delve into the everyday life of the Mekong Delta than by boat, sampling such delicacies as rice wine, coconut candy and »Elephant Ear Fish«?

WHAT TO SEE IN MY THO

Chinese
quarter

On the eastern bank of the canal lies My Tho, the Chinese quarter, still the scene of assiduous trading. Piles of sugar cane, dried fish and watermelon stand outside the narrow shops, awaiting transport to Saigon.

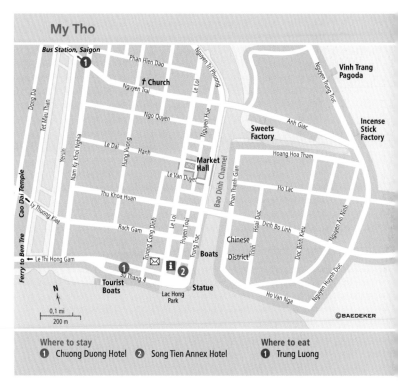

My Tho

Bus Station, Saigon
Phan Hien Dao
Nguyen Tri Phuong
Le Loi
Vinh Trang Pagoda
Nguyen Trung Truc
Phan Hien Dao
† Church
Nguyen Trai
Ngo Quyen
Dong Da
Tet Mau Than
Le Dai
Hung Vuong
Hanh
Nam Ky Khoi Nghia
Yersin
Le Dai
Nguyen Hue
Anh Giac
Sweets Factory
Incense Stick Factory
Hoang Hoa Tham
Market Hall
Le Van Duyet
Bao Dinh Channel
Phan Thanh Gian
Ho Lac
Cao Dai Temple
Ly Thuong Kiet
Thu Khoa Huan
Rach Gam
Truong Cong Dinh
Le Loi
Huyen Toai
Trung Trac
Hoai Duc
Dinh Bo Linh
Nguyen An Ninh
Doc Binh Kieu
Ferry to Ben Tre
Le Thi Hong Gam
30 Thang 4
Tourist Boats
Lac Hong Park
Boats
Chinese District
Trinh
Statue
Ho Van Nga
Nguyen Huynh Duc
N
0,1 mi
200 m
©BAEDEKER

Where to stay
❶ Chuong Duong Hotel ❷ Song Tien Annex Hotel

Where to eat
❶ Trung Luong

Around 1km/1100yd northeast, Vinh Trang Pagoda was built in 1820 and boasts a wealth of Buddha and Bodhisattva figures. Constant alterations and renovations have left the temple looking like an indulgently decorated palace. On entering the pagoda, the dining hall and dormitory of the monks living here can be seen on the right hand side. In the **main sanctuary**, behind the courtyard with its notable miniature mountain, the ornately carved columns are resplendent in gold. The 60 statues, including 18 arhats, are also worth inspection. Ponds, gardens and tombs surround the temple complex.
❶ daily 7.30am–noon, 2pm–5pm

Vinh Trang Pagoda

On the way to the pagoda, smaller enterprises proffer their wares (sweets, for example). On the corner of Anh Giac and Nguyen Trung there is an opportunity to see incense sticks being manufactured. Bamboo shavings are dipped into a perfumed mixture of sawdust and paste, then painted yellow. They are subsequently dried in front of the house.

Incense sticks fabrication
Insider Tip

My Tho

INFORMATION
Tien Giang Tourist
No. 8, 30 Thang 4 (also at: 30/4, Bank Street), My Tho
tel. 073/387 31 84
www.tiengiangtourist.com
7am–5pm

Ben Tre Tourist
16 Hai Ba Trung, Ben Tre
tel. 075/382 23 92
9am–6pm
Both cater for boat trips as well as car and bicycle rentals.

SHOPPING
In keeping with its status as an important trading centre for the surrounding region, My Tho hosts a turbulent market between the Bao Dinh Canal and Nguyen Hue. Heaps of exotic fruits, rice sacks, stalls with freshly plucked chickens, marinated fish delicacies and various types of noodles jostle for position alongside little shops selling fishing nets and household goods.

CUISINE
Insider Tip

Hu Tieu My Tho – a tasty local speciality, not to be missed: served piping hot everywhere in town, this hearty noodle soup is enriched with seafood, chicken and pork

WHERE TO EAT
Countless cookshops are dotted along Le Thi Hong Gam at the riverside night market, serving all manner of tasty dishes from a thousand and one pots (£).

❶ Trung Luong £
tel. 073/385 54 41
Nice garden restaurant on the N 1 at the approach to town.

WHERE TO STAY
❶ Chuong Duong Hotel £
No. 10 on the 30 Thang 4 (beach promenade)
tel. 073/387 08 75
Best hotel in town, situated on the river with air conditioning, some rooms with balcony and river view. Attractive terrace bar on the promenade.

❷ Song Tien Annex Hotel £
33 Trung Trac, My Tho
tel. 073/397 78 83
20 rooms with balcony and river views right on the promenade (very different to each other, better to compare beforehand!). Fine vista into the distance from the airy restaurant on the roof.

AROUND MY THO

Tan Long Island is just a five-minute boat trip away, the vessels departing from Le Loi Boulevard in My Tho. The palm-covered »Dragon Island« offers lovely walks through fruit plantations and the island restaurant offers refreshment.

A few miles outside My Tho lies the so-called Phoenix Island, Phung, the refuge of the Coconut Monk Ong Dao Dua, who died in 1990. The story concerns one of the many **sects** found in the Mekong Delta, which experienced their heyday during partition. In 1945 Nguyen Tanh Nam, the founder of the sect, left his family and became a monk. He developed his own doctrine (Tinh Do Cu Si), preaching a union of Christianity and Buddhism and advocating the peaceful unification of North and South Vietnam, leading to his repeated imprisonment by the government of the south. Like other faiths, the Dao Dua sect was fought by the Communist leadership, but nevertheless maintained a community on the island into the 1980s. At their **peak** in the 1960s, the sect had as many as several thousand members. Their buildings, with dragon columns and a multistage throne where the Coconut Monk would hold audience, are rather like a cross between an amusement park and a spaceport. They no longer look well cared for and the earlier prosperity of the island can barely be recognized.

Coconut Monk's Island

● daily 8am–11.30am, 1.30pm–6pm; admission: approx. 5000 VND

Approximately 10km/6mi to the west of My Tho, cobras and pythons are bred at the Dong Tam Snake Farm. Their **uses** are manifold: serums are extracted from snake venom, the skin is worked into leather and, last but not least, their meat is considered a delicacy by many a connoisseur. The snake farm also features a section with mutant turtles and fish, their genetic deformities probably a result of the spraying of Agent Orange in the Vietnam War

Snake farm

● daily 7am–5.30pm; admission: approx. 16,000 VND

Ben Tre can be reached by means of a good, old ferry, or, these days, one of the many new bridges. The island, some 12km/7.5mi south of My Tho, lies between the Cua Dai and Co Cien branches of the Mekong. During the Vietnam War, Ben Tre was seen as the **stronghold of the Vietcong**, already established here at the end of the 1950s; the town would later become an American military base. Nowhere else were the battles between government troops and the Americans against the insurgents as fierce as here, nowhere else were such quantities of napalm and Agent Orange deployed and nowhere else were civilian casualties higher. Thus Ben Tre became the »Island of a Thousand Widows« and the neighbouring Luong Hoa became known as »Widows' Village«, inhabited only by women. At the heart of the

Ben Tre

town of Ben Tre lies the **Vien Minh Pagoda**, dedicated to the Goddess of Mercy. The central market and the rice wine distillery in the southern part of town are also worth seeing. By car, the journey to Ba Tri in the southeast, with its charming Nguyen Dinh Chieu Temple, takes less than an hour.

Thap Muoi stork sanctuary The marshy environs of Cao Lanh (approx. 95km/60mi west of My Tho) are ideal for studying wildlife. A small bird sanctuary here is largely populated by **white storks**, the heraldic animals of the Mekong Delta, who do not seem in the least troubled by visitors.

Tam Nong Nature Reserve Another nature reserve is situated close to the small town of Tam Nong (barely 50km/30mi north of Cao Lanh) and can be reached on land or by boat, if somewhat laboriously. The area offers refuge to hundreds of species of bird, including **cranes and purple herons**. Great patience is required to watch them as these birds are not used to people and rarely come into view. Hence the region remains the domain of genuine bird-watching enthusiasts.

✶✶ Nha Trang

E 6

Province: Khanh Hoa (capital)
Region: South Central Coast
Population: Approx. 350,000

There can be no place more cosmopolitan in Vietnam to take a dip than the port of Nha Trang. French colonial masters, the former emperor Bao Dai, US soldiers and Russian labourers on holiday have all ambled along the 6km/4mi-long beach with turquoise waters, a ring of mountains in the distance. The famous Cham towers, over 1000 years old, offer an alternative to lounging around on the beach.

International bathing resort Nha Trang is a hotbed of international activity and nightlife, with backpackers, package holidaymakers and Vietnamese families all congregating here. The culinary palette stretches from fried rice and German sausage to excellent seafood in the beachfront beer gardens. An armada of hawkers pampers vacationers at the beach with massages, fresh coconut juice, dragon fruit and iced beer, even fingernail manicures, without having to leave the deck chair. For those seeking more lively pursuits, Nha Trang has a wealth of **water sports** on offer, boasting a higher concentration of diving schools than anywhere else in Vietnam. Around 70 islands off the coast are perfect for boat trips and 25 diving spots wait to be explored.

The harbour fish market is lively and colourful

WHAT TO SEE IN NHA TRANG

Following a sunny spell on the beach , a walk along Tran Phu Street heading north leads to the Pasteur Institute with the Alexandre Yersin Museum. The exhibition centres on the Swiss doctor who settled here in 1893. Yersin (▶MARCO POLO Insight p.338) is something of a hero in Nha Trang. Not, however, for his major achievement – his discovery of the microbe that causes bubonic plague – but primarily as a result of his meteorological knowledge, enabling him to predict **typhoons**, thus saving the lives of many fishermen. Some of his laboratory equipment such as telescopes and barometers are on display, whilst the library illustrates the broad spectrum of his fields of interest – from medicine to horticulture and from bacteriology to astrology. The Pasteur Institute, which houses the museum, was founded by Yersin himself in the year 1895.

Alexandre Yersin Museum

❶ Mon–Fri7.30am–11.30am, 2pm–5pm, Sat 7.30am–11.30am; admission 25,000 VND

Discoverer of the Plague Bacillus

Almost forgotten in Switzerland, yet seen all over Vietnam: the university in Da Lat is not the only institution to bear the Swiss physician's name. A Hanoi hospital, several streets, a museum, a monument, even a Vietnamese bird species – and of course the »Yersinia Pestis« bacterium – have all been named in honour of the scientist Alexandre Yersin (1863–1943).

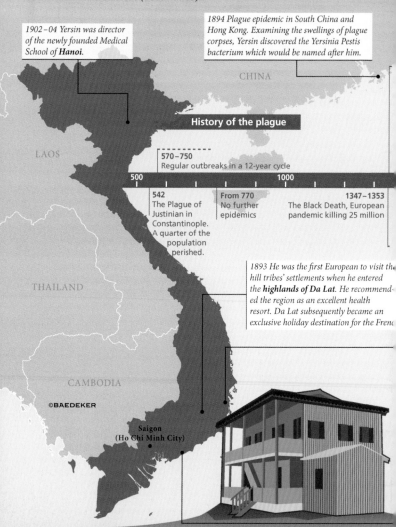

*1902–04 Yersin was director of the newly founded Medical School of **Hanoi**.*

1894 Plague epidemic in South China and Hong Kong. Examining the swellings of plague corpses, Yersin discovered the Yersinia Pestis bacterium which would be named after him.

CHINA

LAOS

History of the plague

570–750
Regular outbreaks in a 12-year cycle

500   1000

542
The Plague of Justinian in Constantinople. A quarter of the population perished.

From 770
No further epidemics

1347–1353
The Black Death, European pandemic killing 25 million

THAILAND

*1893 He was the first European to visit the hill tribes' settlements when he entered the **highlands of Da Lat**. He recommended the region as an excellent health resort. Da Lat subsequently became an exclusive holiday destination for the Frenc*

CAMBODIA

©BAEDEKER

Saigon
(Ho Chi Minh City)

The life of Alexandre Émile Jean Yersins

Born on 22 September 1863 in Rougemont in the Canton of Vaud

❌ **1894**

Discovery of the plague bacterium
Yersin discovered that the bacterium is mostly transmitted via fleabites from rats to humans and then multiplied in the blood.

1910–1911
Pneumonic plague pandemic in Mandchuria (China) approx. 60,000 fatalities

1350–1771
Recurring pandemics in northern Europe

1896–1950
Third pandemic in Central Asia, approx. 12 million fatalities

1888 Doctorate on tuberculosis

1888–90 of the first research group based on Pasteur

1890 Ship's doctor in Indochina

1894 Pestilence research in Hong Kong

1500

2000

1665–1666
Great Plague of London

1678–1679
Epidemic in Vienna, approx. 12,000 fatalities

20 June 1894 Isolation of the »Yersinia pestis« bacterium

1895 Development of an antiserum against the plague (in Paris)

1902–04 Director of the Medical School in Hanoi

1902 First Pasteur Institute outside of France in Nha Trang

*Having completed his medical studies and his work at the Pasteur Institute in Paris, he voyaged as a ship's doctor to the Far East, arriving in **Nha Trang** in 1891. Here he established a laboratory which became the first Pasteur Institute outside France in 1902.*

1904–24
Director of the Pasteur Institutes in Saigon and Nha Trang

In Vietnam Yersin conducted research on cattle plagues and introduced the rubber tree and cinchona tree for the recovery of quinine into the country. He is also credited with the reform of the Vietnamese health service.

A little piece of Switzerland in Vietnam
*Yersin grew plants from his homeland in his **Hong Ba** chalet. He died here in 1943 and was buried in the village of Suoi Dua.*

Died on 28 February 1943

Nha Trang

INFORMATION
Khanh Hoa Tourist
1 Tran Hung Dao, Nha Trang (next to the Vien Dong Hotel)
tel. 058/352 67 53
Also in various hotels and numerous travel agencies

TRANSPORT
Cam Ranh Airport
approx. 40km/25mi south of Nha Trang
tel. 058/382 67 68 and 058/382 21 35.
Flights to Da Nang, Hanoi, Saigon and since 2013 Moscow. Shuttle bus to town (approx. 60,000 VND), taxi approx. 400,000 VND

Railway station
in Thai Nguyen west of the centre: daily trains to Saigon, Da Nang and Hanoi

EVENTS
Merian/Po Nagar Festival
The tutelary goddess of the town, Yang Ino Po Nagar, is taken each year from the Cham temple down to the beach in a procession (March to May) where she is bathed and her robes changed – all accompanied by oblations, music, theatre and dances.

SHOPPING
Not far from the centre of Nha Trang, south of Hon Chong Bay, the Hong Chau Sa family has specialized in »sand painting« from 30 different natural sand tones, all imaginative souvenirs: from Ho Chi Minh's portrait to typical paddy field landscapes at sunset and even western images such as Father Christmas (Hong Chau Sa Sand Pictures, 4 B Nha Tho, tel. 058/383 30 91, daily 8am-6pm, shops

can be fond in the Po Nagar temple ruins and at 81 Tran Quang Khai and 6 Cau Da).

ENTERTAINMENT
❶ *Nha Trang Sailing Club* **£££**
72 Tran Phu, Nha Trang
tel. 058/382 46 28
www.sailingclubvietnam.com
daily 7am–2am
The city's hottest club for years, a place to see and to be seen in: predominantly a meeting place for foreigners on the beach terrace, with Italian-Vietnamese cuisine on offer. Beach parties and campfires, dancing and cocktails.

WHERE TO EAT
❶ *Treffpunkt German Bar and Restaurant* **£-££**
6A Tran Quang Khai, Loc Tho
Nha Trang
tel. 058/352 38 98
Mobile tel. 090/330 54 75
In his small, unassuming bar, Frank serves up homemade burgers, sausage, sauerkraut, schnitzel and potato soup to anyone craving familiar dishes. German beer is also available.

❷ *Lac Canh* **£**
44 Nguyen Binh Khiem
Xuong Huan District, Nha Trang
tel. 058/382 13 91
This simple Vietnamese open-air restaurant has been popular for decades. Fine fare on two levels: seafood, chicken, beef barbecue on the table and, naturally, frogs and other creatures – the prices are not even worth mentioning!

❸ *Cyclo Café* £
5A Tran Quang Khai, Nha Trang
tel. 058/352 42 08
daily 7am–11pm
Attractive little eatery with Vietnamese-Italian menu, vegetarian options, western breakfast, muesli and snacks.

WHERE TO STAY
Six Senses Ninh Van Bay ££££
Ninh Van Bay, Ninh Hoa (approx. 50km/30mi north of Nha Trang on the Hon Heo peninsula) Khanh Hoa province
tel. 058/372 82 22
www.sixsenses.com/
SixSensesNinhVanBay
Island oasis with natural materials in abundance. 50 rustic, yet extremely comfortable villas, typical for the region, situated between the rocks or on the hill above a quiet bay: rocking chairs, small, individual pool and personal wine cellar!

❶ *Evason Ana Mandara Nha Trang* £££-££££
86 Tran Phu, Nha Trang
tel. 058/352 22 22
www.sixsenses.com/evason-ana-mandara-nha-trang
Marvellous first-class hotel and beach complex: 17 bungalows (some with sea view) and 74 luxurious rooms, utterly beautiful décor and canopy beds. Two restaurants, pool, water sports.

Ana Mandara Resort

❷ Sunrise Nha Trang Beach Hotel & Spa ££-£££

12-14 Tran Phu, Hoi An
tel. 058/382 09 99
www.sunrisenhatrang.com.vn
Swanky luxury block on the promenade (some distance from the centre), especially popular with Russian guests. Beautiful pool in temple design, super rooftop bar on the 11th floor and no less than seven restaurants and bars in total! The busy beach road leads down to the beach (serving most of the »beach hotels« in Nha Trang).

❸ Vien Dong Hotel £-££

1 Tran Hung Dao, Nha Trang
tel. 058/52 36 06
viendonghtl@dng.vnn.vn
Getting on in years, perhaps, but with prettily appointed rooms, pool, restaurant, shops.

❹ La Paloma Villa £-££

1 Hon Chong
approx. 2km/1mi north of Nha Trang centre
tel. 058/383 12 16
Mobile tel. 090/350 90 63
Lovely hacienda style hotel in the small bay of Hon Chong. Comfortable rooms (with balcony) arranged around the pool in a tranquil palm tree garden, leafy bathrooms, popular among families with children. Host Bu and his wife Duong preside over a delightful atmosphere

and are happy to drive guests into town. Free bike rental, Wi-Fi and breakfast included.

Whale Island Resort ££

Hon Ong, Van Ninh (island approx. 60km/37mi north of Nha Trang)
tel./fax 058/384 05 01
www.whaleislandresort.com
Stay on the veritable Robinson Crusoe island of the same name in one of 23 original, stylish and yet rustically appointed bamboo bungalows on the beach (mosquito nets, ventilator fans). Lots of wood, rattan and terra-cotta, with the chief attraction being the bamboo beds, along with hammocks outside (some less expensive rooms). Seafood inn (full board including transfer from Nha Trang). Daily shuttle bus at 9am and 2pm from the Rainbow Bar in Nha Trang (90A Hung Vuong, US$20 per person).

Jungle Beach Resort £

Hon Heo peninsula, Ninh Phuoc village, Ninh Hoa (approx. 60km/37mi north of Nha Trang)
tel. 058/362 23 84
Mobile tel. 091/342 91 44
www.junglebeachvietnam.com
Backpacker paradise on a long, wide beach. Communal dining of an evening, sleep in rudimentary palm tree huts or directly beneath the stars.

Cathedral Heading southwest, Thai Nguyen Street leads to two further sites of interest. The cathedral on the corner of Nguyen Trai Street was built in 1933 and features beautiful stained glass windows.

*Long Son Pagoda Hard to miss, the great, white Buddha who seems to watch over the town can be seen from afar. He is seated on a lotus throne above Long Son Pagoda, just a few hundred yards from the cathedral. This temple was built in 1930. An impressive bronze Buddha is enthroned above the main altar, and the walls are decorated with paintings of Jataka scenes. Behind the central columned hall, steps lead past hawkers and beggars up the hill. At the top stands an **imposing statue of Buddha**, erected in 1963 as a symbol of the Buddhists' struggle against the repressive Diem regime. Its plinth bears images of monks and nuns who burned themselves in protest, their number including Thich Quang Duc (►Famous People). The hilltop offers a wonderful panorama of Nha Trang and the coast.

On the south side of town stands Bao Dai Villa, five houses at the heart of a beautiful park. Today, the Art Deco building that stands regally on the cliffs above the sea has been converted into a hotel. The garden restaurant provides a fascinating vista of the coast, harbour and offshore islands.

Bao Dai Villa

A small gallery is dedicated to the works of Long Thanh, a famous Vietnamese photographer. Marvellously atmospheric black and white pictures from the everyday life of his fellow countrymen are on display. Long Thanh is celebrated far beyond the borders of his hometown and has also exhibited his photographs in Europe.

Long Thanh Gallery

● 126 Hoang Van Thu, daily 8am–5.30pm, www.longthanhart.com

From the harbour of the fishing village Cau Da (5km/3mi south of the city centre), boat trips leave for the **karst islands** off the coast. Small, round wicker boats ferry passengers to the coloured barges, where hearty meals of seafood and fish are prepared and served. There is plenty of opportunity to go bathing or snorkelling in the pretty bay. A floating bar is a common sight, offering refreshments to those lounging in the water. Often degenerating into drinking games and inebriated karaoke sessions amongst the younger passengers from all over the world, these tours follow different itineraries, some tours visiting the fish farm on the island of Tri Nguyen, better known as Hon Mieu. The islands, Hon Yen (Swallow Island) in particular, are famed for the **bird's nests** from which »bird's nest soup« is made. Twice a year, when the young have flown, the nests, which largely consist of saliva, are collected from the cliffs. They are considered a delicacy throughout Asia and thought to en-

**Boat trips

! MARCO ⊕ POLO TIP

Eco-boom in Vietnam Insider Tip

The island of Hon Tre (Bamboo Island) is developing its »eco theme«, although, in practical terms, the Vietnamese version includes concrete tree facsimiles, gigantic luxury resorts with golf courses and jet skis shooting across the water. Since 2006, a 3km/2mi-long cable car has connected Hon Tre to the mainland. The journey time is around nine minutes. (Cable car: daily 8am-10pm, approx. 70,000 VND).

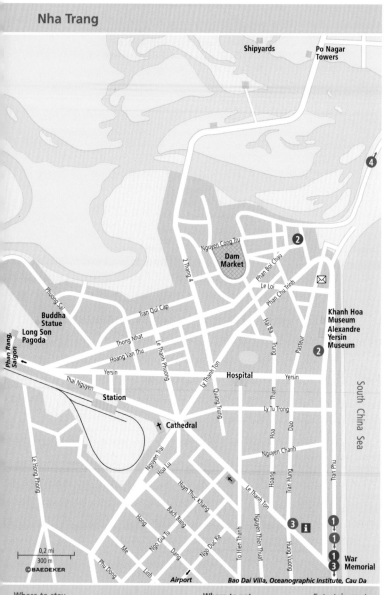

Nha Trang

Shipyards

Po Nagar Towers

Nguyen Cong Tru

Dam Market

2 thang 4

Phan Boi Chau

Le Loi

Phan Chu Trinh

Phuong Sai

Tran Qui Cap

Hai Ba

Trung

Pasteur

Khanh Hoa Museum

Alexandre Yersin Museum

Buddha Statue

Long Son Pagoda

Phan Rang, Saigon

Thong Nhat

Hoang Van Thu

Yersin

Le Thanh Phuong

Ly Thanh Ton

Quang Trung

Hospital

Yersin

Thai Nguyen

Station

Ly Tu Trong

Hoa

Dao

Cathedral

Nguyen Chanh

South China Sea

Le Hong Phong

Nguyen Trai

Hoa Lu

Huyn Thuc Khang

Le Thanh Ton

Hoang

Tran Hung

Tran Phu

Hong

Bach Bang

Ngo Gia Tu

Dang

Ngo Duc Ke

To Hien Thanh

Nguyen Thien Thuat

Hung Vuong

Me

Linh

Phu Dong

Airport

War Memorial

Bao Dai Villa, Oceanographic Institute, Cau Da

0,2 mi
300 m

©BAEDEKER

Where to stay
1 Evason
  Ana Mandara
2 Sunrise Hotel & Spa
3 Vien Dong Hotel
4 La Paloma Villa

Where to eat
1 Treffpunkt German Bar
2 Lac Canh Restaurant
3 Cyclo Café

Entertainment
1 Nha Trang
  Sailing Club

hance potency. On Hon Lao (Monkey Island) lives a family of apes who are happy to let themselves be fed by day trippers. As the monkeys are also happy to bite, however, visitors are advised to keep their distance. Hon Tam (Silkworm Island), with a hotel and parasailing, and the smaller islets of Hon Mun and Hon Mot, Hon Thi and Hon Heo (the last with waterfalls) await snorkellers and sunbathers.

** THE TOWERS OF PO NAGAR

On the way to the towers of Po Nagar (Thap Ba, 1.5km/1mi north of the city centre), the Xom Bong Bridge crosses the Cai River, passing a small harbour with its colourful fishing fleet, red and blue canoes and round wicker boats. At their very heart, a huge rocky outcrop reaches up out of the water. A **Chinese shrine** has been erected on the rock, where local fisherman leave small offerings before they set sail. The temple hill presents a fabulous view of the scenario. The sanctuary was dedicated to Po Nagar, the Mother and Fertility Goddess of the Cham, who, in Hinduistic ritual, became Bhagavati, wife of the god Shiva. Over the centuries, the temples of Kauthara, as they were known under the Cham, were repeatedly attacked by the Malays, the Khmer and the Chinese. So it is that, of the eight Cham towers or kalan which were built between the 7th and 12th centuries on Cu Lao Hill, only four remain today. The complex has since developed into a well-frequented Buddhist place of worship, as made apparent by the variety of oblations and incense.

❶ daily 6am–6pm; admission: 25,000 VND

Visitors ascend a flight of steps up the hill past beggars and traders, whereas the pilgrims of old would have passed through the mandapa (a meditation hall), of which some column fragments remain. From here, steps lead directly to the main temple.

Mandapa

❶ daily 6am–6pm

Three storeys and 23m/75ft high, the northern tower, built by Harivarman I in the year 817, is one of the finest examples of Cham architecture. Reaching up from its base, decorated with double pilasters and lotus-embellished arcades, this is a mighty work of construction. Above the portal, the many-armed Shiva (Nataraja) dances, his foot resting on the head of the bull Nandi, framed by musicians. The lintel and walls of the vestibule bear Sanskrit inscriptions, telling of sacrifices to the goddess. The vestibule tapers to a pyramidal ceiling and into the **sanctum**, where the shadows take a little getting used to. A golden lingam originally stood here, stolen by the Khmer in the 10th century and later replaced by the Po Nagar statue still seen here today. Admittedly, the head has been replaced, as the French removed

*Northern tower with Po Nagar statue

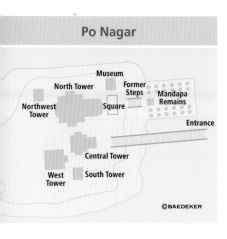

Po Nagar

Museum
North Tower   Former Steps
Northwest Tower   Square   Mandapa Remains
Entrance
Central Tower
West Tower   South Tower
©BAEDEKER

the original. There is something doll-like about the new head, an image accentuated by the yellow cloak which covers her ten arms. Two ironwood elephants stand guard alongside the 8th–9th-century figure, the only surviving Cham sculptures of this type. On the rear wall, a garderobe contains the various different robes that Po Nagar dons during elaborate ceremonies three times a year (Tet, 30 March and 15 July). She is still honoured as the protectress of the town and her statue is bathed in the river during the Merian Festival in March.

Central tower The three smaller towers are less intricate and in poorer condition than the northern tower. Especially worse for wear is the middle kalan (12th century). Childless couples come here to pray for fertility at the lingam.

South tower The southernmost kalan (12th century) contains an impressive lingam. The tower itself comprises two sections, a vaulted roof and an almost square construction with vestibule.

Northwestern tower The northwestern tower dates back to the late 10th century and is no longer accessible. It was formerly dedicated to Ganesha, Shiva's son with the head of an elephant. Still visible on its outer walls are representations of animal gods: Garuda on the south façade, a lion on the north side and a human form with elephant's head to the west.

Museum On display in the small adjacent museum are photographs of restoration work and fragments of the foundations.

AROUND NHA TRANG

Hon Chong Bay For a quiet life on the beach, Hon Chong Bay is the place to go, just 500m/550yd north of Po Nagar. This stretch of coastline may not be quite as well groomed as the town's beach, but the water is crystal clear, glistening turquoise as the sun catches its surface. On the south side, smooth boulders can be seen, one bearing an imprint that is said by locals to have been made by a giant. A number of small hotels and guesthouses have opened for business here in recent years.

Travelling north, the white sands of Doc Let (50km/30mi from Nha Trang) on Hon Khoi peninsula are a good place to break the journey. Casuarina and palm trees provide shade; in addition, two simple beach resorts, a restaurant, changing facilities and refreshments stalls can also be found here. Basket boats from the neighbouring fishing village can be seen bobbing along off the coast.

Doc Let

Enjoy spa treatments Vietnamese style at Thap Ba Hot Springs, relax in mud troughs (37–38°C/98-100F) and hot water springs (40°C/104°F) in pools or underneath a waterfall. Those who feel so inclined can follow up with a decent massage. If the public area feels too busy (particularly the case at weekends and afternoons when large Vietnamese families congregate here with screeching children) or not hygienic enough, there are also (overpriced) VIP zones. In recent

Thap Ba Hot Springs

Bathing in warm mud minerals

times, various superior spa hotels with landscaped pools have established themselves here, such as the i Resort (tel. 058/383 88 33, 333.i-resort.vn).

❶ 15 Ngoc Son, Ngoc Hiep (approx. 10 minutes taxi ride from Nha Trang), tel 058/383 53 35, www.thapbahotspring.co.vn (twin mudbath approx. 400,000 VND; spa packages available including transportation from Nha Trang between 160,000 VND und 2,000,000 VND, depending on booking office).

Hon Ong (Whale Island) A small peninsula and a paradise for divers, Hon Ong inspires dreams of Robinson Crusoe. Jaques-Yves Cousteau dived off »Whale Island« back in the 1930s, exploring the underwater fauna of the depths. With luck, the whales and whale sharks who give the island its name may pass by during a dive, along with rays (the best period is from April to July). Indulge in a spot of surfing, snorkelling, catamaran sailing, diving, sunbathing – or do none of the above and just relax (the island, which lies approximately 60km/37mi north of Nha Trang, is just a short boat trip away, via the peninsula of Hon Gom).

Phan Rang

 E 7

Province: Ninh Thuan (capital)
Region: South Central Coast
Population: 200,000

Phan Rang and Thap Cham are sister cities a few miles from the sea on the Chai River. The place itself holds little attraction, so move swiftly on to the famous Cham towers of Po Klong Garai and the beautiful white beach. Cacti, dunes and flamboyants are the distinctive features of the region along with, surprisingly, grapevines.

✷ PO KLONG GARAI TOWERS

❶ daily 7.30am-6pm; admission: approx. 25,000 VND

Best preserved example of Cham architectural art On National Highway 20 to Da Lat (8km/5mi west of Phan Rang), the four imposing towers of Po Klaung Garai rise up from the xeric landscape. In the late 13th century, during the reign of Jaya Simhavarman III, these Hindu temples were built on top of a granite hill. The sanctuary is dedicated to the legendary Prince Po Klaung Garai, who, in Cham mythology, was the equal of the Hindu god Shiva. Together with the mother goddess Po Nagar, he was superior to the divine king of the dynasty. Steps lead up to the complex, which is sur-

Phan Rang

INFORMATION
Ninh Thuan Tourist
16/4 Street (i.e. 16 Thang 4)
tel. 068/382 26 27
www.ninhthuantourist.com

VERKEHR
Cam Ranh Airport
tel. 058/382 67 68 and 058/382 21 35
Flights to Da Nang, Hanoi, Saigon and
since 2013 to Moscow.

Railway station
approx. 8km/5mi to the west in Thap
Cham, Phan Rang, tel. 068/388 80 29

EVENTS
Kate Festival
A three day festival in the seventh lunar
month (September/October) of the
Khmer calendar, marking the beginning
of the Cham New Year for the Muslim
population; a celebration of traditional
singing and dancing, a procession and
ritual ceremonies in the temple towers.

CUISINE
If tasting roasted gecko (ky nhong, also
called »Dong food«) has been a lifelong
ambition, the time to fulfil it has arrived.
This crispy regional delicacy is to be savoured with (unripe) green mango.

WHERE TO EAT
Com Ga Phuoc Thanh £
3D Tran Quang Dieu (close to the park),
Phan Rang
tel. 068/382 47 12
Small city restaurant, menu includes typical com ga dishes (rice with chicken,
pho with chicken) and breakfast.

WHERE TO STAY
Bau Truc Resort ££
Ninh Chu Beach
Van Hai (6km/4mi outside Phan Rang)
tel. 068/387 60 11
https://www.facebook.com/Bau-Truc-Re-
sort-1480714552237700/
Modern hotel in brick bungalows, some
with sea view, terracotta décor in antique Cham design, tennis court, pool
and camping tents on the beach. Open-
air restaurant with seafood and barbecue. Best to reserve at weekends!

Saigon Ninh Chu Hotel ££
Khanh Hai, Ninh Hai
tel. 068/387 60 11
www.saigonninhchuhotel.com.vn
Three-storey beach hotel belonging to
Saigon Tourist, the reputable travel
group: over 100 spacious, individual
rooms (air-conditioned, telephone) and
bungalows. Two restaurants, karaoke
bar and a lovely pool!

Thong Nhat Hotel £
99 Thong Nhat 343, Phan Rang
tel. 068/82 72 01, fax 82 29 43
thongnhathotel_pr@hcm.vnn.vn
Renovated four-storey hotel (33 rooms),
good location.

Dragonfruit, pitahaya

rounded by cactus scrub. Entrance to the **main kalan**, with its distinctly structured three-level roof, is through a 21m/69ft-high stone archway. The lotus-shaped corner towers and the divine images in the niches are noteworthy. The tower opens to the east onto the meditation hall, the original foundations of which are still standing. To the south is the library, whose saddle-like roof has two bullhorns at its extremities. A similar form can be seen on the windows. Due to Po Klaung Garai's affinity to Shiva, the sanctuary contains many symbols and representations of the god: the dancing, six-armed Shiva (Nataraja) above the entrance to the main tower, Shiva as the bull (Nandi) in the vestibule and the Mukha lingam (stylized phallus), symbolizing creativity and virility, in the sanctum sanctorum. The latter features the face and insignia of Po Klong Garai. In former times, it is said that the Nandi was regularly »fed« to ensure a good harvest. This custom is still practised today during the **Kate Festival** (Oct), the New Year celebrations of the Cham.

 daily 7.30am–6pm

The towers of Po Klong Garai rise up on a small hill

FURTHER PLACES TO VISIT IN THE AREA

6km/3.5mi east of Phan Rang, the splendid sweeping crescent of Ninh Chu Beach stretches out with its yellow sands and clear waters. A few quite bizarre hotels with bungalows and a handful of snack bars are sprinkled along the beach, which is generally empty during the week.

Ninh Chu Beach

The towers of Po Ro Me (15km/9mi south of Phan Rang), built on a hill in the 17th century, are regarded as the **last Cham constructions of significance**. Sadly, the sanctuary dedicated to Po Ro Me, the final ruler of the independent Champa, is practically in ruins. Some interesting features of the late architectural style can still be recognized, such as the distinctive corner towers on the roof of the central tower. A captivating bas-relief presents Shiva as the bearded King Po Ro Me, flanked by two Nandis. West of the complex – in the direction of the deceased forefathers, according to the Cham – stands a roughly hewn memorial stone (kut) for the king. Having been forced to flee their capital Vijaya in 1471, the Cham saw their empire crumble and were no longer able to maintain the high standards of their sculpture. As a consequence they emulated their ancestors and their veneration of natural deities, represented in the form of simple stones. This temple site is also considered to be a Cham sanctuary. The annual Kate Festival is also celebrated here.

Towers of Po Ro Me

> **MARCO ⊕ POLO TIP**
>
> ! *Cham Museum* **Insider Tip**
>
> Those interested in learning more about Cham culture can visit the small Cham Museum in Phan Rang, 17 Nguyen Trai. Pottery fragments, jewellery, some statues and other relics from excavations can be inspected (Mon–Fri 8am–11am, 2.30pm–4.30pm).

Wearing their turban-like headgear, many Cham can still be seen living in the region. Like Muslims all over the world, they celebrate the Ramadan month of fasting. Many living here earn their livelihood from **handicrafts**: to the east of the N 1, the weaving village of My Ngiep produces woven goods and clothing in the traditional manner. In Bau Truc village, pottery wares can be purchased, and the production process of the goods in the ovens may be observed. At the Cham village of Tuan Tu (approx. 5km/3mi south of Phan Rang) the beautiful Nam Cuong dunes stretch out.

Cham villages

Insider Tip

A fine, white beach, turquoise-blue water and a charming coral reef await sunlovers and snorkellers at Ca Na (32km/20mi south of Phan Rang). Refreshment can be found at the few small restaurants and beach huts, albeit rather close to the busy N 1, along with the hitherto basic places to stay and a Korean diving resort. Eucalyptus

*Ca Na

groves and fields line the route, as do fruit orchards with cactus-like, tendrillar plants bearing exotic. The produce in question is **dragon fruit** (thanh long), approximately the same size as a mango. Crimson on the outside with green shoots, they can be sliced open to reveal white flesh with black pips. Some roadside stalls offer them for sale and tropical fruit fans should definitely give them a try. Their taste is a little reminiscent of kiwi fruit (photo ►p.349).Parallel to the N1 Highway, a marvellous coastal road (Coastal Highway 702) is currently under construction, 116km/72mi running through a hitherto sparsely populated stretch of coastal land in Ninh Thuan province: from Ca Na via Mui Dinh Beach, the lengthy Ninh Chu Beach, the gorgeous Vinh Hy Bay (the Aman Resort opened here in 2013) to Bing Tien nea near Cam Ranh. It makes its way past fishing bays, attractive rock formations, sand dunes, brilliant white beaches and jungle-like verdant hills, certain to bring more tourists to this previously underdeveloped region. One cloud on the horizon: a nuclear power station is scheduled to be built near Ca Na in the south by 2020.

Insider Tip

** Phan Thiet · Mui Ne

✦ E 7

Province: Binh Thuan (capital)
Region: South Central Coast
Population: 170,000

It took just a few years for word of this »insider tip« on the south coast near the port of Phan Thiet to spread. That should come as no surprise, as Mui Ne is truly a gorgeous peninsular with a long, broad, sweeping bay laced with coconut palms. Nevertheless, the beautiful beach is still dominated by fishermen with their cutters, baskets and nets, apart from when surfers and kitesurfers breeze in for the »Fun Cup«.

WHAT TO SEE IN AND AROUND PHAN THIET

Beach and dunes

Around 16km/10mi long, the peninsula's beach, reaching as far as the dunes at Kap Ne (Mui Ne), is a real paradise and has long since overtaken Nha Trang as the international beach of choice. Now and again, especially on the eastern stretch of the beach, it is possible to watch the local fisherman in action, particularly in the early morning when there is a coastal current and the trawlers chug out to seawith their dragnets from right in front of the hotels. Fishing has been the prime source of income for centuries and no sooner have the villagers done so than the catch is sorted into baskets and prices negotiated. Under cover of coconut palms, the beach road passes small fishing settlements and an increasing number of bungalow resorts and numerous restaurants. The Mui Ne Peninsula appears to be ever expanding into a mega holiday resort. The beach road, four lanes in places, runs past some 200 3-star and 4-star hotels, the coast has been developed to such an extent that no gaps are left. On Ngyuen Dinh Chieu in the centre of Mui Ne, visitors stroll along a modern boulevard with pavement and no end of tourists descend on cafés, bars and souvenir shops. Mopeds and Jetskis are available for hire, there are massage parlours, diving stores and yoga schools – everything a holidaymaker could wish for, however young or old. Goods are increasingly priced in Russian. In summer, depending on the direction of the wind, the beach can be eroded in places, sucked into the sea, as it were, or scattered with litter (particularly in the northeastern part).

The small settlement of **Mui Ne** boasts a vibrant harbour and is home to a number of small factories making fish sauces. At the end of the Mui Ne peninsula, sand hills casting a reddish-orange and yellowish-white glow wait to be conquered on foot or by Jeep. In Mui Ne, surfers ride the sand as well as the waves – »surfing« down the sand dunes on plastic boards (photo ►p.109). Immediately behind the palm grove, the South China Sea beckons to those wishing to cool off overheated feet. An alternative is the »**White Lake**« (Bao Trang): actually three small and picturesque lakes at the heart of snow-white sand dunes close to Hon Hghe Bay in which the dunes are reflected

The dunes of Mui Ne are reminiscent of the Sahara

Phan Thiet · Mui Ne

INFORMATION
Binh Thuan Tourist
5 Nguyen Du, Phan Thiet City
tel. 062/381 61 08
www.binhthuantourism.com
Information and tours also available in
hotels

TRANSPORT
Railway station
tel. 062/382 11 61
Daily direct rail connection between Saigon and Phan Thiet (departs 7.30am
from Saigon, 1.45pm from Phan Thiet,
shuttle bus service to Mui Ne Beach,
11km/7mi

Buses
from Saigon meanwhile take up to 5 or
6 hours due to the heavy traffic along
the motorway N1, which has dense
housing along both sides.

EXCURSIONS
Binh Thuan Tourist organizes excursions
to the islands off the coast, such as the
tiny local island of Lao Cau and, approximately 100km/62mi off the coast to the
east.

EVENTS
Kate Festival
The three-day Kate Festival of the Cham
is held annually in September/October
with traditional costumes and dishes,
singing and dancing at the Po Shanu
Towers.

WATER SPORTS
Ideal wind speeds for surfers and kitesurfers of 18–30 knots can be expected
between November and early April on
the Mui Ne coast, attracting the international kiting and surfing community.
February sees surfers gather here for the
annual »Fun Cup« when the ****Insider Tip****
boards glide over the waves
and the kiters fly high in the sky.
There are various kiteboarding schools,
the cool people meet up at Jibe's halfway along the beach (90 Nguyen Dinh
Chieu), km 13, www.windsurf-vietnam.
com, www.kiteboarding-vietnam.com).

ENTERTAINMENT
Dragon Beach
120–121 Nguyen Dinh Chieu, Ham Tien,
Mui Ne
Open 8am–2am
The no. 1 dancefloor of Mui Ne attracts
with its chill-out deck and internaational
DJs.

ENTERTAINMENT/WHERE TO EAT
El Latino ££
139 Nguyen Dinh Chieu, Ham Tien,
Mui Ne
tel. 062/374 35 95
Un, dos, tres – salsa dance classes
every Thursday evening at 7pm in this
Mexican restaurant serving fajitas,
burritos and mojitos. Pizza to go is
also available.

WHERE TO EAT
Sandals Bar & Restaurant £££
24 Nguyen Dinh Chieu (at the Mia
Resort, formerly Sailing Club)
062/384 74 40
www.miamuine.com
Trendy fusion locale, if Dongs are not a
problem: stylish, romantic and quiet,
pleasantly attentive service, fine wine selection – worth the high-end price!

Rung Forest Restaurant ££
67 Nguyen Dinh Chieu, Ham Tien
Phan Thiet
tel. 062/384 75 89
daily 10am–3pm, 6pm–11pm
Large, rustic establishment with Cham
décor, classic Vietnamese cuisine as well
as tapas, pasta and salads, grilled dishes,
lobsters, steaks, wine and cocktails. Traditional music with folkloristic accompaniment, cookery courses.

Bamboo Bamboo £
81B Nguyen Dinh Chieu, Ham Tien
Mui Ne
Mobile tel. 090/396 63 75

Tiny family restaurant, simple, cheap
and right on the noisy street (opposite
the backpacker hostel). Tasty local dishes
and curries and a few from Thailand – it
can take a while when busy.

WHERE TO STAY
Victoria Phan Thiet Beach Resort £££-££££
Binh Thuan, Phan Thiet
tel. 062/381 30 00
www.victoriahotels-asia.com
Sprawling four-star complex with 60
palm-covered cottages, sea view from
the terrace, pools and golf course. Quiet

Mui Ne coast attracts the international kiting and surfing community

and a little out of the way, a taxi is needed to get here.

Cham Villas £££
Mui Ne
tel. 062/374 12 34
www.chamvillas.com
reservations@chamvillas.com
Lush green complex on the beach with 14 bungalows decked in palm leaves, kingsize canopy beds, restaurant also serves European dishes.

Bamboo Village Resort & Spa ££-££££
km 11.8, 38 Nguyen Dinh CHieu, Ham Tien, Mui Ne
tel. 062/384 70 07
www.bamboovillageresortvn.com
Beautiful site featuring around 40 closely knit, octagonal bamboo and rattan huts and stone houses with palm leaf roofing, some with sea view, delightfully furnished with carved wooden beds. Pool and open-air bar. Popular with Russian

Insider Tip

guests. Two pools, yoga courses. Kitesurfers practice on the vast beach.

Coco Beach Resort ££-£££
km 12.5, 58 Nguyen Dinh Chieu, Ham Tien, Mui Ne (photo ▶p.100)
Tel 062/384 71 11
www.cocobeach.net
Delightful wooden houses on stilts, air-conditioned, at Mui Ne Beach with Franco-German management. Pool and great food.

Cocosand £
119 Nguyen Dinh Chieu, Ham Tien, Mui Ne
Mobile tel. 0127/364 34 46
cocosandcatdua@yahoo.com.vn
Brand new resort with eight bungalows and rooms in a palm tree garden for bargain hunters (just across the street from the beach) – with everything backpackers could wish for, from free Wi-Fi and TV to hammocks (solar power).

amongst the lotus leaves. As marvellous as the panorama of palms and coastline may be, the rubbish depot is unfortunately also in the vicinity. The commercial exploitation of the sand dunes with all its accompanying excrescence sadly typifies what happens when mass tourism meets Vietnamese entrepreneurial spirit. Nature conservation is left behind: the former idyll is a shadow of itself, no thanks to the Jeeps and quad bikes whose engines roar as early as sunrise.

Suoi Tien (Fairy Springs) A very popular walk (approx. 1 hour) leads from the sea at Ham Tien village (shortly before Mui Ne) along a stream and through the dunes, past the glowing red rock of the little **Red Sand Canyon** to the well at Suoi Tien with its cascading waterfall.

Po Shanu Towers On the way to Phan Thiet, not far from Mui Ne Beach, the southernmost Cham sanctuary can be seen rising up on Ngoc Lam Hill: the three small **Po Shanu Towers** (8th century), restored in 1999. Less ornate than the famous Po Nagar or Po Klong Garai Towers at

▶Phang Rang, they were dedicated to Queen Po Shanu. A wonderful **panoramic view** of the coast and the town of Phan Thiet may be enjoyed from up here.
❶ Admission: 10,000 VND

Built by the French in 1897, the lighthouse of Kap Khe Ga stands some 25km/15mi southwest of Mui Ne. Vietnam's tallest and oldest lighthouse stands on a small island and continues to light up the coastline of Binh Thuan province at night. **Tien Thanh Beach** on the mainland seems to go on forever. Free of shade, the otters spotted here are not the only ones tempted to its shores – construction work for new accommodation is underway. Princess d'Annam Resort was the first top of the range luxury establishment to open, back in 2008 already, www.princessannam.com (££££). The impressive can be seen from the road leading to Khe Ga (tourists are advised only to venture further with official guides due to the dangers of quicksand and old mines – an American military base named LZ Betty was once located here).

Khe Ga Lighthouse

The town of Phan Thiet lies approximately 20km/12.5mi from the sun-drenched peninsula of Mui Ne and is famous for its **nuoc mam fish sauce** (▶MARCO POLO Insight p.359), which is distributed to all parts of Vietnam and is a must on every dining table. This is one of Vietnam's largest fishing regions. A good vantage point from which to observe the early morning hustle and bustle in the harbour of Phan Thiet is the Tran Hung Dao Bridge. When the colourful barges of the municipal fishing fleet return, the fish market (southern end of the Trung Trac) is also a hive of activity to behold. The old **water tower** of the town is a little gem: its triple-gabled roof, curving upwards to the heavens, rises above the Ca Ty River. Van Thuy Tu Temple on Ngu Ong (Fisherman Street, Duc Thang district) was erected in 1762 and is a national monument. A 22m/72ft-long whale skeleton is on display here. Ong Pagoda on Tran Phu Street is frequented by childless women who come here to pray for offspring. The room to the right contains a large mask for the dragon dance.

Phan Thiet

> **!** MARCO ⊕ POLO TIP
>
> *Whale graveyards* Insider Tip
>
> Vietnamese fishermen worship whales as holy animals who will bring them good fortune and protection. »Ngai« is the name they give to them, a title otherwise reserved for kings, and to pay their last respects to the beasts, beached whales in Phan Thiet are buried in their own graveyard at Van Thuy Tu Temple.

On the 694m/2275ft-high Ta Cu (Takou) Mountain in the **nature reserve of the same name** lies what is probably the longest Buddha statue in Vietnam: the reclining Sakyamuni Buddha measures a full

Ta Cu (also: Takou)

49m/160ft from illuminated head to toe and has a shoulder height of 18m/59ft. A cable car ride is the swiftest way to the site; otherwise a hike takes some two hours. At the top, the Linh Son Truong Tho Monastery, over a century old, welcomes pilgrims and visitors (Ta Cu is not far from Tan Lap, approx. 30km/18mi southwest of Phan Thiet, small guesthouse on site).

Monastery: admission 90,000 VND
Cable car: daily 8am–11am, 1.30pm–5pm, at weekends until 5.30pm

✳ Phu Quoc (Island)

✦ B/C 7

Province: Kien Giang
Region: Mekong Delta
Population: 90,000

Tranquility and solitude on a total length of 40km/25mi of beaches against a background of coconut palms and jungle scenery: that is Phu Quoc (pronounced Fu Kwok), Vietnam's largest island, close to the Cambodian border. The holiday islander can enjoy idyllic sunsets on the west coast from small hotels and bamboo huts.

Virtually all communities in Phu Quoc are located on the coast; the jungle terrain of the island interior is almost entirely free of people. Most settlements lie on the flatter, west side of the island, the largest being Duong Dong with around 60,000 inhabitants. Fishing and processing of fish have hitherto been the chief sources of employment for its inhabitants. One major source of income is the famous **fish sauce** of Phu Quoc, favoured all over Vietnam (annual production: approx. 10 million litres/2.5 million gallons).

WHAT TO SEE IN AND AROUND PHU QUOC

Beaches   The new airport will grant the island another tourist boom. The Vietnamese government has big plans for the destination and aims to attract between two and three million holidaymakers by 2020 – that's per year, as many as in all of Vietnam today! There is no doubt that the island has potential: endless beaches to the west and south, the finest bathing bays are often hidden and can only be reached via dusty paths or by climbing tour (Khem Beach in the south is still a restricted military zone, as the Cambodian neighbours also lay claim to the island). **Bai Truong** (Long Beach) south of the main resort Duong Dong boasts a good 20km/12mi of golden sands under palm trees, the beach stretching as far as the small fishing port of An Thoi at the southern tip of the island, punctuated only by rocks and fishing villages. Some 4km/2.5mi have already been developed with groups of bungalows and hotels (some several storeys high). Noise from building sites along the beaches is par for the course these days, the newest trend being ecologically sound bungalows, minimalist design and maximum prices (££). Nevertheless, everybody should still find just what

? Nuoc mam fish sauce

No Vietnamese meal is complete without a dip. The basis is nuoc mam – a salty, spicy sauce made from fermented anchovies and used in cooking and seasoning like salt. Every cook has her own recipe for nuoc mam and varies it according to the dish in question, using it as a dip or salad sauce with lime juice, garlic, chilli and sugar.

they are looking for on Phu Quoc. The beautifully sweeping **Bai Ong Lang** (north of Duong Dong) promises several miles of splendid isolation, with cliffs at intervals. **Bai Sao**, close to An Thoi in the deep south, is quite beautiful and a popular destination for the Vietnamese at weekends and on holidays – and of course the noise of Jetskis is likely to reappear sooner or later. Beach bars offer »covered« hammock-swings and sunbeds for hire to the many day-trippers and picnickers. Two resorts here have already opened their bungalows for business (My Lan Reort, www.mylanphuquoc.com and Gecko Jacks, both ££). On the way to Bai Sao, it is worth taking a look at the Phu Quoc Coconut Tree Prison Museum, a rather peculiar complex with watchtowers, a wealth of photographs and life-size figures between barbed wire and barracks, representing soldiers, guards and Vietcong prisoners (about 5km/3mi beyond the fishing village of An Thoi).
Museum: daily except Sat/sun 8am–11am, 1.30pm–5pm; 25,000 VND

Both the fishermen of An Thoi and pleasure boats from Bai Truong bring tourists looking for diving or snorkelling opportunities to the **offshore islands** such as Turtle Island (Hon Doi Moi) in the north and the tiny An Thoi archipelago in the south, with its coral reefs in crystal clear waters. The diving grounds are amongst the best in Vietnam, with visibility touching 50m/160ft. Staying dry is also an option, however, by trekking to smaller waterfalls and springs in the dense, mountainous hinterland of the **Phu Quoc National Park**, and exploring caves and pepper plantations, as well as pearl farms on the coast. The island's name translates as »99 Mountains«. Some are as high as 603m/1978ft, although most of them lie within the military restricted zone in the north. Winter is the best time for a visit. | Excursions

The main town of Duong Dong holds few tourist attractions. Everything worth seeing is concentrated around the harbour basin: a small fishing fleet, stalls serving Vietnamese snacks, the fish sauce factories | Duong Dong

Phu Quoc

INFORMATION
Phu Quoc Island Information Center
tel. 077/399 41 81
www.visitphuquoc.info
(and in all hotels)

TRANSPORT
International Airport Phu Quoc
(the new inland airport opened in December 2012) approx. 7km/4mi south of Duong Dong
www.vietnamairlines.com
During the high season in winter, around eight flights a day from Saigon, five from Can Tho and Rach Gia and also from Hanoi and neighbouring countries.

Boats
Daily modern hydrofoil crossings from Rach Gia (2.5 hours) and Ha Tien (avoid the cheaper and older ferries, can be dangerous, particularly during the rainy season).

SHOPPING
Asian tourists especially catch the shopping bug on Phu Quoc: ladies' necklaces from 500,000 VND can be purchased at the pearl farm (Bai Truong/=Long Beach, coastal road, approx. 8km/5mi south of Duong Dong) and in the shops of the small harbour town Ham Ninh. In the latter, rice wine is plentiful, promising potency with seahorses, scorpions or fully grown tiger penises in the bottle.

ENTERTAINMENT
Safari Restaurant & Bar (Du Ngoan) £
Tran Hung Dao (=beach road approx. 4km/2.5mi south of Duong Dong, close to the La Veranda Resort)
Mobile tel. 090/522 46 00
Lee, a Brit, and his wife Sinh run this little bar with a garden and TV screen for sports events. Good information about the island as well as a pool table, burgers, chips, local dishes and cold beer.

WHERE TO EAT
Tropicana Resort £-££
Idyllic terrace inn and bar at Bai Truong with good seafood, Vietnamese and European dishes.

Night market in Duong Dong £
Vo Thi Sau, Duong Dong
Insider
Tip
Freshest seafood and fish at low prices (hot pots, giant shrimps, squid and the like) served daily from 4pm.

Sakura £
Access road to Ong Long Beach (close to the Mango Bay Resort)
tel. 077/398 51 37
Mobile tel. 0122/818 24 84
Anyone who eats here is bound to come back for more (even though this family restaurant is a little out of the way, hidden in a jungle-like wood). The pleasant Mrs Kiem cooks up straightforward Vietnamese fare, numerous seafood dishes, fish and tasty curries.

Palm Tree Restaurant £
Tran Hung Dao, approx. 3km/2mi south of Duong Dong, Bai Truong/=Long Beach
(close to the La Veranda Resort and Mai House)

No telephone
Large, comfortably rustic establishment with local dishes, fresh fish and seafood on a barbecue table grill, friendly service.

WHERE TO STAY
La Veranda Resort Phu Quoc – MGallery Collection ££££
Tran Hung Dau (beach road), approx. 4km/2.5mi south of Duong Dong
tel. 077/398 29 88
https://sofitel.accorhotels.com/
Luxury complex on a beautiful beach with a hint of colonial flair. 70 elegant rooms with balconies (and four-poster beds) and villas offering every comfort imaginable. A delightful pool in a lush, verdant tropical garden, although the two restaurants are nothing to write home about, expensive nevertheless. A number of small restaurants nearby however…

Mango Bay ££-££££
Bai Ong Lang
Tel 077/398 16 93
Mobile tel. 090/338 22 07
www.mangobayphuquoc.com
Rustic, close to nature, isolated: 40 spacious wooden huts beneath the palm trees, some with open-air bathroom, some right on the beach whilst others are in the garden or on the lawn. No air conditioning for ecofriendly reasons. Slightly rocky beach with seaweed. Massages, small library and a lovely beach bar with a nice variety of dishes.

Mai House ££
Bai Truong (Long Beach)
tel. 077/384 70 03
Mobile tel. 091/812 37 96
maihouse@yahoo.com
Mai and Gerard's little tropical oasis: one

of the first beach resorts on the island with 25 nicely appointed, palm shaded bungalows, some with sea views. Good for a quiet, relaxing holiday (no TV or indeed any such noise). Romantic, if a little expensive, Vietnamese-French restaurant.

Tropicana Resort £-££

Tran Hung Dao, Bai Truong (Long Beach)
tel. 077/384 71 27
Small, pleasant beach complex with nine air-conditioned bungalows and some cheaper rooms in the garden. Pool, sea view restaurant, bicycles and motorbikes available for hire, windsurfing, boat excursions to the other islands

Beach Club £

Ap Cua Lap, south end of Bai Truong (Long Beach)
tel. 077/398 09 98

www.beachclub-vietnam.com
Six simple rooms and four palm-thatched bungalows on a lovely beach, nice, family atmosphere. The swell can make the beach narrower or »swallow« it up altogether.

Thai Tan Tien £

Tran Hung Dao (beach road on Long Beach, approx. 4km/2.5mi from Duong Dong)
tel. 077/384 77 82
http://resortthaitantien.com
Quiet beach hotel for a smaller budget: 30 rather spartan rooms (some air-conditioned, minbar) are connected to Long Beach by a 50m/164ft wooden path. Terraces with hammocks and sea views, rustic beach bar. The photos on the website are quite misleading…

and Dinh Cau: a temple with a lighthouse dedicated to Thien Hau, Goddess of the Sea. A temple festival is celebrated here in October. The lively night markets with food stalls should bot be missed.

❶ **night markets** daily from 4.30pm

Quy Nhon

✦ E 6

Province: Binh Dinh (capital)
Region: South Central Coast
Population: 300,000

A good place to break a coastal journey is the port of Quy Nhon. The peninsula (between Nha Trang and Hoi An) can serve as a base for excursions to Cham towers, the ►My Lai Memorial and into the highlands. Alternatively, just lie on the beach under palm trees, watch the fishermen in action and dine on fresh seafood.

The provincial capital Quy Nhon can trace its origins back to the ancient Cham harbour, Shri Banoi, and lies around 10km/6mi east of the N 1 on a peninsula at the mouth of the Song Cai. In the 1960s, one of the biggest American military bases was located here, and the tip of the headland is still off limits for military reasons. Today the city possesses two important container harbours and a significant industrial and financial zone. Due to the **severe humidity** – the town is often subjected to typhoons and heavy rainfall – many houses are covered in moss and look rather unkempt. Vietnam's finest Tuong theatre group is based in Quy Nhon!

WHAT TO SEE IN QUY NHON AND ENVIRONS

The focal point of the town is the lively and colourful **Lon Market**,   Centre
where fruit and vegetables from the region are sold. Just a short walk away, between the market and the stadium, the 300-year-old **Long Khanh Temple** stands in Tran Cao Van Street. Its 17m/55ft-high statue of Buddha (1972) can be seen from a distance, rising out of a lily pond. The temple dates back to the year 1700, yet has suffered damage time and again, explaining its current state of disrepair. The last renovation work took place in the late 1970s.

Colourful tombs in the Buddhist part of the cemetery

Quy Nhon

INFORMATION
Binh Dinh Tourist
10 Nguyen Hue (on the beach road) Le
Loi, Quy Nhon
tel. 056/389 25 24

Saigon Tourist
24 Nguyen Hue, Quy Nhon
tel. 056/381 99 22 and 382 82 35
Information also in the hotels

TRANSPORT
Quy Nhon Phu Cat Airport
(36km/22mi north of Quy Nhon)
tel. 056/382 53 13

Railway station in Dieu Tri
10km/6mi beyond Quy Nhon

ENTERTAINMENT
Quy Nhon may seem peaceful by day,
but at night the colourful and kitschy
ocean promenade lights up and comes
to life: karaoke, little parks with foun-
tains, bia hoi (beer) and pils flow freely
in the bars and cafés.

WHERE TO EAT
In the Tha Doi on the northwestern
edge of town by the canal (close to the
Thap Doi Cham Towers) simple, good
value eateries serve seafood dishes, as
on the Xuan Dieu and Nguyen Hue
ocean promenade, all with gigantic glass
tanks of sea creatures to choose from.

Seaview Café £
25 Nguyen Hue
(beach road, adjacent to tourist
information)
tel. 056/389 17 91
Simple open-air establishment with
snacks and refreshments. Rooftop café
of the Saigon Quynhon Hotel (see below)

Dong Restaurant £
26 Nguyen Loc
(close to Lon Market)
Quy Nhon
tel. 056/382 48 77
Mingle with the locals in this two-storey
seafood establishment. Fresh catch and
selected seafood are presented to guests

Cemetery   A vast cemetery is located in the northern part of town, consisting of
a military cemetery as well as Buddhist and Catholic burial grounds.
If time allows, there is much to be discovered here: old and relatively
new gravestones, some simple, some ornately decorated with pictures
and ornaments – all colourfully painted. The Buddhist sites can be
recognized by the lotus blossom placed on top or by a swastika, a
symbol of good fortune.

AROUND QUY NHON

Cham towers   Many relics of Cham culture can be found in the environs of Quy
Nhon, as the former Cham capital, Vijaya, lay just 35km/21mi to the
north, close to Dap Da village. After the fall of Indrapura in the year

who then ask about the weight (prices per kilo). Around the corner on Tran Doc is the equally well-known but larger restaurant Seafood 2000.

WHERE TO STAY
Life Wellness Resort & Spa £££
Ghenh Rang, Bai Dai, Quy Nhon (16km/10mi south)
tel. 056/384 01 32

Insider Tip

Wonderful complex on a beach interspersed with cliffs: 63 rooms with maximum comfort and panoramic views of the sea from the terrace or the bath. Pools, spa with Tai Chi and yoga classes, good internet prices.

Saigon Quynhon Hotel ££
24 Nguyen Hue, Quy Nhon
tel.056/382 01 00
www.saigonquynhonhotel.com.vn
Comfortable hotel with pool from the Saigon chain immediately on the municipal beach Representing good value for money, the 148 rooms are better than expected (many Asian guests so the English language is less common here). Super rooftop bar on the eighth floor with excellent panoramic views. The adjacent Binh Dinh Museum is worth a visit.

Royal Hotel & Healthcare Resort ££
1 Han Mac Tu, Quy Nhon
tel. 056/ 374 71 00
www.royalquynhon.com
150 decent parquet rooms, plenty of wood, at the end of the beach promenade. Rooms to the rear face the street, the ones at the front have wonderful sea views. Wi-Fi, good bathrooms, nice pool, massages.

Hoang Yen I. Hotel £
5 An Duong Vuong
Quy Nhon
tel. 056/374 69 00
www.hoangyenhotel.com.vn
Absolutely beautiful, spacious rooms at bargain prices with sea views from the balcony, high above the (municipal) beach which is empty during the day: flatscreen TV, large beds, bathroom with bath, even a pool. There is also a billiard table but unfortunately the occasional wedding party with noisy karaoke – comes with the territory.

982, the Cham settled here and, in spite of repeated attacks by the Khmer and the Vietnamese, held firm over a long period of time. It was not until 1471 that Vijaya was captured and destroyed as the Vietnamese further extended their empire and advanced into the south. In the area surrounding the **former stronghold**, a number of towers were erected in the 11th and 12th centuries, named after materials (such as silver), although the names had no bearing on the actual construction. At the edge of the town of Quy Nhon (approx. 1km/1100yd north of the town centre), close to the N 1, stand the 11th-century **Thap Doi** twin towers. In contrast to the terraced roofs commonly seen in Cham architecture, the towers of Thap Doi feature curved, pyramidical structures. Garuda figures sit at their corners. With support from UNESCO, the towers have been reconstructed and restored in recent years.

Thap Doi: admission: 10,000 VND

Pleiku A wonderfully scenic road (no. 19) leads into the highland region to the town of Pleiku (Plei Ku), 163km/101mi to the west. Roughly half of the journey twists and turns over the An Khe Pass and it is worth looking across the lowlands, where the Ha Giao River winds its way to the coast. The Giang Pass is also part of the route, as are numerous Bahnar villages, where examples of their traditional communal longhouses can be seen. Rubber plantations, woods and slopes covered in coffee trees point the way to the plateau of Pleiku in the Central Highlands of Vietnam. In this sparsely populated area, the South Vietnamese Army once had their command post for the entire mountain region. Agent Orange was sprayed liberally here, and bombing raids were carried out on a number of occasions – especially in the year 1972. Today, sober, unembellished buildings dominate the townscape, often seen through a misty veil of rain. The **market** is the sole site of interest, filling up rapidly in the early hours of the morning as the inhabitants of surrounding villages arrive to sell aubergines, shallots, parsnips and garlic. Tourists tend to combine a visit to Pleiku with a trip to Buon Ma Thuot to explore the highlands and visit settlements of the minority peoples (Jarai, Bahnar, Ede).

Jarai villages A number of Jarai villages lie on the road to Kon Tum. First, however, comes the Bien Ho Tea Company after 14km/8.5mi; another 1km/1100yd further on are Yaly Falls. The Jarai can already be seen here in the paddy fields and rubber plantations or carrying huge baskets of goods from village to village. Above all, the women's garb catches the eye: it is awash with colour and horizontal stripes. Just a few miles from the waterfall lie the villages of Plei Mrong and Plei Mun, complete with longhouses. The carved wooden statues on the burial grounds are also of interest.

Thap Bac (Banh It) Close to the junction (N 19) at An Nhon (approx. 20km/12mi north of Quy Nhon), four richly ornate 12th-century towers (Thap Bac) rise up amidst the hills. The so-called Silver Towers were one of the first kalan groups to have been erected on a hill – which later became common practice. From these heights, a wonderful view across the landscape can be savoured, taking in the other Cham towers of the area.

The quaint fishing village of *Sa Huynh appears in a crescent-shaped bay of golden sands around 115km/71mi north of Quy Nhon. Fringed with palm trees, its beautiful beach is an inviting place to take a break on the way to ▶My Lai or ▶Hoi An.

The small hotel restaurant serves fine fish. Fruit and drinks merchants are also on hand. Boat trips to the neighbouring island of Genh Nhu are a possibility here.

✷ Red River Delta

✦ C/D 2

Region: North
Area: 15,000 sq km/5800 sq mi

Although the northern Red River delta lies only a few meters above sea level, it has been canalized and cultivated for hundreds of years. Today the landscape is a network streaked with old dykes and dams, strewn with temples, pagodas, churches, family tombs and community houses.

The Red River (Song Hong) begins in the southwest Chinese Yunnan province and flows across North Vietnam for the last 500km/310mi of its total 1200km/750mi length. Adjoining the Red River are other large tributaries such as the **Black River** and the **Clear River**, with which it joins above Hanoi upon entering the lowlands. Here, the Red River spreads out into many arms before flowing into the South China Sea south of the port of Hai Phong. It is worth taking a trip out to the delta area from Hanoi, even though apart from the unique Perfume Pagoda, there are only a few real attractions. Among all of the historic buildings, Thay Pagoda and Tay Phuong Pagoda, (all three ▶Hanoi, Surroundings) located far inland, are the nicest examples of classical Vietnamese architecture. Many cities still heavily bear the signs of destruction from the Vietnam War., but it is worth paying a visit to the villages of Bat Trang and Dong Ky, in which handicrafts are produced. Among the scenic highlights on the other hand are ▶Dry Ha Long Bay and Cuc Phuong National Park.

River network

The rugged mountains and the relatively steep slopes here mean that the watercourses carry off a lot of sediment. The Red River contains mostly iron-rich sediments, which lead to its reddish-brown colour; the Black River in turn carries mainly dark, humus-based material, and the Clear River comes from an area where there is little erosion, so that little colouration is noticeable. Heavy **flooding** is not uncommon. As a result, life on the Red River has always had to go with and against the flow. In order to keep the effects of the summer monsoon floods in check, dams and dykes have been built here since before the Common Era. Their combined length today totals more than 3000km/1870mi. They succeed in taming the masses of water, but this also means that a large amount of the contained sediments no

Colouration from varied sediments

Stage in the Water

Rivers and canals run through the broad delta landscapes of Vietnam. People's lives here are determined by monsoon rainfall. Water is invariably the focal point of events in the region, such as water puppet theatre.

Noisy firecrackers extend a musical greeting to the audience. Members of a small **orchestra** lend their voices to the puppets. They are dressed in festive brightly coloured costumes and sit alongside the »stage«, in this case the water, normally a lake or village pond. Cities like Hanoi, Saigon and Hue tend to have more permanent water puppet theatres with a basin as stage, flanked by two wooden pole balustrades to mark the performance area. The brownish water ripples in little waves and white smoke from the echoing fireworks drifts across the surface.

Teu appears on stage, the **master of ceremonies**, jester and the link between audience and actors. A whitewashed puppet with an impish expression portrays a young peasant, a must in every Roi Nuoc. He opens proceedings and welcomes the public. A bamboo flute strikes up a tune and a musician begins singing.

As if on a thread, a brown **water buffalo** glides across the water. He dips his broad snout into the current again and again, splashing wildly as he does so. Snorting and puffing, he makes his way up and down through the water, a plough and peasant in tow behind him – a scene as typical of the Vietnamese landscape as women in conical hats. All at once, as a folkloristic melody plays, more ploughing peasants, women planting rice and fishermen in boats join the busy scene.

Drawn From Life ...

Most of the imagery in water puppet theatre is drawn from the daily life of Vietnamese rice farmers, related in entertaining little scenes with all of its cheery and sad aspects portrayed, herding ducks, hunting foxes, racing in boats or the perils of fishing.

The fish jump around and the fisherman cast their nets in just the wrong place, time and again. The audience roars with laughter at the fishermen's staged ineptitude as the fish leap to safety and the nets stay empty – particularly when, in the heat of battle, a cheeky little boy ends up in the net rather than a fish.

... or History

Other episodes are rooted in **fairytales**, **legends** or other forms of theatre, in which the heroic figures are usually lifted from national history. One famous and especially popular historical motif concerns the legendary King Le Loi, who drove the Chinese out of Vietnam in the 15th century. In this saga he strikes a victory with a magic sword given to him by the gods. Water puppet theatre performances often like to tell the tale of how the victorious Le Loi embarked on a boat trip across Hoan Kiem Lake in Hanoi after the war. He was challenged by a giant tortoise who prised the sword away from him and disappeared into the depths of the lake to return the weapon to its rightful owners, the gods.

A Damp Profession

At the end of the performance, drums and cymbals sound once more. To a beat that gets faster and faster, the **four holy animals** glide, hop and jump through the water: the wondrous phoenix, the mythical unicorn Kylin, the magnificently coloured dragon and the golden tortoise. When they dance together, peace and happiness reign in Vietnam. After per-forming, the figures disappear into a **water pavilion** that has been constructed at the back of the stage. The requisites, puppets and puppeteers are housed under its curved pagoda roof. The puppeteers, unseen by the public, do their work behind a curtain of woven bamboo. To do this they stand up to their waists in water! The puppets, by contrast, seem to hover above the water. They are moved on **bamboo poles** 3 to 4 metres (10 to 13 feet) long and can be turned and manipulated by means of rudders and strings so that spectators have the impression they have come on stage straight from the rice fields and villages.

longer reach the fields, but are washed straight into the sea. Through this, the ground is robbed of its natural richness, making the use of artificial fertilizers inevitable.

Settlement   The fertile alluvial lands of the Red River are considered the core country and **heartland of Vietnam**. Settlement of this area dates back to the Bronze-Age Dong Son culture. Today nearly 40% of the Vietnamese live in the delta region, which amounts to a population density of nearly 2000 inhabitants/sq km or 5180 inhabitants/sq mi. A characteristic of the region is the close proximity of the rice fields to villages built on hilltops, dunes and dams, protected by bamboo fences. This allows the continuing extensive self-sufficiency of the Vietnamese village. Buildings are constructed on the ground rather than on stilts, as is typical in Laos and Cambodia.

Economy   With 15,000 sq km/5800 sq mi, the agriculturally-oriented Red River delta has only a third of the surface area of the Mekong Delta, but is of comparable importance to the economy of the country. The alluvial soil ensures **high yields**, and the climate is also conducive to farming. As in the Mekong Delta, the high precipitation rate is caused by the summer monsoon. However, winter temperatures of the Red River delta are considerably lower than in the Mekong, leading to fog

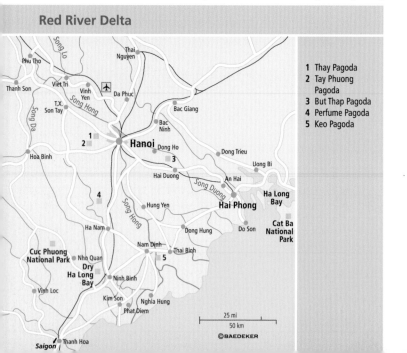

Red River Delta

1 Thay Pagoda
2 Tay Phuong Pagoda
3 But Thap Pagoda
4 Perfume Pagoda
5 Keo Pagoda

25 mi
50 km

©BAEDEKER

formation with a constant drizzle, which keeps the ground sufficiently moist even in the dry season. This means that a second harvest can be brought in without artificial irrigation. Nevertheless, the region does not export rice, as the high population density means that the harvest barely covers local requirements.

** Sa Pa (Sapa)

✦ B 1

Province: Lao Cai
Region: Northern Highlands
Population: 38,000

Situated idyllically between the Tonkinese Alps (Hoang Lien Mountains) and paddy fields on endless terrace slopes, populated by hill tribes in colourful costume and with wondrous walking trails, Sa Pa was bound to attract a flow of tourists sooner or later, no matter how far off the beaten track it lies.

The French developed the mountain village as a climatic spa as early as the 1920s. Today the place is booming; indeed, particularly at weekends, it threatens to buckle under the weight of incoming tourist groups. Not that the hill-tribe traders are complaining. As the flood of tourists grew stronger over the past decade, more and more

Rice terraces in the Sa Pa area

Sa Pa

INFORMATION
Sa Pa Tourism
2 Fan Si Pan Road, Sa Pa
tel. 020/387 19 75
www.sapatourism.com

TRANSPORT
The Lao Cai station is situated approximately 40km/25mi northeast of Sa Pa. State-owned railway trains run daily between Hanoi and Lao Cai (7 to 10 hours; reasonable sleeper cars, varying standards for the same price!); public and tourist buses also run from Lao Cai to Sa Pa.
The beautiful »Victoria« Express from the luxury hotel chain of the same name, runs between Hanoi and Lao Cai several times a week (now exclusively for hotel guests!).

SHOPPING
Hill tribe markets
Every Saturday, countless tourists converge on Sa Pa for the legendary weekend market. The market also takes place during the week (albeit in smaller form) with the hill tribes in attendance; it is less crowded then.
There are other similarly colourful markets in neighbouring villages on different days. Worth noting: indigo clothes dye tends to run (photo ▶p.159)

ENTERTAINMENT
Ta Van Bar ££
24 Dong Loi
tel. 020/387 12 45
On the fourth floor of the Chaulong Sapa Hotel, with a good drinks selection

Nature Bar & Grill

and lovely panoramic mountain views, internet, TV.

Artista Bar £
6868 Thac Bac Street (near the church)
tel. 090/954 71 84
Tiny, quirky bar in a concrete bunker, packed with bric-a-brac and covered in graffiti. Try the local spirits or international beer and wines. Fine music, long after everywhere else has closed – a guitar hangs on the wall should anyone feel like a strum.

WHERE TO EAT
Le Gecko Sapa £-££
Ham Rong, tel. 020/387 15 04
www.legeckosapa.com
daily 7am–10pm
Nice little bar with cosy sofas in the corners (for non-smokers as well) and »La Petite Bouffe« restaurant. French management (five reasonably priced rooms with bath also available) Daily cookery classes from 1pm-5pm, trekking tours.

The Hill Station Café £-££
7 Muong Hoa, Sa Pa
A veritable pearl resides in this little old house: guests feel right at home in the rustic atmosphere with an open fire, just smaller (western) dishes, soups, cake, sandwiches, ciabatta and other snacks, but the excellent wine list (a good Bordeaux, for example) complements French cheese quite perfectly to a soundtrack of gentle jazz.

Baguette & Chocolat £-££
Tha Bac
tel. 020/387 17 66
daily 7am–10pm
Charitable project and school (www.hoasuaschool.com) for disadvantaged children, plus restaurant, bakery, café, bar and small hotel: small dishes and bakery products can be enjoyed in cosy corner seating by the fireplace downstairs, whilst the first floor has four lovely, if basic, rooms with shower and small balcony.

Nature Bar & Grill £
24 Cau May (2nd floor) Sa Pa
tel. 020/387 20 94
Fine Vietnamese fare (from the grill, vegetarian or the house specialty: duck in honey), nice and warm in front of the fireplace – just the ticket for a cosy evening when Sa Pa turns cold in winter. Mulled wine, friendly proprietors and pleasant service.

WHERE TO STAY
Victoria Sapa £££-££££
tel. 020/387 15 22
www.victoriahotels-asia.com
First-class, country house style hotel on the edge of town. Very comfortable rooms, some with canopy beds and balconies. Tennis court, badmintion, heated indoor pool!

Bamboo Sapa Hotel ££   Insider Tip
18 Muong Hoa
tel. 020/387 10 75
www.bamboosapahotel.com.vn
Five-storey hotel with most attractive and comfy rooms, some with decorative fireplace, chaise longue and balcony (satellite TV, telephone, heating), marvellous view of the mountains, good travel agency.

Sunny Mountain Hotel ££
10 Muong Hoa
tel. 020/378 79 98, -9
www.sunnymountainhotel.com

Brand new hotel: 75 sleek, very modern rooms with flatscreen TV, designer bathroom and some with magnificent panoramic mountain views from the balcony. Heated indoor pool, whirlpool, massages. Rooftop restaurant and open-air bar.

Chapa Garden ££
23 Cau May, tel. 020/387 29 07
www.chapagarden.com
Tiny, elegant boutique hotel in an old French villa, centrally located yet still quiet. Small garden and friendly host family: just four, nicely appointed rooms (heated in winter) wih parquet, TV, lovely shower bathrooms, two with mini balconies – be sure to book on time! Own restaurant with open fireplace.

Chaulong Sapa I. Hotel £-££
24 Dong Loi
tel. 020/387 12 45
www.chaulonghotel.com
Once the best hotel in the town centre, now somewhat overpriced, combining a new building (large rooms with balcony and mountain panorama) with an older, castle-like house (ask to see the rooms first!)

Auberge Dang Trung £
31 Cau May, Sa Pa
tel. 020/387 12 43
auberge@sapadiscovery.com
Pleasant guesthouse from the colonial period, reminiscent of a Swiss chalet. Rooms on the top floor have a wonderful view of the mountain scenery.

Thai Binh Sapa £
5 Ham Rong, tel. 020/387 12 12
www.thaibinhhotel.com
Small family establishment close to the edge of town, although Sa Pa is not all that big: 14 large and cozily heated parquet rooms, some with fireplace (Wi-Fi, TV, heaters on wheels and electric blankets, modern bathroom). Good tours with Hmong **Insider Tip** womenfolk as guides.

hotels were built – more than 100 at the last count – gradually creating an urban sprawl. Those who wish to experience the spectacular mountain scenery without having to peer over the roofs of Sa Pa and are keen to shake off the persistent sales patter of hill-tribe womenfolk in pursuit, should set out on foot through the valleys to the more obscure villages – ideally a trek lasting several days (see below). Originally, various ethnic minorities lived around Sa Pa, above all the diminutive Hmong, clothed in indigo blue, and the taller Red Dao, whose women wear impressive red turbans (photo p.24). Since time immemorial, they have cultivated fruit, vegetables, tea and cinnamon in the cool region. Apart from the bustling, colourful markets, Sa Pa has little of interest to offer; visitors are attracted by its location in a thoroughly charming landscape and as a base for undertaking **mountain tours**. The ascent of Fan Si Pan, for example, at 3143m/10,311ft the highest peak in Vietnam, offers a particularly strenuous challenge (allow 3 days). Sa Pa is the coldest place in Vietnam: winter visitors (Dec to Feb) are well advised to pack warm clothing, especially for night time (also in springtime and from August onwards).

Tourists and young Hmong traders at the Cat Cat waterfall

TOURS INTO SURROUNDING AREAS

Sa Pa is a good base from which to take a tour by either moped taxi, Jeep or horse and trap. This can be an expensive undertaking, however, which is all the more reason to choose the more attractive alternative of exploring the region on foot, following narrow, often steep trails. It makes sense to take a guide along. Should the path seem too long, there is always the chance of flagging down one of the moped taxis on the main road (as far as the next valley turn-off). Naturally, North Vietnam now also has its »wilderness«. Moving further away from the well-built country roads around Sa Pa and Bac Ha, the lifestyle of Homestays hosts grows increasingly rudimentary. (Near Sa Pa, for example at the popular Ta Van »Homestay«, do not be surprised to find a hot shower, neon lights and Nescafé served at breakfast – most »adventure holidaymakers« these days apparently need such western standards and refreshments to keep them happy). Indeed, the immediate environs of Sa Pa are already fairly »westernized«, all the way to »luxury travel«. For more tangible »wilderness« and authenticity, longer hikes of several days along rough tracks should be considered. If the pick-up truck gets stuck in the mud, half the village will come out to help. Real adventure instead of ethnohype.

Moped, car or horse

*Cat Cat   Several Hmong villages are within trekking distance of Sa Pa, the most popular of which is undoubtedly Cat Cat in the Muong Hoa valley (approx. 3km/2mi away). Virtually every Sa Pa tourist stops by here, hence the crowds and emphasis on tourists in the high season, complete with countless shops and often pertinacious merchants. Take the street to the west of the marketplace as far as a turreted French villa (National Park office), then turn left onto a path leading down into the valley. Before long, the wooden huts come into view amongst fruit trees and bamboo thicket. Beneath the village, follow the steps and cross a rope bridge to reach a waterfall, a beautiful spot for a breather. From here, it is another 4km/2.5mi to the larger Hmong settlement at Sin Chai.

Lao Cai   Another hike leads south through the Hmong village of Lao Cai to Ta Van (approx. 11km/6.5mi), where Giay and Dao people live. The route passes through pretty villages and wonderful scenery, past baskets of indigo leaves, used by the Black Hmong to dye their clothes, and herdsmen riding water buffalo. At the side of the road, stones are engraved with symbols, thought to be an ancient **Hmong script**. The streams click-clack to the sound of the »coi gia gao«, wooden contraptions which process rice through water power. It is a good idea to carry a stick at all times to guard against snakes and the many wild dogs barking in the villages. The villagers themselves are more attuned to tourists and the majority of them, both old and young, seem to sell souvenirs – with more or less persistence.

**The beautiful landscape more than compensates
for the ardours of the trek…**

Northeast of Sa Pa on the road to Lao Cai lies the Red Dao settlement   Ta Phin
of Ta Phin. After roughly 6km/3.5mi, take a left-hand branch of the
road through a wonderful valley with rice terraces to reach Ta Phin
some 5km/3mi further on. The inhabitants of Ta Phin have concen-
trated their efforts on **handicrafts** (hats, bags, etc.) and sell their
wares through the Craft Link as far afield as Hanoi and Saigon. A
small cooperative with a souvenir shop can be visited in the village.

Trekking tours (3–5 days) up Fan Si Pan are also offered. Vietnam's   *Fan Si Pan
highest mountain (3143m/10,311ft) rises up from the heart of Hoang
Lien Son Nature Reserve, 9km/5.5mi from Sa Pa. The trek is not to
be taken lightly, however: to cover the roughly 14km/8.5mi-long
trail, it is first necessary to descend to 1200m/3937ft and traverse a
rickety bamboo bridge. The real ascent then begins (difference in
height approx. 2000m/6561ft), following sometimes overgrown paths
through pine forests and bamboo thickets. A breathtaking panoramic view of the mountains of northwest Vietnam is the reward for the
endeavour – it extends as far as
the province of Son La in the
south and the peaks of Yunnan
in China to the north. A critical
factor to bear in mind for the
Fan Si Pan tour is the weather: it
is prone to change swiftly and
many a trekker has been obliged
to turn back due to mist, rain or
cold, the paths too muddy or
steep. Overnight camp consists
of basic huts and tents (best to
bring a sleeping bag!). May
would seem to be the ideal
month for the trek, some experienced climbers reaching the
summit in just eight hours at
this time of year. Under no cir-
cumstances is this an expedition to be undertaken alone! A guide
who is familiar with the trails, can negotiate a path through the un-
dergrowth and can find water is essential. Competent guides can be
booked through the »Auberge« and »Mountain View« hotels.

> **MARCO POLO INSIGHT**
>
> **?**
>
> *Rules of conduct amongst the hill tribes*
>
> When paying a visit to the homes of
> one of the hill tribes, under no cir-
> cumstances touch, photograph or
> point at their altar. Houses with a
> bundle of bamboo, chicken feathers
> or leaves hanging above the entrance
> should not be entered – its occupants
> are having a marital row, are sick or
> have had a family bereavement and
> do not want to be disturbed. Children
> should not be photographed, at least
> not without permission, as the Dao
> believe that their soul will be cap-
> tured by a snapshot.

The spectacularly colourful Flower Hmong market in tiny **Bac Ha**   Insider
attracts tourists in droves on Sunday. For centuries, hill-tribe folk have   Tip
sold fabrics and rice wine here, there is also a livestock market. The
shift into the modern age is all too apparent, however, with souvenirs
and cheap timepieces from China also on sale (100km/62mi northeast
of Sapa, the snaking bus ride there is an adventure in its own right).

** Saigon (Ho Chi Minh City)

◈ D 7

Province: Ho Chi Minh City (city state)
Region: South
Area: 2000 sq km/772 sq mi
Population: approx. 6 million (metropolitan area)

Every visitor falls under Saigon's spell: the South Vietnamese metropolis on the river of the same name impresses with colonial buildings in soft shades of ochre and shady boulevards lined with tamarind trees, Chinese temples and a host of sites made famous through literature and film.

Saigon's appeal lies in the mix of districts, each having retained its own distinctive character: the former **French town centre**, the real Saigon, and Cholon, the old **Chinese quarter** are outstanding. Gia Dinh was the third and most Vietnamese of the three districts that grew together to make up the city of Saigon. Even though the Communists gave the city and the neighbouring rural lands the name Ho Chi Minh from 1975 onwards, none of its inhabitants stopped calling the old heart of town on the harbour by the name by which it had been known for centuries: Saigon.

Three districts

Highlights Saigon

► **History Museum**
Vietnam's past is evoked by art relics from the relevant periods in history.
►page 401

► **Thien Hau Pagoda**
If a boat trip is on the agenda, a trip to the most beautiful pagoda of Cholon offers the opportunity of asking the Goddess of the Sea for her protection. This may be followed by a wander through the alleyways of the Chinese district.
►page 406

► **Binh Tay Market**
Few go home empty-handed from a visit to the market and the surrounding alleyways.
►page 409

► **Jade Emperor Pagoda**
Immerse yourself in a world of timbals and swathes of incense.
►page 411

► **Giac Lam Pagoda**
The oldest place of worship in Saigon and one of the most beautiful
►page 416

Saigon's skyline has altered repeatedly in recent years – the Bitexco Financial Tower can be seen here

Upwardly mobile metropolis In recent years, the cityscape has been evolving more and more, with mirror glass hotels and office blocks shooting up. The old Saigon of crumbling façades, colonial villas graced with arcades and greying prefabricated concrete blocks weathered by monsoons, street traders with fruit carts and countless food stalls is being supplanted by an upwardly mobile with a modern veneer as can already be found in the neighbouring countries and so-called tiger states of Asia. Alas, the rapid transformation into an Asian skyscraper city makes no exceptions for splendid old villas, open markets, parks and alleyways. Legendary restaurants and cafés frequented by Graham Greene have felt the wrath of the wrecking ball or given way to multinational corporations and chic shops (Café Brodard, for example, on the celebrated Dong Khoi Boulevard, closed in 2012 after almost 100 years to be replaced by a Sony store). Millions upon millions of mopeds honk and rattle relentlessly through the traffic chaos like miniature battleships – unless they themselves are trapped in the gridlock, at which point they are likely to zoom along the pavement! The days of rickshaws and three-wheeled cyclos are numbered, the leisurely vehicles are largely banned from the centre or are reduced to ferrying tourists in convoys along designated sightseeing routes. The people of Saigon are generally considered to have an **easy-going lifestyle**, in contrast to the inhabitants of the political centre of Hanoi, who are perceived as more reliable and broader in their vision. Not far from the new scenes, however, old traditions persevere in some residential districts beyond the commercial centre: Vietnamese daily life unfolds, as ever, primarily on the street where old men hunch over board games, shoeshiners wave at passers-by and a woman carrying tasty snacks in her shoulder baskets cleans old rice bowls on the kerb.

HISTORY

17th cent.	Vietnamese Nguyen rulers conquer the region.
1862	Saigon becomes the capital of the French colonial empire Cochinchina.
WWII	Japan occupies Saigon.
after 1945	The French defend Saigon against Ho Chi Minh's forces.
1954	Saigon is named as capital of the Republic of South Vietnam.
30.4.1975	Communist troops march into Saigon.
from 1986	Doi Mo reforms
1994	Lifting of the US embargo)

Over 1000 years ago, Khmer villages stood where the metropolis of Saigon stands today. The Vietnamese first settled here in the late 17th century, when the Nguyen rulers advanced from Hue further into the south. The first contact with the French in South Vietnam and in Saigon came through missionaries, but French troops were not far behind the monks. From 1859 to 1975, South Vietnam stood under **foreign rule**. Saigon became the capital of the French colonial territory of Cochinchina. The marshy land on which the town was built was drained and canals were converted into broad streets such as Nguyen Hue Boulevard. An era of French plantation owners, opium-smoking colonialists and elegant coffee houses had begun. The first railway lines were laid. The Governor's Palace, Notre Dame, the Opera House, the Central Post Office and grand villas were all built in this period. Travellers of the age arriving in far-off Vietnam found a place which reminded them of a French provincial town, as Somerset Maugham recorded. During the Second World War the Japanese occupied the city and were thereupon attacked by Viet Minh units from the north.

On 2 September 1945 in Hanoi, Ho Chi Minh declared Vietnam an **independent republic**. The French ignored this and returned as a colonial power to Saigon, reinstalling the former emperor Bao Dai as head of government and defending the town against Ho Chi Minh's soldiers. Following the First Indochina War and the subsequent partition of Vietnam (1954), Ngo Dinh Diem, the first president, initially supported by the United States, declared Saigon the capital city of the South Vietnamese Republic. Saigon's population grew rapidly in this era (up to one million). The skirmishes of war encroached ever closer to the town. On 31 January 1968, during the **Tet Offensive**, Vietcong militants scored their biggest coup to date – forcing their way into the garden of the US Embassy. Far more fundamental changes came with the accession to power of the Communists, who marched into Saigon on 30 April 1975. Countless businesses, workshops and restaurants were forced to close and disappeared overnight. Dispossessed shopkeepers found themselves reduced to penniless boat people by the following day. The pulsating lightness of daily life was surrendered to bureaucracy and five-year plans. In the wake of the so-called Doi Moi economic reforms (from 1986), a more liberal investment law (1988) and the lifting of the US embargo (1994), some two to three million Vietnam-

> **MARCO POLO TIP**
>
> Insider Tip
>
> *Saigon from up high*
>
> To obtain a first overview of Saigon, the panoramic bar on the 33rd floor of the **Saigon Trade Center** (37 Ton Duc Thang) is recommended, permitting a look at the chaos from a safe distance. The first high-rise was built in 1994, but this was dwarfed by the futuristic **Bitexco Financial Tower** in 2010: 68 floors with a shopping centre at a height of 265m/869ft – there is even a helicopter landing pad and a bar on the 50th floor (between Ngo Duc Ke and Hai Trieu. Admission to the Bitexco observation deck on the 49th floor, 200,000 VND, www.saigonskydeck.com).

ese expatriates invested in or returned to Saigon, which has become a »boom town« today. Sadly, this goes hand in hand with the dismantling of over one hundred years of colonial heritage through the demolition of old French villas, as on Le Thanh Ton, for example, where splendid houses made way for a modern tower block in 2008: the Vincom Center containing glitzy stores from Armani to Versace. As the cyclos disappear, so too the authentic stone witnesses to the 1950s are gradually lost, from a era which many visitors actively seek out. The most recent victims are the Brodard Café and Givral Café, both visited by Graham Greene. Also under threat, the Eden Center opposite the Continental Hotel has at least been converted into a shopping centre instead of yet another skyscraper.

Downside of the boom
The economic boom in Saigon also has its disadvantages. Many Vietnamese from the surrounding areas want to grab a share of the business yet fall short of the mark. Many children still arrive in the upcoming towns as orphans or runaways from impoverished rural areas, selling chewing gum and lottery tickets, polishing shoes or performing as fire-eaters outside tourist bars (especially on Bui Vien, Pham Ngu Lao).In spite of compulsory school attendance, child labour is prevalent, as many impoverished parents opt to have their offspring on the streets earning money rather than sending them to school, which is subject to a fee from the sixth grade upwards.

COLONIAL SAIGON (CENTRE)

Colonial villas and mirrored modern buildings
The French bequeathed a rich architectural legacy to Saigon, inspiring 19th-century visitors to describe it as the **»Paris of the East«**. Some of the colonial structures in today's tourist centre (District 1 in particular), such as the town hall and the cathedral, are among the city's genuine landmarks. The remaining villas still convey something of their Mediterranean flair, even though they are mirrored in the neighbouring tower blocks. All of the main tourist sites in the centre of Saigon are less than half an hour's walk from the cathedral.

HÔTEL DE VILLE AND ITS SURROUNDINGS

*Hôtel de Ville (town hall)
The Hôtel de Ville is one of the main attractions in Saigon and pulls in innumerable visitors – tourists by day and Saigon locals by night. Located at the northern end of Nguyen Hue Boulevard, this marvellous example of **French colonial architecture**, in yellow and white with a red tiled roof, was built between the years of 1901 and 1908.

At the heart of Saigon: the town hall and Ho Chi Minh statue

Columns, ornate gables, balconies and decorative stucco, along with a small bell tower, all lend the official building a dignified air. Some visitors may find it a little strange that this Baroque house, of all places, houses the **People's Committee** of the city. Lined with bonsai trees, the square in front of the Hôtel de Ville features Ho Chi Minh(►MARCO POLO Insight p.265) with a child on his lap – Uncle Ho thus poses patiently for photographs with hundreds of Vietnamese every evening. A seemingly endless stream of mopeds, above all at weekends, flows through the neighbouring boulevards. Parents stroll across the square with their spruced up little ones, buying them all manner of tooting toys, balloons and plastic pistols. But beware: pickpockets also tend to make up the numbers in this bustling scene!

The building which houses the Rex Hotel today – identified by the gold crown twinkling on its rooftop – has been standing at one of Saigon's major crossroads (on the corner of Nguyen Hue/Le Loi) for

*Rex Hotel

around four decades. The hotel enjoys a legendary reputation, with the rooftop terrace, adorned with kitsch accessoires, a **popular meeting place** for tourists and rich Saigonese. Bonsai trees draped with fairy lights, bamboo cages with birds in full song, elephant sculptures and even a miniature replica of the One Pillar Pagoda compete for attention. During the Vietnam War, the US Army used the banqueting hall for its press conferences. At 5pm each afternoon, the officers of JUSPAO (Joint United States Public Affairs Office) would invite war reporters from all over the world to take note of the latest successes of their war effort. Graham Greene describes the events of just such a press conference in his novel *The Quiet American*.

Thendayyutt-
hapani
Temple

One block south of the Rex Hotel stands Thendayyutthapani Temple, the most beautiful of the three Hindu temples of Saigon (entrance: 66 Ton That Thiep). Colourful tiles and lamps decorate the interior, with pictures of deities, Nehru and Gandhi adorning the walls. To the right of the sanctuary, a staircase leads up to the roof terrace, crowned by a tower featuring intricately sculpted statues of the gods.

ALONG DONG KHOI BOULEVARD

Dong Khoi
Boulevard
(formerly Rue
Catinat)

The famous Dong Khoi Boulevard – once known as Rue Catinat, the **elegant strollers' promenade** bordered by splendid colonial houses and lined with tamarinds, street cafés and shops, stretches from Notre Dame Cathedral to the bank of the. In spite of all the construction work going on, and the many hawkers on the street, its charm can still be sensed today. As one world-renowned luxury store after another lines up here and rents reach astronomical levels, the future of the last little Vietnamese shops, tailors and galleries becomes increasingly precarious. The authentic Vietnam is most definitely disappearing from the boulevard.

*Notre Dame
Cathedral

At the northern end of Dong Khoi stands the Cathedral of Notre Dame. Saigon's interesting Christian place of worship is hard to miss, rising as it does from a large square at the centre of a busy roundabout. This Neo-Romanesque church was built from reddish bricks in 1880. Its two quadratic towers in Neo-Gothic style dominated the town's skyline for many years. Today they stand in the shadow of plate-glass office blocks and the adjacent Diamond Plaza shopping centre. It is worth inspecting the **altar** with blue Ave Maria lettering and gloriole – both in neon! Notre Dame Cathedral is very popular with Vietnamese Catholics, hence the many wedding parties encountered here.

❶ daily 7am–11am and 3pm–4pm: services 4.30pm, 5pm, Sun also 9.30am and noon

A statue of the Virgin Mary graces the square in front of the cathedral (Paris Commune Square). Saigonese locals gather here of an evening for a chat and a snack. Stalls selling toy helicopters and cars made from old drinks cans can be found amongst the refreshments and postcard stands.

Paris Commune Square

Another building from the colonial era stands opposite the cathedral. The Central Post Office (1886–91) boasts an impressive **dome-shaped roof** with cast-iron supports. The high-ceilinged hall is decorated with copious glass, old maps, ceiling fans and chandeliers. An outsized portrait of Ho Chi Minh watches over the nostalgic postal business in the refurbished hall. There is a bureau de change here and a cash machine, both hidden away to one side in the beautiful, historic telephone cubicles with the world clocks, plus a tourist information office with souvenir shop and a **water puppet theatre**.

*Central Post Office

❶ daily 7am–7pm; **water puppet theatre**: show 5pm, 6.30pm

Exceptional vaulted ceiling in the impressive post office

Saigon (Ho Chi Minh City)

Station

Vinh Nghien Pagoda
Airport

Truong Dinh

Nguyen Thong

Ly Chinh Thang

Ba Huyen Thanh Quan

Women's
Museum

Tran Quoc Toan

Chua Go

3 Thang 2

Dien Bien Phu

Cach Mang Thang Tam

Vo Thi Sau

Tu Xuong

Nguyen Thuong Hien

Pasteur

Dien Bien Phu

Pham Ngoc Thach

Cao Thang

Xa Loi Pagoda

Ngo Thoi Nhiem

Le Qui Don

Nam Ky Khoi Nghia

Nguyen Dinh Chieu

Truong Dinh

War Remnants
Museum

Nguyen Dinh Chieu

Vo Van Tan

Nguyen Thi Minh Khai

Cach Mang Thang Tam

Golden Dragon
Water Puppet Theatre

H.T Cong Chua

Nguyen Thi Minh Khai

Nam Ky Khoi Nghia

Pasteur

Cong Quynh

Bui Thi Xuan

Le Thi Rieng

Reunification
Palace

Le Duan

Notre Dame
Cathedral

Thai Binh
Market

Nguyen Trai

Nguyen Du

Nguyen Du

Cong Quynh

Le Lai

Pham Ngu Lao

Bui Vien

Ly Tu Trong

Mariamman
Temple

Le Thanh Ton

Ben Thanh
Market

Nguyen Trung Truc

Revolution
Museum

Town Hall

Opera

Dong Khoi

Cholon

Tran Hung Dao

De Tham

Co Bac

Nguyen Thai Hoc

Pham Ngu Lao

Yersin

Nguyen Thai Binh

Le Loi

Nam Ky Khoi Nghia

Art
Museum

Thendayyutthapani
Temple

Pasteur

Mac Thi Buoi

Duc Ke

Co Giang

Calmette

Pho Duc Chinh

Phung Son Tu
Pagoda

Ham Nghi

Ton That Dam

Nguyen Hue

Ngo

Ton Duc Thang

Ben Chuong Duong

Ben Nghe Channel

Ben Van Don

Ben Chuong Duong

Nguyen Cong Tru

Ton That Thanh

Ben Van Don

Ho Chi Minh
Museum

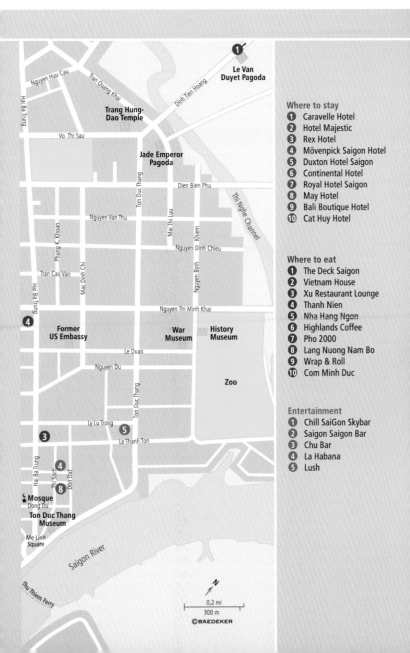

Where to stay
1. Caravelle Hotel
2. Hotel Majestic
3. Rex Hotel
4. Mövenpick Saigon Hotel
5. Duxton Hotel Saigon
6. Continental Hotel
7. Royal Hotel Saigon
8. May Hotel
9. Bali Boutique Hotel
10. Cat Huy Hotel

Where to eat
1. The Deck Saigon
2. Vietnam House
3. Xu Restaurant Lounge
4. Thanh Nien
5. Nha Hang Ngon
6. Highlands Coffee
7. Pho 2000
8. Lang Nuong Nam Bo
9. Wrap & Roll
10. Com Minh Duc

Entertainment
1. Chill SaiGon Skybar
2. Saigon Saigon Bar
3. Chu Bar
4. La Habana
5. Lush

Saigon

INFORMATION
Vietnam Tourism
234 Nam Ky Khoi Nghia, District 3, Saigon
tel. 08/39 32 67 76

also in the Dong Khoi, 18 Nam Quoc Cang and Pham Ngu Lao
www.vietnamtourism.com

Saigon Tourist Travel Services
45 Le Thanh Ton, District 1, Saigon
tel. 08/38 27 92 79
www.saigontourist.net
Tourist information and bureau de change also in the main post office on Dong Khoi

Saigon Kultour
Mobile tel.
www.hanoikultour.com
(for Saigon and Hanoi!)
A different kind of sightseeing.

TOUR OPERATORS
Trails Of Indochina
10/8 Phan Dinh Giot, Tan Binh district, Saigon
tel. 08/38 44 10 05
www.trailsofindochina.com
phong@trailsofindochina.com
toi@fmail.vnn.vn

Focus Asia
138A Nguyen Dinh Chieu, District 3, Saigon
www.focus-asia.biz
tel. 08/38 22 82 22
Long-established tour operator based in Saigon, also offering trips to neighbouring countries.

TRANSPORT
All plane, bus and train tickets can be easily purchased for a small fee in hotels and travel agencies, ideally a few days in advance.

Airport
Tan Son Nhat International Airport
Tan Binh district, approx. 6km/4mi north of Saigonwww.hochiminhcityairport.com
Airport Service Center:
tel. 08/38 48 67 11 and 08/38 44 66 65

Main railway station
tel. 08/38 46 65 28 and 08/38 36 01 05 and Saigon Railway Tourist Center at 275C Pham Ngu Lao (in the traveller district):
tel. 08/38 36 79 70 and 08/ 36 76 40

Boats
Hydrofoils from Saigon to Vung Tau (e.g. Greelines, www.greenlines.com.vn), although not the newest vessels.

Road transport
From the airport to the city
Taxi from approx. 150,000 VND (change!), best to used metered taxis from Mai Linh, tel. 08/38 27 79 79, Vinataxi or Vinasun (»fake« taxis with doctored meters call themselves Vinsun and Vinasum!); shuttle buses from Vietnam Airlines, public bus 152 departs from the International Airport via the domestic terminal to the city centre (Ben Thanh Market, Pham Ngu Lao; 4000 VND, luggage costs the same amount, every 15 minutes from 6am-6pm).
Public buses:.Many set out from the bus station at Ben Thanh Market, such

Sometimes it seems as if half of Saigon is out and about on mopeds...

as the new line 127, which covers a number of important attractions en route (tickets from the conductor from approx. 4000 VND).

Underground: The underground was constructed with German assistance and investment for US$800 million. Two lines are planned to run through the city from 2016 on.

Cyclo (also: Xyclo): be prepared to haggle over the price and do not use at night! Cyclos are banned on many streets, so do not be surprised if they are forced to take a detour...

Moped taxis (price negotiable!) or regular taxis with meter, modern municipal buses (timetable on sale at Ben Thanh Market, for example, see below).

Tips for pedestrians: Saigon traffic resembles a rumbling dodgem car ride at the fair, on both two wheels and four – nobody would dream of applying the brakes on a moped or cyclo at an intersection unless a traffic light is un-

mistakeably red. Tourists aiming to cross the street are advised to »grab the coat tails« of a Vietnamese pedestrian and dodge the motorized chaos in his »slipstream«.

EVENTS

Magazines such as »What's on Vietnam«, »Asia Live MHCMC«, »Time Out« and »What's on Vietnam« are packed with tips for events and can often be found in bars and hotels.

New Year's Festival

For the Tet New Year celebrations, a part of Saigon is transformed into a sea of flowers, particularly on Nguyen Hue Boulevard and Tran Hung Dao Boulevard. The flower markets prosper as the people of Saigon stock up on popular apricot and peach branches and little orange trees to decorate their homes in festive fashion (►MARCO POLO Insight p.114).

Rong Vang Golden Dragon Water Puppet Theatre

Colourful water puppet show with small orchestra for a maximum of 200 spectators in District One (55B Nguyen Thi Minh Khai, tel.08/39 30 21 96, www.goldendragonwaterpuppet.com, shows daily at 5pm, 6.30pm and 7.45pm, tickets US$7.50; further shows during the day in the History Museum's tiny theatre p.377 and afternoons at the main post office.

Cyclo Race

An annual event in March is the Saigon Cyclo Race, a charity event which makes an exception to the usual traffic policy

Rice and spices at Bin Tay Market

by allowing the vehicles to be driven along the boulevards of the city centre (www.saigonchildren.com).

SHOPPING

Most of the souvenir shops, galleries and silk boutiques are located in **Dong Khoi** and **Hai Ba Trung**; Le Loi is also renowned for leather goods. Authentic and replica Asian antiques can be found in Le Cong Kieu, close to the Art Museum. **Thanh Tuy** (125 Le Thanh Ton, next to the Norfolk Hotel, District 1, daily 8am–6.30pm) Visitors to **Lam Son** can not only purchase leather goods but also watch them being made, with a variety of handicrafts on display (106 Nguyen Van Troi, opposite the Omni Hotel) also at **Tay Son**: leather goods, furniture etc. (198 Vo Thi Sau).

Ben Thanh Market: in the southwest of the town, the complete range of Vietnamese goods and merchandise is proffered in several market halls. Numerous galleries can be found close to the Art Museum and in Nguyen Van Troi. Souvenirs around the west entrance, prices negotiable! (Cash machines on hand)

Bin Tay Market in Chinatown is less expensive and worth perusing, as are the alleyways of the **backpacker mile Pham Ngu Lao**. Cheap imitations, T-shirts and everything tourists might hope to find are on sale in **Saigon Square** department store (newly opened in Ton Duc Thang) and in the good, old (value for money!) **Thuong Xa Tax** store (souvenirs on the 3rd floor, on Nguyen Hue to the right of the Royal Hotel). There is an **open-air market** with all manner of goods from clothing to gold at Nguyem Dinh Chieu Market (1 Le Tu Tai), generally decent wares at fair prices (such as tea, sold per kilo).

ENTERTAINMENT/CUISINE

One restaurant after another has opened up on Nguyen Dinh Chieu (District 1), everything from seafood to barbecues and authentic pho diners (no menu), all the way to chic restaurants for the in-crowd.

Ben Thanh Nightmarket: from 6pm in the evenings, the streets to the east and west of Ben Thanh Market present an opportunity to tuck in to some seafood or other regional specialities with the local Vietnamese at one of the many little stalls selling set-price dishes.

A number of **seafood establishments** can be found on Thich Sach and Le Thanh Ton in District 1.

Very popular with the people of Saigon for special occasions and with travel groups are the **restaurant boats** and dining excursions on the Saigon River: Chinese, Vietnamese and international menus with orchestral accompaniment, sometimes vocalists as well, though the latter take a little getting used to (trips lasting one hour depart daily from around 7.30pm from the Bach Dang promenade, e.g. with the triple level Saigon Tourist boat: Saigon Ship Restaurant (££, tel. 08/38 23 03 93, open from 6.30pm-11pm; the ship sets sail around 8.30pm, returning at 9.30pm; tickets approx. 150,000 VND, Sat and Sun also with buffet). It is, however, something of a noisy mass event with western pop music and zany karaoke – not everyone's cup of tea.

ENTERTAINMENT

❶ *Chill SaiGon Skybar & Restaurant £££*   *Insider Tip*

76 Le Lai (opposite Cong Vien 23.9.-Park, close to Pham Ngu Lao), AB Tower, Saigon

tel. 08/38 27 23 72
Reservations mobile tel. 090/72 43 31 34
www.chillsaigon.com (photo ► p.393)
Stylish, cool and pricey.: the open-air Skybar on the 23rd floor of the AB Tower promises a bird's eye view of the glittering Saigon night. The motto is: dress to impress, so leave the flip-flops at the hotel. The 360° panorama makes up for the high prices (a glass of wine/cocktail around £7.5!; Happy Hour Mon-Fri 5.30pm until 8pm). Elegant international dining inside (Danish-French chefs, reservations recommended for bar/restaurant).

❷ *Saigon Saigon Bar £££*

19 Lam Son Square (Caravelle Hotel)
tel. 08/38 23 49 99
live music daily from 11pm
When the house band reel off pop and rock classics at the Caravelle roof bar on the tenth floor, the five-star priced cocktail (inevitably called »Good morning Vietnam«) tastes a great deal better.

❸ *Chu Bar ££*

158 Dong Khoi
daily 6pm to midnight
Modern ambience for a good glass of wine or a cappuccino looking onto Dong Khoi Street. Small dishes available.

❹ *La Habana ££*

6 Cao Ba Quat, District 1
Saigon
tel. 08/38 29 51 80
www.lahabana-saigon.com
Spanish-Cuban-German mix: mojitos, German beer and sangria, salsa and paella, popular with German tourists (German proprietor) and locals. Cosy atmosphere, good live bands every night!

⑤ *Lush*
2 Ly Tu Trong, District 1, Saigon
https://de-de.facebook.com/LushSaigon/
Extremely loud club/disco and open-air
bar, busiest at weekends from 11pm
with youthful in-crowd, mini dancefloor.

WHERE TO EAT
① *The Deck Saigon* £££-££££
38 Nguyen U Di, Thao Dien, An Phu
(District 2, approx. 8km/5mi from the
centre) Saigon   *Insider Tip*
tel. 08/37 44 66 32
www.thedecksaigon.com
Well-hidden insiders' tip in the finer ex-
pat residential district: chic, idyllic river
restaurant with views into the distance
over unspoiled countryside: inventive international and local dishes cooked up
by Vietnamese-French team of chefs. Enjoy a cocktail whilst watching water hy-
ancinths and riverboats float by.

② *Vietnam House* ££-£££
93-95 Dong Khoi, Saigon
tel. 08/38 29 16 23, daily 10am-10pm
www.vietnamhousesaigon.com
Tried and trusted tourist restaurant on
several floors. George Bush has dined
here. Delicious Vietnamese dishes are a
fine introduction to the nation's cuisine.

③ *Xu Restaurant Lounge* ££-£££
71-75 Hai Ba Trung, District 1, Saigon
tel. 08/38 24 84 68
www.xusaigon.com
Those in search of a treat should visit
this stylish, romantic, somewhat extravagant restaurant. Enjoy an aperitif or tasty
cocktail downstairs in the bar and admire the attractively presented fusion
creations in the elegant restaurant (portions are not overly generous, the desserts verge on the ridiculously small). Ex-

pensive wine list covers (almost) the
entire globe, a little glass costs around
€7 (worth dropping in for Happy Hour,
Mon-Fri 5.30pm-8.30pm).

④ *Thanh Nien* ££
11 Nguyen Van Chiem
tel. 08/38 22 59 09
http://thanhnien.vnnavi.com.vn
daily 7am–10.30pm
Lovely open-air location with live bands,
air-conditioned rooms, Vietnamese and
vegetarian dishes à la carte or, on weekdays, buffet (Vietnamese, Thai). Plenty of
locals eat here and have been doing so
for the past two decades!

⑤ *Nha Hang Ngon* £-££
160 Pasteur Street, District 1, Saigon
tel. 08/38 27 71 31
Dine outside or inside the two-storey old
villa: food is prepared in the cookshops,
a feast for the eyes (try the mouth-watering »goi bo bop thau«, a spicy beef
salad with slices of young banana and
starfruit). Full to bursting with tourists
and Vietnamese in the evening.

⑥ *Highlands Coffee (Xa Tax)* £-££
135 Nguyen Hue (to the right of Kim Do
Royal City Hotel), Saigon
tel. 08/39 14 49 92
Popular branch of the Vietnamese coffeehouse chain on the roof of the Saigon Tax Trade Center, a cut-price department (not to be confused with the
Saigon Trade Center tower): a good vantage point from which to observe the
hive of activity at the crossroads of
Nguyen Hue and Le Loi whilst savouring
barbecue beef, shrimps, a cool beer and
typical Vietnamese iced coffee. There is
also Wi-Fi. The rooftop terrace on the
fourth floor is open from 9am to 11pm

Amazing views and a great atmosphere: Chill Saigon Skybar

every day, accessed via the third floor restaurant.

❼ Pho 2000 £
Phan Chu Trinh
(right next to Ben Thanh Market), Saigon
tel. 08/38 22 27 88
daily 6am to midnight
Simple soup kitchen which likes to call itself »Pho for the President«, since Bill Clinton ate what was probably his first bowl of pho here where in the year 2000…

❽ Lang Nuong Nam Bo £
285/C 145 Cach Mang Thang,
District 10 (approx. 6km/4mi from the centre),
Saigon
A little out of the way, but all the more authentic for it, this noisy establishment, well-known to taxi drivers, is always busy. Speciality of the house is bo tung xeo – »execution in slices«. This is, in fact, a Vietnamese barbecue: thin slices of marinated beef fried with ginger and onion.

❾ Wrap & Roll £
97B Nguyen Trai and 62B Hai Ba Trung,
District 1, Saigon
tel. 08/39 25 36 39 and 08/38 82 21 66
http://wrap-roll-com
Popular, modern snack chain serving many types of tasty spring rolls, salads, soups and sweet dishes, fish, vegetarian fare and, of an evening, hot pots.

❿ Com Minh Duc £
35 and 100 Ton That Tung (northwest of Pham Ngu Lao)
tel. 08/38 39 22 40
Typically busy cookshop on two floors, dishes can be selected from the pots at the front (or from the menu). Loud, full and delicious!

WHERE TO STAY

❶ *Caravelle Hotel* ££££

19 Lam Son Square
(next to the Municipal Theatre)
tel. 08/28 23 49 99
www.caravellehotel.com
Renovated five-star tower block from
the 1960s, now equipped with every
luxury, several restaurants, nice pool, spa
& fitness centre.

❷ *Hotel Majestic* £££-££££

1 Dong Khoi
tel. 08/38 29 55 17
www.majesticsaigon.com.vn
On the promenade of the Saigon River.
One of the city's most beautiful hotels
(175 rooms), some rooms rather dingy
and noisy, but with colonial elegance,
some with balconies overlooking the river. A drink on the attractive rooftop terrace above the river on a warm summer's evening is something that can be
recommended to residents and non-residents alike.

❸ *Rex Hotel* £££

141 Nguyen Hue
tel. 08/38 29 21 85
www.rexhotelvietnam.com
Legendary, fantastically situated luxury
establishment with pool, although it has
seen better days. The rooftop
terrace is also an attraction for **Insider Tip**
non-residents – taking a drink
amongst small trees and sculptures to the
sound of birdsong from bamboo cages.

❹ *Mövenpick Saigon Hotel (formerly Omni)* £££

253 Nguyen Van Troi, Phu Nuan district
tel. 08/38 44 92 22

Looking across to the Rex Hotel from the rooftop terrace of the SH Garden

www.moevenpick-hotels.com
One of the city's finest hotels, a short distance outside the centre, close to the airport (10 minutes). Although the area appears more naturally authentic than in the typical tourist districts, it is just as noisy – but intriguing to those on more of a discovery trip. The hotel itself meets the usual Mövenpick standards of comfort, with a pool, five restaurants and its own bakery.

❺ Duxton Hotel Saigon £££
63 Nguyen Hue
tel. 08/38 22 29 99
www.saigonduxtonhotels.com
Chic, centrally located business hotel with 200 rooms, Japanese and American grill restaurant, spa, karaoke, pool.

❻ Continental Hotel ££-££££
132–134 Dong Khoi
tel. 08/38 29 92 01
www.continentalhotel.com.vn
Colonial classic from the year 1880, which does not appear unaffordable (although traffic has increased considerably since then). Bask in the historical surroundings where Graham Greene and Somerset Maugham were residents, amongst precious wood and marble (e.g. Greene's room 214). The »regular« rooms are no less attractive (and are somewhat cheaper), some with a tranquil view of the garden. Marvellous restaurant oasis under the frangipani trees in the courtyard, where (boisterous) wedding parties are often staged, karaoke included.

❼ Royal Hotel Saigon ££ Insider Tip
133 Nguyen Hue Avenue
tel. 08/38 21 59 14

www.royalhotelsaigon.com
At the heart of the city, comfortable and friendly. Lovely views of Saigon activity from the terrace restaurant on the 4th floor, Wi-Fi in the rooms, covered pool and health club. A classic amongst the early Saigon hotels of consistently high standard (although the name has changed often).

❽ May Hotel ££
28-30 Thich Sach Street, Ben Nghe Ward (District 1), Saigon
tel. 08/38 23 45 01
www.mayhotel.com.vn
Central, but quiet and comfortable hotel with 118 pleasant rooms and a covered pool on the roof, sauna and fitness room.

❾ Bali Boutique Hotel ££
82 Bui Vien, District 1, Saigon
tel. 09/39 20 98 04, -5
www.baliboutiquehotel.vn
Family friendly mini hotel which opened mid-2012 in the low budget region: 30 modern, large, tiled rooms on eight floors (elevator), also family rooms with baby beds, a little noisier on the side facing the street. Smartly designed restaurant.

❿ Cat Huy Hotel £
353/28 Pham Ngu Lao, District 1 Saigon
Tel 08/39 20 87 16
www.cathuyhotel.com
Six-storey mini hotel (no lift!) hidden away at the heart of the lively backpacker district, with ten surprisingly large, quiet and comfortable rooms (flatscreen TV, Wi-Fi, minibar, some with balcony, others without windows).

Hotel Continental The Hotel Continental (Lam Son Square, 132–143 Dong Khoi) found fame through Graham Greene's *The Quiet American*. His fictional characters sat at the veranda bar on the kerb to discuss the latest events of war, watching Franco-Vietnamese life come and go, admiring the charming ladies in their long, slit ao dais. It was here that, in the early 1950s, the hero of the novel, the British journalist Fowler first met the »quiet American« and secret agent Pyle, who would poach his Vietnamese girl.

Municipal Theatre Just a few steps further on is the Municipal Theatre, a striking white building standing between two hotels steeped in tradition, the Continental and Caravelle. Designed by the French architect Ferré as an opera house, it was festively inaugurated in 1899. Up until 1975 the South Vietnamese National Assembly sat here. Under the Communists, it reverted to a municipal theatre in 1976. Today, both Vietnamese and Western pieces are performed in the beautiful building, and fashion shows and pop concerts are also staged here.The »Hon Viet Culture and Art Show« (»The Soul of Vietnam«), a musical journey through Vietnam, with bamboo dance, traditional instruments and brightly coloured costumes is performed here on the 15th and 24th of each month.

❶ Tickets 100,000 –300,000 VND. Opera schedule: www.hbso.org.vn and http://hanoigrapevine.com

ON THE BANKS OF THE SAIGON RIVER

The warrior Tran Hung Dao, who defeated the Mongolians under Kublai Khan is remembered with a statue standing tall over Me Linh Square, gazing peacefully into the distance across the Saigon River. Early in the morning, mostly elderly men and women can be seen practising their Tai Chi exercises along the river promenade. Not so many years ago, entire families would stroll through the evening air in their pyjama suits. Now, honking horns and clattering engines dominate the day and night. Restaurant ships offering lunch and dinner cruises into provincial waters provide brief respite from the traffic chaos, although these too can be noisy affairs, popular with Asian groups and local families. For decades, until they were discontinued in 2011, the Tu Thiem ferries left from the pier below the Renaissance Riverside Hotel, crossing to the more tranquil District 2 (Thao Dien); today, in the age of modern bridges and tunnels, hydrofoils still depart from here to Vung Tau and half-day private charters are available to Cu Chi. At the southern end of the street along the river bank, a bridge crosses the water to the **Ho Chi Minh Museum**. Erected in 1861–62, the administrative building was once the seat of the French Shipping Company. It was here that, on 5 June 1911, a young man by the name of Nguyen Tat Thanh boarded the ship that would take him around the world. Approximately three decades later, he returned to his homelands and ultimately became the unanimously revered President Ho Chi Minh (►MARCO POLO Insight p.265). The five exhibition rooms contain many photographs, documents, newspaper articles, models, sculptures and everyday personal possessions of Ho Chi Minh on two floors; on display in Room 4, for example, are articles of Ho Chi Minh's clothing, his rusty typewriter and a walking stick. Activity in the harbour can be well observed from the terrace or the small café in the courtyard.

❶ Tue–Sun 7.30am–11.30am, 1.30pm–4.30pm; admission: approx. 15,000 VND. The Ho Chi Minh Museum is also known as Nha Rong or Bao Tang and is situated on Nguyen Tat Thanh street, District 4 (not to be confused with the similarly named City Museum!)

History lesson at the Ho Chi Minh Museum

BEN THANH MARKET AND ITS SURROUNDINGS

Ben Thanh Market is situated at the opposite end of Le Loi, in the southwest of the city centre. The market hall is characterized by its distinctive clock tower, a veritable emblem of the city. The halls were built on the traditional market square in 1914. Both the market hall and the square out front, with its lively and chaotic roundabout, have sadly become a popular meeting place for **pickpockets**, so take care in the market crowds!

The Art Museum (Bao Thang My Thuat, 97A Pho Duc Chinh) is housed in a quite lovely cream-coloured building. One of the most interesting national collections can be seen here: from Oc Eo culture via works of Socialist Realism to contemporary trends. Some works are available for purchase. The garden attached is very attractive.   **Art Museum**

❶ Tue–Sun 8am–6pm; admission: approx. 10.000 VND

REUNIFICATION PALACE AND SURROUNDINGS

*Reunifica- West of the cathedral, all roads lead to Reunification Palace (visitors'
tion Palace entrance: 106 Nguyen Du Street). In complete contrast to the mag-
(Thong Nhat) nificent colonial architecture, the three storeys of Reunification Palace, which served as presidential residence until 1975, seem rather
sober. The modern building was constructed in 1966, designed by the
Vietnamese architect Ngo Viet Thu. Previously, in 1868, the Noro-
dom Palace had been erected on this site for the French Governor
General. In the 1950s the **dictator Ngo Dinh Diem** lived in and ruled
from the colonial building with his family. On 27 February 1962, the
structure was badly damaged by bombs, as rebel soldiers of the South
Vietnamese Army attacked the presidential residence from the air.
Diem survived the offensive and had the ruins demolished. Four
years later, the new, larger building, with over 100 rooms and a helicopter pad on the roof, was opened. It was to become the centre of
the battle for Saigon: on the morning of 30 April 1975, viewers
around the world were able to witness on television« how a North Vietnamese T-54 tank crushed the iron gate and Communist soldiers
occupied the building. On the roof, the flag of the Democratic Republic of Vietnam was hoisted. In the winter that followed, the negotiations for reunification were held here – hence the present name.
Inside, the style is dominated by a Western, functional aesthetic with
cavernous assembly and conference rooms. The banqueting halls,
however, are rich in pomp. On the first floor, the former reception
rooms and living quarters of the president can be found. Also open
to visitors are ballrooms, a small cinema and countless rooms with
red carpets and flowing curtains, leather armchairs and antique
chairs. The cellar leads on to subterranean **escape tunnels** and a
form of command centre. As well as being a museum, the palace also
hosts international congresses and receptions.

❶ daily 7.30am–11am, 1pm–4pm; admission 30,000 VND
There is a drinks stall on the roof (fourth floor).

**War The former »Museum of American War Crimes« (28 Vo Van Tan
Remnants Street) awaits with many facts and figures, documentation and pho-
Museum tographs from the Vietnam War. A few years ago, the place was re-
named the War Remnants Museum so that the many visiting US
veterans did not feel insulted. The museum was opened as early as
September 1975 and expanded to incorporate six exhibition rooms
and an open space with tanks, war planes and gun defences from the
Americans. Visitors should steel themselves to witness images (large-
ly by US photographers) illustrating all conceivable **horrors of war**.
The first two rooms, entitled »Historic Truths« (1st floor) and »War
Victims« contain the bulk of the horrific war images, e.g. from ▶My
Lai, where, on 16 March 1968, a total of 504 villagers were shot dead.

Vietnam War relic

Display boards also describe the struggle for recognition of US veterans as »Agent Orange victims« in the USA. Foetuses deformed by the chemical agent are conserved in preserving jars which, until just a few years ago, were stored in a Saigon hospital. Various weapons can be seen in the third room, while the final room is dedicated to Vietnamese war heroes. At the end of the site, an iron door set in a mighty wall leads the way to an exhibition concerning the **Con Dao Island Prison** (►Vung Tau). In three sections of the building, models of the so-called »tiger cages« (cells measuring 2.7m/9ft x 1.5m/5ft x 3m/10ft), some instruments of torture and a guillotine from French colonial times can be inspected. The guillotine was used as a means of execution as late as the year 1960. Souvenir shops sell war memorabilia (ostensibly genuine cigarette lighters, watches, shell cases) and all manner of handicrafts. Diagonally opposite, a water puppet theatre awaits an audience.

❶ daily7.30–6pm (last admittance 4.30pm); admission 15,000 VND; http://warremnantsmuseum.com

Xa Loi Pagoda, a modern Buddhist structure from the year 1956, is of interest primarily for its historical significance. In the early 1960s, the sanctuary (89 Ba Huyen Thanh Quan Street, close to Dien Bien Phu Street) was seen as the **centre of the resistance** against the dic-

*Xa Loi Pagoda

tatorial president Ngo Dinh Diem. Some 400 Buddhist monks and nuns congregated here to find sanctuary from the reprisals of his regime. Some even went as far as self-immolation by burning to underline their protest, among them the monk Thich Quang Duc (►Famous People), to whom a monument now stands, close to the pagoda at the crossroads of Nguyen Dinh Chieu/Cach Mang Thang Tam Street. The pictures of his spectacular act of desperation were seen all over the globe and weakened the reputation of the Catholic president considerably. Finally, in August 1963, soldiers stormed Xa Loi Pagoda, arresting the monks and nuns. Today the temple is a popular destination for Buddhist Vietnamese, especially at weekends and on holidays. Many traders proffer their incense sticks, flower garlands and other devotional objects, whilst birdsong and drums blend in with Buddhist chants. At the entrance to the pagoda, an impressive tower of seven storeys reaches skywards. On the right-hand side of the site, religious believers with incense sticks bow before a white Quan Am statue. The building with a double roof is typical of real socialist design. Its interior is dominated by a roughly 5m/16ft-high **golden Sakyamuni Buddha**, meditating on a lotus pedestal. On the walls of the great hall, 14 paintings depict important stages in the life of the Enlightened One (a board to the right of the entrance explains the numbered paintings in English, to the left in French). Behind the statue of Buddha to the left is a shrine dedicated to Thich Quang Duc and the other monks who set themselves alight. He is portrayed in the figure to the left, holding pearls.

❶ daily 7am–11am and 2pm–5pm

ALONG LE DUAN BOULEVARD

*Zoo/Botani-cal Gardens
At the end of Le Duan Boulevard is the gateway to Saigon Zoo and Botanical Gardens. Swiftly leaving behind the clatter of mopeds and the accompanying exhaust fumes on the busy streets, visitors can immerse themselves in a world of peace and quiet, where the air is filled with the aroma of freshly cut grass and frangipani blossom. Created by the Frenchmen Germain and Pierre in the year 1864, the gardens still hold great charm for young couples and anyone who enjoys a stroll. There is a particularly fine **orchid collection**. Big cats and elephants as well as many birds can be seen in the enclosures and cages, some of which are rather cramped. The latest star turn in the renovated zoo, for example, is provided by two white tigers. Of particular note are the Komodo dragons, a present from the Indonesian government. Fairground stalls and children's roundabouts are also to be found on the same grounds.

Insider Tip

❶ daily 7am–5pm (usually very busy on Sundays); admission: 12,000 VND

Within the walls of the Botanical Gardens stands the city's History Museum, founded in 1929. It is well worth investigating this beautiful building as it boasts a wealth of interesting exhibits, including a Dong Son drum from the Bronze Age. Not to be missed are the ceramics from the Le dynasty (15th-17th century), model ships, items of clothing and instruments from the Tay Son dynasty (18th to early 19th century, room 8), as well as ceramic vases from various Asian countries (room 10). In rooms 11 to 14 are a number of well-preserved artefacts excavated from the Mekong Delta and the environs of Saigon. In Room 7, an almost 4m/13ft-high replica of the famous »Lady Buddha with A Thousand Arms« (Quan Am, ▶p.1) from But Thap Pagoda is especially noteworthy. Also on display in the museum are Buddha statues from various eras and parts of Asia, along with clothes and furniture from the Nguyen dynasty. Costumes and everyday articles of minority peoples from southern Vietnam can be admired in Room 15. Room 11 leads to the little **water puppet theatre**, where performances are held during the day as soon as five spectators have taken their seats. The plays star legendary creatures such as dragons, lions, turtles and phoenixes. Three or four puppeteers stand behind the stage up to their waists in water and move the figures on long bamboo sticks. There is a good chance that those sitting in the front row will get wet (▶MARCO POLO Insight p.78 and p.368).

**History Museum

❶ Tue–Sun 8am–11.30am, 1.30pm–5pm; admission: approx. 20,000 VND, no photographs. **Water puppet theatre** on the hour 9am–11am, 2pm–4pm, provided there are enough spectators (approx. 40,000 VND)

A single Buddha dominates the empty space of Xa Loi Pagoda, a sanctuary of Hinayana Buddhism

Buddha & Co

Anyone visiting the impressive sacred sites of Vietnam will be confronted with no end of statues very different to the ones they are used to seeing. Each has its own special »characteristics« by which they may be identified and, given time, they do not appear so strange after all.

Buddha is honoured in various different guises. **Sakyamuni**, the historic Buddha Siddharta Gautama, can most readily be recognized by his simple appearance as an ascetic, often as a teacher with his favourite pupil. He usually sits on a lotus throne, sometimes with elongated earlobes, a third eye on his forehead and curly hair. **Amitabha**, the Buddha of the Past, accompanies mankind on the way to purification. In some representations, he has an especially long right arm, with which he can embrace all people, or he joined by gracious Bodhisattvas (see below). The Buddha of the Future, **Maitreya** or Di Lac, is commonly found laughing and with a fat belly. He is said to return to the Earth every 5000 years to save mankind. **Bodhisattvas** are enlightened beings who do not enter Nirvana, but stay on Earth to help others. Most popular of all is undoubtedly **Quan Am**, Goddess of Mercy, often depicted as a female Bodhisattva in white. She can be seen in various forms: holding a bottle of pure water, with 100 arms and eyes as a symbol of her power, or standing on a lotus leaf with a child on her arm, promising childless women fertility. The most famous male Bodhisattva, meanwhile, is Avalokiteshvara, usually seen in the meditation pose, holding a jar of water and lotus. Sometimes he has four arms and holds rosary beads and a book.

Judges of Hell et al

Buddhist pagodas also house **guardians**, groups of the ten Judges of Hell and 18 Arhat. The benevolent **Ong Thien** with the white face and the malevolent **Ong Ac** are guardians of the Buddhist faith. The ten **Judges of Hell** (usually arranged in two rows of five) await man after his death. Each is responsible for a different sin (murder, betrayal and so forth) and when one has passed judgement, the next takes his turn. After the final verdict from all of the judges, the poor soul is handed over to **Mother Meng**. She serves the soup of forgetfulness, so that the soul can be reborn completely pure and unburdened. Realistic depictions of the **Arhat** (La Han), holy ascetics, can be seen above all in the pagodas of North Vietnam.

Other Figures

Statues of pagoda founders or benefactors may be found at the side altars, meritorious monks in particular, along with ancestral spirits, heroes and other non-Buddhist tutelary gods. Taoist gods and demons certainly also have a place in Buddhist sanctuaries. The

Strange, unusual figures populate temples and pagodas

most important is the **Jade Emperor** with his adjuncts Bac Dau (Star of the North) and Nam Tao (Star of the South), who keep record of the dead and the living. Courtyards often contain grottoes for spirits of nature. Chinese pagodas and assembly halls are likely to feature **Thien Hau**, Goddess of the Sea, and **Quan Cong**, the Chinese General of the Three Kingdoms, with his three aides and magical horse, must not be missed. Thien Hau, originally the daughter of a Chinese provincial fisherman, is usually seen in a seated position with a flat crown. The green-faced Thien Ly Nahn and the red-faced Thuan Phuong help the goddess to predict the weather.

Lucky Charms

All manner of lucky charms or symbols of fortune may be found adorning the holy sites, such as **dragons** in many forms, considered divine and a positive force in Asian lands, not dangerous or evil as in our fairytales. Some visitors may be taken aback to see a **swastika** on graves or coffins in temples, but this is originally a symbol of good fortune for Buddhists, appropriated by the National Socialists and given a wholly different meaning. The swastika symbolizes the heart of Buddha and stands for a long life. It is shown in both left and right rotations. The **Yin-Yang symbol** has its origins in Taoism. A circle is divided by an S line, separating light and dark, symbolizing the duality in all things.

CHOLON (CHINESE QUARTER)

The oldest surviving part of Saigon is Cholon in the southwest of the city, home to the descendants of the Chinese who fled here from Southern China some 300 years ago. The pavements, markets and narrow alleyways are busy with traders, but today the air is no longer laced with the sweet smell of opium. As in days of old, red strips of paper with Chinese characters still hang in the doorways of the houses – talismans from a recent visit to the temple. On the main streets, meanwhile, there are few reminders that this is the exotic Chinese district. The best way to get to know the area is by straying into the side streets. Exotic aromas emanate from the markets, which seem to vibrate with human activity and noise. Most of Saigon's more than **180 pagodas and temples** can be found in Cholon, many of them on Nguyen Trai Street. A visit to one is an absolute must: join the religious followers and enter a world of idiosyncratic deities, colourful adornments and coils of smouldering incense. A temple and pagoda tour through Cholon should begin at Binh Tay Market, the ochre-

Insider Tip

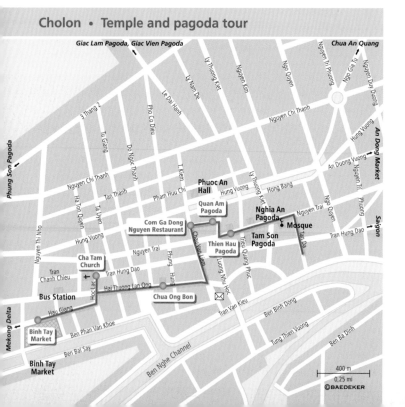

Cholon • Temple and pagoda tour

coloured central market of Cholon selling everyday wares. From here, follow Hau Giang into the heart of the Chinese quarter (but not before taking a look at the Cha Tam Church/Francis Xavier behind the small park to the left in Ho Lac). Go down Hai Thuong Lan Ong looking for a God of Happiness, following the countless red lanterns, garlands and fortune banners – shops for Chinese wedding decorations – past traditional apothecaries and the Cat Dang coffee shop (no. 279) as far as Chua Ong Bon: the pagoda of the bearded god is busy with visitors at all times, as donations here are thought to bring financial blessings in the future.Continuing through the bustling myriad of mopeds, turn left at the post office into Chau Van Liem. The restaurant Com Ga Dong Nguyen appears after some 400m/450yd, where, for decades, hungry souls have feasted mostly on Com Ga (rice and chicken). An English menu also features ginger rice, lotus soup, fried tofu, crab-meat, sweet roast pork and sausage. Hot and spicy pig's brain may tempt a few (house number 87–91). Amidst all the chaos, it is worth looking up now and again to admire old colonial facades in places with colourful or fading wooden slats, some with beautiful wrought iron balconies (in Hai Thuong Lan Ong and Nguyen Trai, for instance). The old opium dens may no longer be in evidence, but tall

In the pagodas of Cholon: smoke to honour the dead mingles with the scent of many candles

The legend of Thien Hau

One day, around 1000 years ago, the girl Thien Hau who lived in the Chinese province of Fujian, asked the rich owners and captains of the large fishing vessels if she might accompany them out to sea. As they refused her request, she had to make do with a small boat. A sudden storm spated the girl, whilst all other boats which had set out perished. Since then, Thien Hau has been revered as the patron saint of seafarers and fishermen.

incense coils (a metre or 3ft high) cast their smoke from under the ceiling inside the pagodas and countless incense sticks burn before the altars – bearing the wishes of the faithful to heaven. Some coils burn for half a year – quite a wish list! As in the next sacred site, Chua Quan Am (in Lao Tu p.401), dedicated to Quan Am, the Goddess of Mercy, dressed in white. Here, Taoism and Buddhism, Lao Tse and Buddha, meet for all to see, whilst Ngoc Hoang the Jade Emperor and many others are also represented. But first, take time to admire the little figures adorning the roof ridge, telling stories and relating Chinese legends.Immediately around the corner, the highlight of the temple tour awaits. Probably the finest example of southern Chinese temple architecture in the world stands on Nguyen Trai Street: Chua Ba (also known as Thien Hau Pagoda, see below) is dedicated to Thien Hau, the maritime goddess and protector of sailors and fisherman and to Kim Hue, goddess of fertility. Delve into a world rich in sandalwood vapours, Chinese character, red and gold décor. Note the little devils on the roof in the second courtyard and pink strips of paper bearing donors' names on the walls – the receipts for the Taoist finance office, so to speak. A Cholon tour lasts three to five hours, depending on the degree of interest. Cyclo riders also offer this temple tour, which can be a good idea if it is raining. To bring proceedings to a sumptuous, sensous conclusion, the short Tan Da alley on the corner of Pham Don is host to numerous cookshops (»Cholon Best Food in Town«, turn right off Nguyen Trai).

** THIEN HAU PAGODA (CHUA BA)
❶ daily 6am–5.30pm

The most beautiful pagoda in Cholon

The »Temple of the Heavenly Lady« was constructed some time between the end of the 18th and middle of the 19th century, a more exact date has not been determined. It was built by the Chinese and is dedicated to the goddess of the sea. Restoration work has been carried out on several occasions on this popular Taoist place of worship at 710 Nguyen Trai Street. The picturesque temple is above all worth visiting for its **elaborate façades and ornate roof** with coloured ceramic figures. The structure is typical of South Chinese temple architecture. In the 17th century, many Chinese sought to escape the warring factions of the Ming and Qing dynasties, fleeing to Vietnam by boat and placing their trust in the goddess to protect them from sea monsters, storms and pirates. Having arrived safely, they built this richly decorated temple in her honour. Thien Hau can be seen s on a mural above the main entrance. Colourful mandarins in headdresses stand guard on both sides.

In the first courtyard, numerous marble tablets and red strips of paper with Chinese characters hang along the walls – these are the names of donors, sometimes with the amount donated (►see p.73). The fruits of the many good deed hangs above the pieces of paper: pictures of buildings financed by the donations, including a clinic and a school. From this atrium it is possible to study the many colourful figures along the **roof crest** more closely: the scholars, guards, kings and princesses, dragons and witches relate stories from Chinese legend. It looks something like a puppet theatre – yet so realistic, that they might jump to life at any moment. ***First courtyard**

In the second courtyard, horned devils can be seen on the edge of the roof. Huge coils of incense, made from sandalwood and leaves of the Kapok tree, permeate the air with their smoke: they burn for between two weeks and six months – the longer the better, for the smoke is said to carry the wishes on the red slips of paper to the heavenly goddess Thien Hau. In the small ovens in the courtyard, relatives send symbolic paper gifts to their dead in the afterlife: money or clothing such as shoes or hats, cars and houses made of paper are burned. Incense sticks are also lit in their memory in bronze basins. ***Second courtyard**

The main shrine features three gold-painted statues of Thien Hau in embroidered garb; the central figure is carried through the streets during a procession in the third lunar month. The shrine to the left is worthy of attention, with the **Goddess of Fertility, Kim Hua**. Married couples often pay homage to her, praying for a child. A small bed stands on the altar complete with a curtain, to help them in their wish – purely in symbolic fashion, of course. A wooden model ship in the corner serves as a reminder of Thien Hau's adventure at sea. **Sanctuary**

On the left hand side is a bronze bell, 200 years old, which is struck every time a donation is made. Temple employees sit behind a counter and paint the wishes of believers onto coloured strips of paper – these are then hung in the doorways of people's homes. In the rooms to the rear and to the sides, more gods and heroes can be seen, including General Quan Cong and the god of Prosperity and Happiness Than Tai. Particularly on holidays, large numbers of believers stream into the temple. On the 23rd day of the third lunar month, the annual procession is accompanied by Cantonese singing and dancing. **Further rooms**

WHAT TO SEE AROUND NGUYEN TRAI STREET

The Nghia An Hoi Quan Temple was constructed in 1840 in honour of the legendary General Quan Cong, who was worshipped like a god. The courageous **hero of the »Three Kingdoms«** is revered for his bravery, sense of justice and his wisdom. The structure of the sanctuary recalls that of the temple described above; with two green courtyards before the main altar. A magnificently carved wooden boat catches the eye above the entrance. This is said to be the vessel with which the General of China made the journey to Vietnam. A 3m/10ft-high statue of the general stands on the main altar in a glass case. He is flanked by his fellow warriors, generals Chau Xuong and Quan Binh. In the shrine to the right is a statue of the Goddess of the Sea, Thien Hau, and to the left squats the God of Prosperity, Than Tai. Every year, **several festivals** take place in honour of Quan Cong, for example on 24 June and the 15th day of the first lunar month.

Nghia An Hoi Quan Temple (Chua Ong)

❶ daily 6am–6pm

In front of Quan Am Pagoda (12 Lao Tu Street) hordes of hawkers await customers who purchase incense sticks or set birds free from their cages to boost their karma. It is worth taking a moment to observe the exterior of the sanctuary more carefully. The roofs are adorned with scenes depicting small figures, houses and temples. Two fierce-looking guards and two stone lions watch over the entrance to the pagoda to ward off evil spirits. Gilded panels depict scenes of courtly life with dancers, musicians and chess players. When the community of Fujian built the place of worship some 200 years ago, it was dedicated to Quan Am, yet it is the Goddess of Heaven (A Pho) whose statue stands in front of the main altar. The open courtyard behind it contains many deities and idols, including Quan Am, clad in white, who attracts many believers. In a small room to the right, the calligraphers can be seen at work, inscribing the red prayer slips and **contribution receipts**.

*Quan Am Pagoda

* BINH TAY MARKET (CHO BINH TAY)

All kinds of market stalls stand alongside each other on the two levels of Binh Tay Market, its courtyard and the surrounding alleyways. Ceramic pots and plastic bowls on one corner, colourful sweets and dried fish piled up on the next. Virtually everything the heart desires can be found here. The traders are used to tourists, who can browse

As long as the incense spirals in Thien Hau Pagoda burn, the smoke carries messages to the gods and departed ancestors

undisturbed. It is nevertheless advisable to keep an eye on one's personal possessions! The market is located on Thap Muoi Street in the west of Cholon.

Vietnamese medicine In Hai Thuong, Lan Ong Street, named after an old 18th-century healer and founder of the »Encyclopedia of Vietnamese Traditional Medicine«, south of Cha Tam Church, there are shops specializing in traditional Vietnamese medicine. The manifold aromas wafting through the air betray their location. In the shadowy shops, old men and women weigh powder and mix ingredients in mortars. Sometimes it might seem preferable to remain ignorant of the contents. Recent health warnings circulated to the effect that dried placenta powder, back in fashion as an ancient healing remedy, is being illegally imported from China and may contain bacteria or even plastic. 100g costs 400,000 VND, by the way. Traditional medicine has been practiced in Vietnam for at least 2000 years. A pharmaceutical company displays around 3000 exhibits in a museum featuring 18 rooms (the exceedingly beautiful brick building incorporating different architectural and ethnic elements from all over Vietnam, replete with woodcarvings merits a visit to this quiet residential street in itself). Mortars and antique weighing scales, tea services and herb containers, old documents and ancient books are amongst the artefacts, whilst a documentary film in English offers further background. Tea made from Ling Zhi mushrooms rounds things off and, naturally, it is possible to purchase teas and remedies for headaches or coughs in the museum shop.

MARCO ❓ POLO INSIGHT

Superstition

It is still the case today that superstition still plays an important role in the healing power of substances and animal extracts in Vietnam. Boiled monkey brain for a healthy life, tiger penis for potency, rhinoceros horn against nosebleeds, with delicacies such as snake meat, frogs and tiger wine regular components of the Asian diet.

❶ 41 Hoang Du Khuong, District 10; daily 8.30am-5pm; admission: 120,000 VND; www.fitomuseum.com.vn

SANCTUARIES IN THE NORTH AND WEST OF THE CITY

*Pagoda and temple tours Adding together all the pagodas, temples, monasteries, mosques, Hindu shrines and other religious centres, there are in the region of **one thousand places of worship** in Saigon. Some of the most noteworthy examples can be found to the north and west of the centre, albeit fairly far apart. The taxi drivers, motorbike taxis and cyclos are, however, used to dealing with foreign tourists in Saigon and have

The Jade Emperor Pagoda: a beautiful courtyard leads to the Taoist sanctuary

maps of the town with sightseeing highlights clearly marked, enabling visitors to plan their own itinerary.

** JADE EMPEROR PAGODA AND ITS SURROUNDINGS

❶ daily 6am–6pm. The monks pray between 4pm and 5pm. The pagoda festival takes place on the 9th and 10th day of the new year following the Tet Festival.

The magnificent Phuoc Hai Tu Temple is also known as Chua Ngoc Hoang (Jade Emperor Pagoda), the Vietnamese name for the Jade Emperor. He is one of the most revered figures of Taoist philosophy, ranking higher than all the mythological saints and kings. Ngoc Hoang is worshipped as **ruler of the heavens**. He and his ministers are said to be able to decide the fates of life and death, victory or defeat. The well-frequented temple (73 Mai Thi Luu Street) comprises two buildings standing next to each other. It was built by Chinese

Buddhist-Taoist pagoda

Saigon • Jade Emperor Pagoda

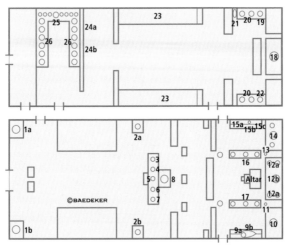

1a Tho Than (Tho Dia, God of Earth)
1b Mon Quan (God of the Gate)
2a General who defeated the White Tiger
2b General who defeated the Green Dragon
3 Phat Mau Chuan De (mother of the five Buddhas of the cardinal directions)
4 Diang Vang Vuong Bo Tat (God of Hell)
5 Sakyamuni (Buddha of the Past)
6 Quan Am (Goddess of Mercy)
7 Thich Ca Buddha (bas-relief)
8 Duoc Su Buddha (glass case)

9a Dai Minh Vuong Quang (riding a phoenix)
9b Die Tien Nhan (god persons)
10 Phat Mau Chuan De (mother of the five Buddhas of the cardinal directions)
11 Sun God
12a Tu Dai Kim Cuong (the »Four Big Diamonds«)
12b Ngoc Hoang (Jade Emperor)
13 Goddess of the Moon
14 Ong Bac De (reincarnation of the Jade Emperor)
15a Thien Loi's guardians (above)
15b Thien Loi (God of Lightning)
15c Military commander of Ong Bac De (below)

16 Bac Dau (God of the Northern Polar Star and Longevity)
17 Nam Tao (God of the Southern Polar Star and Happiness)
18 Thang Hoang (Chief of Hell)
19 Am Quan (God of Yin)
20 Thuong Thien Phat Ac
21 Thanh Hoang's Red Horse
22 Duong Quan (God of Yang)
23 Dia Tang Vuong Bo Tat (King of Hell)
24a Dia Tang Vuong Bo Tat (King of Hell)
24b Thi Kinh (Protector of Mother and Child)
25 Kim Hoa Thanh Mau (Chief of All Women)
26 Figures of 12 women

from the province of Guangdong in the late 19th century and consecrated in a celebration in the year 1906. Unremarkable from the outside, it is, in fact, a masterpiece of Chinese temple architecture, featuring impressive wood carvings, sculptures and colours. The pagoda has been renovated several times, the most recent being in 1985. Inside, innumerable Taoist deities and Buddhist figures stand in unified splendour. Visitors to this temple are allowed to leave their shoes on, but should step over, not on, the high doorsill.

Entrance area: In the centre and on the right of the parvis, **turtles** swim in small ponds, donated by believers. The Vietnamese and Chinese worship the turtle as a symbol of a long life. Offering the gift of a turtle to a temple promises a long and happy existence. A small guardhouse, with an impressive bronze cauldron for incense sticks, stands immediately in front of the temple entrance. In the building itself, visitors first pass the guardhouses and shrines of the two gods of the earth (left) and the gate (right), followed by devotional stands. At the entrance to the actual temple, two colossal generals of the Jade Emperor stand guard: on the left, a white tiger lies beneath one general (Bach Ho), on the right another heavenly general strikes a victory pose on a green dragon (Thang Long). The next small altar is decorated with various Buddhist figurines and chains of lights. Inside a display case in the centre sits a Sakyamuni Buddha made from sandalwood. To the left stands **Quan Am with 18 arms** (Goddess of Mercy), also worshipped as a Bodhisattva. In her hands she holds a shell, the book of Buddhist teaching, a chalice and a willow branch, various weapons such as a sword and hatchet, a chain and the Wheel of Dharma.Beyond this space is the main altar with the Jade Emperor resplendent in his glittering robes. Smoke wafts through the room and a bell or drum is sounded for each oblation. In front of the altar, donations are piled up, e.g. fruit and incense sticks or a sack of rice for the monks who live here. The centrepiece of the shrine is the **figure of the Jade Emperor**, made from papier maché and painted gold. He is joined on both sides by his four guards and students. Six life-size figures stand in line in front of him, with the heavenly gods Nam Tao (God of the Southern Polar Star, to the right) and Bac Dau (God of the Northern Polar Star, to the left) closest to him – these two determine the fate of the living and dead. In the altar case to the right of the Jade Emperor is the 18-armed Phat Mau Chuan De with three faces. To the left is another of the Jade Emperor's aides: Ong Bac De, standing on a turtle with a snake in his hands. Further heavenly figures and heroes are lined up on the walls. A dark wooden frame with magnificent animals and mythological scenes surrounds the altar.

In a smaller room on the left, usually thick with smoke, visitors can catch **a glimpse of hell** and the fate of the departed – the gods who reside here reward good deeds and punish evil acts. Behind the altar, which believers or the bereaved sometimes circle in a clockwise direction, the Chief of Hell, Thanh Hoang, with his red wooden horse, the Gods of Yin (female) and Yang (male) and mandarins are gathered. To the far left in white robes and headdress sits the God of Wealth, Than Tai, with another collection box – business people commonly turn to him in the hope of his blessing and a good income. Ten wooden panels along the walls depict the innumerable torments of hell for those whose karma was bad. The graphic **torture scenes**

Further rooms

The Jade Emperor flanked by his guards and students

hauntingly bring home to believers the fate which then awaits them. Ten Judges of Hell watch over the gruesome representations. On the rear wall opposite the altar, the faithful can clutch at hope once again, for it is here that Thi Kinh (one manifestation of Quan Am) offers her blessing and the chance of reincarnation. The figure on the wooden panel is shown holding a baby, as she is also seen as the patron of mothers and children. On the other side is a tiny room, often filled with acrid smoke, containing twelve ceramic figurines, each carrying a baby. They represent the heavenly women and twelve zodiac signs of the Chinese lunar calendar. Most of those who come to pray here are parents or childless couples. Furthermore, each figure clad in silk exemplifies a positive or negative characteristic of mankind. Returning to the main altar chamber, a narrow corridor on the other side points the way to another room containing photographs of the two founders of the temple and another statue of Quan Am. Steps lead up from here to the **balcony**, which provides a view of the colourfully designed roof. Like most Taoist temples and older Vietnamese buildings, it is decorated with green ceramic tiles and the four mythological beasts: dragon, unicorn, phoenix and turtle.

✳ LE VAN DUYET TEMPLE
❶ daily 6am–6pm

A pleasant, tranquil temple, well worth a visit, lies off the beaten tour-ist track in the erstwhile rural region of Gia Dinh. The northern dis-trict is known today as Binh Thanh. This beautiful old wooden struc-ture was built as a memorial tomb for General Le Van Duyet (126 Dinh Tien Hoang/on the corner of Bach Dang). Le Van Duyet (1763–1832), perceived as a **benevolent regent**, ruled in Gia Dinh prov-ince under the Nguyen dynasty. During this period, he allowed for-eign ships access to the harbour, granted Catholics religious freedom and consented to the Chinese conducting free trade with Cambodia. As supreme commander, the general also played a decisive role in subduing the Tay Son uprising.

The temple consists of several lofty halls and is exemplary of so-called Khai Dinh architecture. Colourful mosaics and ceramics in the form of small savants, dragons and tigers greet visitors on the outer wall and on the roof. Decorative details and antiques can be discovered in the temple, whilst the rituals of the Vietnamese visitors can discreet-ly be observed. These include the shaking of numbered wooden sticks from a wooden beaker (for prophetic purposes) and the throw-ing of wooden blocks, also said to bring luck depending on how they fall. Dragons, phoenixes and unicorns wind their way around carved wooden columns in red and gold and marble pillars which surround the **splendid altars**.

Two portraits of the honoured general hang in the middle and rear rooms. Temple servants sound the gong when donations are made, although on some days they can barely be seen through the swathes of incense. Particularly on the anniversary of the general's death, the 1st day of the 8th lunar month, and on the day of the Tet Festival, the temple is overrun with visitors come to honour the dead.

✳ VINH NGHIEM PAGODA
❶ daily 6.30am–11.30am and 1.30pm–6.30pm

Built during the Vietnam War (1964–71) Chua Vinh Nghiem is the most important pagoda for the Buddhist community of Saigon. The gables of its wide, sweeping double roof take the form of heads of dragons and phoenixes. With the help of the Japanese, the structure was erected in the style of North Vietnamese pagodas.

Centre of the Buddhist Community

A 40m/130ft bell tower, seven storeys high, rises up directly at the side of the road leading to the airport (339 Nam Ky Khoi Nghia), each storey housing a statue of Quan Am.

The pagoda tower is only opened to the public on special Buddhist holidays.

Main hall   In the vast main hall, **ceremonies** such as burial services are often held, the participants clad in white and wearing white headbands. The altar is graced with three large statues of Buddha: in the centre, a 6m/20ft-tall Sakyamuni Buddha is flanked by his students Van Thu (the Wise) and Pho Hien (the Talisman). Nine paintings on each of the two side walls relate the story of the La Han, the 18 Bodhisattvas and religious figures. On the shrines to the rear of the hall, countless ancestral tablets are on display, featuring photographs and the dates of birth and death of deceased relatives. To begin with, a picture of the departed is placed on the altar and then replaced by the wooden tablets after 100 days – thus enabling the soul to find peace in the holy rooms. For the recently deceased or on the anniversary of a person's death, complete (meatless) meals are sacrificed before the Quan Am statue, commonly small bowls of rice, vegetables and soup, with tea or water.

✶✶ GIAC LAM PAGODA AND ITS SURROUNDINGS

❶ daily 7am–noon, 2pm-6pm

Oldest sanc-   Giac Lam Pagoda (Chua Giac Lam) is not only the oldest sanctuary
tuary in   in Saigon, it is also one of the most beautiful – in spite of the flat
Saigon   building with yellow and red tiles looking fairly ordinary from the outside. To the left of the entrance, on Lac Long Quan Street (north of Cholon), comes the first sighting of the seven-storey **pagoda tower**, which can be climbed via a spiral staircase. It contains symbolic relics of famous monks along with Buddha statues on every level. From the top, visitors can enjoy a wide panoramic view of the vibrant Tan Binh district and Saigon. When the pagoda was built in 1744 by the Chinese-born Ly Thuy Long, students and poets often wandered amongst the many trees and blossoms on this hill, writing or reciting poetry. In the **garden** within the complex, the tall Bodhi tree to the left was a present from Sri Lanka, brought to Vietnam in 1953. In front of the tree is a white Quan Am statue, standing on a lotus blossom. The Goddess of Mercy holds a bottle of holy water in her hand. Eight abbots were buried in stupas further back.

Main altar   When entering the pagoda through the small side entrance, shoes should first be removed. Turn left immediately to reach the main altar. Mighty columns fashioned from the wood of jackfruit trees catch the eye straight away. Their intricate carvings on dark palisander wood depict, amongst other things, bats, water lilies and the four mythological creatures – dragon, unicorn, turtle and phoenix. The

Monk at the main altar of the Giac Lam Pagoda

altar pedestal is encased in a gilded, richly decorated wooden frame and boasts an impressive collection of various wooden Buddhas, Bodhisattvas and guards. On a dais at the centre of the back row is a **Buddha of the Past**, between his favourite students Ananda and Kasyapa. Standing in front of them, in the middle row, are the bronze Sakyamuni Buddha and the fat, laughing Di Lac Buddha. Alongside Di Lac, the Jade Emperor is enthroned in bronze. Four Bodhisattvas occupy the front row, flanking another Sakyamuni Buddha. Some of the statues are very old and were brought from Hue to Saigon. On the walls, the 18 wooden La Han and the ten Judges of Hell stand guard. In the left-hand corner of the room, a bronze bell is struck when believers place their wish slip here after making a donation. Often the wishes written on the paper ask for the old or sick to make a healthy recovery, with name, address and age noted for good measure. The right hand corner also contains an interesting feature of traditional Vietnamese belief: the Den Duoc Su – a kind of wooden medicine tree. Believers feed its 49 small oil lamps with kerosene and hang their paper wishes to the tree.

Returning to the entrance, coloured portraits of nine monks who lived here come into view. Opposite is a shrine for the 18-armed Quan Am and two more bronze figures. A smaller altar at the back of the room

Further statues

is easily missed, but harbours the oldest Buddha: a wooden Sakya-muni, over 300 years old. Altogether, there are more than 120 Buddha statues in the pagoda. On the 1st and 15th of the lunar month, the monks living in the temple hold a ceremony in memory of their deceased abbots, whilst on other days they congregate several times a day for prayers. Funeral services are held here frequently – hence the proliferation of benches and tables with tea services.

*Giac Vien Pagoda (Chua Ho Dat) This pagoda is very similar to Giac Lam Pagoda and is located in the same street – roughly 500m/550yd away, yet somewhat hidden at the edge of a leisure park close to Dam Sen Lake. A dusty path through a residential area leads to this dreamy wooden construction in rural surroundings. Containing some 140 statues, it was built by the monk Hay Tinh in around 1850 on an island at the heart of an area of marshland. The **main altar** is at the rear of the building: again, Buddha and his various manifestations are to be found here, along with the Buddhist students Ananda and Kasyapa. The ten Princes of Hell look down from the walls, as do the 18 Bodhisattvas and a number of guards. Intricate, artistic carvings in teak adorn the altar, its frame and the columns. In a shrine to the right sits the Goddess of Mercy. Another medicine tree with 49 lamps and wishes written on paper can be found in the corner. A door leads onto an **idyllic garden veranda**, where many bonsai trees stand tall. Splendid stupas mark the final resting places of monks who have died.

❶ daily 7am–6pm

Dam Sen Water Park A wooden bridge at the eastern extremity of the complex connects the temple to the neighbouring leisure park, which can also be accessed via Hoa Binh Street. The Dam Sen Water Park is one of the largest and most modern leisure parks in Saigon for all ages, with rowing boats, giant water slides, »Space Spiral« and miniature railway. The predominantly Vietnamese visitors can eat or drink at one of the innumerable refreshment stalls, soup kitchens and cafés or at a floating restaurant. The sports centre comprises a tennis court, billiard tables, bowling and fitness centre, whilst the health & beauty club offers a range of relaxing treatments and services including acupuncture and a Jacuzzi (3 Hoa Binh, District 11, Saigon).

❶ Tue–Sat 9am–5.30pm, Sun8.30am–5.30pm. (Sat/Sun very crowded!); admission: adults 100,000 VND (depending on the time of visit), children: approx. 60,000 VND

AROUND SAIGON

Excursions Having explored the turbulent streets of Saigon, it is well worth venturing into the beautiful region outside the city. As public transport is relatively slow and unreliable, it is advisable to book a tour or hire a car plus driver. Most head northwest to the infamous tunnels of ▶Cu Chi and the exotic temple of the Cao Dai in ▶Tay Ninh. ▶My Tho is less than a day away, offering a first impression of the ▶Mekong Delta. Those who might prefer to investigate this unusual landscape by boat should, however, allow several days for the expedition. The bathing resort of ▶Vung Tau is also worth a visit, or indeed a stay of one or two nights. Nature lovers should make a point of visiting the Cat Tien National Park on the way to ▶Da Lat.

The region is famous for its **mangrove forest**, the first Vietnamese biosphere reserve to be recognized by UNESCO. Formed by alluvial sand in the Saigon River, the »island« of Can Gio (approx. 80,000ha/198,000ac, 55km/34mi southeast of Saigon) is described as the »green lung« of Saigon. The mangrove forest, where the trees stand in the murky water as if on splayed stilts, provides shelter for many varieties of **wildlife**, including 137 types of fish and 31 species of reptile, such as monitor lizards. A colony of some 800 macaques (long-tailed monkeys) lives here, happy to be fed by visitors. Tourists can negotiate the dense mangrove canals by motorboat and find overnight accommodation in a simple »eco« guesthouse or middle-class hotel on the beach.

Can Gio

The tour through the biosphere reserve can be made on foot or with a tandem kayak: rope bridges and wooden boardwalks cross the numerous canals and green swamp in dense mangrove forest – the absence of exhaust fumes and engine noise makes this a more ecological excursion than those undertaken with common motorboats, as favoured by indigenous trippers. On the southern side is an approximately 10km/6mi-long, fairly wild and windy beach, the closest to Saigon – refreshment stalls proffer fish and seafood.

❶ Can Gio Ecotourism, tel. 08/38 29 29 6,

✶✶ Tay Ninh · Cao Dai Temple

✦ D 7

Province: Tay Ninh
Region: South

Tay Ninh (population approx. 42,000) lies at the foot of Nui Ba Den and is famous for its colourful Cao Dai Temple. This unique religious community has its headquarters in the provincial capital – it is possible to participate in the prayers and rituals of the Caodaists during the four services held from the early morning until late into the night.

In the 1940s the Cao Dai enjoyed great financial and political influence, as well as a private army of some 20,000 men, which engaged in shifting alliances. Due to their **oppositional stance**, the Cao Dai sect were earlier attacked and oppressed by the Catholic President Diem. Nor were the Caodaists able to maintain harmonious relations with the Vietcong or the North Vietnamese – they periodically fought at the side of the South Vietnamese Army against the Communists. When the latter were in power (from 1975), the Caodaists were hindered in practising their faith and their estates were confiscated. Only since the mid-1980s have relations eased with the political incumbents of power.

Cao Dai Holy See | Cao Dai means »High« or »Great Palace« and is synonymous with God. A certain Ngo Van Chieu founded the Cao Dai faith in the year 1926, when God is said to have made his third and final appearance on earth. Thus was created a **potpourri** of the moral teachings of Buddhism, Confucianism, Taoism, Christianity and Islam. Its followers still adhere to occult practices to receive heavenly messages from the universe: mediums are put into a trance and suddenly messages appear in sealed envelopes. The bizarre sect enjoyed its heyday in the 1950s, with, by all accounts, around 4 million Vietnamese members. Today, the total number of followers worldwide is estimated at between one and two million.

** CAO DAI GREAT TEMPLE

Temple design | The beige structure of the main temple is reminiscent of a Baroque church, featuring two square bell and drum towers at the front. Between the towers, a Di Lac figure (Buddha of the Future) sits upon a throne on the curved roof. The resplendent first lady cardinal crowns the left tower, the first pope of Cao Dai the right. The symbols below stand for evil (left) and the divine (right). A ubiquitous feature, for example above the main entrance and on the altar, is a **huge eye**, emanating bright rays and seeing everything – it symbolizes the Divine Eye (photo ▶p.47). On the side walls of the temple, the eye is surrounded by a triangle; some observers see the symbol which appears on the one dollar bill, whilst Caodaists interpret it as a sign of justice. The numerous illustrations are joined by the talismanic mythological figures: dragon (wisdom), turtle (longevity), unicorn (peace) and phoenix (prosperity). In addition, the Hindu trinity of Brahma, Shiva and Vishnu must not be forgotten.

The **interior** of the sanctuary features a cabinet containing figures and statues from religion and mythology, international literature and politics. A mural by the entrance includes representations of the French poet Victor Hugo and the Chinese revolutionary Sun Yat Sen

At first sight, Cao Dai Temple is a dazzling potpourri of colour

as saints, signing a tablet with the Caodaist motto »God and humanity, love and justice«. Gathered at the main altar are Laotse (at the rear, to the left), the Sakyamuni Buddha (centre) and Confucius (to the right), in the middle row the Bodhisattva in the form of the benevolent goddess Guan Yin (left), in the centre the holy Pope Ly Tai Pe and the legendary General Quan Cong (right), Jesus Christ at the front and another figure by the name of Khuong Thai Cong. Since 1934, the papal chair has remained unoccupied, as no worthy successor has materialized in real life. The huge globe with the Divine Eye at the centre of the altar is impossible to miss. Relics and genealogical trees of deceased dignitaries are also kept here. The **mosaic floor** rises to the altar in nine flat steps. The number nine symbolizes the nine steps of the beatitudes and perfection as well as the nine different hierarchies in Caodaism, from the pope via the bishops and cardinals down to the simple followers. The hall is vaulted by a blue, whitewashed heavenly ceiling, dotted with sparkling mirror stars and crescents and supported by mighty columns: dragons and tendrils wind their way around the richly decorated, motley pillars in two rows of twelve.

Tay Ninh

INFORMATION
Tay Ninh Tourist
210B Duong 30 Thang 4
Tay Ninh
(in the Hoa Binh Hotel, see below)
tel. 066/382 23 76

EVENTS
Cao Dai Festivals

Insider Tip

The Cao Dai sect holds its main festivals on the 14th and final day of each month (30th) at midnight. Further annual festivals take place on 15 January, 15 July and 15 October. Days before, thousands of Caodaists and pilgrims in colourful dress gather in the main sanctuary of Tay Ninh to pray together. (www.caodai.org)

Festival of Spring at Nui Ba Den
Thousands of Vietnamese follow the Tet holidays (February/March) by making a pilgrimage up the mountain and into the temples, offering heaps of fruit and whole pigs as a sacrifice.

CUISINE
Scorpions add spice to the menu in the Tay Ninh region – fried with date sauce or deep-fried with chilli. The poisonous creatures have become serious competitors for the traditional delicacies of crickets, termites, grasshoppers and locusts. A crispy, tasty scorpion is said to cost more than the average daily wage.

WHERE TO EAT
Thanh Thuy £
next to the Hoa Binh Hotel
tel. 066/382 76 06
Classic Vietnamese fare revolving around noodle soup, chicken and pork.

Lan Phuong £
on the main road from Tay Ninh
Many tour buses stop at this Vietnamese restaurant, hence the wait can be lengthy at peak times.

WHERE TO STAY
Hoa Binh Hotel £
210–30 Thang 4
tel. 066/382 13 15
Simple hotel with socialist charm and 97 unostentatious rooms, the best the town has to offer.

Conduct in the temple Visitors enter the temple through a small entrance on the right of the building. Shoes should be left here. **Suitable clothing** is also an important consideration. A good place to observe the service is from the balustrade inside, as unobtrusively and quietly as possible, of course. **Photography and film recordings** are permitted during the ceremony, although some believers do not like to be filmed or photographed individually – it is better to ask them for permission. When looking around the temple after the ceremony, do not walk through the centre of the hall, but stay between the rows of pillars. The believers enter the temple through separate entrances, divided by gender, although this no longer seems to be expected of tourists.

There are four services in total every day. Each ceremony lasts for roughly one hour and is a most impressive spectacle, following a strict **hierarchical composition**, with designated seating arrangements and predetermined prayer positions. In the lower area, the priests congregate four times a day in their blue, red and yellow robes, along with the laymen, the Tin Do, dressed in white. The Confucianists wear red, the Buddhists yellow and the Taoists blue. Women are theoretically also allowed to be dignitaries, but always wear white. Orchestra and choir accompany the prayers. Services at 6am, noon, 6pm and midnight

Religious service

> **?**
> *MARCO ⊕ POLO INSIGHT*
>
> *Ceremony without the crowds*
>
> The noon service is often overcrowded with tourists, as day-trippers from Saigon can only reasonably attend this one in the time they have. Therefore it makes sense to plan one or two days for Tay Ninh and attend one of the other services. A visit can be combined with a trip to the tunnels of Cu Chi.

IN AND AROUND TAY NINH

One destination, some 11km/6.5mi northeast of Tay Ninh, is the mountain of Ba Den, usually shrouded in cloud. Standing at a height of 986m/3234ft, »Black Lady Mountain« is tied to a **romantic legend**: the young, pretty seamstress Ly Thi Thien Huong often came here to pray. One day the damsel was threatened by a robber, but a young man by the name of Le Si Triet came to her rescue. They fell in love and wanted to get married, but Le Si Triet had to go to war and Thien Huong again found herself alone as she prayed on the mountain. This time, nobody could come to her aid as she was attacked by the robber. As she fled, she fell down a cliff. Another version claims that a third person was involved – a mandarin, to whom she had long been promised. Today, centuries later, the Black Lady still occasionally appears to the pilgrims who have travelled great distances to make her offerings as if she were a goddess, hoping for a miracle. In the Vietnam War, the almost impassable mountain was used as a hideout by the Vietcong, although, for a period, it was also used as a helicopter landing site by the Americans. Today, paragliders can be seen in action up on high. The sometimes arduous climb across cliffs and streams, past souvenir stalls and refreshment booths, temples and grottoes, takes around two to three hours. Foreigners are at least officially only allowed as far as the simple Black Lady Pagoda (Chua Ba) at approximately 300m/985ft (approx. 45 minutes up stone steps or with the chair lift a third of the way up the mountain). A great temple festival is held on the mountain during the Tet holidays, attracting thousands of Vietnamese. The simple guesthouses at the foot of the mountain are completely booked up at this time. If the weath-

Nui Ba Den (Black Lady Mountain)

er is fine, **Mieu Son Than Temple** at the summit offers a panoramic view of Dau Tieng Lake and the idyllic Vam Co Dong River, lined with palm trees.

Trang Bang On the way to ▶Cu Chi is a small town whose name resounded around the world during the Vietnam War. The Vietnamese photographer Nick Ut arrived here shortly after a **napalm bomb attack** on 8 June 1972, as villagers and peasants fled from the flames. A naked, nine-year-old girl ran screaming towards him – the photographer pressed the shutter. All around the world, the public was shocked by the picture (▶p.57), which remains today the most striking image of the Vietnam War. The young Phan Thi Kim Phuc (▶Famous People) had suffered serious burns, which still incapacitate her years later. In 1996, at a personal meeting in the USA, she forgave the commanding officer for the attack, as so many Vietnamese have done. The former officer, who had claimed he believed the village to be free of civilians, has been working for decades as a reverend for peace in America. Nick Ut was awarded the Pulitzer Prize for his historic photograph.

✴ Vung Tau

✦ D 7

Province: Ba Ria–Vung Tau (capital)
Region: South
Population: Approx. 250,000

A hilly peninsula on the south coast attracts hordes of Vietnamese, lending the harbour town of Vung Tau a certain Rimini flair, particularly at weekends and on holidays. Does it have something to do with the heartrending legends concerning the region? It cannot be due to the beaches, as there are more beautiful ones elsewhere – oil is extracted right off the turbulent coast.

This brings a certain amount of wealth to the town, however. Many Russians (employed in the oil industry) and surfers seem to have found their Vietnamese Eldorado here. Vung Taus Bai Sao (Back Beach) is, along with the Central Vietnamese town of Da Nang, one of the top spots of the surfer scene in Vietnam. At weekends, Vung Tau belongs to trippers who arrive en masse from Saigon.

Special economic zone In 1979 Vung Tau was declared a special economic zone with international participation, for rich oil and gas deposits lie in the offshore shelf. The small town has grown into the **largest oil extraction centre in Vietnam**, initially with much Soviet support. The Soviet influ-

Fishing boats on the beach of Vung Tau

ence can still be felt today, with some Vung Tau menus offering Russian dishes such as borscht – in Cyrillic lettering. Western companies have now also set up here and exploit the oil reserves side by side with the Vietnamese. As a consequence the province, with its important deep-sea harbour, has become a magnet for foreign investment in South Vietnam. The first mirror-glass office blocks already overshadow the palms on the beach promenade.

Vung Tau is awash with legends. A love story is entwined with the mountain of Nui Lon, the highest in the north. It was here that a courageous man rescued the girl from the claws of one of the tigers that roamed the dense forests of the mountain. He cut off the tiger's head with his sword. To show his thanks for the heroic deed, the girl's grandfather offered her to the hero as his wife and henceforth named the mountain Tuong Ky (the happy meeting). The legend of the smaller Nui Nho in the south concerns a princess of the sea who was transformed into a goldfish and was only able to meet her fisherman husband in human form every five years on the small mountain.

Legends

Vung Tau

INFORMATION
Ba Ria – Vung Tau Tourist
207 Vo Thi Sau, Ward 2, Vung Tau
tel. 064/385 64-45

TRANSPORT
Boats
Hydrofoils commute between Saigon and Vung Tau (45 minutes)

Con Dao flights
Air Mekong (from Can Tho) and Vasco/Vietnam Airlines (from Saigon, Hanoi) fly daily to the islands in under an hour (airport on Con Son); helicopter charters from Vung Tau, there are also hydrofoils and a ferry to Con Son (around 11 hours, small cabins).

EVENTS

Nghinh Ong Festival
On the 16th day of the 8th lunar month (September) the fishermen of Vung Tau celebrate the anniversary of the stranded whales: offerings are made at Lang Ca Ong Temple accompanied by the sound of gongs and festive processions.

Greyhound races
At weekends, Lam Son Stadium, the only dog racing stadium in the whole of Vietnam, plays host to greyhound races. This represents a great opportunity to mingle with the locals as they place bets and cheer on the hounds who race at speeds of up to 60kmh/37mph – but do not expect a jackpot on a stake of

20,000 VND (15 Le Loi, Vung Tau; twelve races from 7.30pm to 10.30pm on weekends, admission approx. 48,000 – 80,000 VND; although most of the action is in the public area: approx. 13,000 VND).

Surf Bar – Vung Tau Beach Club

8 Thuy Van, Bai Sau Beach (= Back Beach, opposite the Sammy Hotel), Vung Tau
Mobile tel. 016/87 55 88 02
www.vnkite.com
The only true beach bar and surfer hang-out: BBQ and snacks, campfire parties on Fridays until sunrise, cool beer and delicious cocktails. Surf and kite gear and tuition (from 9am). A fine alternative to all the »girlie bars« in Vung Tau.

WHERE TO EAT
Hue Anh Restaurant £

15A Truong Cong Dinh
tel. 064/385 66 63
daily 9.30am–10pm
Large garden restaurant with air-conditioned rooms (seats 300), vast array of Vietnamese dishes.

Nine Bistro ££–£££

9 Truong Vinh Ky (at the Rex Hotel) Vung Tau
tel. 064/351 15 71
Many locals consider this to be the best »western« restaurant in town: café, bakery and restaurant all in one, guests sit pleasantly close to the greenery and the service is friendly at breakfast, brunch and dinner. The chef is French, with French and Italian dishes dominating the menu. Delectable ice cream, chocolate cake and decent, reasonably priced, wines.

WHERE TO STAY
Six Senses Con Dao ££££

Dat Doc Beach, Can Dao
tel. 064/383 12 22
www.sixsenses.com/sixsensescondao
The ultimate in luxury and 24/7 pampering thanks to a personal butler. Much wood, bamboo and other natural materials went into the construction of the beach villas with pools. Everything else is high-tech (from the espresso machine and air-conditioned wine cupboard to Wi-Fi and iphone/ipod station). The perfect place for those seeking exclusivity and seclusion and do not need to worry about the bill!

Binh An Village £££–££££

1 Tran Phu (1km/0.6mi outside the centre)
tel. 064/351 00 16
www.binhanvillagevungtau.com/
A chic, architecturally outstanding beach refuge (at a price): just ten beach villas with terrace, each designed individually and beautifully appointed with antique Asian décor and furniture, some with murals, lots of terracotta, inspired al fresco bathroom. Two lovely pools (saltwater and freshwater) overlooking the sea, an open-air bar built into the rock, restaurant with jazz concerts on some weekends. Notably cheaper if booked via hotel websites (e.g. agoda); food and drink are expensive here, but there are plenty of restaurants in the vicinity, such as »Ganh Hao Seafood«.

The Imperial Hotel & Residences £££

159 Thuy Van, Bai Sau Beach, Vung Tau
tel. 064/362 88 88
www.imperialhotel.vn
Six-storey palatial beach hotel with a

romantically dreamy landscaped garden with pool and pavilion. 131 elegant rooms and suites, perhaps too much Victorian kitsch for some, but the best choice in Vung Tau.
Three restaurants. Chic beach club with wicker sun loungers and a 30m/100ft long infinity pool (a bridge leads across to the beach). Fitness club and adjacent shopping plaza.

Anoasis Beach Resort & Residence ££–£££

Insider Tip

Domain Ky Van, Long Hai (approx. 20km/12mi northeast of Vung Tau) tel. 064/386 82-27/-28
www.anoasisresort.com
Prize-winning, rambling complex situated on a lovely, yet remote, beach: from studio apartments to luxurious penthouse villas in a tropical garden (30 bungalows in total), some with a private Jacuzzi. Olympic standard pool, two restaurants, bars, business centre, kids' club.

Petro House ££

63 Tran Hung Dao, Vung Tau
tel. 064/385 20 14
http://petrohousehotel.com.vn
Elegant colonial building in town, with 71 rooms and apartments, small pool,

Chinese restaurant and small casino. Popular with business guests.

Green Hotel £–££

147C Thuy Van, Bai Sau Beach
tel. 064/625 10 03
A modern hotel, also popular with Vietnamese, with 50 light and cosy balcony rooms, sea views and Wi-Fi on seven floors. The beach is just across the street. Modern bathrooms, copious breakfast buffet. Rooms are more expensive on Saturdays.

Nathalie's Vung Tau Hotel & Restaurant £

220A Tran Phu, Bai Dau Beach
tel. 064/355 16 51 and
mobile tel. 062/384 73 71
http://nathalies.hotels-in-vung-tau.com/da/
A pretty little guesthouse, built in wedding cake style complete with towers in 2010, stands some way above the fairly remote Bai Dau Beach.
Seven rooms with tiled or parquet floors, some with wonderful sea views from the balcony (although a little noisier to the front), lovely, modern bathrooms, Thai décor right down to the royal portrait in the lobby. The only Thai restaurant in town, authentic to boot.

WHAT TO SEE IN VUNG TAU

*Bach Dinh Villa
The White Palace, or Bach Dinh Villa, stands proud above the Tran Phu coastal road, accessible via a steep track. The restored colonial building was erected in the late 19th century and initially served as a summer residence for the French gouverneur Paul Doumer. In the years 1909–10, the anti-colonialist Nguyen emperor Thanh Thai was held captive here by the French before his exile to Réunion Island. Later on, Emperor Bao Dai and the South Vietnamese presidents Ngo Dinh Diem and Nguyen Van Thieu used the house for recreation. Frangipani and bougainvillea cast their sweet smell

throughout the garden. A fantastic view of the town and Bai Truoc Beach can be enjoyed from here. The interior of the villa exudes the captivating **charm of days long since past**. The original furniture and items rescued from a shipwreck can be admired on the two floors, the latter including rusty muzzles, Cambodian bronze statues, porcelain relics of the Qing and Ming dynasties and a large bronze drum.

❶ daily 7am–5pm; admission: 10,000 VND

Bai Truoc Beach is a sweeping bay between the two hills of Nui Lon and Nui Nho, running parallel to Quang Trung Road. This stretch of coast is not really suitable for swimming, but Bai Truoc is an excellent place to watch the fishermen at work.

Bai Truoc

A small path leads from the broad coastal road close to the Hai Au Hotel onto the summit of Nui Nho (approx. 3km/2mi). At a height of 170m/557ft stands a lighthouse, built in 1910, casting its light a distance of 35 miles from the shore. Looking into the hinterland, the landscape is characterized by fruit trees and coffee plantations, rubber trees, paddy fields and sand dunes.

Nui Nho lighthouse

❶ admission: approx. 8000 VND

The Buddhist Tinh Xa Pagoda was constructed from 1969 to 1974 on the western face of Nui Nho. The sanctuary is well worth a visit to see the lying Buddha, although weekends should ideally be avoided. A 21m/68ft-high flagpole can be seen from a distance, marking the location of the pagoda. Its 42 rings represent the 42 pages of Buddha's prayer book. A small street, lined by stalls purveying souvenirs and devotional objects, climbs to the unremarkable entrance portal, which is flanked by the gods of goodness (Than Thien) and evil (Than Ac), the guards standing at the entrance to nirvana. The main shrine features an impressive 11m/36ft-long **lying Buddha**, encased in marble. The wonderfully carved wooden frame is decorated with peacocks, apes, flowers and twiners, designed to evoke the place where Buddha entered nirvana. Leave the main hall on the left to enter a higher room containing three meditating Buddha statues. A narrow staircase on the left-hand side leads to the roof terrace, where a Thuyen Bat Nha dragon boat stands, 11m/36ft long, with plants and colourful ceramic mosaics. It symbolizes the Buddhist vessel with which man crosses the sea of suffering and finally reaches the other side – like Buddha himself. Also worthy of note is the 3½-ton tower bell cast in bronze, onto which believers stick slips of paper bearing their wishes. One of the nuns rings the bell with a massive bolt so that the wishes may come true. This spot provides a splendid view of the numerous religious statues watching over the coast of Vung Tau.

*Tinh Xa Pagoda

The star attraction in the Tinh Xa Pagoda is the lying Buddha

Bai Dua Bai Dua Beach can barely be seen beneath the coloured parasols but turns out to be a narrow sandy beach between the quay wall and gently rolling waves, bordered by black cliffs.

*Statue of Jesus This figure lends Vung Tau a certain Brazilian flair: as in Rio de Janeiro, Jesus stretches his arms out protectively over the peninsula. Any Western guests taking a cyclo tour are sure to be driven behind Bai Dua Beach to make a stop at the »Catholic Buddha«. Steps lead up to the 33m/108ft-high Jesus monument, built by the Americans in 1971. Inside the white concrete figure, 130 further steps can be ascended. From its 18m/59ft-wide outstretched arms, which are accessible, a broad view from a final height of 36m/118ft over town and sea can be savoured.

❶ daily 7.30am–11.30am and 1.30pm–5pm

Back on the main street, the small island of Hon Ba comes into view, where a man named Ho Quang Minh built a temple in 1881. In the year 1939, it came under fire from the French and was partially destroyed, only being completely repaired in 1971. Beneath the structure, there is said to be a **cellar** where Vietnamese patriots held clandestine meetings against the colonial rulers. The 200m/218yd separating the island from the mainland can be negotiated at ebb tide without getting wet feet by crossing the rocks. It can get rather crowded here on the 15th of the month, when pilgrims swarm onto the tiny island, bearing incense sticks and other offerings.

Hon Ba Temple

Bai Sau, the 8km/5mi-long rear beach, is largely hidden behind a row of street-side restaurants and booths along the extended Ha Long Street, called Thuy Van at this point. Sunshades, deck chairs and casuarina trees are dotted along the beach, whilst jet skis roar across the water. There are changing rooms and restaurants, and anyone who has forgotten a bathing costume has the opportunity of purchasing a new one in the boutiques of the Ocean Park Center. Although the central portion of the beach does get busy at weekends, the extremities of this stretch of coast are far less frequented.

Bai Sau

The three sections of the building complex in Hoang Hoa Tham Street house the bones of a number of whales who were stranded and perished on the Vung Tau coast. Almost all fishermen in the south believe reverentially in the miraculous powers of the impressive mammals, honouring whales until this day. In the year 1911, the fishermen of Vung Tau had finally collected enough money to build a suitable tomb for what are now three whales buried at Bai Truoc. In the temple, the bones are preserved behind the three altars decorated with wood carvings (►MARCO POLO Insight p.357).

Lang Ca Ong (whale tomb)

Bau Dau Beach in the northwest of the peninsula is surrounded by the wooded slopes of Nui Lon, on which a temple or giant statues (like the Virgin Mary or the Goddess of Mercy) may break the tree cover. This small, tranquil beach sits beneath a less than picturesque quay wall. The water in the bay is shallow and calm, the sand riddled with stones. Above the beach, small restaurants and simple cafés are especially inviting at sunset.

Bau Dau

Tran Phu Street leads to Thich Ca Phat Dai Pagoda, situated on the north side of Vung Tau at the foot of Nui Lon. Large statues in the sprawling park (created in 1961–63) depict the various stations in the life of Buddha. As the 5ha/12ac park is so popular, large numbers of children stick to the visitors like glue. Immediately to the left beyond the entrance is a small **exhibition** on the past and contemporary history of the former prison island of Con Dao (see below). Steps lead

*Thich Ca Phat Dai Pagoda

up to the main attractions: to the right, a 10m/32ft-high Sakyamuni statue sits atop a lotus blossom, to the rear, an octagonal, 19m/62ft-high Bao Thap tower, said to contain the ashes of the Enlightened One. At the four corners of the tower base stand urns containing holy earth from the four important places in Buddha's life: from Lumbini, his birthplace in what is now Nepal, from Bodh Gaya, where he achieved enlightenment, from Sarnath where he preached, and from Kushinara, where he attained final nirvana. Another figure to the left portrays the Enlightened One as he receives fruit from an ape and an elephant.

● daily 7am–5pm

AROUND VUNG TAU

Long Hai If Vung Tau gets to be too hectic and noisy, it is worth venturing 25km/15mi further north to the more peaceful Long Hai, away from the tourist crowds. Long Hai and Phuoc Hai beaches lie side by side with palm trees offering some shade along the **miles of white sand**. A small villa at the northernmost point of the little fishing village serves as a hotel. Nevertheless, prepare for large numbers of Saigonese to materialize here on weekends.

Binh Chau (Xuyen Moc) North of Vung Tau, more than 70 hot springs bubble in the mangrove woods near the coast. The largest pool measures approximately 100 sq m/120 sq yd and is 1m/3ft deep. The area close to provincial highway 23 is a popular weekend destination for many Vietnamese. Around the springs, a large **leisure and relaxation centre** has been developed. The Saigon Binh Chau Eco Resort welcomes visitors to its range of different bungalows (200 rooms; tel. 064/387 11 31, www.saigonbinhchauecoresort.com, admission to pool and mud baths: approx. £4.50). A large restaurant is on site, as are tennis courts and a golf course. As well as hot baths (also in smaller, separate family pools) massages and mud baths, there is also the opportunity to relax in the sauna.

Con Dao Islands Approximately 200km/124mi off the Vung Tau coast lie the 14 islands of the Con Dao archipelago in the South China Sea. The hilly main island Con Son was used from 1862 by the French and later by the South Vietnamese and Americans to detain **political prisoners** and opponents of the regime. 10,000–12,000 Vietnamese were held captive and tortured in cells known as »tiger cages«. Amongst the most famous inmates was Ton Duc Thang, Ho Chi Minh's deputy and later president of Vietnam. The island kingdom was declared a nature conservation area in 1982 and boasts a wealth of **flora and fauna**, with 360 species of tree alone. Whales, dolphins, seabirds, turtles, sea cows and monitor lizards are some of the wildlife to be found here. As well as possessing marvellous sandy beaches, the islands also boast wonderful coral reefs. At present, Con Dao is inhabited by fishermen and several thousand soldiers. There are, however, plans afoot to increase tourism. Following a mid-range hotel complex and smaller guesthouses, the trendsetting Six Senses chain entered the field with a dream complex a few years ago. A casino is also on the drawing board, along with the ambition of granting the islands duty-free status. So far, there are several daily flights from Saigon, Hanoi and Can Tho, as well as ferries from Vung Tau.

PRACTICAL
INFORMATION

Is bird flu dangerous for tourists in Vietnam? How do you address the Vietnamese? When is the best time to visit? Practical tips for a successful holiday.

Arrival · Planning the Journey

By air There are seven international airports in Vietnam: Saigon (Ho Chi Minh City, 6km/3.7mi north of the centre), Hanoi (30km/19mi from the centre) and Da Nang at the heart of the country, joined by Can Tho in the Mekong Delta in 2011 and the island of Phu Quoc in 2012. There are also international airports in Cam Ranh (approx. 40km/25mi south of Nha Trang) and Hai Phong in the north. European flights only land in Hanoi and Saigon, apart from a few connections from Moscow.

British Airways does not currently fly to Hanoi. It offers flights from London Heathrow to Saigon, with a change of planes in Hong Kong or Singapore. Indeed, many airlines fly from Heathrow to Saigon, but there are no direct flights: Thai Airways fly via Bangkok, Air China via Beijing, Cathay Pacific via Hong Kong, and so on. Vietnam Airlines offers services from Heathrow to Saigon and Hanoi via Paris Charles de Gaulle, and to Hanoi via Frankfurt. A direct flight from Frankfurt to Saigon is also operated by Lufthansa. Vietnam Airlines flies from Sydney direct to Saigon, and continues on to Hanoi without changing planes. Qantas flights to both Hanoi and Saigon involve changing in Hong Kong, Bangkok or Tokyo, for example. There are numerous flights from US and Canadian airports to Vietnam, but they always involve changing planes at an Asian airport (or Paris or Frankfurt). American Airlines, for example, flies from both JF Kennedy International Airport in New York and San Francisco International Airport to Saigon by way of Tokyo.

> **Note:**
> Service numbers which are not toll-free are marked with an asterik *0180...

Stopovers are of course possible in places such as Dubai, Bangkok, Singapore, Kuala Lumpur or Hong Kong. Most Asian capitals and neighbouring countries have daily flights to Saigon and Hanoi. Flights from Europe take around 11–13 hours, depending on the route and layovers. It is advisable to book early for the travel season which begins in October. Tickets become scarce around January/February when many Vietnamese from overseas return home for the Tet Festival.

The exchange rate at airports (and hotels) is often inferior to rates available at licensed bureaux de change in town centres. It is not possible to change currency at Hanoi Airport after 10pm, but there are cash machines on site and taxis will accept US dollars for the ride to the hotel. Flights must be confirmed by telephone with the airline two to three days prior to departure.

Overland It has recently become possible to travel by train to Vietnam, although it is not necessarily cheaper than flying. Specialized agents can organize the entire trip, including the necessary connections.

AIRLINES
Vietnam Airlines in the UK
7 Lower Grosvenor Place
London SW1W 0EN
tel. 020 3263 2062
www.vietnamairlines.com

in the USA
88 Kearny Street, Suite 1400
San Francisco, CA 94108
tel. 415 677 0888
And 1-866 677 8909
www.vietnamairlines.com

in Australia
Level 25, 31 Market Street
Sydney NSW 2000
tel. (02) 9285 4700
www.vietnamairlines.com

in Vietnam
in Saigon: tel. 08/38 32 03 20
in Hanoi: tel. 04/38 32 03 20
in Da Nang: tel. 0511/383 23 20
www.vietnamairlines.com

Jet Star Pacific
in Saigon and Hanoi: tel. 19 00 15 50
in Da Nang: tel. 0511/358 35 83
www.jetstar.com

Lufthansa
in the UK: 0871 945 9747
in Saigon: 19-25 Nguyen Hue (14 St.),
Bitexco Tower
tel. 08/38 29 85 29 /-49
www.lufthansa.com

British Airways
tel. 01805/26 65 22
www.britishairways.com

KLM
tel. 01805/21 42 01
www.klm.com

AIRPORTS
Saigon
Tan Son Nhat International Airport
Tan Binh district, approx. 6km/4mi north
of Saigon
http://www.hochiminhcityairport.com
Airport Service Centre:
tel. 08/38 48 67 11 and 08/38 44 66 65
(bus 152, approx. 8000 VND without luggage) or Vietnam Airlines shuttle bus (approx. 25,000 VND) from around 7am-
6pm; taxi ideally only with Mai Linh or
Vinasun cars, can be booked at Saigon
Tourist desk from approx. 150,000 VND,
depending on traffic and destination.
Mai Linh Taxis tel. 08/38 27 79 79

Hanoi
Noi Bai International Airport
tel. 04/38 84 35 63
www.hanoiairportonline.com
shuttle bus to town
taxi approx. 300,000 VN

Da Nang
International Airport
tel. 0511/382 33 91
www.dananairportonline.com

Hue
Phu Bai Airport (approx 15km/9mi
southeast of Hue): tel 054/382 32 49,
386 11 31
Saigon/Hanoi flights: shuttle bus (approx.
100,000 VND) and taxi to town
(approx. 200,000 VND)

TRAVEL AGENTS
Trails of Indochina
10/8 Phan Dinh Giot (nahe Airport)
Tan Binh district, Saigon
tel. 08/38 44 10 05
www.trailsofindochina.com
Reliable agency with imaginative programme, also for neighbouring countries

Trains run twice a week from Hanoi to Kunming (Yunnan province) and Beijing in China. The journey time is approximately 32 hours or longer (couchettes; route is via the border crossing of Lao Cai–Heiku). Despite separate handling, formalities may take a long time for foreign nationals. Make absolutely sure that the border crossing at Lao Cai is entered on the visa. The train has 2nd and 3rd-class compartments, which should be reserved several days in advance.

By bus or shared taxi: Coming **from China**, the border crossing of Lang Son (Dong Dang/Ping Xian) in Guangxi province is also open to Europeans. It is another 160km/99mi from here to Hanoi. There is another crossing at Hai Ninh (Mong Cai/Dong Hung) in the northeast (Road 18) and at Lao Cai (Heiku) in the northwest, on the way to Yunnan.

Travelling cross-country, the now tarmacked Route 9 **from Laos** (Savannakhet) leads via the Dansavanh/Lao Bao border crossing to Central Vietnam (Dong Ha) and further north across the Keo Nua Pass at Nam Phao/Cau Treo (near Vinh), as well as via Na Naew/Nam Xoi (to Thanh Hoa), Phou Keua and Ngoc Hoi/Bo Y (to Kontum and Pleiku), Sop Hun/Tay Trang (to Dien Bien Ph) and the remote border district of Nam Can (Tien Tieu/Nong Het).

From Cambodia (Phnom Penh) it takes approximately 4 hours to reach Vietnam on the N 22 in Tay Ninh province (Moc Bai border crossing), Ba Vet/Moc Bai border crossing. Express boats (air-conditioned) cross daily from Phnom Penh into the Mekong Delta to Chau Doc (Khorm Samnor or Kaam Samnor/Vinh Xuong, see below). The following border checkpoints are also open: Phnom Den/Tinh Bien (to Chau Doc), Prek Chak/Xa Xia (to Ha Tien) and O Yadao/Le Thanh (to Pleiku).

Important note: for most border crossings, it is necessary to apply for a visa for Vietnam in advance and have this ready inside your passport! Visas are of course also required to enter the transit countries. They must be applied for in advance and are valid for all international border crossings. Embassies and consulates can be found in all countries neighbouring Vietnam.

By ship   Vietnam has a coastline of more than 3200km/2000mi, and there is a port in every large coastal town, making it an ideal destination on board a freighter or cruise ship. Though it is fairly expensive, travelling by cruise ship is increasingly popular.

Cruises start in various countries in Asia, e.g. Thailand, or they travel from Vietnam to Thailand, Hong Kong and Singapore. The ports of destination in Vietnam are Hai Phong, Ha Long City, Da Nang, Nha Trang, Saigon Phu Quoc and Vung Tau.

For a number of years now, it has been possible to travel **from South Vietnam to Cambodia** (apply for a visa in advance) along the Mekong River from Chau Doc via the border town of Vinh Xuong (boat

BEHAVIOUR IN PUBLIC

In Vietnam, it is uncommon to tip. In hotels (and often in bars and restaurants) up to 15% tax and service charge is already included, but considering the average monthly salary is only £32 it is polite to give a small tip. When invited to **pray** at a temple by monks or nuns, it goes without saying that visitors should drop a donation into the wooden boxes provided as a sign of gratitude. Usually one or three incense sticks are lit (the latter is common for deaths or problems), five means they are dedicated to the Mother of the Forest and seven to the wandering souls.

Tipping

Quite often, travellers in Vietnam will still encounter war veterans. As there is no longer free public healthcare in Vietnam, travellers may wish to make a donation (small dong notes). Beware that large numbers of gangs now deliberately inflict injuries and mutilations, or even »stage« injuries fit for Hollywood films with extra dramatic effect. Beware of begging women with half-unconscious babies in their arms – apparently the children are not theirs and have been sedated with tranquilizers.

War veterans and begging children

It is up to the traveller whether to give sweets or money to begging children; just keep in mind that at some point children will earn more money begging than their working parents, so they may end up not going to school anymore. Child labour is widespread and is supported by buying postcards or cigarettes from them. Often children are exploited by gangs who will take away all their earnings at the end of the day. Of course, visitors can invite children to a meal, which most will happily accept.

> **!** MARCO POLO INSIGHT
>
> *Salutations*
>
> The Vietnamese have a whole range of salutations, depending on age and social or Confucian rank, and, to make it even more complicated, some even vary from the north to the south, resulting in absolute confusion for tourists. Foreigners cannot go wrong, however, with this general greeting: xin chao (pronounced: sin chao).

▶Prices · Discounts

Bargaining

Do not under any circumstances bathe naked or without a bikini top. Also the beach (generally public) is an unsuitable place for acts of love, as romantic as the ocean sunset may be. This would clearly conflict with proper conduct in Vietnam.

On the beach and by the pool

Before taking a photograph, locals should always be politely asked in advance; a »no« or disapproving nod should be accepted, even if it is accompanied by a hearty laugh. Women might be embarrassed when

Taking photographs

photographed in their street or work clothes. Also street vendors with black market products and certain hill tribes dislike being photographed. A nice gesture: buy something, ask them for their address and send them a copy from Europe.

INVITATIONS

Forms of greeting — Nowadays the common way to greet in Vietnam is with a western-style handshake (seniors first) – those who wish to greet the traditional way should cross their arms in front of their chest and bow slightly. When visiting a Vietnamese family at home the **shoes** of all residents are usually kept out on the doorstep. Taking one's shoes off is never wrong, even if the host waves it off with a smile. The only real discourtesy toward Buddhists is to face the soles of one's feet towards others.

Dinner invitation — When invited to dinner, it is customary to bring a small, nicely wrapped gift and present it with both hands (such as flowers, drawing pens for the children, fruit or cigarettes). Never forget to exchange business cards if the dinner is business-related – this is considered an obligatory ritual.

Outside Saigon and Hanoi don't be surprised if dinner is served on a mat on the ground if there are not enough chairs or space at the table (first the host and guests, then the rest of the family). It would be deemed impolite to refuse being served first as a guest. »Xin moi« means please start! Eating with the Vietnamese is usually a loud and leisurely affair, even at public restaurants: slurping, belching and the clicking of the tongue is just as common as talking on a mobile phone and smoking. Non-edible leftovers such as meat or fish bones and napkins are often just whisked off the table at the end. Never leave chopsticks standing in leftover rice – this will conjure up someone's death!

Health

Particularly during your first days in Vietnam, beware of dishes that include raw vegetables, salads and non-peelable fruit. After that, consider every meal individually rather than categorically avoiding eating regional specialities. At a private dinner, it may be perceived as impolite to refuse dishes – especially when you are a guest or are being served first. In Vietnam, your body will perspire a lot more than at home, so it is vital to drink at least 2 litres/day. As a rule, **ice cubes** are free of health risk as they are made from boiled water. Those who

It is advisable to drink plenty of liquid in tropical climates

do not want any ice in their drink should tell the waiter: »khong co da« means »no ice, please«. Soups are harmless even for sensitive stomachs, as they are served boiling hot and the accompanying un-cooked vegetables can be avoided.

Meat should always be well done and nevereaten raw or lukewarm. In inland regions, it is best to avoid fish at simple restaurants because it may not have been properly cooled during transportation.If, de-spite all preventive measures, digestive problems do occur, charcoal tablets, sufficient liquid and electrolytes often help.

To avoid sunburn and heatstroke, gradual **exposure to the sun** is advised. Use proper sun block with sufficient UV protection.

There are no mandatory vaccinations required for entry to Vietnam, unless you are entering from a country affected with yellow fever. It is recommended that travellers get booster vaccinations for polio, tetanus (also in combination with diphtheria), if it has been more than ten years since receiving one, and hepatitis A, (B for lengthier stays), rabies and Japanese encephalitis plus an oral vaccination for typhus.

Cholera has been a hazard since 2008, especially in North Vietnam (Hanoi, Ninh Binh) but also in the Mekong Delta, hence drink only boiled or bottled water and use the same for brushing teeth. Avoid ice cream and ice cubes and only eat peeled fruit! Dengue fever is on the rise worldwide and has appeared throughout the country since 2010, even in urban areas such as Saigon, especially after the mon-soon season. Mosquito sprays and long-sleeved clothing, keeping skin covered, can help to avoid catching the disease.

Vaccinations

SOS International Clinic
24 hours
51 Xuan Dieu, Hanoi
tel. 04/39 34 06 66
(another clinic in Vung Tau)

AEA International SOS
24-hour emergency number, also for
dental clinics
65 Nguyen Du Street, Saigon
tel. 08/8298520 and 8298424

AEA International SOS
31 Hai Ba Trung, Hanoi
tel. 04/9340555 and
9340666

Bach Mai International Hospital
Giai Phong Street, Hanoi
tel. 04/8693731

? | Bird flu

MARCO ⊕ POLO INSIGHT

Bird flu has been rife in Vietnam since 2004 and people can become infected. There have been fatalities in Vietnam, so direct contact to fowl is to be avoided. Steer clear of poultry markets and farms. Eating chicken carries no risk, however.

Malaria Malaria is prevalent in Vietnam, and in particular the more dangerous strain of malaria tropica, often fatal for Europeans. There is a greater risk in the rural regions of the north during and following the monsoon season, whilst the south is at risk throughout the year, above all in the Mekong Delta and in Ca Mau, Bac Lieu, Tay Ninh and the Saigon region in particular. The coastline as far as Nha Trang is classified as medium risk during the rainy season. Mosquitoes are most widespread during and shortly after the **monsoon season**. It is advised, therefore, to take prophylaxis (prescription) or at least bring stand-by medication in case of emergencies (e.g. Doxycicline or Malarone). Consult a doctor or tropical institute approximately 6 weeks prior to departure. There have also been some cases of dengue fever, with similar symptoms to those of malaria. To lower the risk of contracting malaria, bring a **mosquito net** (especially for hotels without air conditioning) and use mosquito repellent at dusk and at dawn. Thick, long socks as well as long-sleeved, light shirts offer some protection against mosquito bites. Mosquito coils also help. In the case of flu-like symptoms such as fever, shivering, dizziness and headache go to the doctor immediately, even if they occur months after returning from Vietnam!

HIV/AIDS Vietnam now counts among the countries with rapidly rising AIDS rates (the foreign office states: 300,000 infected, predominantly prostitutes). To avoid any risk of infection through foreign blood, bring disposable syringes and plastic gloves to any doctor's appointment and use condoms. Prostitution is illegal in Vietnam and foreigners often face fines of up to €400. Sexual abuse of minors is severely pun-

... department store
... food store
... market
When does the department store
open/close?
What does this... cost?

... Cua hang
... Hang thuc pham kho
... Cho
Cua hang bach hoa tong hop mo
cua/dong cua/vao luc may gio?
Quyen ... nay gia bao nhieu?

Bank
Where is the...
... bank?
... bureau de change?
I would like to change... euros
(US dollars) into dong.

O dau co ...
... ngan hang?
... doi tien?
Toi muon doi ... tien Euro
(tien Dola) ra dong.

Post office
How much is ...
... a letter?
... a postcard?
... to Britain?

Bao nhieu tien ...
... mot bi thu?
... mot thiep goi?
... toi nuoc Vuong quoc Anh?

Accommodation
Could you please recommend
... a hotel/... a B&B
Do you still have...
... a single?
... a double?
... with shower/bath?
... for one night?
... for one week?
How much is one room with...
... breakfast?
... half-board?

Ong co the tim cho toi ...?
... Khach san./... Phong tro.
Ong co con can ...
... Phong rieng?
... Phong doi?
... voi Phong tam?
... cho mot dem?
... cho mot tuan?
Gia tien bao nhieu mot phong voi ...
... an sang?
... an sang va an chieu?

Doctor
Can you recommend a doctor?
I have...
... pains here.
... fever.
... diarrhoea.
... headache.
... toothache.

Omg co the tim, cho toi mot Ong bac si?
Toi co ...
... dau o' day.
... sot.
... tieu chay.
... dau dau/nhu't dau.
... dau rang/nhu't rang.

Eating out
Where can I find ...
... a good restaurant?

O dau co ...
... nha hang ngon?

... a cosy bar?
Please reserve us
a table for tonight for four.
Cheers!
Nice to meet you!
The food was delicious.
The bill, please.

... tiem bia lich su?
Ong/lam on, cho chung toi mot ban
bon nguoi toi nay.
Chuc mung Ong!
Han hanh duoc gap ong!
Thuc an rat ngon.
Tinh tien, lam on!

Food and drink
Breakfast
caphe den
ca phe sua/da
tra denh/xanh
bahn mi
bo
pho mat
mut nhu
doi
trung/luoc/chien
trung op la
yoghurt

Bua an diem tam/bua an sang
black coffee
coffee with milk /icecream
black tea/green tea
bread/toast
butter
cheese
jam
sausage
soft-boiled egg/hard-boiled egg/fried egg
omelette
yoghurt

Soups and starters
nuoc leo
bun thang
chao

canh chua ca
lau
pho (bo/ga)
mien luon/ga
an chay
cha gio

xup
chicken broth
stew
rice soup with added chicken, pork,
mushrooms, spices, etc.)
fish soup (sweet-and-sour)
fish and vegetable soup
rice noodle soup (with beef/chicken)
glass noodle soup with eel/chicken
vegetarian dish (with tofu)
spring roll

Fish and seafood
ca
ca luoi
ca thu
ca ngu
ca map
cua
tom nho
tom lon/to
muc
so

ca/do bien
fish
sole
tuna
pikeperch
shark
prawns
shrimp
king prawns
squid
oysters

Meat and poultry
thit bo

cac mon thit
beef

List of Maps and Illustrations

Photo Credits

Publisher's Information

2nd Edition 2019
Worldwide Distribution: Marco Polo
Travel Publishing Ltd
Pinewood, Chineham Business Park
Crockford Lane, Chineham
Basingstoke, Hampshire RG24 8AL,
United Kingdom.

Photos, illlustrations, maps:
200 photos, 45 maps and and
illustrations, one large map
Text:
Martina Miethig with contributions by
Beate Szerelmy, Dr Heinrich Motzer,
Sabine Stahl, Helmut Linde
Editing:
Robert Taylor, Rainer Eisenschmid
Translation: Margit sander, Gareth
Davies, Alex Paulick
Cartography:
Christoph Gallus, Hohberg;
MAIRDUMONT Ostfildern (large map)
3D illustrations:
jangled nerves, Stuttgart
Infographics:
Golden Section Graphics GmbH, Berlin
Design:
independent Medien-Design, Munich
Editor-in-chief:
Rainer Eisenschmid, Mairdumont
Ostfildern

Printed in China

MARCO POLO Travel Publishing Ltd
Pinewood, Chineham Business Park
Crockford Lane, Chineham
Basingstoke, Hampshire RG24 8AL
United Kingdom
Email: sales@marcopolouk.com

MIX
Paper from
responsible sources
FSC
www.fsc.org   FSC® C124385

MARCO  POLO

HANDBOOKS

MARCO POLO
TRAVEL HANDBOOK
ANDALUCÍA
NEW

MARCO POLO
B
BALI

MARCO POLO
TRAVEL HANDBOOK
BARCELONA

MARCO POLO
TRAVEL HANDBOOK
BERLIN
NEW

MARCO POLO
TRAVEL HANDBOOK
BUDAPEST
NEW

MARCO POLO
TRAVEL HANDBOOK
DRESDEN
NEW

MARCO POLO
TRAVEL HANDBOOK
DUBAI
NEW

MARCO POLO
TRAVEL HANDBOOK
FLORENCE
NEW

MARCO POLO
TRAVEL HANDBOOK
FLORIDA
NEW

MARCO POLO
TRAVEL HANDBOOK
GRAN CANARIA
NEW

MARCO POLO
I
ICELAND

MARCO POLO
TRAVEL HANDBOOK
IRELAND
NEW

MARCO POLO
TRAVEL HANDBOOK
LONDON
NEW

MARCO POLO
M
MADEIRA

MARCO POLO
TRAVEL HANDBOOK
NEW YORK
NEW

MARCO POLO
TRAVEL HANDBOOK
NEW ZEALAND
NEW

MARCO POLO
N
NORWAY

MARCO POLO
TRAVEL HANDBOOK
PARIS
NEW

MARCO POLO
TRAVEL HANDBOOK
PRAGUE
NEW

MARCO POLO
TRAVEL HANDBOOK
ROME
NEW

MARCO POLO
S
SRI LANKA

MARCO POLO
TRAVEL HANDBOOK
TUSCANY
NEW

MARCO POLO
TRAVEL HANDBOOK
VENICE
NEW

MARCO POLO
V
VIETNAM

Vietnam Curiosities

Telephone calls with the spirits and particularly exquisite varieties of coffee: There are so many curiosities to discover in Vietnam:

►**Oktoberfest in Vietnam**
The largest and perhaps the most exotic Oktoberfest in Southeast Asia is staged annually in Saigon, where the ballroom of the »Windsor Plaza« is transformed into a beer tent.
(www.oktoberfestvietnam.com)

►**Fakes and Ccopies**
Copies of everything and anything abound all over Vietnam: from counterfeit fashion labels and pirated CDs or DVDs to brands with names deceptively similar to the originals. Even »Picasso« paintings are a snip for US$30!

►**Expensive Sh... coffee**
The most expensive coffees in the Vietnamese export trade are the ones which involve the beans first being eaten by cats, squirrels, weasels or foxes and then »discharged« – they are of course then cleaned and roasted! A kilo of cat coffee (ca phe chon) weighs in at around US$150!

►**Compulsory Helmet Chic**
The helmet is a modern accessory, available in the most striking colours and forms: ladybirds for kids (complete with antennae), military style for adults or decorated with kissing lips and hearts.

►**Supernatural Beliefs (I)**
There are 54 different ethnicities in Vietnam, some with apparently archaic customs: women of the Black Dao wrap the hair of their deceased ancestors inside their own braided headgear. The Lu, another of the hill tribes in the north, stain their teeth black with a tincture of bamboo leaves, mothwings and honey.

►**Supernatural Beliefs (II)**
Seeking advice from benevolent spirits and forefathers in the temple, believers throw »xin keo« – wooden blocks – into the air. How they land on the floor (in three attempts) should help them to answer the question posed to the spirit.

►**Supernatural Beliefs (III)**
The toolkit of the Red Dao shamen includes an old, dog-eared book with Chinese symbols and drawings, handed down from one generation to the next, two split lengths of bamboo and a stone which is heated in the embers of the fire. A thread is wound around the hot stone to create a »telephone to the spirits«.